LIMITING PRIVILEGE

C0-BXA-482

CENTRAL EUROPEAN STUDIES

The demise of the Communist Bloc and more recent conflicts in the Balkans and Ukraine have exposed the need for greater understanding of the broad stretch of Europe that lies between Germany and Russia. The Central European Studies series enriches our knowledge of the region by producing scholarly work of the highest quality. Since its founding, this has been one of the only English-language series devoted primarily to the lands and peoples of the Habsburg Empire, its successor states, and those areas lying along its immediate periphery. Salient issues such as democratization, censorship, competing national narratives, and the aspirations and treatment of national minorities bear evidence to the continuity between the region's past and present.

SERIES EDITORS

Howard Louthan, University of Minnesota
Daniel L. Unowsky, University of Memphis
Dominique Reill, University of Miami
Paul Hanebrink, Rutgers University
Maureen Healy, Lewis & Clark College
Nancy M. Wingfield, Northern Illinois University

OTHER TITLES IN THIS SERIES

Imagining Slovene Socialist Modernity: The Urban Redesign of Ljubljana's Beloved Trnovo Neighborhood, 1951–1989
Veronica E. Aplenc

Przemyśl, Poland: A Multiethnic City During and After a Fortress, 1867–1939
John E. Fahey

Combating the Hydra: Violence and Resistance in the Habsburg Empire, 1500–1900
Stephan Steiner

Transleithanian Paradise: A History of the Budapest Jewish Community, 1738–1938
Howard N. Lupovitch

Finding Order in Diversity: Religious Toleration in the Habsburg Empire, 1792–1848
Scott Berg

Unlikely Allies: Nazi German and Ukrainian Nationalist Collaboration in the General Government During World War II
Paweł Markiewicz

Balkan Legacies: The Long Shadow of Conflict and Ideological Experiment in Southeastern Europe
Balázs Apor and John Paul Newman (Eds.)

LIMITING PRIVILEGE

Upward Mobility Within Higher Education in Socialist Poland

Agata Zysiak

Purdue University Press ▪ West Lafayette, Indiana

Copyright 2023 by Purdue University. All rights reserved.
Printed in the United States of America.

Cataloging-in-Publication Data is available from the Library of Congress.
978-1-61249-881-2 (hardback)
978-1-61249-883-6 (epub)
978-1-61249-882-9 (paperback)
978-1-61249-884-3 (epdf)

This book will be made open access within three years of publication thanks to Path to Open, a program developed in partnership between JSTOR, the American Council of Learned Societies (ACLS), University of Michigan Press, and The University of North Carolina Press to bring about equitable access and impact for the entire scholarly community, including authors, researchers, libraries, and university presses around the world. Learn more at https://about.jstor.org/path-to-open/.

Cover layout by Purdue University Press using the following assets:
Foreground image—Professor lays the first brick for a new University of Łódź building. From the collection of the Institute of Sociology, University of Łódź.
Background image—*Polychrome* by Leon Kunka, which hangs in the reading room of the University of Łódź Library. Reprinted with permission from Halina Kunka. Photo by Adam Musiałowicz with the support of the University of Łódź Library.

CONTENTS

ACKNOWLEDGMENTS

BOOKS ARE SOCIAL FACTS, ONE MIGHT JOKE. THEY ARE ALWAYS THE PRODUCT of social context and intellectual community as well as effort on the part of an author. This particular book has its roots in my dissertation, written in Polish during my time at the University of Łódź, the Central European University in Budapest, and the University of Michigan in Ann Arbor. I need to start by going back as far as a decade to my first visits to the University of Łódź Archive, where I received support from Kamil Piskała and Andrzej Pielat. The biographical interviews were gathered for a collective project run by the University of Łódź and a local NGO, the Topografie Association, and collected also by Kaja Kaźmierska, Katarzyna Waniek, Joanna Wygnańska, Ada Szczerba, Anna Rawicka, and Sebastian Zaborowski. These materials were closely discussed with Kaja Kaźmierska and Katarzyna Waniek, resulting in another book.[1] A few dozen recorded hours and over 1,000 pages of interviews were supplemented by several hundred press articles digitalized thanks to Izabela Smuga, Adam Musiałowicz, and Anna Zaremba. Insightful comments and encouragement from my PhD committee: Kazimierz Kowalewicz, Paweł Starosta, and Michael D. Kennedy, and also Łukasz Biskupski, John Bukowczyk, Piotr Filipkowski, Wiktor Marzec, Brian Porter-Szucs, Magdalena Rek-Woźniak, Włodzimierz Wincławski, and Genevieve Zubrzycki, enabled the dissertation to become a book: *Points for Social Origin. Postwar Modernization and a University in a Working-Class City*.[2] The Polish predecessor of this publication has received awards in Poland and has been honored with a generous reception.

Due to a calm and productive time at the IAS in Princeton, I was able to rethink and rewrite the book for an English-speaking audience and find a supportive and enthusiastic publisher (which would not have happened without the expertise of Johanna Bockmann, Michael D. Gordin, David Ost, and Angela Zimmerman). As a native Polish speaker, I was supported by Magdalena Szuster and Ben Koschalka in my struggles with English. The final version was assiduously copyedited by Julia Podziewska—I wish I could always have such a devoted and attentive reader for my work. This book is not a translation of the Polish one. It is based on the same sources and argument, but has a new structure and was adapted for a non-Polish audience. This reincarnation, including finding a publisher, was a struggle, and was possible thanks to incisive consultation, comments, and support. I would like to thank my colleagues at the IAS Social Science School (2017/2018), my coworkers at the University of Łódź, University of Warsaw, and University of Vienna, participants of the Centre for Cultural and Literary Studies of Communism seminars at IBL PAN, the Copernicus Program in Polish Studies and the Culture and History and Politics Workshop at the University of Michigan, and the Institute of Slavic, East European, and Eurasian Studies at UC Berkeley. For the inspiration I received for some final touches at the very last stages of my work at the Research Center for the History of Transformations, I would like to thank John Connelly, Thuc Linh Nguyen Vu, Aga Pasieka, Philipp Ther, Tomasz Zarycki, and for day-to-day steadfast support, Kasper Ługowski. I gratefully acknowledge the effort of the Purdue University Press team, whose guidance and patience helped close this project. During over a decade's work on this project, I became much indebted to many brilliant people. However, for all errors I alone am responsible.

INTRODUCTION

Each dustman shall speak, both in Latin and Greek,
And tinkers beat Bishops in knowledge.[1]

"One day a poster announcing the preparatory course[2] at the university appeared in a village. Pokusa [a surname that means *temptation* in Polish] was the first to enroll. He was accepted after passing an exam. Now he is one of the best students!—You just have to want to do it—he explains." In 1953, that is how a local newspaper encouraged peasant children to study at the University of Łódź—a model socialist university established in 1945 in Poland's largest industrial city. Mr. Temptation was awarded a scholarship, a place in a dormitory, and access to subsidized dining. A state-guaranteed job awaited him after graduation. If he ever managed to graduate, that is. Working-class children[3] dropped out of their courses more often than those from the intelligentsia.[4] In addition, their peers regarded them as a "mob" or "boors."[5] Despite structural obstacles and everyday classism, people like Mr. Temptation exemplified state socialism's greatest achievement—unprecedented upward mobility. After all, what once might have been more a miracle than an exception[6] was slowly becoming the rule.

The book is about this difficult attempt to build a society anew by democratizing access to universities in postwar Poland. The word "democratization" was used without reference to the direct rule of the people. Instead, it meant simply equal access. The desired state of affairs was that the social structure of students would reflect the social structure of society as a whole. It was also not only an attempt to construct a new elite but a new society and a new educated citizen. Therefore, the book tackles several more general questions: How and for whom was state socialism built? What visions of society and the university drove the postwar changes? How did these shape the horizon of expectations of people from the working class and peasantry? And finally, what were the limits and paradoxes of socialist modernization?

I focus on the perspectives of those who experienced upward mobility during state socialism. This comprised over one-third of the Polish population, but their stories remain untold. Despite the so-called Soviet reform's negative effect on the autonomy of academia, for the education system and society as a whole, state socialism meant new paths of upward mobility for millions. Polish reformers planned to provide higher education for as many as 80 percent of each year's cohort of high school students.[7] This reveals an attempt to construct a new kind of educated citizen and an egalitarian society. During the 1950s, the project became more realistic: workers' children were supposed to make up 30 percent of students, and peasants 20 percent.[8] In 1945, in comparison with the interwar period, the number of students almost doubled, and spending on education rose from 0.5 percent of the annual state budget in 1939 to 11 percent.

I argue that the reform of universities was not a case of the oppression of Polish academia by a foreign superpower or the political brainwashing of naive students—the two most widespread notions about academia under state socialism. That is an incomplete and unjust story. At the beginning (1945–1948), it was not known how the political situation was going to develop, which allowed considerable latitude for the accumulation of wide-ranging support for the new political project. During the Stalinist period (1949–1953),[9] rapid modernization, upward social mobility, and simply postwar stabilization were important factors that, for many Polish citizens, helped build support for the new order. Over time, more women and more workers graduated not only from universities but also from high schools and trade schools, the latter becoming the main channel of upward social mobility. All subsequent generations brought up during the Polish People's Republic (Polska Rzeczpospolita Ludowa—the PRL) had greater chances of attaining a higher level of education than ever before, and educational inequalities decreased—for example, there was a sixfold increase in the selection of working-class children for higher education. Still, we know little about this group.

Based on extensive primary sources, press queries, and oral histories, my research recognizes the limitations of social change and contributes to how we understand what state socialism was. I am especially interested in the first postwar years and the Stalinist period (1945–1956), but the social and biographical processes examined here extend beyond any strict periodization; therefore, the timeline of this book stretches from the 1920s to the 1990s. My approach fixes its sight on the industrial city of Łódź. This working-class textile capital occupied a very special place in the postwar period. The industrial giant Łódź was nicknamed the "red" city because of the role it played in the 1905 revolution and its labor movement tradition. Historically, it operated as the "Other" in Polish culture, distinctively different from the urban centers of the Polish intelligentsia like Warsaw, Cracow, or Lviv, as well as sleepy rural townships.[10] Following the end of the war in 1945, only 30 percent of the city's former citizens remained, but its material structure was well preserved, and together with the influx of internally displaced Poles, it became the temporary, informal capital of the country, welcoming 200,000 newcomers in the following three years. It also became a "magnet for leftist intellectuals."[11] Although it had been the second-largest city after Warsaw since the 1870s, it had no previous academic structures nor higher education institutions to reproduce. Overall, it was the ideal place to build a university for a new era, and one could easily feel and become part of this change. In contrast to the conservative Jagiellonian University in Cracow or the hegemonic University of Warsaw, the University of Łódź became a perfect case of the socialist university—a working-class university in a working-class city.

I continue John Connelly's research on state-socialist universities,[12] but I deemphasize the authoritarian context, because it obscures the upward mobility of the working class and peasants. My argument focuses on other factors and sources. At the center of my attention is the proletarian city of Łódź, an initial flagship of socialist modernization, which has not been analyzed before. This gap leaves a conspicuous lacuna in the existing expertise on the topic. I trace the state-socialist elite's reproduction and higher education and use Pierre Bourdieu's theory to explain a triumph of cultural capital over political capital, epitomized in the reproduction of the academic intelligentsia. I tell the story of building a socialist university and planned emancipation, the unimagined success of many, a story also full of startling paradoxes and zealous pitfalls.

The "limiting privilege" in the book's title is the most important paradox of socialist mobilization. On the one hand, the socialist state tried to privilege peasant and working-class children in getting into and staying in higher education. It wanted to break down the reproduction of the social structure and democratize access to universities. On the other hand, these efforts were constrained by the privilege of the intelligentsia, whose domain was higher education, universities in particular. Throughout the book's chapters, I trace how these privileges—socialist and traditional—limited each other.

WHEN THE FUTURE WAS SOVIET

Worldwide, industrialization, as well as statism, became a paradigm for postwar economic thought and modernizing ideas. A classic 1947 work by Edward H. Carr, *The Soviet Impact on the Western World*,[13] introduced the United States to the notion that the Soviet system, or "a new and more progressive form of democracy," had developed in the USSR. The Soviet world was creating an alternative social project. It created a new modus operandi and an implicit reference point (or threat), facilitating a political adjustment to Western Europe and the United States. State socialism was inspired by (and in turn inspired) Western economic and philosophical thought[14]—the two were inseparably entwined and shaped postwar reality globally.[15] And sixty years after it could be still noted:

> Of all the deliberate social experiments which have taken place in human history, Soviet society was one of the largest ever undertaken [. . .] it claimed to offer an alternative to capitalism, providing full employment for its citizens, cheap housing for all, free health care and free education.[16]

I follow the revisionist paradigm and see the postwar decades as a time of social revolution and a spectacular modernization attempt.[17] Socialist modernization was limited and sometimes paradoxical, yet it was still a form of modernization aimed at, among other things, emancipation and the promotion of working-class mobility, largely by providing open access to education.[18] Nondemocratic, totalitarian environments can sometimes foster these processes. While not forgetting the terror that Soviet-style modernization wrought, and the victims it took, it was still a time of great social experiment—both in Soviet Russia from the 1920s, and in Central Europe after 1945, where political pressure was incomparable to that in the USSR. Socialist modernization refers here to the project of a new social system, state socialism in its historical and regional context, in particular postwar Poland.

Another question this book poses is exactly where in education and scholarship did state-socialist modernization achieve the most?[19] As late as the 1980s, the USSR had the biggest system of research and scholarly institutions in the world,[20] producing a rising number of publications, as well as students and graduates.[21] All countries of the Soviet bloc except Albania reached high rates of college education, leaving behind Latin America—a reference point that is often seen as more relevant than Western Europe when judging Eastern Europe modernization. Even some countries in the West had lower rates.[22]

The postwar reform of universities in Poland was a parallel process with the global shift from elite toward mass university education, which occurred in most developed and developing countries, both in socialist and capitalist systems. What was universal was rising accessibility for the first-generation students, and in Łódź socialist modernization was the way to implement it. An alternative version of society was emerging: based on collectivism, a planned economy or internationalism, promoting equal and open access to education, placing universities as a symbol of the new project—an elitist intelligentsia's institution was opening up to the masses. In Eastern Europe, postwar changes paved the way for the building of a socialist university, something seen as one of many possible solutions to a rising need for university reform and education for the working classes.

On the one hand "communism as a modernization project"[23] influenced Polish academia at the political and institutional level, bringing a pattern of uniformity to a whole region. On the other hand the local specifics of Poland show less obvious aspects of the change, especially in the case of the city of leftist intellectuals and the working class, which became a melting pot of Polishness, reformist spirits, and Soviet influence. In comparison to the other socialist republics, Poland serves as a great example through which to examine the latter processes thanks to its relative freedom in the Soviet bloc, historically strong intelligentsia, and also because of its dramatic starting point after World War II—the social revolution caused by wartime damage reinforced the scale of reform. Over 16 percent of the prewar population lost their lives and 38 percent of university professors perished. From 1945 onward, there was no going back to the interwar model of academia. Postwar Poland was not only about Zbigniew Brzeziński's "totalitarian" regime nor was it only Czesław Miłosz's "captive mind." It was also about modernization aimed at building an egalitarian society, modernizing the economy, and reforming the education system. For many it was a time of hope, agency, and possibilities. Engineers, teachers, and doctors were needed more than ever before. As elsewhere, intellectuals debated and quarreled over the shape of future academia; politicians struggled for power and influence; the daily press and public speeches reshaped everyday language; the social imaginary was being reconstructed; and the educational desires of the masses grew.

TOTALITARIANISM STRIKES BACK

One might think that the totalitarian paradigm is dead, but this is definitely not the case in Eastern Europe. In contemporary Polish bookstores, it is very easy to find the section containing literature on the country's postwar history. One need only look for the most black and red corner, where bookshelves display covers full of storm clouds, threatening red stars overshadowing the map of Poland, and bloody hammers and sickles. In recent years these images have been joined by wolves, partisans, and foggy forests. While narratives about Stalinist terror, the captivity of professors, and the seduction of students came to dominate contemporary historiography after 1989,[24] this book focuses on modernization and emancipation.

Though it might seem redundant to reconsider the old totalitarian–revisionist debate, this discussion is by no means over in Eastern Europe where the totalitarian perspective is still the hegemonic one—supported by institutions, job offers, and funding. What had seemed to be a long-gone and outdated way of thinking underwent a revival in peculiar local conditions. That is why I propose to refer to it as neototalitarianism: an Eastern European revival of the totalitarian approach that developed in the region after 1989. A paradigm clash between revisionists and totalitarians, which had lasted for several decades, took yet another turn after 1989; however, this time its main arena of dispute was located not in the United States, but in Eastern Europe and Russia itself. As Stephen Kotkin predicted,[25] a totalitarian hegemony overtook the field of history production in the region and gained support among transition elites.[26] The accessibility of new archival materials in the 1990s[27] and the need to build an alternative project to the PRL might explain the focus on oppression, terror, and censorship.[28] It was not only readership and publishing market currents that were causing the shift toward more sensational subjects, but a wider political project. The Institute of National

Remembrance in Poland, established in 1998, hegemonized historical writing about the PRL and public debate.[29] In consequence, the postwar period is often misleadingly framed by the two totalitarianism arguments: with the fascist occupation followed by the Soviet one.[30]

Polish research on universities and higher education was no exception. I would claim that those areas of study were even more strongly influenced by neototalitarianism alongside those of political affairs and underground movement studies. Universities are crucial institutions for social reproduction and traditionally they remain an important focus for the over-reflective intelligentsia who hegemonized discourse production even further after 1989. During the last decade a growing number of scholars have contested the above-mentioned neototalitarian paradigm through which Poland has been viewed. The shift has been based not only on translations of mainly American scholars, but new generations of scholars, mostly educated after 1989. Their contributions have not significantly impacted the available literature on higher education reforms in the postwar period.[31] A recent "people's turn" focusing on a peasant and working-class perspective in Polish history is slowly shifting the focus of the social sciences and humanities but concentrates mainly on serfdom and the pre-1945 period. However, the same approach is equally needed for postwar history.

Universities as the traditional domain of the intelligentsia still seem to be regarded as politically dominated by the state under state socialism, a view that includes two main narratives: either about the captivity of professors, or the subjugation of students, or both.[32] The existing literature in the field deals mainly with the problems of higher education policies as best reflected in Piotr Hübner's series of monographs.[33] These carefully reconstruct the postwar political influence on scholarship and its organization at the national level and are the most available literature in Polish.[34] Beyond this work, little attention has been paid to the topics covered in my book. Most available scholarship describes the working conditions of select academic disciplines during the period, taking into account the ideological pressure on academia.[35] With respect to the Polish background, the works closest to my area of interest are the historical books and the collection of sources published by Bohdan Baranowski,[36] as well as those by generations of Łódź-based sociologists, which will be discussed in more detail later on. However, the problem I would like to bring to light is only marginally treated in these works. One of the professors who worked most of her life at the University of Łódź, an anticommunist historian originally from Lviv, appealed:

> "Collaboration with the new occupant"—what an offensive simplification, inadequate in respect of reality. [. . .] Everyone, regardless of their political orientation, wanted to somehow cope with this new reality. [. . .] We, the Polish intelligentsia, responded to the country's needs, the needs of that difficult time.[37]

One sociologist, a student of Florian Znaniecki and a future rector of the University of Łódź, noted in his diary in 1945: "Although it is difficult to deny the unheard-of political primitivism of people from Lublin [communists—AZ], their program should be the program of tomorrow."[38]

Indeed, it did become the program of tomorrow and the argument of this book goes against dominant notions about the PRL, and in particular against two widespread notions about higher education in the postwar period: captivity and seduction.[39] Either one can speak about terror, the decline of academia, and a loss of autonomy, or about the ideological allure that attracted uneducated masses to support the evil regime. The two, seemingly contrasting, are actually complementary plots of the same approach—those two notions interact with each other within a framework of generational conflict. This totalitarian interpretation offers a vision of an endangered university. Its traditions and values, undermined by political forces that demand the production of specialists, appealed for support for industrial development and expected the implementation of positive discrimination in favor of young people of working-class origin, and so on. Therefore, these processes are seen as the domination of academia and the captivity of professors. Similarly, the postwar generation of students is considered to have been seduced by the vision of a new society and the creation of a "new intelligentsia." In this perspective there is no place for any kind of working-class or peasant perspective—the view of those who were for the first time addressed as legitimate citizens, who were encouraged and supported to study, and many of whom experienced social advancement. I focus on the socialist university in a working-class city to answer the question of what was possible within the new political circumstances for the first-generation students and how socialist modernization worked on the ground.

I argue that the old intelligentsia and interwar university shaped the biographical paths of academics more than any political factors, which are usually brought to the forefront by contemporary researchers. The main factors in the latter debate were brought up by Joel Andreas in his book on communist China, where he argued, against the classic interpretation that Communist parties claimed to represent the proletariat, that they were actually the vanguard of the intelligentsia.[40] Andreas shows that the emergence of a technocratic socialist class was not an achievement of state socialisms, but rather a failure of their class-leveling efforts, which were abandoned halfway.[41] His approach uses a frame of competing claims between political and cultural capital, and announces a final triumph of the latter. I fully agree, but in contrast to those claims, my argument lies closer to John Connelly's and Benjamin Tromly's works, which focus on the intelligentsia and its stubborn reproduction—enforced rather than captivated by political influence.[42] From my findings, cultural capital—the domain of the intelligentsia—defended itself against political influences. The narrative of the captive university produced by the totalitarian paradigm masks the highly conservative character of academia and its high level of autonomy, especially with regard to the values and criteria for granting positions to newcomers. It reveals how the contemporary narrative about state socialism was hegemonized not by the beneficiaries of social changes, but those whose position was endangered by the newcomers.

CHAPTER-BY-CHAPTER OVERVIEW

What is essential for understanding postwar reality is for it to be set in context. The first two chapters lay the groundwork for further analysis by drawing on a pair of crucial reference points for the postwar project: interwar academia and the impact of World War II. During the Second Republic of Poland (1918–1939), only five public universities and over thirty institutions of higher education were in operation before World War II, and none in Poland's second largest city—Łódź. The conditions prevailing in interwar academia were far from satisfactory. One of the main obstacles to be overcome was the lack of funding, which blocked the academic careers of many young scholars. On the eve of World War II, 3,000 faculty including 1,000 academic professors worked in Poland. Most of them (60–80 percent) were of intelligentsia origin, and only a few (4–8 percent) came from the working classes.[43] The universities had a rather conservative profile with respect to both their methodological and political aspects. Anti-Semitism at universities was just one element among an increasing number of dangerously ethnic tensions throughout the entire country, reflected in the educational reform of 1933 and the strengthening of the authoritarian regime. Many leftist intellectuals[44] could not find a place for themselves and some got involved in more progressive projects like the private Free Polish University. By the late 1930s, a quarter of the population was illiterate, educational selection took place even prior to the elementary level, the number of students per capita was low, and only 13.7 percent of the 50,000 students came from peasant or working-class families (which made up 80 percent of Poland's thirty-eight million multicultural citizens). Against this background, debate about the role of the university made slow progress. However, class and ethnic tensions indicated that reform was desperately needed. The most radical academics faced the challenge of how to think and design society anew, and how to deal with a hidebound institution like the university.

The interwar period established a reference point for the postwar period; later, World War II brought an end to this milieu, and it might be described as triggering a social revolution.[45] Therefore, the postwar period was a time of "Revolution and Modernization" (chapter 2), when leftist intellectuals saw in the aftermath of the war a very special historic moment for the implementation of utopian projects, for instance, reforming the social order by creating a new type of university—democratic, egalitarian, and free. Nineteen-forty-five was consequently the beginning of an unknown social order, possibilities, and dreams. Who the new social project was being designed for was still in the making.

The debate about the vision of the university is examined in the third chapter, "The University for New Times." I trace progressive intelligentsia discourse, which resulted in two contentious models for the university: a "liberal" and a "socialized" one. Analyzing speeches, articles, and memoirs, I reconstruct these models for the future university and the tensions between them. The main protagonists in this part of the discussion are the two first rectors of the University of Łódź: the philosopher Tadeusz Kotarbiński and the sociologist Józef Chałasiński. Kotarbiński's liberal university had three principles—accessibility based on individual skills, liberal content of curriculum, and democratic management. Likewise, Chałasiński argued for radical change and a break with interwar academia. He wanted a university open to the needs of society and accessible to all social strata, especially to the working classes. His vision evolved into the socialist university supported by the governmental reforms of the late 1940s. The vision of a socialist university that was discussed and the political reforms that were declared were only abstract ideas. How was the socialist university put into practice?

In the fourth chapter, "Rising Expectations," I offer an overview of policies proposed and tools aimed at democratizing the universities. The academic year 1949/1950 was crucial for Polish academia as it was then that the reform of higher education was implemented. Universities were transformed into institutions critical for the emerging state socialism. As elsewhere in the world, institutions of higher education became sites where national history and ideology would be delivered, and where the future elite would be shaped and produced. However, the socialist university was supposed to operate with a different horizon of values: collectivity, social responsibility, utility of research for the economy and society. It was supposed to provide education at a higher level for the people and bring an end to the reproduction of the old intelligentsia—the state aimed at limiting so-called privileged classes, but how was it possible to achieve this with legal and political tools? A variety of solutions was supposed to reshape higher education and, in turn, society as a whole.

To understand social change, we need to look at more than the political level of changes and intellectual debate. To effect a profound social change, a new hegemonic language was needed, but not the barely understood language of academic papers and political documents. During the first postwar decade, the influence of the press on society rose dramatically thanks to diminishing illiteracy, an expanding readership, as well as higher printing rates and better circulation (through, for instance, factory subscriptions, networks of libraries, and cultural centers). How this widely available language shaped expectations and how the press explained and mediated the meanings of the new reality is explored in the fifth chapter, "The Future Designed." Here I examine discourses introduced in the daily press after 1945 and a new configuration of meanings proposed by socialist modernization. I propose that postwar transformation effected a deep reconstruction of a social imaginary and the creation of educational desires among the working classes—in opposition to both the seduction argument and the newspeak interpretation. Instead of framing the press as a propaganda tool of totalitarian ideology, I look at it as any other hegemonic language. Moreover, this press language has its roots in socialist pamphlets and revolutionary speeches from the nineteenth century and the 1905 revolution. Instead of focusing on features of totalitarian languages, I trace the creation of new subjects and the discourse's emancipatory potential for a proletarian and peasant reader.[46]

Chapter 6, "Educational Desires," traces how those ideas were brought into practice. What were the results of the implemented reforms and a profound change in public discourse? Could a new privileged position of the working classes be secured? And how was it possible to measure a possible success, indeed how was it possible to reach to the level of daily practices, individual choices shaping and shaped by the social structure? Policies of enrollment, points for class origin, preparatory courses, and learning groups were supposed to privilege those unprivileged by history and social structure—to make the vision of a socialist university a reality. Insight into that time is possible thanks to the return of sociology, banned in the late 1950s. I examine rich research materials, reports, and analyses conducted by sociologists over a long period. However, when in the 1970s 40 percent of each year's high school graduates entered universities (before World War II the rate was 4–5 percent), 20–60 percent of students did not finish even their first year of education. Moreover, most of this group were of working-class origin—what was the reason for this and what kind of obstacles did they face?

While political careers and even management positions were more open to working-class people, academia served as a testing ground for upward mobility, which is examined in the last two chapters. What then were the limits of social change and the reproduction of the intelligentsia and the traditional university? By the 1950s, a new generation of scholars had entered academia and taken agency at universities. This postwar generation was supposed to become true comrades and to build the university-factory for a new era. I reconstruct a typical professor's biography in chapter 7, "Academic Biography." Although prospects of mobility were available, universities remained highly elitist with only a minority of working-class students. I argue that the intelligentsia and the traditional university shaped the biographical paths of academics more strongly than political factors, which are usually brought to the forefront by contemporary researchers. To give a brief example: during the reforms, eleven assistant professors lost their jobs, yet nine of them continued their academic careers later on. Furthermore, while academic titles were granted to 302 people in 1951–1954, only 41 were Communist Party members.[47]

Finally, only a very small group of students decided to continue in academic careers after graduation—a fact that ultimately reveals the limits of postwar social change. What course did the clash of old and new privileges take? Which would be stronger: the state-guaranteed privilege of the working classes or the traditionally secured high position and capital of the intelligentsia? A final chapter, "Newcomers to Academia," focuses on the tiny group of working-class children who actually became professors. How did their paths differ from those of intelligentsia children? Tracing the biographical trajectory of Polish academia, I shape my final argument based on oral histories. I compare the academic biography described in the previous chapter with biographies of professors from working-class and peasant backgrounds, and conclude that the differences are minor. Those who formed a seemingly perfect "new intelligentsia" were socialized by the traditional academic habitus. The few who entered the new academic world from working-class or peasant backgrounds had to embrace the interwar university ethos in order to justify their own claim to belong. I propose a model of opposite hysteresis vectors to explain tensions between the academic and political fields.

The reforms, the repressions of the time of Stalinism, or even the simple influx of students from the working classes and the massification of universities opened up new opportunities for academic careers and reconstructed the academic habitus. At least, this would seem to be the intuitive interpretation from the perspective of today's view of that period as a time of a captive and shackled academia and the idea of the formation of a new intelligentsia. In light of the collected materials, however, another dimension of the work of hysteresis seems much more important: not the process whereby the habitus of academics was adapted to the changed rules of the field (which also took place), but the changing habitus of people entering the academic field on the back of those changes. Accordingly, the question I pose concerns the adaptation of the "select few"—the people from lower classes who embarked on the path of a university career. Which privilege would be limiting: the old privilege of the intelligentsia or the new privilege of the socialist state?

The case presented here also contributes to an explanation of the intersection of individual agencies and institutional trajectories. Where there is power, so the story goes, there is resistance as well. No administrative or policy reform is carried out solely on paper. It is always constituted and put into practice by various institutional changes, working its way down through different levels where it is contested, reestablished, reciprocally induced through conjoining and differentials, and thus rearticulated. When power, however ruthless and forceful, "hits the ground," it is met with various interactive dynamics and reshaped along different structural and personal vectors. The book gives voice to this first generation of previously marginalized students. It tells their story in all its specificities, with all its paradoxes, and also with an understanding of and empathy for its protagonists—those who experienced social advancement under state socialism.

1

INTERWAR TRAPS

The Polish intelligentsia in its structure is related to the underdevelopment of Polish civilization in technical and economic terms.[1]

ALTHOUGH THE UNIVERSITY OF ŁÓDŹ FOUNDATION ACT DATES BACK TO MAY 24, 1945, the processes that enabled the establishment of the institution begin much earlier. There is no point in tracing these back to the redbrick university revolution or the popularization of the German university as a model, which was especially favored by the Polish intelligentsia. My scope of interest here is more pragmatic and also less focused on academia itself. This chapter provides a brief historical context, which aims to provide an in-depth understanding of the origins of the socialist university and the most important reference points that shaped its possibilities and defined what could be imagined.

The first reference point is that of interwar Poland, a highly mythical period in Polish history, during which a reestablished, independent state provided a new context for universities. Both the continuity and the disruption represented by the Second Republic of Poland (1918–1939) would leave visible marks on the later project of the socialist university. The second reference point, as will be discussed in the next chapter, was World War II, which I understand mainly as a social revolution. The war years reshaped the social, political, and economic structure of the Polish state and society in a particularly cruel manner. Prewar values were undermined, population losses were enormous, much of Poland's basic infrastructure was destroyed, and the state's geopolitical situation was profoundly changed. There was no going back to the Second Republic of Poland.

These two historical periods not only shaped and defined future developments at the level of inevitable chronological consequences, but more importantly, they rendered postwar ways of thinking and coping with social reality. Both historical reference points are crucial to the telling of the story about Polish state socialism, as they were crucial for the generational formation of socialism-builders. The interwar and the wartime periods were a necessary antithesis for the creation of a new social reality. I also introduce, at this point, the book's case study—the University of Łódź—and explain the city's history as well as the specific role that this industrial giant played in Polish culture.

MYTHICAL REPUBLIC

Only a dozen years after the war, the period of the Second Republic of Poland began to be regarded in the collective memory as a mythical time.[2] This sentiment, first put forward in the mid-1960s, appears to still hold. Perhaps it is even more compelling in the context of the post-1989 idealization of the interwar period and attempts to construct an image of the Third Republic of Poland as a direct continuation of the Second Republic, with an almost total omission of the 1945–1989 period, which in some quarters is referred to as a "second occupation," after that of World War II.

After World War I, in "the East," as the colossal modernization of the Soviet Union was being cast in the fire of the revolution, the countries of Central Europe, including Poland, were faced with the equally difficult modernizing challenges of finally building independent nation-states. The Second Republic of Poland was the long-awaited fulfillment of the intelligentsia's dreams of an independent homeland. For the entire long nineteenth century, that is, for just over 120 years, 1795–1918—a period key for industrialization, urbanization, as well as the universalization of education—the territory of the future republic was divided between three separate powers, a phenomenon known as "the partitions." This meant three separate and distinctive education systems and related social policies, which conditioned the availability of educational paths. Furthermore, a series of failed insurrections and several years of war (first, World War I, and soon after, the Polish-Bolshevik war) reinforced a sense of the role of the intelligentsia as the guardian of national identity, and of education as a means of preserving jeopardized values. In 1918, a completely new country was being built that would have very little in common with the gentry's "democracy," the First Republic of Poland (1569–1795). At the same time, its implementation was not easy and became increasingly complicated during subsequent years due to the economic crisis of 1929, growing political tensions, the authoritarian direction of the 1930s, and a radicalization of social tensions.

Under these difficult conditions, the primary function of education and the university was to integrate the nation in the postpartition period and build up Polish culture. Initially, the main challenge was primarily that of rampant illiteracy[3] and to tackle this the introduction of compulsory schooling. A scarcity of educated people, drawn from three different education systems, hindered reforms at both the elementary and higher education levels. Academia was made up of professors who came from each of the three partitions along with those returning home after years of working abroad, as well as middle school teachers and even clerks.[4] Some faculty came from pauperized gentry backgrounds, their earlier lives derailed, while others, whose social origin will be discussed later, came from assimilated bourgeois Jewish and German families.

There were five public universities in the country: in Warsaw, Poznań, Lviv (the Jan Kazimierz University), Vilnius (the Stefan Batory University), and Cracow (the Jagiellonian University), as well as a nonpublic Catholic University in Lublin. However, before World War II over thirty "institutions of higher education" were in operation, including technical universities, academies, and colleges. The best-known institutes of higher education, apart from the universities, were the Warsaw School of Economics and the Academy of Mining in Cracow. The most important from our perspective was another nonpublic initiative, the Free Polish University in Warsaw, with a local branch in Łódź.[5]

The oldest university, the Jagiellonian, had for over a century been little more than a local academic center on the margins of the Austro-Hungarian Empire, where intellectual life primarily took place in Vienna and Budapest; nevertheless, the Jagiellonian continued to be the heart of Polish academia. The Jan Kazimierz University was considered the second most vibrant center of Polish intellectual life at the time. Now in the Second Republic of Poland, previously also part of the Habsburg Empire, the university in Lviv offered the best opportunities for social advancement and was relatively open to peasant students. The situation of universities that had been under the Russian partition was quite different. After the November Uprising (1830–1831), Nicholas I had ordered the closure of all universities in the territory of the Kingdom of Poland, an edict that affected both the ancient, and at that time czarist, University of Vilnius as well as the University of Warsaw, which was then barely a dozen years old. The latter, however, operated with interruptions and under various names until it became polonized in 1915. It was not until Poland regained independence that higher education in Vilnius was resumed, under the name of the Stefan Batory University; and at the same time, a new university was founded: the Polish University in Poznań.

In the 1930s, Warsaw dominated all other academic centers, attracting nearly half the entire country's students: 10 percent at the Warsaw University of Technology and 20 percent at the University of Warsaw; and considering nonpublic universities, it attracted around 40 percent of the entire student body.[6] The second largest academic center was Lviv, which accounted for a fifth of the student body, at the Jan Kazimierz University, the city's Polytechnic, its Academy of Veterinary Medicine, and other nonpublic universities. Size-wise, the next was Cracow with three public universities, and following this, the smaller universities in Poznań and Vilnius. The last was Lublin's private Catholic University.

Łódź was not alone in aspiring to become an academic city. Katowice, Toruń, and Bydgoszcz also applied for support with opening universities. All these cities had a considerable German population and a proletarian character. At that point, in terms of its population, Łódź was five or even ten times the size of any other of these aspiring cities. Compared with the academic cities, it was twice as big as Lviv and over four times the size of Poznań. Why Łódź's pursuit of a university, which dates back as far as the 1860s, would always end in failure will be the topic of later discussion.

THE SHACKLES OF UTILITARIANISM

After World War II, debate about the education system and academia pictured the interwar period as its main, and mostly negative, point of reference. It was criticized for being conducive to the formation of a traditional, frequently termed "liberal," model of the university. Indeed, the first legislation to be passed during the interwar period was inspired by the German model, and it secured, first and foremost, the university's autonomy and the independence of its faculty. Professors given tenure became practically unremovable. They were not obliged to report on their activities, and the authorities were able to enter the university campus only with the rector's permission.[7] Higher education institutions were also highly autonomous in terms of their finances.[8] The challenges of everyday life and the difficult situation of Polish academia distanced reality from theory and, in the 1930s, political circumstances almost entirely undermined the groundbreaking concepts of a liberal university.

As early as 1918, a debate was triggered on the mission of academia and its relation to the state, economy, and society. There were voices that called for the inclusion of academia into public life. In 1919, a discussion about the university–state relationship started in the pages of the academic journal *Nauka Polska* (Polish Science). Some believed that the state should publicize its demand for research at the same time as academics should play a practical, utilitarian role in the development of the reborn motherland. In 1919, the historian Kazimierz Tymieniecki made an appeal, using his own discipline as an example: "While non-specialists should not evaluate the scholarly methods and means of a historian, a historian owes the nation a view of its own history that is accessible and comprehensible to all."[9]

However, the opposition immediately raised their voices. Protesters argued that public clerks did not understand the role of scholarship. Only academics could decide on and engage in topics deemed to be useful. This dispute resurfaced at the meetings of the First Congress of Polish Science in 1920. The voice of another historian, who called for the planned and collective efforts of all academics instead of anarchy and individualism, was marginalized as a threat to the intrinsic value of knowledge and the autonomy of the scholar.[10] The same situation occurred during the Second Scientific Congress of the Józef Mianowski Fund[11] on April 2–3, 1927. This time, one of the professors criticized the government for its lack of interest in the issue of scientific utility and research policies, but the majority of attendees did not support him. These were lone voices against a background of the dominant vision of academia as an independent community and *universitas* of scholars (also financed mostly by private funds).

While the polemics on whether knowledge production should be pure or subject to the "shackles of utilitarianism"[12] continued, this took place on the margins of university life. In 1929, the director of research at the Baltic Institute, Józef Borowik, wrote: "The autonomy of Polish scholarship is not jeopardized by etatism. [...] A bigger threat is the lack of resources for laboratories, stipends and libraries."[13] Planned research, "utilitarian" engagement, and teamwork were supposed to alleviate this.[14] It was not until the 1930s that changes to the research policies of the authorities were introduced and government attempts were made to engage researchers in industry and agriculture. In 1936, the Council of Applied Sciences was founded. Nonuniversity research centers began to emerge: the National Institute for Rural Culture, which employed sociologists and the future rectors of the University of Łódź: Józef Chałasiński as well as another protégé of the famous sociologist Florian Znaniecki[15]—Jan Szczepański. However, this type of initiative was not at all typical of academic life of the time whose imagined ideal was "pure knowledge" and the model of a liberal university, which was becoming increasingly detached from the actual state of the country.

Generally, universities had a rather conservative profile with respect to both methodology and policies. On a declarative level, academic circles were largely apolitical. However, two of the postpositivist trends shaping the Polish intelligentsia were palpable: nationalism and socialism. The strong influence of the nationalist camp was predominantly felt in Poznań and Cracow. Warsaw, Lviv, and Vilnius were perceived as pro-Sanacja[16] centers whereas leftist researchers found themselves either outside academia, in niches such as the Free Polish University, or part of nonuniversity scholarly initiatives.[17] While few professors were members of political parties, many fulfilled administrative functions or were members of Parliament.[18] The May Coup of 1926, carried out by Marshal Józef Piłsudski, installed a professor from Lviv, Kazimierz Bartel, as the new prime minister. The coup opened the door to the reinforcement of the authoritarian regime. The Brest trials of 1932, during which the leftist opposition was persecuted and sentenced to eighteen months to three years in prison, became a symbol of that change.[19] Just a year later, higher education reform was introduced.

Key changes were triggered by the 1933 Higher Education Act, a part of the broader Jędrzejewicz education reform policies.[20] These included granting the minister of religion and public education the right to approve rectors selected by universities, and to form and to close down departments, chairs, and institutes; extending rectors' terms to three years; and capping the powers of the university senate and student groups. The act considerably augmented the powers of the minister. It also treated a number of issues in such a generic, broad-brush fashion that it left several areas open to interpretation, thereby inviting even more intrusion by the administrative authorities into university life.[21] Considering earlier stages of education, it also made it harder for young peasants to progress from elementary to middle schools and for middle school graduates to move on to general secondary schools.[22] The Act was opposed in academic circles, which resulted, among other things, in professors known for their antigovernment views being forced into early retirement as well as the liquidation of twenty or so chairs. At the same time, new nominations for the positions of rector and professor clearly hinged on candidates' positive, or at least neutral, attitude toward the authorities (one of the newly formed chairs was given to the partner, and later the second wife—a rare female scholar—of Janusz Jędrzejewicz). The new Act was at odds with the liberal model of the university with which many wished to identify. It transferred the powers of university senates to the central authorities and, ultimately, it streamlined the liquidation of fifty-three chairs according to political views. The autonomy of universities was used against the protesters (if they wanted to keep its autonomy, they were not to engage in politics). The act remained in force until 1948.

From the 1930s onward political and social problems arose. Following the Higher Education Act, the state's control over academia increased. At the same time, growing anti-Semitism reached the universities where young nationalists were stirring up trouble; this would become a growing problem during the immediate prewar years. One of the main obstacles to be overcome by institutes of higher education was a lack of funding: In 1938 they were awarded only 0.43 percent of the annual budget, while private funds were scarce. This had a very negative impact on the experimental sciences and blocked the academic careers of many young scholars.[23] In the 1930s, the number of associate professors (*docent*) grew but a faculty position was assigned effectively for life. Hence, the most privileged positions were restricted to a very small group of professors—the majority of whom were men, and over 60 percent of them were older than forty-five.[24] This lack of job openings and perspectives led to the migration of many talented scholars of the younger generation. Furthermore, a majority of the educated intelligentsia, primarily teachers, became unemployed as a result of the economic crisis and education reforms.[25]

Despite the fact that in order to decentralize the academic map of Poland, new institutions were founded outside the traditionally academic cities, Warsaw, Cracow, Lviv, and Poznań remained the unquestioned centers of learning, while the rest of the country stayed poorly developed. Industrial Łódź and the Silesia region were the most disadvantaged as well the most populous areas. Students were mostly recruited from the landed gentry, the bourgeois, and the intelligentsia, and one of the most common modes of recruitment continued to be the infamous student corporations. In the eyes of left-wing public opinion, members of these corps symbolized the "golden youth"; they were presented by the press as slackers who earned their diplomas with egregious delays, engaged in fights, partied endlessly, and treated their studies as a time for fun and entertainment rather than a period of intensive effort and work.

Obóz Wielkiej Polski (Camp of Great Poland, a far-right organization), Młodzież Wszechpolska (All-Polish Youth, a right-wing nationalist youth organization), and other such groups were gaining popularity among students. They operated by infiltrating existing student organizations, above all Bratnia Pomoc (Brotherly Help), which refused membership to Jews. They increased the influence of nationalists on students through the distribution of support measures, such as offering places in dormitories.[26] They openly advocated the removal of Jews from universities for "spreading pacifism" and "internationalism." Ghetto benches[27] were introduced at the Lviv Polytechnic, the University of Warsaw, and the Jagiellonian as bottom-up initiatives spearheaded by anti-Semitic militia. Debate around *numerus clausus*, which limited the Jewish student enrollment to 10 percent of the student body, had its origin in Russian Empire policies, but its introduction was discussed in the 1920s (along with a proposed total ban on Jewish students—*numerus nullus*).[28] With regard to the wave of interwar anti-Semitism, such debates also took place in other European countries as well as in the United States.

Numerus clausus also targeted women on the grounds that it was not worth investing in female students as, first, they were less bright and, second, courses were too demanding for them and put pressure on the state budget—women wasted public funds by going on to choose family instead of academia.[29] This was a litmus test of patriarchy regulating academia. Female students faced chauvinistic comments, were ignored or verbally attacked in university lecture halls, threatened in university corridors. While these might have been exceptional incidents recalled within stories of overall success, they define the social imaginary of the period. In addition, the notion of academia as an ivory tower and the scholar as detached genius devoting his whole life to science served against the feminization of studies. Again, being a scholar was not a profession but a vocation, a calling, therefore emotional women burdened with family obligations could not possibly meet such expectations. Still, during the interwar period more and more women entered and finished the secondary level of education, in particular general secondary schools. This resulted in the changing composition of the student body. In the 1930s, 27 percent to 40 percent of university students were female—the majority in the humanities (except law) and arts; within the medical faculties, in dentistry.[30] Unfortunately, those proportions diminished at higher levels such as completing studies and graduating, not to mention defending a PhD thesis or being awarded a habilitation. Before 1939, there were only six women professors.[31]

The professors of the interwar years constituted a very narrow group, whose separation from the rest of society was augmented by their privileged origin. Demographic factors that theoretically could have favored the mobility of the lower classes into the intelligentsia, such as a low birth rate among this group in comparison with the peasantry, did not change the status quo. On the eve of World War II, half of all white-collar workers were the offspring of the intelligentsia, a quarter of the propertied class (the gentry and wealthy bourgeois), while a fifth were the children of peasants, factory, and blue-collar workers.[32] However, the category of white-collar workers is a very broad one, which includes the lowest ranking officials as well as factory clerks. The popular belief that during the interwar period a secondary school–leaving certificate was a ticket to the intelligentsia or at least to higher society is a myth. The periodical *Głos Nauczycielski* (The Teachers' Voice) illustrated the issue succinctly, referring to a situation in one of the middle schools in Łódź: "The daughters of councilors do not talk to the daughters of clerks while the latter do not speak to the daughters of craftsmen."[33] Social divisions were strong and with only a secondary school–leaving certificate, the only way one would ever feature among the intelligentsia would be in a statistical table. In 1933, only 11 percent of the intelligentsia (white-collar workers) had a higher education.[34] The professors were the intelligentsia's elite.

The range of social origins of members of faculty and staff was different from that of the white-collar class in general. Out of the thirty million people making up the Second Republic of Poland, only around a thousand held the title of professor. Several thousand served as university lecturers and researchers while very few engaged in ad hoc scientific and scholarly research. When universities were being formed in the wake of World War I, 60.4 percent of professors came from the intelligentsia (i.e., mostly from families of officials, doctors, and engineers), 15.4 percent were from the gentry, and another 10 percent were from the bourgeois (industrialists, merchants, and owners of tenement houses and urban property). Five percent came from the peasantry (mostly from Galicia, that is, the section of Poland that had formerly been part of the Austro-Hungarian Empire). Only 3.3 percent had working-class origins, and of these the majority came from the families of railwaymen, that is, they were state employees with a high social status and a stable income.[35] By the 1930s, little had changed with regard to the social profile of the academic community. It remained a very elitist group: 84 percent of academic employees came from the professional intelligentsia, 7 percent from petit bourgeois circles, 5 percent from the gentry and bourgeoisie, and still only 4 percent from the working class and peasantry.[36]

In order to grasp the egalitarian foundations of the educational policy of the Polish People's Republic, it is crucial to better understand the educational policy of interwar Poland, which excluded and hindered many from accessing higher education on class, gender, and ethnic grounds. To recapitulate, the interwar academic intelligentsia was politically divided, which became transparent during the disputes that took place at the end of the 1930s. In the final years of the Second Republic of Poland, the institutional life of Polish academia became dominated by the nationalist and pro-government camp.

A uniform reaction by some professors to prison sentences in Brest[37] and anti-Semitic incidents in Cracow, Warsaw, and Lviv helped unite liberal and leftist academics. That only a relatively small section of the academic community[38] chose to speak out publicly against the ghetto benches points to the general sentiments in Polish academic circles and an ever-widening rift in world view. These experiences, along with the later Nazi occupation, turned a number of intellectuals toward the left of the political spectrum. This was not a new tendency by any means. To use Andrzej Mencwel's phrase, it was more of a continuation of the "left's ethos,"[39] a tradition of the generation that Bohdan Cywiński refers to as "the defiant."[40]

Beyond the institutionalized group of professors, researchers without academic chairs, who had to support themselves with a mixture of teaching, ad hoc research work, tuition, and publications, were also an important factor. A significant number of interwar researchers were unable to secure themselves any position whatsoever, and due to their nationality, religion, or political views, they were excluded from universities and technical universities. The most radical researchers feared ending up in the Bereza Kartuska internment camp, while others did freelance work at universities, sought employment at research centers, or joined the most progressive university with a liberal, even leftist profile—the private Free Polish University (Wolna Wszechnica Polska—the WWP).[41] In 1928, this university opened a branch in the working-class city of Łódź, thereby laying the foundations for the development of higher education in this working-class city.

THE RED CITY

So far as we know, the first cornerstone of the university in Łódź was laid in 1928; not only did this happen very late, but it was also a truly modest event. The "Polish Manchester" was the largest industrial textile center in Eastern Europe and despite rare calls from a progressive intelligentsia to educate the illiterate proletarian masses, education was definitely not its forte. Throughout the nineteenth century, industrial hubs like Łódź had faced massive migration, ethnic and class struggles, rapid modernization, and the rise of peripheral capitalism. In the 1820s, Łódź was nothing but a forgotten town in the Kingdom of Poland, a semi-independent part of the Russian Empire. The intensity of social change brought about by rapid government-driven modernization at the beginning of the 1800s was of course much more significant than in the countries where these processes occurred over a more extended period of time. Urbanization and industrialization were not evolutionary, but revolutionary, and the capital of this revolution was Łódź. Throughout the Russian Empire, industrialization was founded first and foremost on cheap labor and easily accessible natural resources. Simultaneously, the government's economic policy was a mixture of laissez-faire and protectionism. Consequently, this meant that the authorities, in the hope of rapid industrialization, supported capitalists rather than paying attention to improving the conditions of the working class. Economic inequality, and consequently social unrest, gradually grew. Neither the czarist regime nor the local administration took responsibility for urban policy, labor legislation, or education. Areas now dealt with by the public sector were handled by private benefactors or by charity.

As a result, Łódź was soon nicknamed "the Polish Manchester," and like the original had the tarnished reputation of a "shock city,"[42] and even, less ambiguously, of "a bad city"—anti-intellectual, other, and barbarian.[43] By the interwar period its time of economic prosperity was over, but its bad reputation remained. Until World War II, "Łódź [was] treated as a tumor in a traditionally agricultural country, as a center not only without history but also without a myth with which it could be positively associated."[44] One of the first scholarly books to be written on Łódź, in the late 1920s by Edward Rosset, was titled *Łódź—miasto pracy* (Łódź—City of Labor); it diagnosed the following:

> If Łódź is an eyesore, if the urban facilities are blatantly scarce and neglected in the capital of Polish labor, if, finally, today's Łódź is a caricature of healthy city expansion, this is a result of nothing else but the abnormal conditions of Łódź's growth.[45]

The first national report on the academic life of Łódź, published in *Nauka Polska* in 1933, can be considered as symptomatic. Before reporting on the state of science and scholarship in Łódź, the author devotes half the material to justifying the mention of Łódź in the first place:

> The power of opinion, particularly in literature, which refer to Łódź as "a bad city," "a domain of business and bankruptcy, a land of ruthless materialism," the power of arbitrary judgments of newcomers from other districts who call our city "Europe's largest village" is so suggestive that even a native of Łódź, who, let's say, has been taking part in the city's cultural life for a couple decades, is affected by these critical opinions and often asks himself if academic life in Łódź exists at all?[46]

Furthermore, in the closing section, thanks are given for taking Łódź into account and an appeal is made for this city to be written about in order to "rectify the erroneous and hasty judgments about Łódź's lack of education," so "the world can know the extent to which we serve the highest purposes."

The coming of independence to the Polish state after World War I did not change much in this working-class city; indeed, compared to its years under wartime German occupation, one could say that there was some regression. Years of neglect, war damage, economic crises on various scales, and finally, central policies toward Łódź did not facilitate its growth. A number of issues typical for nineteenth-century industrial cities were exacerbated. Industry became increasingly consolidated and nearly half of all factory workers were employed in several of the largest companies. The population of Łódź remained stable thanks to a constant influx of a young workforce. Residential density remained at the same level despite the city's depopulation during numerous epidemics, the war, and the subsequent economic turbulence. The population of Łódź struggled with poor housing conditions and malnourishment: the nutritional value of the working-class diet was worse than in Warsaw and other industrial areas such as the Dąbrowa Basin. On the other hand, in many respects, the interwar period was a time of positive change: Attempts were made to combat illiteracy, the urban expansion of the city was supervised, a network of public institutions was established, and the further regulation of labor law was instituted.[47]

Education in Łódź visibly improved, primarily thanks to the newly elected city council. Łódź was the first city in the territory of the former Russian partition that actually implemented compulsory elementary schooling. Promoting education at various levels and building several modern schools required a substantial effort. This issue was also hotly discussed in the local press.[48] Despite the introduction of compulsory elementary schooling and fines for not complying with the new regulations, one in three working-class families failed to educate at least one child. At the level of secondary education, the percentage of working-class children fluctuated between 3 and 5 percent.[49] Slowly, the reproduction of the factory workforce was taking place, although professional mobility was minuscule.

Despite the fact that for most residents of Łódź it was difficult even to enter the education system, the issue of setting up a higher education institution had been raised as early as the 1860s. Several attempts were made to open a technical university; first in 1865, and again throughout the interwar period until the late 1930s, when the Ministry of Treasury blocked an initiative to establish a medical university in the city. Every effort failed, whether responsibility lay with the czarist administration in Petersburg, the German occupier during World War I, or the government of the Second Republic of Poland. The reasons for the rejection varied. However, it seems that a fear of creating an intellectual base for the labor movements, which had a far-reaching influence in Łódź, played the key role.

While it is true that the interwar period produced the first generations of educated people as well as local literary and artistic circles, this was a small and not very active group. Its activity could be measured in the journals devoted to art and culture that it produced (occasional and not widely read). Due to a lack of readership, there appeared only one issue of the first journal on art and culture, *Tańczący Ogień* (Dancing Fire). Later, there were others, such as *Nowe Drogi* (New Paths) and *Prądy* (Currents).[50] Łódź, still the second largest city in the Second Republic, attracted the Galicia intelligentsia, which emigrated to the motherland after the drawing of new borders. It is noteworthy that Austria-Hungary had offered the best and most egalitarian conditions for education, relatively speaking.

In response to a lack of state support, independent initiatives were taken. Small groups of the local intelligentsia organized campaigns that tackled illiteracy among the wider public. It was then that the first research projects were undertaken in Łódź and about Łódź (primarily historical works). In the early 1920s, the independent and short-lived Teachers' Institute and the College of Social and Economic Science were founded. However, both institutions were disbanded in 1928 due to the politico-economic crisis. Both schools mostly attracted adults; the schools were not authorized to issue higher education diplomas, and the entire teaching staff was drawn from beyond the city, with people commuting into Łódź to teach. As so few faculty members resided permanently in Łódź, they were never able to reach the critical mass necessary to speak of this city having its own academic community.

The most serious attempt at creating a university was the aforementioned foundation of the Free Polish University.[51] Dating back to 1916 in Warsaw, it was a non–state university whose goal was to disseminate knowledge. It drew on the model of the "free universities," which were popular at the turn of the century in Western Europe, and on the tradition of alternative education in the Kingdom of Poland. At that time, the Free Polish University was a prototype of an egalitarian university. Its aim was to educate social, political, and local government workers. In terms of the selection of faculty and the university's atmosphere, the Free Polish University was commonly perceived as a domain of leftist and liberal circles.[52] One might say that if the conservative Catholic University of Lublin was at one end of the spectrum, then the Free Polish University was at the other, with its clear social engagement and left-leaning tendencies.[53] For a long time, it was not treated as a "serious" university. Once it obtained the right to award diplomas, its position was strengthened. However, its basic problem was its leftist image.

The political profiles of the Free Polish University and the Łódź city council most certainly had a major impact on their working together and opening a branch of the university in Łódź. This was also why a group of councilors and numerous other groups in Łódź protested, in opposition to the importation and subsidizing of a "Bolshevik university." As an alternative, it was proposed that a branch of the Catholic University of Lublin be opened in Łódź. The city authorities were responsible for all attempts to organize higher education in Łódź. Thanks to the socialist majority, the Free Polish University was granted access to buildings and a high annual operational subsidy, amounting to 3 percent of the city's annual budget. This naturally met with protests again from nationalist circles. It is interesting to note the elitist bent of their argument. The Free Polish University was presented as a crucible of mediocrity. It was accused of attracting those who had failed to pass the *matura*, the school-leaving exam, and of producing an intelligentsia proletariat. It was also called "a cesspool of socialism and atheism."[54] The Free Polish University was spared the anti-Semitic incidents plaguing other universities in the late 1930s. It was also constantly monitored by the National Democrats.[55]

Throughout its existence, the Free Polish University in Łódź struggled with a difficult situation in terms of both finances and infrastructure. Initially, three departments were formed: humanities, political sciences, and pedagogy. Sixty-six people were employed, of whom forty-three commuted from Warsaw. The rest—primarily young people—were mainly recruited from Łódź.[56] The faculty totaled around 100 people but faculty numbers fluctuated. Aside from Seweryn Sterling (who died in 1932), none of the academic employees was local and none could be persuaded to move to the city, even when offered a full-time position and remuneration by the rector of the city's branch of the Free Polish University. As a result, lecturers, who were constantly in a hurry to catch a train home, did not have the chance to build rapport with students. Their first conversations often only took place after the end of term exam, and there was no chance to build any academic community around the university.

The branch in Łódź did not succeed in terms of teaching, either. The number of students fluctuated between 300 and 400.[57] The local intelligentsia rarely sent their children there. Most students from Łódź—as many as 57 percent—studied at various universities in Warsaw, while 20 percent studied in Poznań and only 10 percent at the city's Free Polish University branch. Overall, it was one of the smallest universities in the Second Republic of Poland. The largest, the University of Warsaw, had a student body of over 9,000. The Catholic University of Lublin, which resembled the Free Polish University with respect to its organization, attracted as many as 1,000 students. It was not only its size that distinguished the Free Polish University but also the social makeup of its students. According to the data in the *Atlas Szkolnictwa Wyższego* (The Higher Education Atlas) from 1937, by A. Witlin, as many as 35 percent of the students came from a peasant or working-class background, whereas the country's average stood at 13.7 percent for both groups. Also, its faculty was the most feminized, hiring thirty-five female scholars among whom five were professors (out of the six holding this title).[58] The students at the Łódź branch of the Free Polish University were recruited mainly from among the Polish section of society (87 percent came from the Łódź region) and female students made up the majority. Moreover, tuition was not free and despite the activity of self-help organizations and a flexible schedule enabling students to both study and work, few could afford to. The university did not operate long enough to influence either accessibility to or inclusiveness of education, the local intellectual environment, or the image of Łódź. Despite this, the tradition of the Free Polish University later played a crucial role in the formation of the university in Łódź in 1945, which was largely based on the community of Free Polish University professors from Łódź and Warsaw, the so-called *wszechnicowcy*.

Following the outbreak of World War II, reformist tendencies in Polish academia intensified along with the feeling shared by the intelligentsia that a certain era had come to an end. Those, like the *wszechnicowcy*, who remained on the margins could fight for a change.

2

REVOLUTION AND MODERNIZATION

Łódź—the working-class heart of Poland
is starting to beat strongly.[1]

WHILE WORLD WAR II WAS FIRST AND FOREMOST A CATASTROPHE, IT WAS also a revolution.[2] Indeed, those few dreadful years witnessed profound shifts, redefinitions, and transformations in almost all aspects of social, economic, and political life. Writing about Poland, both Michael Fleming and Padraic Kenney refer to Tadeusz Łepkowski's "two revolutions."[3] They have described World War II and its aftermath as a double revolution: a social and economic one until 1947 and a political one between 1948 and 1950.[4] In turn, Polish scholars such as Krystyna Kersten, or more recently Andrzej Leder, see it as one social revolution lasting from 1939 to 1956.[5] Following the war, reconstruction was imperative and its scale was immense.

Poland suffered social and economic losses estimated as the most damaging in the whole of Eastern Europe[6]—over 16 percent of the prewar population lost their lives during the war, including 90 percent of the prewar Jewish population.[7] Postwar, the country became extremely homogeneous in terms of ethnicity, nationality, and religion; however, it was more the class structure that fueled the social revolution. Entrepreneurs, an urban bourgeois, tradespeople (mainly of Jewish or German origin) had never been particularly numerous. For traditionally agrarian Poland, the war also meant the loss of most of its urban population—five million people.[8] Another 3.2 million migrated and three million were left outside the new Polish borders, which were moved west.[9] The eastern borderlands, so-called *Kresy*, with cities like Lviv and Vilnius, became parts of Soviet republics—this area constituted nearly half the country's prewar territory, and the redrawing of borders forced 1.1 million people to move.[10] In return, Poland was assigned some considerably smaller, but better developed, formerly German territories in the west (Gdańsk/Danzig, East Prussia, Pomerania, Silesia). A great migration of people began: Germans and Poles from eastern parts of the Second Republic headed west, thousands relocating, searching for their families and for new places to live. The population was devastated on both physical and psychological levels.[11] The entire base

of the urban population had gone. An enormous gap in the social structure appeared. Highly stratified, postfeudal Polish society was lacking its highest social strata. The old landed elite, the nobility, was declassed and practically liquidated as a separate class.

As for the intelligentsia, it has been roughly estimated that 37 percent of the people with a higher education perished during the war[12] and 30 percent of scholars and researchers had disappeared—around 700 professors had died[13] while 160 never returned to the country.[14] Specific calculations indicate that exactly 641 scholars and researchers, that is to say, university lecturers and professors, lost their lives: 191 as prisoners of war, 163 in executions, 147 in prisons and camps, 114 from emaciation after returning from the camps, 26 went missing. This totals 38 percent of the prewar professors and 20 percent of other university employees.[15] To give Polish wartime underground teaching its due, it is also estimated that between 7,000 to 12,000 students were educated clandestinely.[16] As estimates vary so profoundly, it is almost impossible to calculate how many of them actually survived the war, stayed in Poland, and were eager to reveal their educational past.

In addition to the loss of personnel, the academic infrastructure was largely destroyed, including 90 percent of library and archive collections. For instance, the Central Archives of Historical Records and New Files burned down completely.[17] There were severe shortages of experienced faculty members who were able to fill the newly opened chairs and run the departments. To a large extent, institutional continuity had been severed. One of the first students of the University of Łódź recalls that time as follows:

> The prominent, exterminated intelligentsia [...] I estimate that it wasn't those 30–40 thousand officers in the Soviet Union but [those who had perished] in the camps. The Soviets and Germans excelled at destroying the intelligentsia. It was necessary to build universities and educate these people. I remember perfectly how they would say that there aren't enough professors. There were no doctors, no lawyers, no engineers or chemists! They had all gone! There were huge shortages. Not enough of everybody! We faced a vastness of opportunity. We could go anywhere we wanted, really, you just needed to go steady.[18]

A new social structure emerged and new groups of people had to enter positions of power and influence. They were recruited through the spectacular promotion of members of the lower classes, mainly from rural areas in central Poland, and also from the eastern borderlands. Peasants and the working class became the base of postwar society—not only on a symbolic level but chiefly thanks to sheer demography. This had tremendous consequences for the industrial cities, among them the largest one, Łódź.

The situation in Łódź, furthermore, was even more dramatic than in the country at large as its population had been multinational before the war. Accordingly, the city suffered serious losses in the face of the absence of both its Jewish and German inhabitants.[19] During the war, Łódź was directly annexed to the Third Reich and renamed Litzmannstadt. In 1940, the Nazi administration established a Jewish ghetto in Bałuty, the most underdeveloped part of the city and the historic area of its Jewish population. The Łódź ghetto was the largest after that of Warsaw; it was also the longest in operation and known for its unconventional and controversial productive role in the German war economy.[20] Under the shadow of the Shoah, Polish elites in Łódź were arrested and often murdered.[21] Although most prominent *Lodzermenschen* were replaced by Nazi leaders, when the occupation ended on January 19, 1945, desire for revenge was widespread and local Germans were almost all brutally expelled from Poland in 1945.[22]

After 1945 only 30 percent of its former residents remained in Łódź, that is, fewer than 250,000 to 300,000 inhabitants from a prewar (1939) population of 672,000, or if talking in terms of its metropolitan area, 300,000 to prewar 800,000.[23] In 1945, the city served as the de facto capital of Poland and in terms of population size was bigger than Warsaw.[24] At the same time, it was a symbol of a new city for new times, as well as a symbol of historical justice after years of capitalist negligence:

> It is no exaggeration to say, that after WWII Łódź—for the second time in its history—became a peculiar phenomenon. [. . .] After the war, it was extraordinary on a country level as well as an international level. The fact was that within just in few months Łódź, a semi-literate city with no proper material base, became the center of cultural life and a respected academic center.[25]

It is important to note, however, that although industry was the main reason for the city's rebirth, it had much more to offer. In its first three years, Łódź gained ten higher education institutions and dozens of trade schools and high schools, and training courses were made available. Furthermore, the city became a magnet for leftist intellectuals.[26]

AFTER THE CATASTROPHE

Therefore, the postwar period was the beginning of a new social order.[27] In Polish historiography, the term "gentle revolution,"[28] introduced in 1945 by the prominent intellectual and editor Jerzy Borejsza, is often used to describe the early postwar years. There was a lot of hope and energy aimed at shaping the world anew, especially on the part of leftist intellectuals, many of whom viewed the postwar reality as a very special and unique historic moment that offered a chance for rapid modernization, for the implementation of utopian projects, and for reforming the social order by, among other things, creating a new type of university—democratic, egalitarian, and free. This group of progressive intellectuals, mainly liberals and leftists, associated interwar Poland less with the idyllic manor houses of the nobility than with rising authoritarian tendencies, censorship, poverty, economic stagnation, and mass anti-Semitism, discussed in the previous chapter. These intellectuals wanted to build a new Poland that was the very opposite of its interwar past, an egalitarian and modern state. Immediately following the end of the war, they got a chance to try this.

The scale of changes in thinking about a future independent state is exemplified by a passage from the document "What the Polish Nation Is Fighting For."[29] Published in March 1944 by the Armia Krajowa (the Home Army), the main underground movement during the war, this document presents a consensus among a wide range of parties, from the social democrats to the nationalist right. A striking contrast with the interwar milieu is visible at a glance:

> The state will have the right to acquire or nationalize firms that are useful to the public, as well as key industries, transportation, and financial institutions whenever the general welfare demands it. [. . .] Private property shall be treated not as an unlimited personal privilege, but as the basis for fulfilling delegated social and state functions. [. . .] The goal of social policy will be the complete liberation of working people. [. . .] Labor itself will not be a commodity; the working person will receive the dignity s/he deserves and be freed from the yoke of hired labor.[30]

Paradoxically, a step in the direction of nationalizing large companies had already been untaken during the Nazi occupation. Given the transnational shift toward a paradigm of planning and the rising role of the state, together with the regional situation defined by World War II and the post-Yalta geopolitical setting, postwar Poland headed toward a more responsible and engaged state, protective policies, and a planned economy. This was common for most twentieth-century modernization projects: the intensive pace of reforms, central planning and control, the public sector's domination over the private, industrialization based on heavy industry, and protected trade circulation.[31] Even if these features were presented as apolitical and technocratic, they all were political; they were rooted in different systems of values but remained focused on the state and industry.[32] The gentle revolution was a step in the direction of a socialist state.

A PLACE FOR EXPERIMENT

Postwar Łódź became a magnet for thousands of refugees, as well for central-government agendas, artistic groups, and intellectual circles. As has already been mentioned, in 1945 Łódź became one of the main centers of Polish academic and scholarly life, in part for practical reasons: its material structure had not been destroyed, living conditions in

Łódź were bearable, and it was both centrally located and close to Warsaw (120 kilometers away, with a reliable railway connection). However, one should not lose sight of the fact that political considerations also played an important role. The focus on a "workers' city" had symbolic meaning in terms of historical justice and compensation for the grievances suffered through the decades when it was considered too radical and too proletarian for Polish academia and the Sanacja regime.

State institutions migrated from the eastern borderlands[33] and the intelligentsia flocked to the city as Warsaw had been razed to the ground and stood in ruins. Jewish survivors congregated for reasons of safety. The number of inhabitants began to grow extremely fast as newcomers from Warsaw and from the territories annexed by the Soviet Union poured in. As one intelligentsia immigrant recalled:

> After the Warsaw Uprising, half of Warsaw moved to Cracow, it was impossible to breathe there. And then my husband left me in Cracow and went traveling. [...] Wherever he went, there was rubble. Wrocław—ruins, Gdańsk—terrible. In a word, there was nowhere to stay, because everything had been destroyed and it was Łódź that surprised us, because everything was in its place, there was no rubble. This was something very strange.[34]

After the biggest wave of migration, in 1945, another 125,000 new city dwellers arrived over the following years, 1946–1950. From the end of the war until 1948, over 200,000 people settled in Łódź.[35] In 1951 a mandatory registration of residence was introduced to deter any further influx of rural migrants to the city. Hopes were high despite a difficult situation and they were additionally boosted by dozens of leftists and liberal intellectuals coming to Łódź and making this strange city their new home.

From 1945 onward the city underwent a period of rapid development that took it beyond its industrial past. Now that it was an administrative unit of national importance, outposts of culture and academic hubs emerged—for the first three postwar years it was the most important city in the state.[36] During Łódź's initial 110 years of development (for most of that time as the second-largest city in the Kingdom of Poland and later in the Second Republic of Poland), it had neither any central administrative function nor any robust intellectual community. However, this all changed abruptly after the war. By 1946, five public institutes of higher education had been established (among them a university, a technical university, and a state academy of arts); and later on, in 1948, the famous Film School was founded. Higher education was a completely new branch of the city's development, resulting in thousands of students coming to Łódź in a search of an education. They were looking for new opportunities, but at the same time would contribute to building a rising research center focused on local specificities and problems.[37] For example, in decades to come, the sociology of work and mass culture would become an especially strong field in this industrial city. Many editorial offices and publishing houses[38] settled in Łódź, and local cafés were full of writers, artists, literary figures, actors, and intellectuals.[39] As a specialist in Łódź history noted, "In just a few months, Łódź, a semi-literate city with no proper material base, became the center of cultural life and a respected academic center."[40] An influx of the intelligentsia resulted not only in the development of an academic culture and higher education, but in a wide range of initiatives, from open lectures, theaters, and cabarets to preparatory courses designed to facilitate enrollment in universities.

The deputy minister of education, Władysław Bieńkowski, promoted the concept of what came to be called the "representative Polish university." During the official inauguration ceremony of the first postwar academic year at the newly established University of Łódź, in January 1946, the deputy minister said:

> The opening of the University of Łódź has a symbolic significance. Łódź, a great city and, today, after the destruction of Warsaw, the largest in Poland, was unable to obtain a normal institute of higher education before 1939. [...] Today, the day of the inauguration of the University of Łódź symbolizes an act of historical justice, and the desire of Polish Democracy to open its doors wide to higher education for the working masses; it symbolizes the convergence of knowledge and work, and cooperation between workers and scholars.[41]

SOCIALIST CITIZENSHIP

What seems to be of crucial significance for 1945 is the enormous gap that opened up in the social structure. Entrepreneurs, the bourgeoisie, tradesmen (who were mainly of Jewish or German origin)—who formed the substructure of the urban population—were gone and the nobility had been de-classed.[42] This permitted the founding of a new social structure based on a spectacular promotion of the lowest classes, who came mainly from the rural areas of *Kresy*, the eastern borderlands. One of the most important elements of this new modernization narrative, in the press and political speeches, was the securing of historical justice for both the working classes and the workers' city, neglected by capitalism, cared for by socialism. An important reference point for this postwar reality was both a long tradition of anti-urbanism and the exclusion of the peasantry from urban spaces.[43] It is crucial to be aware of those changes as the social revolution opened up the social structure, undermined former hierarchies, and allowed for profound changes: A new group of citizens was rising. What also needs to be underlined here is that the postwar period was a time of a dual working class: the urban proletariat and peasants. Both had been marginalized and discriminated against during the interwar period. Nonetheless, the first group was extremely small, geographically specific, and also difficult to govern (it retained a prewar work ethos, had a developed strike culture, displayed critical attitudes toward the new government, etc.).[44] Year after year, the urban working class changed in its composition and the position of interwar workers was taken by rural newcomers.

The vision of a future Poland shared by social democrat intellectuals and Communist Party members moved in a similar direction. Nowadays, the achievements of this period are all too often forgotten: Chronic illiteracy was tackled; schools, hospitals, and cultural centers were built; there was an impressive improvement in living conditions for thousands of workers;[45] social security was provided, which ranged from crèches and a full-employment policy to pensions that were worth something—these were crucial achievements.[46] As historian Brian Porter-Szűcs reconstructs that time:

> Workers and peasants were publicly honored, and they experienced real improvements in their lives. Education and health care spread to the small towns and villages, and jobs were readily available for the first time in anyone's memory.[47]

The preamble of the PRL constitution from 1952 spoke of a "republic of working people," which "realized the liberation ideas of the Polish working classes"[48] in the overwhelming presence of the working classes in public discourse—socialist citizenship was being built.

Press articles and political speeches underlined this move to inclusion. Their discursive strategies did not have to be too sophisticated—subjects are constructed by the use of language, by denomination. Therefore, a simple usage of words such as "peasants" or "working people" was a key part of establishing a new social imaginary.[49] An example of this can be seen by looking into a large database of press articles about Łódź in 1945–1949. In several articles about working-class heritage and the sacrifices made during the recent war, peasants are spoken of as standing alongside workers as equal protagonists—heroes and heroines of the war effort:

> Workers clenched their fists, but hope entered their hearts, at the sound of the giant Red Army offensive, in which Polish worker and peasant marched arm in arm in uniforms with a white eagle on their caps, ushering in the great days of Red Łódź.[50]

The minister of agriculture and agricultural reforms, Jan Dąb-Kocioł, at the convention of farm workers in 1947, when the establishment of state agricultural farms was announced, proclaimed:

> We have the most pioneering political system. In this system, unfortunately, we have a prewar man, who often has not changed and cannot grasp today's reality. Since the

> political system is pioneering, it requires pioneers [applause]. We must particular attention to that, to working-class people, we must change, modernize, train, and socialize them.[51]

The question was: Who would change, modernize, and train them?

PEOPLE'S INTELLIGENTSIA

Discussions about this matter lasted for decades with the most vigorous debate in the literature focusing on an idea from the 1920s in the USSR, the idea of *Proletkult*. It was then that none other than Vladimir Lenin sarcastically asked: Who is going to teach the new scientists how to, say, build a locomotive?[52] These dilemmas were not alien to the communist Polish Workers' Party (Polska Partia Robotnicza—the PPR), although as early as 1945, Władysław Gomułka, the vice prime minister at that time, emphasized Poland's need to raise its own intelligentsia,[53] at the same time declaring, in a speech during the First PPR Convention, in 1945: "We shall not put education on hold!"[54] and:

> There should not be a negative attitude toward the intelligentsia overall [. . .] the broadest group of the intelligentsia are those who haven't decided, who are dissatisfied but who are not fundamentally reactionary. We, as the Labor Party, as the leading party, must help the intelligentsia overcome their hesitation.[55]

There was a demand not only for specialists such as engineers and administrators, doctors and teachers, but also for intellectuals, people of the arts and sciences, without whom it was impossible to imagine how the country would be brought out of the war crisis. Hence, in the first years, there were efforts to form the broadest coalition and convince those who were hesitant to rebuild the new Poland "arm in arm" with the Democratic Bloc. At the All-Poland Education Convention in Łódź (June 18–22, 1945), Stanisław Skrzeszewski, the minister of education at the time, demanded that "education stop being the privilege of the rich and involve peasants, workers, and the working intelligentsia."[56] Overly radical voices demanding a revolution and violent changes were at the time rejected by the mainstream of the PPR, and even considered dangerous.[57]

Only three weeks earlier, on May 31, Władysław Nieśmiałek, the first secretary of the PPR's committee in Łódź, had appealed: "The most urgent task is to step up efforts among the intelligentsia in Łódź."[58] However, the PPR's academic circle in Łódź totaled only thirty members. The vast majority supported the moderate Polish Socialist Party (Polska Partia Socjalistyczna—the PPS).[59] Łódź might have been a magnet for leftist intellectuals, but not communist ones. One PPR activist reported that "working in the area of the intelligentsia is especially hard."[60] Adam Schaff, a young philosopher educated in Moscow during the war and a future pro-Stalinist politician, put forward a plan for gaining wider support among the intelligentsia in Łódź. First, it was necessary to attract the moderates and figures respected in the city such as the liberal philosopher Tadeusz Kotarbiński and the agrarian sociologist Józef Chałasiński and use their authority to legitimize the PPR's propositions. Second, there should be more education in the field, hence, more open readings, club campaigns (the Democratic Professorship Club), and work among students where Catholic organizations like Caritas and the Sodality of Our Lady had considerable influence.[61] The outcomes of these undertakings were rather poor. Only eight members of the PPR were recruited from among the employees and students of all of Łódź's higher education institutes.[62] However, this number would grow over the next few years (but not through the participation of the prewar professors). Despite the fact that certain reforms were widely considered necessary, support for the communists was very low. In 1947, only fifty members of the PPR were active in all the universities.[63]

HEGELIAN BITE

However, it quickly became apparent that dreams and visions for modernizing the university varied, and in this respect a split developed between the radical and the moderate factions. The postwar map of Polish state universities was split in two. There were the academic centers reconstructed along prewar lines and traditions, that is, reproducing the older social structure of departments and the academic environment. These included the universities in Cracow and Poznań, and later Warsaw, as well as some that found themselves outside Poland's new borders and accordingly relocated to new cities in the so-called Regained Territories (*Ziemie odzyskane*), such as the Jan Kazimierz University, which was relocated to Wrocław; the transfer of Vilnius's academic tradition would be used to found a new institution in Toruń. As J. Connelly notes, these actions constitute proof of temporary political weakness among the Polish communists, who were not yet strong enough to risk more radical actions and prevent this reproduction of prewar Polish tradition.[64] Then there were the universities that were established from scratch, often with a clear political agenda: for instance, the University of Lublin, established to neutralize the influence of the Catholic University of Lublin, and the University of Łódź, which sought to bring "historical justice" to a hitherto intellectually neglected city of workers.

There was strong opposition to both interwar academia and contemporary conservative circles, and especially to Cracow, the location of the two institutions most closely identified with the interwar vision of academia: the Polska Akademia Umiejętności (Polish Academy of Arts and Sciences) and the Jagiellonian University.[65]

As T. Chrościelewski, one of Łódź's new intellectuals, put it, "In Cracow, in the Trenches of the Holy Trinity[66] the patriotic intelligentsia took up its position, fideist and conservative, while the Łódź intelligentsia was largely progressive and laic [...] from liberal-democratic to radical and even leftist."[67] The antagonism was mutual, as scholars from the Jagiellonian University opposed the establishment of new universities, especially the University of Łódź, which soon became the second-largest university in Poland.[68]

On January 26, 1946, the Jagiellonian University along with the Polish Academy of Arts and Sciences held a conference in Cracow on the needs and organization of Polish academic life. The proposals drafted there and later announced in the periodical *Życie Nauki* (Academic Life) spoke in favor of a postwar revival of the idea of the liberal university.[69] The university was to be founded on autonomy and self-governance, the development of scholarship only in an atmosphere of freedom and an understanding of its needs, the kind support of the government, and freedom of word and print. Any reforms were to be initiated exclusively by universities themselves.[70] It was also proposed that the state Council of Scholarship be transformed into a committee nominated by academic circles, which would manage the state budget for higher education. Conducting research based on dialectical materialism was strongly and clearly opposed. Importantly, in relation to the University of Łódź, the formation of new research centers was also contested, due to scarce resources and a shortage of a professional workforce.

But it was too late. In Łódź, progressive scholars had begun many bottom-up initiatives, and it was sociologists who were the most actively engaged in establishing these new projects. The preliminary year and the preparatory course were new institutional tools designed to widen universities' intake of people whose lives had been affected by the war or who were from a working-class background or both. As in Western Europe, most socially aware Polish intellectuals supported the socialist model of modernization, even if many resisted using that particular adjective. To illustrate the scale of change and the rise of the state's engagement, in 1945 11 percent of the state's annual budget was earmarked for scientific and educational investment in contrast to the 0.5 percent spent on the sector during the interwar period.[71]

As we know, before the war, access to universities and higher education in general was extremely limited.[72] Considering this as well as the change of circumstances and the passing of time, a reform of academia, scholarship, research, and higher education was necessary, not only from the point of view of the communists. Almost immediately after the war, the matter of intake at secondary schools—and as we know, at universities—became politicized. Initially, ill-prepared people, often with fraudulent documents, were accepted. The educational level of students as well as their age, their life, and their wartime experience varied considerably. However, what mattered most was the reconstruction of the country, hence, the low educational level of many students was often overlooked. It was not until several years later that the unevenness of students' preparedness for education was discussed and turned into a subject of class warfare. Nevertheless, over time, these proposals became ever more extreme, alongside the discourse on the intelligentsia. Only "working intellectuals," who evolved into the category of white-collar workers, were supposed to be the builders of socialism. Next to the working class and peasants, this was to be the third class included in the modernizing leap[73]—the new intelligentsia, which needed to distance itself from the "past of idleness." The equal value of all occupations was stressed and their mutual closeness was emphasized. For instance, the press would print photographs of an intellectual and a factory worker engaged in conversation to highlight the shared qualities of their work and not its specificity. Joining forces for the common good was within arm's reach, it was said, if only the intelligentsia would drop their air of superiority.[74] Their privileges were to be limited. At the same time, transition into the intelligentsia, viewed as the dominant class (that is, education that enabled the shift "from peasant to gentleman"), was problematic at a time when class equality and working-class power were being promoted. Intellectuals were called on to abandon their privileged position and think of themselves as "technical officers of production" and creators of the new order.

The incredible speed of the reconstruction could be felt as early as a year after the war. In 1939, 49,500 people were studying at thirty-two existing higher education institutions in Poland[75]—thirteen state and two private universities exercised academic rights. Together, all the universities employed a total of 4,400 people, including academic institutions, which had hired 2,450 independent workers and research assistants.[76] One year after the war, there were already 56,000 students. While in the academic year of 1937/1938, 782 chairs had hired 1,064 professors (along with their deputies), in the year 1946/1947, there were already 1,229 chairs with 1,462 professors.[77] As the periodical *Przegląd Akademicki* (The Academic Review) wrote in its program text in 1947 about prewar academia: "The entire edifice of our psyche collapsed, destroyed by the bombing, and we are yet to find out whether that was because it was a house of cards or because the blast was so powerful."[78] All this made Polish academia appear to be one great building site, which stimulated the imagination of leftist intellectuals. There was hope that the revolution that was knocking at the gates of the universities would radically erase all the weaknesses of the conservative and elitist interwar academia.

Jerzy Szacki, an expert on the history of the social sciences in Poland, has argued that continuity rather than a rupture with interwar academia defined postwar sociology.[79] This might be true for Poland in general, with conservative strongholds at the Jagiellonian University and the transfer of entire academic communities from Lviv to Wrocław and from Vilnius to Toruń. However, the case of the working-class city of Łódź was different. Already in 1944, a group of scholars, including sociologists like

Józef Chałasiński and Stanisław Ossowski, headed to Lublin during the establishment of the Provisional Government of the Republic of Poland to lobby for the reconstruction of sociology.[80] Later on, together with the new government and university administration, they moved to the working-class city of Łódź. Those who traveled from Lublin were not only prominent sociologists of the younger generation; they were also leftist and liberal intellectuals. Even if their party affiliations were different, they shared the common heritage of the interwar coalition against anti-Semitism, rising nationalism, and the authoritarian Sanacja regime. After the war, the members of this disparate group grew closer to each other, and they hoped to build new institutions for the new times. For better or worse, in the particular case of Łódź, this meant building everything from scratch.

Even if this group of scholars ended up in Łódź partly by chance, it was no coincidence that this working-class city became the most prominent center of sociological experimentation in the early postwar years. By the first months of 1945, prominent scholars such as liberal philosopher Tadeusz Kotarbiński, sociologists Stanisław and Maria Ossowscy, Jan Szczepański and Józef Chałasiński (both pupils of Florian Znaniecki who remined in the United States), and leftist historians Nina Assorodobraj, Witold Kula, and Natalia Gąsiorowska had settled in Łódź. A Marxist academic press was established and began publishing the influential journal *Kuźnica* (Forge), which boasted leftist radicals like Stefan Żółkiewski and Jan Kott on its editorial board.[81] It also published the pro-agrarian *Wieś* (Country)[82] and the progressive journal *Myśl Współczesna* (Contemporary Thought),[83] among numerous other periodicals. The city's cafés were full of intellectuals engaged in lively debates.[84] Adam Schaff initiated the Democratic Professorship Club, which gathered members who espoused a wide range of political views.[85] A young Jan Kott, at the time a Marxist activist and the future Shakespeare scholar, recalled:

> We were sure that we were changing history by writing it as if it belonged to us. All that time we engaged in this "Hegelian bite"—although we did not know this term at that time, nor that it was we who were breathlessly biting history, like mad, demiurges of a postwar time. It seemed to us that you could mold everything, as if from clay.[86]

All in all, a large, diverse, and politically progressive academic environment flourished in Łódź.[87] It is worth recalling that, following the tumult of the interwar period and buoyed by postwar hopes, the leftist viewpoint as an authentic choice and not political opportunism was *widespread*. "[After the war] one became a Marxist as easily as in the previous century one became a positivist. [. . .] It was about taking advantage of historical circumstances and about doing the most fundamental work for Poland."[88] This general trend, however, did not apply to all academic circles across

Poland. It was true for those in Łódź, especially social scientists, but it did not affect many other cities.

Therefore, Łódź became the hotbed of postwar progressive academia, a possible capital, and a place for social experimentation. It was in such an atmosphere that the University of Łódź was created. The act authorizing its establishment was issued on May 24, 1945. Conditions were difficult: Lectures were held in cinemas or professors' flats (if they had one, as many lived in hotels or in their friends' flats), books were looted from the Regained Territories, and charity collections for starving students were organized. As many as ten new higher education institutions were established, and the number of inhabitants was greater than in Warsaw, which meant that Łódź at that time was the largest Polish city and the University of Łódź was the second largest after the Jagiellonian University in Cracow.

During several intensive months after the end of the war, discussions and quarrels about the future shape of the postwar university took place. Some opted for the so-called Poliuniversity, a large institution that would gather all disciplines in one place from the humanities to technical subjects—specific for polytechnics. However, the main struggle was rather over any future institution's continuity with interwar academia. The radical tradition of folk high schools, workers' universities, and the Free Polish University was not the main reference point, even in Łódź. Instead, the model followed was the German model of the liberal university—an imagined reference point.

3

THE UNIVERSITY FOR NEW TIMES

In a fight, neutrality equals flight. [. . .] The place of scholarship is by the side of socialism.[1]

AFTER A SHORT PERIOD OF GENTLE REVOLUTION, GOVERNMENT-DIRECTED reform followed, and then overtook the initiatives of the mostly leftist and liberal grassroots reformers. This chapter examines this brief period of individual agency during which progressive social scientists and activists were able to put their radical educational visions into practice. These reforms were the fruits of a coalition of unevenly reform-minded state officials, Soviet-influenced legislation, plus academics themselves. I focus mainly on two important individuals, the first and second rectors (officially the second and the third since the first rector died before assuming his duties) of the University of Łódź, one a philosopher and the other a sociologist. Both were leftists, but outsiders to political structures; both focused on university reforms; both thought about and were involved in social change; and finally, both, as high-placed officials, had some agency to implement their ideas. These are Tadeusz Kotarbiński (rector from 1945 to 1949) and Józef Chałasiński (rector from 1949 to 1952). Both put forward and advocated their respective visions of the university: "the liberal university" of Kotarbiński and "the socialized university" of Chałasiński.[2] The latter would somehow be taken hostage and became the socialist university—not without active input from the sociologist himself—by the government as Stalinization intensified, the result of which was the total victory of the central command policy over rank-and-file academic projects and initiatives.

Parts of this chapter were previously published in Agata Zysiak, "Science for Modernization: Between a Liberal, Social, and Socialistic University—Case of Poland and the University of Łódź (1945–1953)," *Science in Context* 28, no. 2 (2015): 215–36, https://doi.org/10.1017/S0269889715000083.

Chałasiński can be seen as an example of a leftist intellectual who hoped to create a new, egalitarian university, and who played a role in the modernization of a rural and destroyed country. He serves as an example of the dilemmas and vicissitudes faced by leftist intellectuals under state socialism. He and his model of the university enable us to trace postwar visions of higher education reform. Debate around the social, the socialist, and as a counterpoint to these, the liberal university offers an understanding of the dynamics of the battle for hegemony in public debate, the battle for setting new norms of dispute, and last but not least the battle for becoming a subject, not an object of social change.

THE LIBERAL UNIVERSITY

Following the tragic death of the first rector—Tadeusz Vieweger, a well-respected biologist from the University of Warsaw who died just two days before officially assuming his chair, in May 1945—Tadeusz Kotarbiński was appointed the new rector of the University of Łódź. This philosopher, also from Warsaw, was well known for his tolerance, anticapitalist views, sensitivity to social injustice, and reformist—rather than revolutionary—approach.[3] He was considered to be a leftist and was viewed by some interwar academics as a controversial choice; still, his election was an attempt to reconcile radical and conservative groups. To some, Kotarbiński's nomination seemed to be a sign that Łódź was going to take over the central functions of Warsaw.[4]

In the postwar debate on universities, Kotarbiński introduced the concept of the liberal university based on the ideals and structure of the interwar period and the nineteenth-century German model, which at that time were a doxa for academics.[5] This imagined model of the university was founded on ideas of academic freedom, a strong primary focus on research with teaching subordinate to the scholar's individual vision. As was pointed out by another sociologist from the younger generation, the so-called German model was unable to withstand the challenges of modernity and was blind to social selection and its own elitist context.[6] What Kotarbiński sought to defend was rather the university as a space for unfettered discussion, free from any kind of political influence. On the one hand he was defending continuity with interwar academia, on the other a need for egalitarian and social-sensitive reform, with separation from the Catholic Church, which was still seen by many conservative scholars as the main "guide" in conducting research. What he shared with the latter group was an assumption that academia was an autonomous, independent "temple of knowledge" serving the truth. Kotarbiński proposed that the university be reformed mainly with respect to three points: accessibility based only on individual ability, a liberal content of teaching, and democratic management. At the inauguration of the first academic year, he declared:

> The University of Łódź wants to be accessible to working-class children, it wants to be truly innovative [. . .], it wants to be assertively secular, it wants autonomy from all inflexible systems: ideological, historiosophical and others. It wants to serve the truth in the best understanding of every scholar and teacher. Let the truth arise from thorough and free discussion. (*Dziennik Ludowy* 1946)[7]

The social background of students and the reproduction of university structures were mentioned but treated generally. He was not enthusiastic about the implementation of a preparatory course or a preliminary year, ideas designed to help students without formal secondary education, mostly workers' and peasants' children, to enroll in the university. He was concerned that the quality of education would drop if preferential enrollment procedures for the lower classes were introduced, arguing that only the most "able and prepared" should enter universities.[8] He sought to tackle the problem of enrollment by means of a system of bursaries, scholarships, and subsidized dormitories.[9] Furthermore, he also undertook the building of democratic structures, including student representation in the university's management. In general, his aim was to preserve a traditional model of higher education, while avoiding the pathologies of the interwar period.

During this time, Kotarbiński's main opponent was the deputy-rector, Józef Chałasiński. A younger and more radical sociologist, his sharp criticism of the intelligentsia and the reproduction of academia had originated much earlier, during the interwar period. However, both men were committed democrats and overlapped on some issues, such as the need to preserve the university's autonomy and freedom of expression. Where they differed was primarily in their attitude to interwar academia and their assumptions about postwar reality. While Kotarbiński could be described as a reformer who was at the same time sensitive to historical continuity, Chałasiński was, rather, a revolutionary, who was trying to break away from interwar academia.

Chałasiński, an agrarian activist and radical thinker, was a prominent figure among progressive scholars. His academic career had begun in Poznań in the 1920s under well-known sociologist Florian Znaniecki's supervision. Coming from a small town, fascinated with peasant culture, and active in the peasant popular movement, Chałasiński did not fit comfortably into interwar academia. He became widely known after publishing a four-volume work entitled *Młode pokolenie chłopów* (The Young Generation of Peasants), an edited selection of peasant memoirs. Not long after its publication, it was classified by the Sanacja government as a subversive book that posed a danger to state order.[10] There were even plans to confiscate all printed editions of the work.[11] Personal attacks followed: He was called a "sociologist from a barn" and was threatened with hellfire.[12] In the late 1930s, he, along with other progressive social scientists such as Ludwik Krzywicki and Jan Bystroń, protested against anti-Semitic regulations and the atrocities then taking place in Polish universities. As a result of this activism, these prominent intellectuals were called "ersatz-Poles, *shabbos* goyim" in the University of Warsaw journal *Alma Mater*.[13] He later recalled his ambivalent role in academic structures as follows: "I was not able to settle down among the university's intelligentsia, but they didn't want me either. Besides, I was already a professor with several heavy tomes to my name, so neither was I attracted to them. I was not able to love knowledge and scholarship solely for the sake of giving lectures and writing books."[14]

Chałasiński's views about social inequality were widely known before World War II, and during the war, he wrote a book entitled *Chłopi i Panowie* (Peasants and Gentlemen), more incisive in its critique than all his previous works about interwar Poland and its social structure. The manuscript was lost during the war, but he drew on some of its ideas in his famous speech, given as a deputy-rector under Kotarbiński's rectorship, at the inauguration ceremony of the 1946/1947 academic year.[15] It contained such radical statements) as: "Here every generation of the intelligentsia starts its work anew and always in the same manner. Always the same phraseology about rescuing Western culture in Poland, always the same Poland—the Bulwark of Christianity. Always the same indolence, rendered sacred by hackneyed, grandiloquent phrasing."[16] According to the comments of those who read the lost manuscript, it was still toned down in comparison with *Peasants and Gentlemen*. However, in a book published just a year later, summarizing his lost manuscript and latest thoughts, he reverted to sharper language, writing: "The intelligentsia ghetto was a tremendously reactionary force, parasitic on Polish cultural life."[17] He saw the intelligentsia as nobility's heirs reproducing their values and privilege,[18] which should be limited.

Given his usage of the phrase the "intelligentsia ghetto," it is hardly surprising that Chałasiński was reluctant to support any project that aimed to restore the interwar model of the university, thereby, in his opinion, reproducing its pathologies. For him, the university's main predicament was that an academic ivory tower, detached from reality and social needs, would, in the long term, only lead to the further isolation of scholarship from society and the further backwardness of Poland. Thus, he was convinced that there was no way that older forms could be modernized, but rather, that the new reality and the opportunities it offered begged for the construction of a completely new project. Chałasiński was both critical and radical, even in terms of governmental discourse and the PPR rhetoric of the day. Not surprisingly, the "Marxist" label, which followed him from the interwar period, became reinforced, despite the fact that the label was not accurate. A more fitting term was proposed many years later by his favorite pupil, the sociologist of culture Antonina Kłoskowska, whose attitudes toward that time were highly critical. She described him as a "democratic populist."[19] Probably the best example of this democratic populism was indeed his vision of university restructuring during the years 1945–1948—his vision of the socialized university.

THE PLACE FOR AN EXPERIMENT

From the very outset of their cooperation, the conflict between Kotarbiński and Chałasiński was over issues of policy. Kotarbiński's vision of the liberal university did not, according to Chałasiński, meet the needs of the postwar period. In his opinion, Kotarbiński's seemingly progressive "modernized academism" in fact reproduced the model of the university as an ivory tower, out of touch with society's needs. Chałasiński recognized the political changes that had taken place and claimed that the preservation of traditional academia in the form of a liberal university would be detrimental to Polish scholarship, and by extension, to Polish society as a whole. Division between scholarship and wider reality, that is, between academia and political, social, and cultural life, would cause the further isolation of academia and its colonization by bureaucratic discourse. Paradoxically, the very idea of an apolitical university would lead to its politicization. The university as an institution could no longer remain passive and neutral, as sooner or later confrontations with political structures were bound to arise.

Therefore, from Chałasiński's perspective, the university was obliged to fight for its controlling role in the forthcoming historical changes, to produce its own ideas for its existence, and not simply become an object of government reform. For Chałasiński, who was probably more realistic about the political future of Poland, it was clear that what was at stake was the general role of the university in the postwar reality, and it was high time to act, which meant presenting a vision elaborated in a public debate in academic society, in anticipation of attempts at its colonization by political and bureaucratic discourses. In this spirit his most explicit statement can be found in an article he published in *Kuźnica*, entitled *O społeczny sens reformy uniwersytetów* (About the Social Sense of University Reform).[20]

This text can be seen as a manifesto promoting the second model of the university—put forward in opposition both to party-driven governmental ideas and to that of the liberal university—the model of the socialized university. Starting out from the same premises as Kotarbiński, Chałasiński saw his project within the framework of the unquestionable autonomy of universities and the democratic order. Furthermore, at that time he believed in a kind of deliberative democracy, based on developed public opinion (for which he used the synonym "intellectual opinion"). In Poland, he argued, the self-governance of citizens was very underdeveloped, therefore for the further modernization of the country it was essential that robust public opinion be developed, as a guarantor of democracy. Only via discussion and confrontation with multiple opinions would the construction of a people's republic be possible.

In a similar vein, he claimed that universities are obliged to take responsibility for building and shaping this public opinion. Thus, he repeatedly stressed the special role of culture (and scholarship) as autonomous spheres of social life, the autonomy of which should even "increase with the nationalization of economic life."[21] He claimed that "from the point of view of democracy, the stronger the tendency to nationalize other fields, the more indispensable was the full and comprehensive autonomy of scholarship and culture."[22] This was also a clear message to the government, which was already preparing the central reform of higher education. Chałasiński warned that the academic field was not a place for moves as revolutionary as the land reform in the field of agriculture. He advised that universities be reformed in an experimental manner, and the place for such social experiment was Łódź.

The first component of the socialized university was, then, its autonomy. The second was its social utility. However, scientific and scholarly purpose was fundamental and had to be preserved as a prior domain of its activity. There was another set of aims to be achieved as well, that is, to become an independent center of public opinion formation and the foundation of democratic order. This was precisely the social dimension of the university. As such a center, the university had to be engaged in the process of social change, not through the "dogmatic propaganda of one scientific theory," but rather by means of the "critical method of scholarly thinking." At the socialized university, there was no place for cliques and people devoted to their social groups or individual interests. On the contrary, everyone was obliged to be devoted to society as a whole and to democracy. This was a subtle critique of Kotarbiński's notion of scholars' individualism.

The years 1945–1947 were propitious for utopian thinkers, as everything seemed to be subject to and ready for action and change. Chałasiński's article, however, created a lot of trouble for him, which was just one of the many signs of forthcoming Stalinism, and a signal that the "gentle revolution" was coming to an end.[23] In the same edition of *Kuźnica*, but printed on the first page, ahead of Chałasiński's manifesto, was a polemical article. Its title said it all: "A fight for the freedom of research or the preservation of the old order?" It was not even Kotarbiński's liberal university anymore, which symbolized the past, but a freshly proposed socialized university. Chałasiński knew that time was running out and that room for maneuvering was shrinking, but he probably still believed that it was possible to benefit from the forthcoming changes. Just a few months later he published another paper, entitled "*Współczesne reformy szkolne a idea narodu i socjalizmu*" (Modern School Reform and the Idea of the Nation and Socialism), which turned out to be nothing more than a paean on the Soviet model of education. It was an apology for criticizing the government, and accordingly, Chałasiński managed to regain his position and some political agency.[24]

By this time Kotarbiński had paled in significance.[25] He defended the values of truth and free discussion.[26] Dialectical materialism was for him nothing but a hypothesis, impossible to verify.[27] His philosophic notions had much in common with Marxism, but he never recognized the latter as a scholarly theory. A declared humanist and individualist, he did not feel suited to the new times and their holistic solutions. At the same time, when Kotarbiński was advocating academic freedom and following the truth, another of his deputy-rectors, Zygmunt Szymanowski, publicly defined freedom differently: "We talk about politics, about victory, about liberation. There is another type of yoke that burdens people, which is the bourgeois monopoly on science, its monopoly on knowledge, through which it tries to keep the people away from knowledge, and as such, from freedom."[28]

In the spring of 1947, the PPR put forward a plan to step up educational reform. Among other things, it was suggested that associate professors and assistant professors should be appraised at universities by party circles: this was not going to be met enthusiastically within academic circles. Soon, the decree of October 28, 1947, "on the organization of scholarship and higher education" was passed, replacing the act of 1933, which had been reinstated after the war. This substantially curbed the autonomy of the university by allowing the central authorities to actively participate in faculty policies and in the granting of habilitation and the nomination of rectors. That same year, a meeting of rectors took place at which "the tasks of the people of science"[29] were presented. These were clear signs that the political course was intensifying. In the fall of 1947, representatives from outside academia were introduced to recruitment committees, and Marxism was included in the curriculum. At the same time, censorship (and self-censorship) intensified. The victory of the Democratic Bloc in the elections and the passing of the so-called Small Constitution[30] heralded further changes. The planned reforms of the Council for Higher Education were being discussed. The freedom of education and autonomy of universities were presented as under threat, to which the supporters of the reform replied that under capitalism, scholarship could not be free because it was determined by the profit motive and scholars had to fight for their economic survival. Viewed through this prism, scholarship was likewise regarded as impeded by chaotic measures and academic individualism; after the reform, the efforts of researchers would be coordinated and planned by the state, which would bring true freedom. As a result, the time and efforts of highly qualified specialists, as the modernizing project viewed academics, would not be wasted.

The party realized that at universities, the professorate were the authority figures. During one of the Polish Workers' Party education activists' meetings in 1948, Skrzeszewski said: "We have to admit that the ideological offensive which we augured has generally not materialized beyond the sphere of wishes and slogans. [. . .] Right under our noses, professors expound with impunity incredibly reactionary gibberish just as they did during the Sanacja regime and fascist times."[31] The end of "the gentle revolution" was approaching and the reforms undertaken in 1948 concluded it altogether. It still seemed that Chałasiński's position was getting stronger. In 1949, he replaced Kotarbiński—who had long lost the authorities' support—as rector of the University of Łódź.

VISION AND PRACTICE

Chałasiński, as the new rector, opened the academic year 1949/1950 once again with a significant speech:

> Workers and leaders, professors and employees of the University of Łódź, young people, citizens! [...] It is no coincidence that our ceremony takes place outside the walls of the university, in an open and public space. We want to emphasize that we are fully conscious that we are breaking with the tradition of the social isolation of the university, and in this manner, we declare that creative scholarly ideas are going to engage in a powerful stream of transformation of our Polish life, in all its areas. With this display of the breaking down of the isolation of the university, we open the new academic year![32]

Although it is impossible to reconstruct exactly when and on what levels the interplay between Chałasiński and the party took place, it was certainly already far advanced when he took the rector's chair. The academic year 1949/1950 was crucial for the University of Łódź not only because of the person who was the new rector but also because of the forthcoming central reform of Polish scholarship. Chałasiński, finally holding the reins of power, tried to put into practice his idea of the socialized university. Of course, it was no longer the right time for an "independent public opinion center," but still Chałasiński tried to force a bottom-up reform of the University of Łódź. Unfortunately, as he himself had noted earlier, many years were needed to develop a socialized university, and he was running out of time. Central reform, inspired by what the radical communist philosopher Adam Schaff called "the N Operation" ("N" for *nauka*—scholarship in Polish), was about to be implemented.[33]

Starting from smaller decrees dating back to 1947 up to the final act, passed in 1952, the central reform of higher education aimed at transforming universities into one of the many tools required for the implementation of the six-year plan—"By Industrialization to Socialism!" The autonomy of the university authorities was revoked. The rector was nominated by the minister of higher education, and furthermore, all other nominations had to be approved by him. The rector's scope of authority was limited to developing and managing the work schedule, monitoring educational outcomes and work discipline, supervising the physical education of young people and their state of health, as well as managing administration. The rector became, above all, an official who coordinated the work of an institution. Rectors lost their *primus inter pares* position and rather became managers who made sure that plans were implemented. The notion of planning, the bureaucratic nature of the student-professor relationship, and the introduction of teamwork were likewise alien to the concept of the liberal university.

The university structure and its organization was changed by the introduction of a hierarchical system of reporting and authority. Chairs, grouped into institutes and faculties, became the basic organizational unit. The academic degree system was changed too: Instead of earning a PhD degree and then a postdoctoral habilitation degree, a person advanced to become an aspirant and a candidate of sciences. As a matter of fact, both systems functioned in a parallel fashion in subsequent years (although only new degrees were officially awarded) until the Thaw in 1956, when the pre-1949 system was reinstalled. Additionally, at the same time as new degrees were introduced, so too were they linked to functions carried out at the university. An assistant professor with habilitation, that is, a docent, was appointed by the minister to the position of an associate professor, while assistant professors were appointed by the rector. (See figure 3.1.)

The "period of quantification" began.[34] Academia was parameterized with indicators such as *studento-godzina* (number of students per hour) or *studento-egzamin* (number

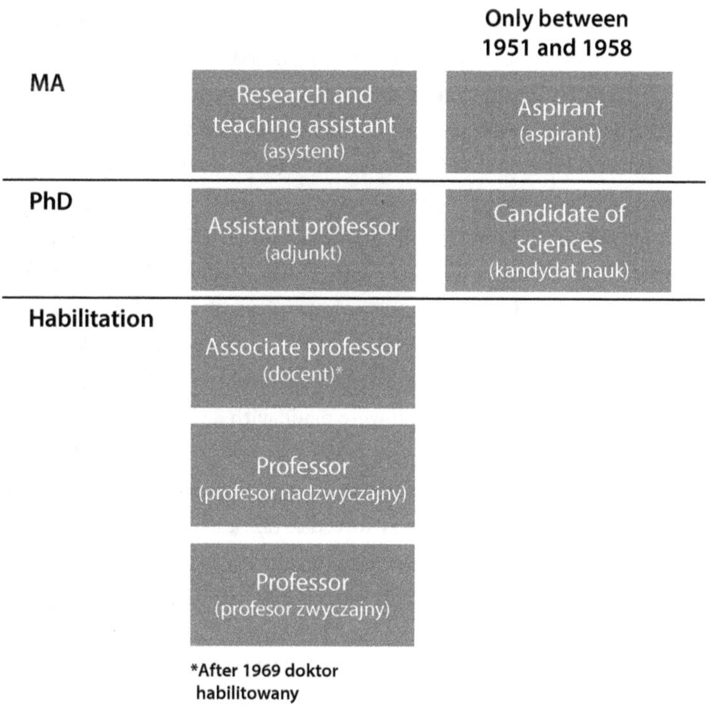

Figure 3.1 Academic degrees 1945–1989.

of students per exam), which were then documented on enormous charts to be sent to the ministry; the universities were also obliged to respect assigned quotas of students and graduates according to their social origin.[35] Courses became compulsory, and in opposition to the so-called "aristocratic manner of studying," students were expected to work along the lines of factory workers, with almost eight hours per day of classes, roll call, and supervision of their efficiency. Under the prewar system attendance was not compulsory at lectures; students had been free to choose what to attend, and graduation had depended on passing final exams and defending a master's thesis.[36]

The first three years of a degree course were designed to prepare students for practical tasks, and the additional two years to give them more advanced skills and the *magister* (master's) degree. Students were advised to contact a future workplace during their studies to obtain work experience in a factory or public institution. Universities were thus to become part of a production process aimed at training skilled specialists. One of the key goals was to prevent the reproduction of academia. Several measures, such as the removal of habilitation, the centralization of the academic title award system, and the introduction of time limits on obtaining subsequent degrees, focused on the younger members of faculty to hinder the reproduction of the prewar academic habitus.[37] It was anticipated that a new intelligentsia would emerge thanks to planning, the unity of scholarship, teaching and educating based on dialectic materialism, the change of university structures and its divisions, teamwork methods, and competition.

The humanities, in which prewar notions of the university were preserved, remained the most dangerous field of "reaction." Hence, a revision of professorial positions took place, alongside the gradual removal of inconvenient people, who were then replaced with progressive faculty members with Marxist views. Even before the founding of the Polish United Workers' Party (Polska Zjednoczona Partia Robotnicza, the PZPR) in 1948, what became known as "the university sixes" (three activists from the PPR and three from the PPS) had been introduced. They were tasked with drawing up lists of the professors to evaluate their academic activity and world outlook. In 1948 alone, 1,093 decisions about staff were made with a view to changing the structure of universities.[38] Among those sent on leave were Lviv-Warsaw school philosophers Władysław Tatarkiewicz, Kazimierz Ajdukiewicz, and Janina Kotarbińska (Kotarbiński's wife), while a number of professors were forced to take early retirement. Furthermore, individuals were moved from one institution to another in an attempt to weaken prewar relationships. Stefan Żółkiewski attacked the humanities overall whereas Adam Schaff targeted sociology in particular from 1949 onward. This situation was challenging for sociologists themselves—including Chałasiński—because sociologists "in most cases, actively supported at least some of the transformations taking place in the country."[39] A theory of the distinctive natures of bourgeois and of socialist scholarship was promoted. Naturally, the "bourgeois" discipline needed to be abolished. Sociology[40] in particular was considered as its stronghold, along with psychology and the theory of organization and management.

A decision was made to separate vocational, agricultural, economics, and medical faculties from the universities, making them into specialized colleges.[41] What was crucial for Łódź was the new national hierarchy that was implemented: (1) The main academic center—the Great University—was of course the University of Warsaw. (2) A group of the larger universities, chosen for their geographical location, was to serve as local growth centers: Cracow, Poznań, and Wrocław. (3) A group of small universities was to meet the needs of the regional population: Lublin, Toruń, and Łódź.

Each group was assigned enrollment limits as well as faculty quotas, with only the University of Warsaw designated as highly specialized. The "smaller" universities were only able to teach law, biology, geography, math, physics, chemistry, history, and Polish philology. Additionally, in 1950, a specialized institute modeled on the Institute of Red Professors in the Soviet Union[42] was organized in Warsaw. The Instytut Kształcenia Kadr Naukowych (Institute for Academic Faculty Training) was a part of the party structure and trained future socialist professors to replace the interwar academic staff, who were no longer seen as a potential ally.[43]

The academic faculty at the University of Łódź were disturbed by the rumor that the whole university was going to be closed down, or, in the best-case scenario, that the humanities were going to be disbanded and chairs moved to Toruń. While the University of Łódź had previously recruited students in fourteen humanities faculties, as a provincial university, it accepted students in philosophy, Polish and Russian philologies, and—after the personal intervention of the doyen of Polish Marxist historiography, Natalia Gąsiorowska-Grabowska—history.[44] The recruitment freeze also affected sociology, which was the key department in the view of Rector Chałasiński. Most chairs continued to operate but professors could not teach. The "socialized university," it appeared, was becoming the "socialist university."

As well as the University of Łódź being demoted to a provincial university, further consequences of the reform were even more catastrophic than the loss of professors or institutional mimicry that had been carried out in previous months. Between 1948 and 1955, student numbers fell by 46 percent (partly because of the secession of medical universities); and only three out of fourteen humanities programs were preserved, and then only after protests by well-known professors. History was kept, but sociology—most important for Chałasiński—was closed.[45] Although departments were still operating, teaching and recruitment were stopped.

Taking the example of sociology: Most of the faculty continued to work, although some, for example sociologists Stanisław Ossowski and Maria Ossowska, were banned from teaching. The names of departments and research projects were changed, too. Chałasiński was still the head of the Sociology Department, although this was renamed the Department of Historical Thought. He also created a special unit officially devoted to research on the nineteenth-century press at the newly established Polish Academy of Science in Warsaw. One of his most prominent students, the future sociologist of culture Antonina Kłoskowska, who defended her doctoral thesis in 1950, was taken on there.[46] When the final issue of *Przegląd Socjologiczny* (Sociological Review) was published in 1950, a new periodical was established, *Przegląd Nauk Historyczno-Społecznych* (Social-Historical Sciences Review), which provided a platform for stable and durable sociological exchange.

During the last months of 1948, with the rebuilding of Warsaw a general migration of intellectuals to the "real capital" began. Many of them, who during the years of chaos had stayed "in transit," were returning home.[47] The University of Warsaw was now becoming "the most politically active university" in the PRL. Most leftist intellectuals had begun to leave Łódź in 1948, with even the most committed Marxists fleeing to Warsaw, accusing Łódź intellectuals of dogmatism. After his dismissal, Kotarbiński moved to Warsaw as well, where he played a notable but neutral role in academic life. Chałasiński, who was always impulsive and stubborn, fiercely attacked those who left,[48] accusing them of a lack of responsibility, a lack of a sense of common good, and of careerism. He appealed to the ministry,[49] lamenting that "the needs of Łódź were being ignored."[50] He emphasized the achievements of the university and its excellent results of democratization. He illustrated how close the University of Łódź was to implementing the model of the socialist university and demanded more resources and support for the growth of the institution: "When we talk about the development of the University of Łódź, which is at the heart of the greatest working-class center, we are not talking about matters of a small local university but matters of one [of] the largest national universities in Poland!"[51]

However, the drain of individual people was partly a consequence of the fact that the University of Łódź had lost its position in the government's developmental policies and that it was going to be downgraded as a result of the higher education reform. The university, once envisaged as heralding the avant-garde of the revolution and whose formation was inscribed in the rectification of historical injustice, was demoted at the first opportunity. The difficulties that the Polish Workers' Party had encountered as early as 1945 among the working class of Łódź were not without significance. Although the blue-collar city was praised in the press and speeches, in reality, Łódź was being swept with strikes[52] and its working-class population, whose tradition dated far back to the revolution of 1905, had its own, bottom-up idea of the people's power, which was at odds with government plans.

RELICS

During this period, changing so rapidly and with such an uncertain future, Chałasiński's main statement concerning his vision of the university was delivered in his speech at the fifth anniversary of the founding of the University of Łódź, in 1950, entitled: "From a Liberal to a Socialist Idea of the University." On some levels, this message had much in common with his previous statements, but a radical change of language can be observed with the disappearance of words such as "independent" and "autonomous" in the context of the university. It should be noted, too, that it was no longer a "socialized" university, but an outright "socialist" one. Once again Chałasiński's acute criticism of the interwar university provided his main point of reference, but he now added a much stronger criticism of the traditional university in general, and by implication, of Kotarbiński's liberal university. In addition, he engaged in self-criticism, popular at that time, of his previous writings, criticizing them as too liberal and seduced by Kotarbiński.

The first part of his speech was an elaborate and systematic criticism of the traditional model of the university as a place that reproduced an intelligentsia ghetto, where scholarship is treated in a utilitarian manner, either as a source of profit or as entertainment for the privileged (i.e., the university as a "kindergarten for wealthy young people"). He criticized the policy of his predecessor, Rector Kotarbiński, who was present at the event.[53] Responding to Kotarbiński's slogan "Truth and Liberty," he pointed out:

> Seeking the truth and enjoying the freedom of the individual was never neutral, but always associated with a positive interest in a specific historical direction. [. . .] The University of Łódź is historical nonsense if it is to be understood as a liberal improvement of the prewar University of Warsaw, moved to Łódź. [. . .] The university not only stands on the field of class struggle but is involved in it. Awareness of this fact is essential to ensure that universities are no longer relics of the past but become centers of socialist intellectual culture![54]

He concluded that freedom of discussion had become a slogan for capitalistic freedom and that this would lead simply to the appearance of freedom and tolerance. It was not enough to raise a voice in a discussion. Society would not shape itself, especially not a socialist society; it needed "lead management centers for public opinion in all fields, scholarship included." He stressed that scholarly research could not be treated as private property; it needed to focus on its public role, and for that, central planning and management were necessary. The difference between his statements and his former ideas about public opinion and freedom of expression was striking. He underlined the need to put an end to the concept of scholarship as private property, to allow it to regain its public functions. New institutional frameworks were needed, "on the one hand to enable intellectuals' free discussion, [...] on the other to inform society about the agreed-upon view of scholars and the subjects of controversy among them."[55] Freedom not controlled by the state might lead to anarchy. An important shift was also visible in Chałasiński's attitude to the democratization of scholarly research—he stressed that such a process could not take the form of popularizing the culture of higher classes, but should be focused on creating a completely new type of culture, one that responded to the aims and experiences of the working masses. Earlier he had been rather interested in the creation of new types of institutions, supporting the democratization of culture, which seemed to be—along with pluralism and democracy—universal.

An even more ideological tone was visible in a speech Chałasiński made a few months later at the inauguration of the academic year 1950/1951. Using newspeak, he underlined the special role of scholarship in the six-year plan and its strict and close relationship with and place on the path to industrialization and a socialist society. At the same time, in the second part of his speech, he tried to argue that the humanities were also indispensable in these processes (and irreplaceable for promoting Marxism and Leninism). This was one of his many attempts to restore sociology to its place at the university. Chałasiński wrote: "An awareness of the irreversibility of the historical process that leads to socialism is ever more pervasive in our universities; more and more young people of working-class or peasant origin are undertaking higher education, and workplaces in agriculture, industry and culture are waiting for all of them." The involvement of universities in the six-year plan "is not limited to the technical and economic foundations of the socialist system based on modern research, but it affects all the social and cultural relations of the nation. In the same way as the reconstruction of the economy and the class structure was proceeding, so too did the renovation of culture and mentality have to proceed."[56]

Chałasiński, a committed idealist, had taken on the role of rector at the worse possible moment, just before the implementation of the reform. Furthermore, he was bereft of diplomatic skills: quarrelsome, stubborn, and fierce. His overzealous implementation of the ministry's instructions only made his efforts, and his person, preposterous.[57] Finally, to demonstrate his disappointment, Chałasiński pleaded with the minister of higher education and scholarship for permission to resign from the rector's chair, but his request was rejected.[58]

The convening of the First Congress for Polish Science (in July 1951) was a culmination of Stalinism.[59] The liminal time of the postwar period was over; a new order was proclaimed. Centralization, parameterization, and control intensified. International contacts became subject to strict control, the publishing market was nationalized and centralized by the creation of the National Scientific Publishers (PWN), and the Polish

Academy of Sciences (PAN) was created. The goal of higher education establishments was to prepare professionals with the highest level of qualification. Particular emphasis was put on teaching and the formation of a people's intelligentsia.[60] In this constellation, universities were divorced from research. They were supposed to focus on teaching and the production of new professionals (*nowe kadry* in Polish) necessary for the modernization of the country. Following the reform, the number of higher education institutions increased to eighty-three, including eight universities. Split structures were supposed to be more easily supervised. A new university structure was imposed and its plan was to limit humanists to one faculty, depending on the institution: either the faculty of philosophy or philosophy and history (for example, in Łódź). The number of students enrolled in technical subjects grew dramatically due to the recruitment freeze in most humanities subjects. Education, on the whole, implemented the six-year plan and was subject to heavy parameterization and intense reporting. Curricula were modeled on Soviet programs.[61]

Chałasiński became part of the "old guard," inadequate for the new times. He maintained his position as rector until 1952, playing the role of an enthusiast of governmental reforms, reforms that led to the subjugation of scholarship to state bureaucracy. That year he went on the attack[62] and— although he never joined the PZPR—he wrote a few propaganda papers.[63] At the same time, Kotarbiński remained on the margins—too liberal and individualistic for the new era. In a response to Chałasiński, he warned that it was very easy for progress to regress.[64]

Based on later memories of that time, Chałasiński's engagement—in contrast to that of many others—does not seem to be related to conformism, but rather to be a crude exercise of his "democratic populism," with him believing in the possibility of social change and persuading himself of the rationality and necessity of Stalinism. In describing that period in the 1960s, he wrote that he was not only the "revolutionist of humanistic socialism," but also the "altar boy of an established order—a cult of Stalin" which he became because of "having a habit of acting with real results, a habit, whatever the regime, of working for myself and the liberal university community; that is, of never accepting stagnation that was satisfied with contemplation of its loyalty to spiritual beauty, but rather, of taking part in an ongoing social revolution."[65]

He was once called "the regime's decoration"[66] and just two years later "the Claudius of sociology," an emperor secretly preparing to reestablish the republic.[67] These examples show how difficult it is to evaluate Chałasiński's choices. He was quite convincingly compared to a householder who salvages everything after a flood,[68] acting like a peasant, not an honorable gentleman, too proud to get his hands dirty. His later involvement in the Polish Thaw and his criticism of the Stalinist period helped to repair his reputation. Who had the recipe for progress? What steps could lead to the country's modernization? Land reform was widely supported, nationalization of industry less so, but still, for many, democratization of education was an absolute must. Postwar debates had shown the complexity of the issue, but rapid postwar modernization left Kotarbiński, Chałasiński, and hundreds of other progressive intellectuals far behind.

UNIVERSITY MODELS

The rethinking of academia that took place in postwar Poland was framed by a pull between two models of the university, the traditional and the modern. The struggles of both rectors can be seen as an attempt to mediate between the two poles: the former the reality of interwar academia with its pathologies (such as preservation of the elite and anti-Semitism) at one end, and the forthcoming Sovietization of scholarly research at the other. At a symbolic level, the traditional model was based on Humboldt's idea, *universitas,* the imperative autonomy of scholarship, and its elitist character. This was combined with the opportunity of bringing high culture to the masses by providing access to higher education for the most able young people from all social strata—simply avoiding the direct reproduction of the intelligentsia. In contrast, the modern model aimed at the massive and rapid production of skilled workers. According to this modern model, the university was transformed into a tool, a measure, and a component of the industrialization of Poland and with a strong egalitarian impulse to democratize Polish academia. It was thought that this way it would play the role of a new type of university, one closer to meeting the social and economic needs of workers, open to as many people as were needed to build a socialist welfare state.

The question of whether to bring high culture to the lower classes or to create a new type of egalitarian culture was not only framed and articulated in the local debates mentioned above but elsewhere. The main framework for the debate about the democratization of higher education was also taking place in the Soviet Union. The issue, widely discussed in *Pravda* (Truth) from 1922 onward, was not how to institute reforms, but rather, the basic meaning of modernization and the democratization of science/culture.[69] On the one hand cultural revolutionists and the avant-garde opted for the creation of a completely new model of society; on the other hand more moderate communists wanted to bring former high culture to the masses and popularize "old values" as universal. It is this division that is crucial for understanding the sense of modernization and social change.

The university is a specific domain of practices, carried out in situ with a high degree of reflexivity. At the same time, the university is saturated with habitual immersion and inertia to prevent any systemic imperatives from being embodied in day-to-day practice; accordingly, the revolutionary ideas of reformers and government generally failed. Nevertheless, in Chałasiński's case, this operated as a Trojan horse as well, injecting a new rationality into the thoughts and practices of leftist visionaries. Consequently, they acted on behalf of the new logic, thereby betraying their own dreams. On the other hand, however, the moral authority and the leftist radicalism of intellectuals were wittingly employed to protect vestiges of independence and the benign institutional efforts that they had sacrificially made. This demonstrates the tragic stakes of institutional rearticulations of Stalinism made by particular people in particular places. Such a conjuncture of the institutional and the personal is probably representative of a fair share of every writer who strives to pursue his or her goals in actually existing society, be it socialist or capitalist. Personal navigation in such circumstances is always a tragic choice. Its outcomes always easily fall prey to retrospective criticism of the untainted, the morally superior, and the, in effect, passive. (See table 3.1.)

After 1956, the University of Łódź reverted to a more general academic profile. It was no longer so specialized and approximated the model of the liberal university. There were efforts to make it more like other universities. The decision of the new rector, Adam Szpunar, an alumnus of the Jagiellonian University, to return to the custom of wearing robes at university ceremonies was a symbolic change in 1956. In 1945, Rector Kotarbiński had discontinued this to indicate the modernization of the university. Professor Krystyna Śreniowska, an alumna of the Jan Kazimierz University in Lviv, who had been associated with the University of Łódź for years and was skeptical of Chałasiński's revolutionary zeal, commented on this change as follows:

> The traditions of medieval universities with male clergy as professors have been transplanted into the reality of an industrial city of the second half of the twentieth century. This fancy-dress party in postindustrial halls and other spaces failed to conjure up medieval structures with cloisters but verged on the grotesque. And in later years, when a theater auditorium was hired for the inauguration of the academic year—that, indeed was an operetta. Female professors tried on birettas in front of the mirror, tilting them as if they were fashionable hats. The company in costumes would sit on the stage, sweating under their heavy robes. The rector, who wore red gloves and wrapped himself in an ermine cape, tapped a golden scepter. Only Professor Szpunar—a fine, strapping man—looked magnificent in that costume.[70]

Post-Thaw liberalization saw the unfreezing of subjects earlier closed: archaeology, ethnography, sociology, Polish and English philologies, and from 1960/1961, classical philology as well. New staff were hired, new buildings built, and the number of students rose to 4,000 and soon to 8,000 in full-time and weekend studies (introduced in 1956).[71] This grew until the mid-1970s when the ministry put a cap on recruitment. University of Łódź graduates mostly worked as teachers, chemists, lawyers, and administrative employees.[72] The parameters from the late 1940s that mattered most to the

TABLE 3.1 THE MODELS OF THE UNIVERSITY, BASED ON CHAŁASIŃSKI'S MAIN ARTICLES (1945–1950)

	LIBERAL UNIVERSITY	SOCIALIST UNIVERSITY
SCHOLAR	Intellectual aristocrat	Builder of a socialist society (socialist humanist)
ROLE IN SOCIETY	Isolated from society Focused on the internal affairs of academia, on his/her issues, and "esoteric science"	One of the tools of social change Translator and interpreter of scholarly achievements for society
TASKS	Undertaking pure scholarship Securing space for free academic debate	Implementing the "historical tasks of scholarship" Planned, changing class relations in science
ACADEMIC PERSONNEL	The craft model of pupil and master Only the "master" is interested in the development of young scholars Restraint in the promotion of researchers	The factory model—a predetermined and measured number of scholars Directly planned development of young scholars
STRUCTURE AND ORGANIZATION	A federation of departments, neither restricted nor planned	Team research stressed All disciplines subordinated to "social philosophy"
CONCEPT OF SCIENCE	A way of getting to know oneself in complete isolation from society Isolated from society Pluralism of scholarly theories	Scholarly research as a public good, serving the needs of a socialist society Scholarly research has a class character The domination of Marxism in the field of scholarly theories
POLITICAL ATTITUDES	Isolation	Scholarship as part of the political line of the government
CLASS BACKGROUND AND DEMOCRATIZATION	Students taken from the intelligentsia, the bourgeoisie, and the landed gentry Neutral actor in the democratization processes	An institution based on young people from the working class The university as one of the tools of class struggle

authorities, that is, the social makeup of the student body, did not much change. The share of working-class students fluctuated between 38 and 44 percent while young people from peasant backgrounds never exceeded 12 percent of the student body.

The growth of the university in Łódź in the 1960s and 1970s, even if it never realized postwar ambitions, had a major influence on the city and the region. Its graduates filled postwar staff shortages in institutions. Students in Łódź were graduating not only from the university, but also from the University of Technology, the Medical University, and the Academy of Fine Arts and Film School. The city overall, which before the war had had the lowest ratio of intelligentsia and the highest rate of illiteracy, could boast over 10 percent of residents with a higher education. These data illustrate the scale of the modernizing leap. While in 1957 over a third of the population were illiterate, 7 percent of adults had never attended any school,[73] and only 57.4 percent of the city's residents had had a secondary education, by 1988, when the city's population exceeded 850,000, this figure had reached 95.8 percent.[74] At the same time, Łódź's capital expenditures were decreasing compared to other cities,[75] as a consequence of which it would later suffer, especially after 1989.

During the turbulent year of 1968, the university compromised itself with the removal of a section of its academic staff, the appointment of so-called March docents, and the repression of defiant students, all amid the general crisis of power.[76] The authorities once more restricted the autonomy of the university, and a new organizational structure was introduced, which replaced chairs with departments. In the area of learning, compulsory classes in basic political science and workers' training were introduced. The University of Łódź was by now a project with many years of experience, an intellectual tradition, a campus, and a growing number of faculty, staff, and students.

A parallel process to that of building an academic institution in the working-class city was the reconstruction of a social imaginary. While the country was being revived materially, its young builders stood at the heart of the social imaginary. Not only were the young people the protagonists of the official discourses,[77] but a new horizon of expectations was being shaped for them as well.

4

RISING EXPECTATIONS

Newspapers have always created readers, not news, as their primary function.[1]

AT THE END OF THE 1947/1948 ACADEMIC YEAR, STUDENTS COULD READ THE following in one of the Polish newspapers:[2]

> We are raising a free man, a man who knows that he is unleashing all of his creative individual powers. [. . .] We are raising a fellow fighter in the battle of all working people striving for a better tomorrow. [. . .] We are raising a man ready for any sacrifice, tireless in his fight for the ideals of the ultimate freedom, collectively reborn into our nation and the entire progressive humankind. (*Nowa inteligencja ludowa*, KP 06/48)[3]

This fragment was about them. Every day, the press reported new scientific and technical advances, called for the rebuilding of the country, encouraged work and education. Education was supposed to be available to everyone and universities wide open to all, especially to those who had struggled to pass through their doors before. The modernizing spurt, social shifts, and institutional changes also took place in the form of discursive processes that unfolded at the level of linguistic transformations. The everyday press, even though censored and manifestly using agitation speak, co-created the postwar social reality and offered a new vision of the world. This new vision generated educational desires, a wider horizon of expectations, and richer possibilities for a generation of postwar young people to imagine.

The new narrative language was not only a tool for seducing the masses through totalitarian propaganda, as a newspeak frame suggests.[4] It also influenced an increasingly greater number of groups in society who were gaining political empowerment. In this chapter, I analyze the discourse the daily press deployed in Łódź between 1945 and 1956[5] as a tool for transforming the social imaginary. I attempt to refute the argument about the manipulation of the masses—if the press was sufficiently persuasive and potent enough to "seduce," why did it not have the potential to emancipate? I suggest a view of the controlled socialist press that enables us to go beyond the limitations of analyzing totalitarian language. Even if what was taking place was solely discursive emancipation based on hegemonic rhetoric and did not translate directly into calculable indexes of social mobility, it still constituted a significant element in the postwar modernizing project and one of the few moments in Polish history when the working class found itself at the heart of the social imaginary as a motor for change.

The daily press depicted and constructed a sense of reality—it shaped the social imaginary,[6] the way in which people grasp things that allows for the realization of a society through a common understanding of the world. The social imaginary is a set of expectation horizons, ideal types, and knowledge about our relation to the world and other groups. It is a map of social spaces. It also specifies what can generally be conceived within a given historical period—it defines a repertoire of collective actions that are at the disposal of a given group or class. Stories or narratives that featured in the postwar press built anew conceptual frameworks and constellations of meanings. It was the daily press that continued to be the most dynamic platform of language use and the creation of new meanings, and it was on pages of the papers that the social imaginary was materialized and transformed. During the first period, the aforementioned boost was related to the "nodal moment"—a time of restoration and the establishment of the new, post–World War II social order; the second period, after 1947, refers to a time when the PPR, and later the PZPR, attempted to create and enforce a coherent program of modernity.

The socialist press assumed a shift in the readers of the press, from the well-read, urban intelligentsia to workers and peasants. In the postwar period, the significance of the press and its impact escalated: (1) new titles and publishers emerged; (2) circulation increased and distribution grew; (3) readership, particularly among workers and peasants, increased.[7] Rejecting the analytical frames of totalitarian language, newspeak, and propaganda, I treat the postwar press as a discursive tool of modernization policies, a powerful platform for redefining meanings and shaping the social imaginary.

BEYOND NEWSPEAK

After the war, the number of press titles was much higher than during the prewar period and so too was their circulation. Enthusiasm for liberation and the rebuilding of the country was funneled into publishing. From 1944, the number of titles rose—in 1948, almost 900 different magazines were published in Poland.[8] Furthermore, print runs increased significantly. Newspapers were more available simply because of the number of circulating items. For example, in 1938, about 210,000 newspapers were distributed daily among more than half a million Łódź residents, the most popular title,

Express Ilustrowany, achieved 100,000.[9] After the war, in 1948, when the city's population was close to its prewar numbers, 234,465 newspapers were distributed daily. Even the local *Dziennik Łódzki* was printed in a run of seventy thousand copies (although a large section ended up pulped).[10] Moreover, reaching readers from the working class became an important target—not only were papers cheap and sold below their cost of production but they were also available in a growing network of libraries and reading rooms.

In the interwar period, it was typical for a single copy of a newspaper to be circulated among a group of workers. Reading aloud was also common. However, the readership patterns were different.[11] Many of these newspapers ended up in the newly opened public libraries and reading rooms. Compulsory subscription was introduced to factories—it accounted for 42 percent of newspaper circulation[12] and boosted the availability of the daily press to working-class readers. In some factories, newspapers were read aloud at the plant to entertain the workforce. In addition, "the fight against illiteracy" was broadening the reading public.

Additionally, literacy levels were rising. A great deal had already been accomplished during the interwar period with the introduction of compulsory education; over twenty years, the level of illiteracy had fallen from 33.1 percent in 1920 to 22.1 percent in 1931, only to start inching back up again in the mid-1930s. In 1945, when it was found that three million Poles could neither read nor write, that is, 18 percent of the population, an extensive "war on illiteracy"[13] was launched. Courses in reading and writing reached over one million people. As mentioned in the previous chapter, in working-class Łódź, over a third of the population were still illiterate in 1957,[14] but access to the written word was increasing at a rate that was probably the fastest it would ever be in the history of the country.

How many workers were reading the press in Łódź? We have insight into how newspapers spread among working-class readers thanks to sociologist Józef Kądzielski and his research into readership among workers from 1958. He notes that newspapers came to be disseminated among working-class readers later than books or magazines, mainly, that is, after World War II. His research offers a comparison of readership rates among workers for the prewar and postwar periods. In general, in 1958, as many as 87.7 percent of Łódź's working class read newspapers (in comparison with 61.7 percent in 1938); predictably, the percentage was highest among skilled male workers.[15] Even if unqualified workers and women still read less, readership rates were wider than ever before.

Furthermore, what makes arguments about newspeak even less convincing is that the language of the researched press has historical continuity. The rhetoric of the socialist press in Poland, which sounds jarring today, has its roots in the language of nineteenth- and twentieth-century agitational rhetoric of workers' parties operating before the partitions.[16] In terms of international models, the agitational language of the Second International produced the framework for socialist language, which would be enhanced in the interwar period by the Soviet Union's influence. This historical continuity was most clear to the working-class or left-wing activist reader. The reader of the postwar press was no longer first and foremost an intellectual in a café but a worker on a lunch break in a factory (where the compulsory subscription had most probably been introduced). This was a new type of proletarian reader.[17] The totalitarian view universalizes the position of the liberal intellectual, ignoring how this type of language was experienced and received by the working class, and its empowering potential. The reception of news releases by a left-leaning intellectual (not to mention an intellectual who viewed the postwar reality critically) would have been extremely different from that of a worker seasoned in reading interwar socialist pamphlets or an illiterate worker listening to the news read out loud in the workplace—news that for the first time was officially directed at him—or even more importantly: at her—making them the subject of the change.

Finally, several features of the totalitarian language can be found in any dominant language—whether it be the modern military discourse of the United States or neoliberal economic language. The claim that the language of communism equalized to the Nazi language cannot be examined without considering its particular values and purposes, different from those conveyed by fascist or neoliberal language. Although similar forms might be used by a range of languages, the basic message of socialist language was an attempt at emancipation, equality, collectivity, and rationality. These values are not canceled out by the mechanics of the language itself nor by the problematic elements of the system of socialist rule. Hence, we should consider the performative consequences of statements made in a given place and time, what they do to the recipient, and what their material results are in the here and now, including in the area of modifying the social imaginary.

The postwar press in Łódź no longer addressed a well-read, urban audience but turned to workers. At the same time, the model of the prewar press circulation that had shaped the expectations of Polish readers coupled with a preserved journalistic ethos allowed for the retention of much of the press's national specificity.[18] In the USSR, a popular audience was created in part by the socialist press—mass readership, modern press circulation, and the fight against illiteracy had already taken place under the Bolsheviks. The situation in Poland was different. Even if illiteracy was still a grave problem, Polish readers, including those from working-class backgrounds, were relatively better educated. Therefore, existing institutional patterns ensured the preservation of a network of intellectuals, among them journalists, alongside readers with certain expectations, and this forestalled the verbatim implementation of the so-called Soviet model.

A NEW CONFIGURATION OF MEANINGS

One of the key dimensions of creating the social imaginary was that of giving a new meaning to already existing subjects. New terms for the university, professors, and students were emerging. Also, completely new words were coined for new meanings, such as: new professionals (*nowe kadry*), democratization, economic plan, and the fight for peace. The following sections of this chapter reconstruct how language was used to depict and create the default role of students, professors, and the university as well as the scope of activities, agency, and role models ascribed to them. Thereby new subjects-objects were established, such as: students/studying young people/attendees of universities; academic staff/professors/academics/university lecturers, and finally a university/higher education institution/academy and scholarship/knowledge/research. The terms grouped in this list obviously differ in the scope of their meanings and their use, however, to such a small degree that they were treated as common groups of synonymic terms referring to relatively fixed concepts—subjects conveying new meanings. It is not without significance that a university was referred to as a higher education institution, students as attendees of a higher education establishment, and education as research for the economy.

The proposed "democratization" assumed that the structure of students' and graduates' social background was to reflect the structure of society as a whole—in accordance with a socialist notion of meritocracy whereby more or less the same proportion of people composing each social class were to undertake studies. The state was obliged to create a system in which each able citizen had the opportunity to access higher education. At the same time, it was assumed that "both, a metalworker and a professor, are needed. Both jobs should be given equal respect and support. However, in order to be a professor and a researcher, one needs different talents than to do metalwork" (*Ci, którzy dzieło ojców swoich rozwiążą i udoskonalą*, KP 06/46).

The most significant change in the social imaginary consisted of expanding the possible opportunities for those from the lower class through the prospect of undertaking studies. "Thanks to the conditions that have changed since the war, the son of a small farmer or the daughter of a worker or of a working intellectual will be able to hold the reputable title of an engineer, a doctor or a magister [having a master's degree]" (*Bramy wyższych uczelni szeroko otwarte*, GR 8/48). The titles of the articles alone (for example, *The doors of universities are wide open*) explicitly conveyed the availability of university places, employing the metaphors of "open doors," "being wide open," "filling universities with the children of workers and peasants." The proclaimed equality of occupations did not contradict the democratization of higher education but was supposed to foster it.

From 1948, the recruitment process was ever more often the subject of news articles. Its mechanics were presented as "the most urgent issue," due to the relation between the social makeup of candidates and the makeup of future graduates. The press reported on and explained complicated procedures. In order to provide equal opportunities as early as the recruitment stage, the preferential treatment of certain candidates was introduced, a positive discrimination that the press presented as a necessary step in equalizing educational opportunities. This was also the explanation behind the preliminary year and preparatory courses.

> The examination takes into account the social background of a candidate. This does not mean any favoritism, however, as it is understandable that the children of a peasant or a worker who do not have suitable conditions for learning are entitled to certain considerations. Hence, there are two guidelines to the committee's work: 1) offsetting the consequences of war and 2) scouting for valuable individuals from the working and peasant environments, which will entail a change in the face of our universities. (*Ponad 1000 osób zakwalifikowało się*, DŁ 04/46)

A great deal of attention was devoted to these policies. They were not only directed toward the past, that is, related to a narrative about compensation for past loss and the remedying of past injustices, but they were also oriented toward the future, hence, the creation of a new order, modernization, rebuilding the Polish economy, culture, and the entire social structure.

At times, press texts took the form of reportage, recounting heart-wrenching stories about individuals with whom a reader could easily identify. The success of these individuals made the reader believe that his or her own success was attainable. There were even some melodramatic features, not so much outlining pertinent examples as offering entire stories—like that of comrade Temptation who was mentioned in the introduction. Workers' or peasants' children could easily gain entry to the university, not only thanks to the preparatory courses and preliminary year but mainly on account of their hard work. Such success was the result of the habit of diligent and systematic work, which characterized people from a working-class background. They tried harder, appreciated educational opportunity, and had a good work ethic:

> It is noteworthy that, contrary to the opinion of skeptics, the standard of education is improving while young people from working-class and peasant backgrounds, despite initial difficulties, soon surpass prewar students with their perseverance and abilities. (*Od przedwojennej pustyni kulturalnej . . .*, GR 05/52)

It was argued that these young people underwent an even more rigorous selection than those from the intelligentsia. The "floaters" used erudition brought from home to essentially mask their lack of expertise. In fact, this argument was the main weapon used against those who opposed democratizing the university too radically on the grounds that it would lead to the lowering of standards. As a result, representatives of the working class not only had an inherently democratic (socialist) worldview but also a predisposition to work hard and to be well organized.

It was emphasized that the attitude of worker-parents and peasant-parents also needed to change so that they would not be propelled primarily by a desire to secure their children's personal prosperity—"so that their sons would become 'Gentlemen.'" It had to be impressed on parents that the goal of educating their children was to "build a new world and common prosperity and not [...] to provide one privileged human group with better living conditions."

The coinage of the term "new faculty" not only related to the ideological change, which was almost mechanically dependent on the social background of students, but also to another term, the "new generation." This notion existed somewhat synonymically; however, the factor of the social change was rooted not so much in the class structure but in demographics. It referred to young people born in the 1930s, whose formative years took place during or after the war, and who therefore did not remember prewar times very well.

> This young generation of Łódź scholars and the new intelligentsia shaped by our university are playing an increasingly crucial role in the development of our university. [...] the new generation is a real social power which is making its mark on the development of our university and our city. (*UŁ po 5 latach*, GR 01/50)

Aside from expanding the horizons of expectations and raising educational desires, press reports, one by one, outlined new visions of who a student or professor was, and what learning and university meant. Thus, the children of peasants and workers were encouraged to take up studies while, overall, a new meaning of studying was emerging; workers and peasants were being persuaded to enter university at the same time as the roles of this institution were being redefined.

STUDENTS AND STUDYING

Tadeusz Wilk from the tiny village of Rudków, in central Poland, was a son of a small farmer. Time and again, he read in the newspapers that there was a shortage of doctors in Poland, particularly surgeons. He also heard a lot about the immense progress made by Soviet surgeons and their modern surgical techniques. These matters were of great interest to him so he decided to study medicine (*Wyższe uczelnie stoją otworem*, GR 04/49).

From the moment of liberation, tens of thousands of students, including Tadeusz Wilk, stood out in Łódź's streets because of their student caps. At both a general level and in the discourse defining who a student was and what studying meant, there were tensions typical of the friction between town and gown, the Łódź of workers and the Łódź of the university.

The press presented this in terms of an unbalanced social composition of the student body and the risk of a replication of the prewar elites. This was the starting point for change:

> We are witnessing the phenomenon of typical occupational continuity, which causes young people to study en masse the law, the humanities, or mathematical and natural sciences. Occupations are passed on from father to son. (*Uniwersytet u progu nowego roku . . .*, GR 09/46)

There was a looming threat of conflict between the peasants and workers' group, whose aim was to transform the country and who were positioned as the spearheading modernizers, and the elitist young people, who were purportedly trying to hamper this transformation. The critical voices included accusations of students living in an ivory tower, separate from the problems of wider society, warnings that they were "anchors of reactionary forces," "a bunch of slackers" who were taking advantage of the privilege provided by the people's state through the efforts of society as a whole (particularly workers). When students "made trouble," for instance, in 1945, by protesting following the murder of the student Maria Tyrankiewicz[19] or by neglecting their studies or even selecting their field of study recklessly, it was always the "reactionaries" or the aforementioned "prewar youth" who were to blame.

On a few occasions, the press voiced the collective concerns of workers, rebuking students and reminding them how much they owed their country and other members of society, thanks to whose labor they could study and advance:

> Placing a great mass of academic young people within the city walls is a great challenge. But young people have no patience, hardly do they start to learn and they already bring trouble to the city and to those who are its true hosts—the organized workers. (*Studenci muszą się liczyć . . .*, DŁ 12/45)

It was the working class and the rest of society who made sacrifices to maintain the privilege of this one social group, which meant they gained the right to control and review students' actions as well as those of the university as a whole. Hence, they could even demand that academic autonomy be revoked in order to curb the excesses of the "reactionary section of the student body."

However, the majority of press coverage was positive and favored students, calling for joint efforts to build a better future. Students, as a social group, were placed on the same side of the barricade as the workers, hence, as taken advantage of and unprivileged during capitalist times, but today, cared for by the state and society as a whole. For instance, when Arturówek—a district surrounded by forest north of Łódź, known as a district for the wealthy before the war—was designated as a site for student dormitories, this decision was presented as an act of social justice. Even the postwar president of Łódź, Kazimierz Mijal, famous for his skeptical views on the university, called for students to be supported and no effort spared so they could "feel at home" (this occurred under the ambivalent slogan of "student socialization"). Rather than being regarded as "slackers," students were more often considered the potential cornerstone of social change and the new socialist professionals who would ensure the progress of the economy and the country as a whole.

Students themselves, not as a body, but as the voice of student organizations playing the role of a synecdoche in the press, often defined themselves as "the avant-garde of progressive youth." Outlining the prewar vs. postwar division in a "Manifesto" from *Dziennik Akademicki* (Academic Daily), students defined their role and tasks as follows:

> We would like to show that having begun a new, postwar life as students of the University of Łódź [...] we have persistently striven to create new values and score as many successes a possible—in a word, to create a new type of scholar. We wish to become a public-spirited and creative element. Besides learning, which is our basic goal, we also engage in cultural, social, and self-educational work. [...] We are part of society and if we stand out in this society, we hope that the reason for this distinction is not just white caps or academic badges, as some still believe. We strive to earn this distinction with learning, work, our attitude toward life and its current issues. We wish to be seen as the avant-garde of progressive youth, consciously and persistently aiming to implement democratic ideals. (***, DA 10/46).

The statements of students associated with the organization AZS *Życie* (Life) were couched in a similar tone:

> We demand education and we demand knowledge that enables us to build a new world, a world of social justice which will never permit exploitation, where the bloody horror of recent years will never recur. We do not want to listen to dry platitudes, we do not want to become craftsmen, we want our wisdom to be the wisdom of living men, we want the knowledge passed on to us to be a weapon of progress, to become conscious fighters of society, its avant-garde in the fight for human rights. Hence, we demand a social education, we demand that the inseparable and inherent

> tie of an individual to the community be highlighted. We demand that this simple call for democracy, which one would think does not require any elaboration, be emphasized, that the interest of an individual shall be subject to the needs of society. We simply demand democratization, democratization in the full meaning of the word. (AZMW—Akademicki Związek Młodzieży Walczącej, a publication titled *Życie*, as quoted in *Nowe pismo akademickie*, DA 10/46)

Thus, the voice of students in the discourse was represented by "social warriors" who demanded a new world and democracy. The voice of the entire academic environment was presented as coherent and unambiguous. The new professionals were to stand shoulder-to-shoulder with workers in the process of historical change. Soon, student representation at the university was completely taken over by the Union of Polish Youth and a small number of field correspondents, that is, select students commenting on academic issues "from within." It was the voices coming from within the academic environment that most convinced the average reader about the real change along with the engagement of students who, for instance, cheered each other on to reinforce work discipline (*Nauka w walce o wykonanie planu . . .*, DŁ 10/50).

The tasks of the socialist student included first and foremost choosing the right field of study, effort and commitment to study, activity and engagement in social issues, and— after graduation—service to the country and society.

1. CHOICE OF STUDIES

Dozens of articles were devoted to this subject. A shortage of professionals caused by wartime losses and the immense "effort to rebuild" the country meant that each individual choice made a difference. Hence, with every year's university enrollments, an appeal was made that decisions be made carefully and responsibly, not from the perspective of benefits to oneself but to society more broadly:

> The influx of university applicants, recorded directly after the war, is not diminishing. Luckily, there is a place for everyone interested. It is less fortunate that young people are driven by purely materialistic reasons—they apply en masse to medical or legal faculties, etc. disregarding the value of other fields that are just as important, such as the humanities, natural sciences, and so on. (*Młodzież garnie się do nauki*, DŁ 09/47)

There was no place for prewar individual whims nor wasting time and money from the state budget. This meritocracy promoted in the socialist press did not aim to direct the highest number of people into fields directly connected to a given industry but, rather, to provide opportunities for advancement according to an individual's interests. This in turn was to ensure dedication to work and consequently to improved efficiency and provide a greater benefit to the public. Papers also reported that "oftentimes, candidates who for various reasons wanted to forgo studies were openly urged by the recruitment commission to reconsider" (*Dlaczego wybieracie ten kierunek*, DŁ 06/52). Students were warned not to follow the advice of relatives who suggested "lucrative" subjects because this was a secondary consideration (*Nad właściwym wyborem studiów*, GR 12/53). Potential students were also advised not to take up studies in cities other than their family's place of residence, so as not to burden them and the state with unnecessary expenses. On the other hand, it was emphasized that studying was not for everyone and that higher education was not a mandatory educational path, even for those who held secondary school–leaving certificates (*matura* certificates; see figure A.1 in the appendix). Study for study's sake, as a result of social pressure, was a prewar relic:

> A similar view was highly characteristic of the bourgeois environment where a university degree, next to one's level of wealth, decided an individual's social status and was a tool in their assessment. Today, this view is a thing of the past; nor should we allow another relic to resurface, the so-called perpetual student. (*Uwagi o studiach*, DA 09/47)

2. EFFORT AND COMMITMENT TO STUDYING

Having chosen an appropriate subject, the young person was next expected to study diligently, that is, to attend classes regularly and punctually, to sit for exams, not "slack," to systematically work on the material and not take shortcuts. From the 1950s, there was a particular emphasis on productivity and learning outcomes with students being expected to plan and manage their time well:

> A substantial number of classes and the need to prepare for them will force students to manage their time most efficiently. They will want to make the most of each minute, either in lectures or practical classes, or alternatively, preparing for them. Accordingly, the university authorities need to spread classes suitably throughout the day and academic personnel must strictly follow this timetable as well. (*Socialistyczna dyscyplina*, DŁ 11/51)

Increasingly greater emphasis was placed on planning work, organization, "active competition," and teamwork. A success was supposed to be collective, not individual. The new discipline of studying introduced in 1948 was to distinguish the socialist university from the prewar liberal one:

> The previously popular "stock," where students camped outside the exam room to inquire "How does the professor examine?" and "Which questions are asked most

> often?" is no longer practiced. A student of the liberal university had usually prepared for the examination based on this hastily copied "information." Serious changes have been introduced in this area. Today—instead of the "stock," organized student groups meet for classes according to the timetable. Students who attend lectures together, do homework together, should also study together. (*Dyscyplina studiów i zespołowa praca*, GR 09/51)

This was linked to the revolutionary rhetoric that had gained momentum from the outset and couched academic issues in military terms. Education, much like the iron and steel industry or textiles, became an area of struggle for the execution of the six-year plan—groups of students and even entire universities were to join in the competition, challenging one another. Graduates were to form "a massive army of socialism-builders" or become "the officers of building socialism" (*Nowy rok—nowe zadania*, GR 10/53). As on the battlefield, universities faced "pivotal days," "offensives," and so on. *Dziennik Łódzki* cheered on the competitors as follows:

> "Leaders take the most challenging paths"—announces the call of the Union of Polish Youth on the pioneer draft. The students of the University of Łódź shall respond to this call with the movement of mass leadership in education and social work. Raising the bar and mobilizing strength—they shall keep up with their colleagues from coal mines and steel works. (*Studenci Uniwersytetu Łódzkiego podejmują ruch masowego przodownictwa*, DŁ 03/53)

Political awareness and the approach adopted to perform tasks played a key role in this valiant march. The indicators of success reported by the press were primarily exam session results, the percentage of students sitting for exams as well as their pass rate. Hence, the exam period was a time of strenuous "fight," testing both students' abilities and the effectiveness of the entire institution. After every exam period, the sifting rate was reported, that is, the number of people who failed exams, and the dropout rate of people who did not sit for exams. As early as 1950, the press reported that students themselves were debating how to bring these numbers down (*Młodzież akademicka podnosi...*, GR 04/50). Student effort was also measured in terms of class attendance and the social background profile.

3. ACTIVITY AND ENGAGEMENT IN SOCIAL ISSUES

A student was to remain a conscientious citizen, to engage in extracurricular activities as well as resist and fight against reactionary forces. From the beginning, this emphasis was particularly visible in Łódź:

> The youngest city in Poland has the youngest university in the world, without ancient traditions, without the past that other Polish universities have, and this fact puts a great responsibility on its young people to answer to the future generations of Łódź academics. Students of the higher education institutions in Łódź ought to become the frontiers of new thought, a bastion hewing the new intelligentsia from the reborn, democratic Poland. (*Inauguracja roku*, DŁ 10/45)

Students were expected to participate in cultural life, student organization projects, harvests, censuses (as interviewers), and ideally, not be gainfully employed. If there was to be a double burden, then it would be academia as work (but not additional employment), and activism.

The latter was frequently deliberated in the press. The gainful employment of students was a subject that caused considerable tension: Young people ought to come from the working class and devote themselves solely to their studies. Although a system of scholarships, dormitories, and cheap or even free meal provision was developing year by year, a vast number of students had to work to be able to study. To a large extent, this body consisted of those arriving from the countryside and those from working-class backgrounds who, although studying in their city of residence, still had to supplement their income to support themselves or their family, or both. In 1948, there was alarm that most students had no free time because 90 percent of them were in paid work (*Studenci maja dużo humoru, ale mało pieniędzy*, DŁ 11/48).

One response to this took the form of calls to adjust class and lecture timetables as well as the dean's office hours to suit those who worked, while likewise supervisors at workplaces were requested to enable class attendance or reduction of the workload during the exam period. Another response depicted the situation otherwise, as if it were the ineptitude of young people that led them to seek employment to earn additional money instead of studying. At the same time, students were certainly able to do social work, and in that way give back to society what they were being gifted during their studies. Social work was supposedly the less burdensome option while it also enabled more growth and entailed fewer clashes with studies. The model student, aside from being intensely interested in the country's situation, was to be active at the university, participate in student organizations (from 1948, membership in the Polish Youth Union, Związek Młodzieży Polskiej, the ZMP,[20] was compulsory), and engage in social interactions and various cultural activities.[21] Students were also encouraged to participate in various kinds of undertakings, such as building tramway lines and dormitories for fellow students, an achievement that was proudly reported in the press, digging foundations so that streets could be laid, and so forth. In later years, they were obliged to help peasants during harvests. Activity during studies meant meeting the requirement for "student socialization" and bonding with society, policies fostered by the authorities.

4. WORK — SERVING THE COUNTRY AND WIDER SOCIETY

Qualified professionals, whether they had graduated from language studies, chemistry, or medicine, were to help modernize the country, first by rebuilding it and later, when the drumroll of revolutionary rhetoric intensified, by implementing the six-year plan. The prewar period was often a crucial reference, depicted as a time of growing unemployment when universities were interested in neither the needs of society nor the country's economy. The future for graduates in the postwar reality was to look different—one of the key policies of the authorities, and the flagship slogan of the PZPR, was that of tackling unemployment. The phrase "the right to work" was inscribed in the vision of modern society:

> Graduates from every faculty are awaited by factories and schools, ironworks and agriculture, all branches of the national economy are waiting. The phenomenon of unemployment has vanished. There are no privileged occupations, every citizen of People's Poland has the right to work, each job is an honor. (*Ważna decyzja*, GR 05/53)

It was essential that everybody find a job according to their qualifications and that this effort was not wasted. The right to work was assured by the people's state. This guarantee was a crucial message to the many who, after the years of wartime unrest, desired practical skills promising employment regardless of circumstances, whether for themselves or their children. As often indicated in biographical interviews and memoirs from that period, for many people, practical skills had ensured survival in difficult times and thus had been highly valued. In the well-planned structure of a socialist university, if faculty were recruited and students accepted, it meant that society had a place for this profession.

To recapitulate, the press created a typology of the ideal postwar student. This was to serve as a model for young people from the working class.[22] Examples of individual students, a rhetoric of care, a vision of challenges that could ultimately be overcome, were to render the decision to study a realistic option for a wide range of social groups.

PROFESSORS

The new faculty were still to be recruited. The press underlined tensions between the new generation of academics and those from the prewar period. As with students, the intelligentsia was divided into a progressive section belonging to the postwar era and the reactionary rest, who remained shackled to the prewar era. Each group was distinctive. Those in the first group were referred to as "researchers" or "academic staff," less often as professors or academics, although neither of these words had gone out of use. Consequently, progressive faculty had an incredibly important role to play—they were to train a new generation of professionals, including new faculty members for the new times.

Professors, as presented in the press, should—like students—be supported by society and the state. In the first years after the war, there was a shortage of housing for professors, hence, there were appeals to improve their living conditions. One example was Professor Sym[23] who had to prepare his lectures in the only place available—his own bed; and others who had no place whatsoever to work, either at the university or at home. Conditions of academic work was a public concern and the press alerted and monitored this issue.

There were attempts to show that a change was taking place among the initially skeptical faculty. Confronted by reality itself, academics were supposed to play their new role and miraculously transform from "diehard supporters of the old system" into apostles of the new—"a professor ought to take on the role of a pedagogue, teacher, organizer" (*Przed Kongresem*, GR 04/50). By ridding themselves of their old habits, they were to form a bond with the masses and get involved in building the new order. While the student body could be molded from nothing, professors had to "find common ground with the masses"—and transition from the prewar to the postwar era. From the very beginning, the press called for and reported this fight for souls, which was key to the country's future:

> Regrettably, not all academic employees realize the benefits of liberating human thought from the shackles of the capitalist dictatorship and backwardness. The sooner the entirety of Polish scholars finds a common language with the Polish working masses, who are toiling to sculpt a new improved social system in most difficult times, the sooner Polish culture, maimed by the occupier, will revive from the horrible destruction of the war. (*Ludzie nauki muszą znaleźć*. . . , KP 09/46)

A professor—whether progressive or a convert—was primarily to be a teacher rather than a researcher, bringing down the torch from the heights of knowledge to the masses; she or he was to be a motivated worker devoting a lot of care and "sacrificial effort" to his/her mission. In 1949, *Dziennik Łódzki* summed up the tasks faced by academic circles under a notable title, "Knowledge Is Not a Commodity on a Stall":

> The tasks before us in this area (of combating the backwardness of scholarship) come down to the following essentials:
>
> 1. Modernizing the scope and methods of teaching.
> 2. Supporting young scholars.

3. Encouraging experienced professors and scholars to review their outdated views on education. (*Wiedza to nie towar w kramiku*, DŁ 11/49)

The reader of the press could follow how this change was unfolding, how academics were leaving their ivory towers and becoming "scholarly workers."

Aside from the main teaching goal of their work, academics were also to contribute to the socialization of the university—they were to popularize knowledge and their activities. Therefore, they were expected to give external lectures on popular scholarship, visit factory cafeterias, help students, and engage in the life of the university, the city, its citizens, and ideally the entire country. The press regularly provided information about the current activities of Łódź scholars, their research, and its potential benefit to society and the growing economy. Newspapers proudly reported on conventions and conferences held in Łódź, and also about events nationwide and abroad attended by the local professors who represented the workers' city (and the socialist motherland) before the world. There were even mentions of scholarly journals published in Łódź, most celebratory events, and initially also doctoral defenses and professorial appointments. Reports on issues of the university as an area of public interest brought the world of academia closer to the average reader.

Following the offensive of the six-year plan, from around 1950, scholars were expected to take on new challenges to implement it. It was communicated with pride that increasingly more was expected from faculty, such as extending office hours, using a smaller amount of reagents in laboratories, producing additional publications, or devoting work to important social matters, for instance, the issue of workers' lives in Łódź.

Another mobilizing effort intensifying in the 1950s was the peace movement. In this context, the academic community was portrayed as united and uniformly progressive (e.g., *Apel naukowców łódzkich*, GR 03/55). During the peace pact campaign, where the peaceful use of science played a crucial role because of nuclear weapons, the rhetoric intensified and culminated during the World Peace Council (WPC) in Warsaw in 1950 and the National Peace Plebiscite in May 1951. Citizens' signatures were gathered under the Peace Treaty between five world powers in a form of referendum (are you for or against it), and the WPC gathered 600 million signatures worldwide,[24] including in Łódź:

> Professors and students of the city's young workers' university expressed their steadfast will to serve the cause of peace and progressive science. [. . .] The scholars and students of the University of Łódź have confirmed that they are unwavering fighters for peace and progress. (*Plebiscyt na Uniwersytecie*, DŁ 05/51)

In the "Polish Film Chronicle" reporting on the referendum, professors and university students were mentioned right after the "first fighter for peace," president

Bolesław Bierut, miners, and workers in the newly built steelworks named "Peace" in Silesia. Therefore, they occupied considerably high positions, before peasants or construction workers (and also "progressive priests and nuns").[25]

Student poverty and the need to create a comprehensive system of social benefits that would enable studying was a frequently discussed problem. It particularly applied to those who were not learning a profession per se, but who could essentially devote themselves to academia and, in the future, join the new faculty, thus continuing the traditions of the progressive group of professors. Such devotion required much better conditions—hence, the demand that students be protected and supported was more urgent in the context of the new academic faculty:

> A minimum. Let's say it's enough to do a practical job. But where will we get replacements for the old generation to continue the labor of transferring knowledge? Where will we get the scholars to work for progress?
>
> It's sad to say but we won't raise them until the material existence of the student masses improves, until the burden of worries and mundane problems isn't taken off young people's shoulders. This needs to be seriously considered. (*Jan drzemie na wykładzie*, DŁ 09/48)

The new intelligentsia—that is, thousands of young doctors, engineers, economists, and teachers—needed to have secure career paths, and an academic career needed to become an attractive option for young people. In the meantime, concerns were being raised:

> Who is supposed to be a future lecturer at higher education institutions: a working student waiting around the dean's office to apply for an exam deferment? Or perhaps a student on a scholarship, a representative of the proverbial student poverty? Or maybe a student who is a regular at a café? Surely none of them. (*W trosce o kształcenie naukowców*, DŁ 10/47)

Teaching assistants were an important group in this process. This group was not only numerous because of the postwar demography and the educational boom, but it was precisely this young generation that was key to breaking the reproduction of the faculty and democratizing it. It was emphasized that its current situation, compared to prewar times, was better and more stable, and that it was supported "unlike during the Sanacja government" (*Pod troskliwą opieką*, DŁ 09/51).

Column inches were given to demanding clear promotion criteria in an academic career and warning against reactionary views spreading among teaching assistants. The press cautioned that "often, the functions of teaching assistants are performed by people hostile to the system of People's Poland" (*Robotnik—wzorem dla studiującej młodzieży*, DŁ 04/50). A lack of transparent procedures was condemned and there were continuous calls for socialist meritocracy—promotion should be awarded for merit as well as passion for the profession. In 1952, *Głos Robotniczy* wrote:

> Curricula, contents, and forms of teaching and education are transforming, young people, as well as professors, are changing their ideological face. We are witnessing the gradual obsolescence of the previously dominant type of scholar who isolated himself in his ivory tower and walked around on platforms so high that from way up there he couldn't see life or what transformations were taking place below. (*Od przedwojennej . . .*, GR 05/52)

The roles of both students and professors were redefined and connected to new sets of activities, responsibilities, and new descriptors—both for the undesired state and the target or proclaimed state. The reconstruction of the subjects shaping the social imaginary was underway.

EDUCATION AND UNIVERSITY

The model of the liberal (prewar) and the socialist (postwar) university remained a key point of reference in the construction of the subject of the university. This was amplified by other terms used in the discourse on the prewar-postwar spectrum, such as an aristocrat-scholar vs. a builder of socialism, isolation (pure science) vs. engagement in social issues (engaged science), unsupervised freedom vs. planning, elitism vs. egalitarianism. All these elements were connected to the notion of socialized education, which, depending on the context, meant both the usefulness of knowledge, the democratization of universities, planning and discipline, and later Marxism-Leninism, as the only method for scholarly activity. In 1948, *Dziennik Łódzki* wrote:

> Previously, the issues of learning, universities, and higher education overall remained somewhat on the margins of Polish public opinion. At the same time, professors, researchers, the entire apparatus of higher education were shut off behind their office walls and research facilities generally kept away from issues affecting wide swathes of the nation. The few exceptions only confirmed the new arrogant isolationism. (*Nauka bez izolacji*, DŁ 01/48)

An important component of the prewar era was its alleged capitalist economic model. This was expressed in two vital anticapitalist demands made of the university.

First, knowledge is not a commodity—despite the departure from the idea of "pure science" (that is, science was to be subjected to the needs of the society); the autonomy of producing knowledge was to be maintained, perhaps not from social (or political) pressure but from market pressure. Therefore, there appeared in print the slogan: "KNOWLEDGE IS NOT A PRODUCT ON A SHELF" [original capitals] (DŁ 11/49) or as already mentioned, "Knowledge Is Not a Commodity on a Stall" (DŁ 11/49), that is, as it had been under capitalism—in the PRL it served to build society, not private wealth and exploitation.

Second, the university is not a venture—however, it should work efficiently, similar to a factory, cooperate with the whole system of production, manage and plan; but it should not have profit in mind but effectiveness and progress.[26] This would guarantee funding for research, would make it independent of capital, and would ensure its true freedom and autonomy: "Research and researchers cannot fund themselves" (*Ludzie nauki muszą znaleźć . . .*, KP 09/46).

Third, universities were no longer for privileged elites: "The representatives of the broadest people's masses should be educated at the universities first of all, and not, as was the case before the war, the sons of people from the privileged classes—capitalists and landowners" (*Wyższe uczelnie stoją otworem*, GR 04/49). One privilege was to be replaced by another:

> Suppose there were not enough places for everyone at the university. In that case, priority admission will be given to children of workers, peasants of the working intelligentsia and indigenous youth of the Recovered Territories. This privilege will also be enjoyed by candidates who took part in the 1939–1945 war, candidates who have demonstrated one year of community service in youth organizations or one year of professional work related to their chosen field of study, and teachers. (*Przed nowym rokiem akademickim*, DŁ 11/54)

The historical process that led from the liberal to the socialist university was supposedly inevitable, and according to press presentations—especially after 1948—truth and progress were not on the side of the prewar university: "Every year, the old, liberal university is shrinking. It is being pushed out by the socialist university. [. . .] The young people of People's Poland have taken over the university" (*Dyscyplina studiów i zespołowa praca . . .*, GR 09/51). As *Dziennik Łódzki* reported in 1953, universities "have one purpose: to shape the new face of education in the service of the masses working for the peaceful creation of socialism" (*Współpraca wydawnicza*, DŁ 01/53).

From the postwar vantage point, four basic groups of functions emerged, which would characterize the new socialist university:

1. Teaching (Didactics)—The university above operated to teach; it was to be a place for educating professionals and enabling the country's growth. In the process of meeting this function, the university was to support the aforementioned process of democratization, which also meant making young people from peasant and working-class backgrounds feel at home in an institution that was foreign to them. The education goals were to be based on several essential components, such as an effort to provide the highest possible level of education, the suitable ideological profile of the education, and the adjustment of activities to the needs of the country.
2. Research—The second most important function that the press attributed to the university was that of the production of new knowledge. The country was taking a difficult modernizing leap, and, aside from staff, it needed technology, modern techniques of work, knowledge about work organization, and so on. Let us not forget that this was the time of the Cold War; the Marshall Plan was rejected, and hence, the whole burden of proving to the world that socialism was superior to capitalism fell on socialist countries.
3. Dissemination—A socialized university was obliged to disseminate its outcomes as well as the findings of its research, presenting them in an accessible form to the rest of society, that is, reporting its tasks back to those who had enabled its existence. There was a conscious effort to demystify the university and bring its activity closer to the rest of society as well as to shape its mission of disseminating knowledge. Hence, there were numerous notices about open lectures and leading articles on important university events, from the granting of doctoral degrees to statistics relating to academic output. In the 1950s, *Łódzki Ekspres Ilustrowany* published a series of articles titled "*Z łódzkich ośrodków badawczych*" (From research centers in Łódź), which reported on the activity of Łódź researchers. These articles aimed to explain what a given faculty was doing and to what end, focusing on the practical dimension of this research and its impact on the life of the average person.
4. Consultancy—Higher education institutions, including universities, were ultimately places of knowledge production and for conducting research. It was only an additional step to translate this practical knowledge into concrete activities, which would help workplaces and institutions operate more efficiently.

Another component, which was aggressively advanced after the reform of higher education and following intensified Stalinization, was the ideological profile of the university. Previously, there were references to the progressive, democratic, or open character of the university, toning down the overt pointers to socialism, not to mention those of Marxism-Leninism. As with the level of political speeches, this was primarily connected to the attempt to include as wide a range of social groups as possible into the modernizing project. However, in the later period, a correct approach to research was enforced, openly and rather aggressively, particularly in *Głos Robotniczy*. For instance:

> The mission of the party organization will be that the leadership of Marxism and Leninism in scholarship is commonly recognized. We must streamline the transition of the former materialists-formalists to the ideological viewpoint of Marxism. We shall do this not by obscuring ideological opposition or suppressing it, but by showing it in full light, revealing its class roots, and consequently, by inevitably choosing between the positions of progress and backwardness. (*Kadry decydują o wszystkim*, GR 10/49)

DEMOCRATIZATION AND SOCIALIST MERITOCRACY

At each historical moment, there is a certain repertoire of practices available to a given social group—activities considered to be natural, acceptable, or even desirable—and it is clear how to perform them. In the postwar period, there was a major shift in this area, based on the modification of the entire conceptual framework and the rebuilding of the repertoire of practices—this was also part of constructing the socialist imaginary of society. As *Dziennik Łódzki* stated: "Among the many victories of People's Poland, making education accessible to the widest masses of our society is number one" (*Otwarta droga*, DŁ 50/01). *Kurier Popularny* echoed this, reporting that "among all the social movements, socialism has always been driven by the greatest care and support of the advancement of science, education, and art" (*Ludzie nauki muszą znaleźć* . . . , KP 09/46). Democratization and socialized higher education—an attempt to build a socialist university—were supposed to be the most crucial outcomes of this change. (See table 4.1.)

The result was a new constellation of subjects, granting agency and awakening educational desires among numerous social groups, primarily the working class. For most Poles, the prospect of higher education, especially studying at a university, had been unimaginable. The prospect of taking up studies became real—for some suddenly, for others gradually from year to year. It was an option worth considering from the perspective of one's own life, of one's children, and even one's co-workers and neighbors. Higher education was supposed to be available to everybody; moreover, it was almost designed with the working class in mind. Furthermore, studying and the work of a university became public issues. As a result of the collective socialist surge, individual

TABLE 4.1 REDEFINITIONS OF MEANING IN THE POSTWAR PRESS

SUBJECT	PREWAR	POSTWAR
Students	Fear of unemployment	Right to job
	Skills not leading to a job	Useful skills
	Against progress	Working for society
	Detached from society	Supported by working classes
	Elitist	Egalitarian
Intelligentsia /faculty	Serving elites	Serving working classes, society, and nation
	Detached from society's needs	Close to society
	Elitist	Egalitarian
	Few progressive—marginalized	
University	A monastery out of reach	A forge of progress
	Reactionary	Open to everyone
	Supporting fascism	Academic freedom despite pseudoscience
	Stagnation hidden under academic freedom	Responsibility to society

decisions also became public, transparent, detached from private life, and worthy of discussion. Grasping this attempt to transform the social imaginary is key to attaining a fuller understanding of the postwar social reality. However, what was the situation of the students themselves? Who went to college? Who was welcome at the University of Łódź and other universities in the PRL?

5

THE FUTURE DESIGNED

It's easy to die knowing that nothing threatens future generations.[1]

OUR SUCCESSFUL MR. TEMPTATION, MENTIONED IN THE INTRODUCTION and the previous chapter, had seen in his village a poster announcing a preparatory course at the university. He was the first of many hundreds of peasant children to enroll in n a degree course at the University of Łódź, a model socialist university. As a student Mr. Temptation received a scholarship, a place in a dormitory, and access to subsidized meals. A state-guaranteed job awaited him if he managed to graduate. As I demonstrate in this chapter, studying at university was not that simple for working-class and peasant children, who dropped out more often than the descendants of the intelligentsia. In addition, they were regarded as "trash" or "boors" by their peers. Yet despite structural obstacles and everyday classism, people like Mr. Temptation exemplified the greatest achievement of postwar educational reform. After all, what once had been even more than an exception, that is, a miracle,[2] was slowly becoming the rule. However, this was a difficult and complex process. What happened to the postwar idea of the democratization of higher education and the dream of universal education for the working class? What were the results of the efforts to transform the social imaginary, and what was the fate of the first generation of socialist university graduates? This chapter attempts to assess the effects of the educational reform at the University of Łódź, which after 1949 lost its pioneer position as the largest working-class university but which was still considered to be "the most democratic."[3] The protagonists of this chapter are the postwar participants of preparatory courses, students and graduates from a working-class background. By examining how they prepared for university, the stages of their education, and how they took up their first jobs, I intend to answer the question about the reach and role of the socialist university project. This and subsequent sections are primarily based on sociological studies from the researched period, which requires several preliminary comments.

REVISITING THE SOCIOLOGY OF THE DAY

The official report data that we have at our disposal cannot always be considered fully reliable—like all sources, these are not free from the context of production. They tended to be warped at a number of levels: from statements by individuals, which concealed the truth to a smaller or larger degree, through the minor or even considerable roundups at the level of university administration and the local authorities, up to the actions of ministries and agencies of the PZPR. Furthermore, discrepancies in the collated data are even found at the level of official reports—different numbers were given at meetings at the Sejm (the Polish parliament), in internal documents, and in the press. For instance, out of the 22,000 students who participated in voluntary surveys in the spring of 1947, only 4.1 percent were of working-class descent, only 0.2 percent had a peasant background, while the majority of those taking the survey came from the intelligentsia (47.3 percent) and petite bourgeoisie (36.1 percent).[4] This was at a time when, according to official data, the number of working-class students supposedly exceeded 20 percent. Perhaps the last two groups were more willing to take part in the survey, or it may be that a less official context led working-class people to adjust their background to the situation and fit into the new environment. Frequently, discrepancies in statistics resulted simply from the application of different definitions and criteria. How people were assigned or assigned themselves to individual classes or professional categories was particularly problematic. The classification of those who had socially advanced right after the war added another layer of difficulty. Many of these were working-class people who, following the war, had become white-collar workers or management. Some of them had children, who, however, had not been raised in the type of household that their parents' position would suggest.[5]

Notwithstanding these methodological challenges, after 1948 some officials and party representatives (and as a result, the press) seemed to become obsessed with the magic of numbers and the persuasive appeal of statistics. In the first years of the reform, in particular around 1950, reports featured various kinds of numbers. It was at that time that the impact of the reforms should have surfaced and the data served as evidence. It was a necessary tool for further mobilization and a demonstration of the system's effectiveness. Archival folders from that time are filled with pages of hand-drawn tables and charts, time-consuming breakdowns and calculations. Nearly everything could be parameterized and turned into a report.

Despite discrepancies in collected data, the message was clear—the changes in the social profile of applicants accepted by the university were significant but not entirely satisfying. Depending on the breakdown, around half the students still came from the intelligentsia, optimistically referred to as "white-collar workers" or "working intelligentsia." Their advantage in the most popular programs, where the selection mechanisms manifested the most, was even greater. Just as during the Second Republic, law, medicine, and foreign philologies remained elitist (the situation changed at the faculty of law when enrollments became largely regulated at the central level). In addition to official data, research project materials are another important source. These afford an insight into the paths taken by University of Łódź graduates when entering the workforce in the second half of the 1950s. These students—the generation of the new professionals—had been educated as part of the socialist university project. This variety of sociological works allows us to trace social change among first-year preparatory course participants from their ideas about the socialist modernizing project all the way through to the aforementioned graduates' career paths.

Following the Thaw of 1956, sociology was no longer considered a "bourgeois relic." The first signs of a Thaw appeared in 1954,[6] initially at the University of Warsaw where sociological lectures were first reinstated.[7] By 1957, most universities had opened enrollment for sociology, and larger organizational changes followed. Sociological journals experienced a revival with the publication of both new and old titles; the Polish Sociological Association was founded; and many Polish sociologists began to engage in international academic associations. At the University of Łódź, the Department of Sociology, headed by Chałasiński, was quickly inaugurated, although it is worth noting that, by this time, he was beginning to lose his status in academia in the eyes of both the government and other sociologists. His term as rector had ended in 1952 as a result of his unsuccessful attempts to protect the University of Łódź from the impact of the governmental reforms. In addition, he was marginalized as both a university official and an academic, initially because he was considered too pro-government and later because he was too critical of the state. After many career highs and lows, he moved to Warsaw to take a chair at the Polish Academy of Sciences.

The most important shift, however, was that sociology regained its role in public life. Once again, sociologists became desirable experts commissioned by the government to teach and, more importantly, to diagnose social ills and recommend improvements. All in all, sociology was just one of many disciplines that exemplified "science subordinated to society." From the mid-1950s, Chałasiński, Jan Szczepański, and Nina Assorodobraj, all of whom were educated by the interwar fathers of academic sociology, led many research projects carried out by the postwar generation of sociologists. Despite the break in enrollments during the early postwar years, its limited presence in the curricula, and its mimetic adaptation to Stalinist reforms, the scholarly environment seemed to be stronger for having overcome wartime disruption and the rupture that marked the postwar period.

Sociology received funding and government support. Research was resumed with double force and attempts were made to diagnose Polish society. Most of this focused on the sociology of work but the trend to examine social mobility, hence advancement via education, was almost as strong. Studies on higher education graduates began as early as the mid-1950s. Far-reaching research projects were also conducted in the 1960s and 1970s. These produced considerable databases, numerous reports, analyses, and scientific monographs. Based on current assessments of this work, there appears to be no reason to doubt its reliability as its authors have had many an opportunity to rectify the results. Instead, they and subsequent generations of researchers continue to make use of these findings and thus they can still be considered a "solid reference point."[8] Scholarship from the time of the PRL such as ethnography, history, and other fields is similarly valued abroad and recognized as reliable (unlike, for instance, certain findings made in the Soviet Union).[9] Simultaneously, we should be aware of its drawbacks as well, which are (among other things) synthetically discussed by Jan Lutyński, a renowned methodologist employed at the University of Łódź.[10] He points out that socialist research after the Thaw was characterized by complimentary reviews, a small number of polemics, and a focus on "uncontroversial coexistence." Furthermore, interviewees treated research in which they were taking part as an official situation and gave "politically correct" answers. Lutyński's criticism also seems to hold for research conducted today; therefore, it is hard to treat his accusations as pertaining exclusively to the social sciences after 1956. Consequently, the aforementioned comments do not negate the substantive value of this research and the relevance of its numerous findings. We cannot use research from sixty years ago as the foundation of our study here, as would be the case in a classic revisit.[11] This material does, however, allow us to take a closer look at the social reality of the time and to interpret materials and results from today's perspective. It is problematic, though, that while a substantial pool of research from the time of the PRL has been preserved, it is mostly incomplete. Authors argue and present selected issues convincingly but they do not offer a comprehensive picture of a given situation.[12] Nevertheless, such a fragmentary insight is better than none, hence, sociological research from the time of the PRL will be the main data source for the two subsequent chapters.

PREPARATORY COURSES

Initially, in the first months of 1945, only a few applicants from the working class applied to the university, and the process of regulating enrollment was rather chaotic. At the University of Łódź, in the 1945/1946 academic year, due to a high number of applicants, out of 4,470 people, 862 were not accepted (from that number, 735 were rejections from the faculty of medicine alone).[13] The recruitment process was neither well planned nor coordinated. This continued until the publication of the first regulations, which included Circular (*Okólnik*) no. 46 from August 28, 1945, reserving a pool of university places at the ministry's discretion. This was aimed at providing access to knowledge for people who had fought the occupying forces during the war, political prisoners, and camp survivors. The ministerial quota was also employed in political battles only to later become a tool for reproducing political capital. During the first recruitment, the unrepresentative social profile of the intake was shaped by the fact that prewar education paths were still determining who would study. For this generation, selection had taken place at the level of elementary education. Most probably, the social profile of the first intake of university applicants from 1945 roughly corresponded to the prewar structure. The preserved data is incomplete. However, among other things, it is known that in Łódź in 1945, the recruitment commission sent 300 people to do a preliminary year, of whom 23 percent came from the working class.[14]

The "preliminary year" was a bottom-up initiative devised by members of the academic community, the purpose of which was to help bridge the educational gaps that had resulted from the war. Some academics supported the introduction of these courses (they voiced some concerns but were nevertheless prepared to engage in the experiment), while others were skeptical and perceived this procedure as heralding the downfall of universities and the "production of a pseudo-intelligentsia."[15] The concept itself worked in the interests of both left-wing academic circles and the PPR of the time, which viewed this initiative as a sustainable tool for democratizing access to higher education as well as its supervision. It comes as no surprise that the preliminary year, and later preparatory courses, started to be viewed with increasingly more skepticism the more they departed from their original premise of compensating for war disadvantages and moved instead toward the Polish version of the Soviet *Rabfaks*.[16]

Soon, this initiative was legally regulated and, in 1948, was transformed into a preparatory study year. Prospective students were only required to have completed seven grades of elementary school and to have a working-class or peasant background. Further legislation provided paid leave from workplaces for the duration of the course to entice working people to take up studies. According to this legislation, preliminary studies could be undertaken by people between the ages of eighteen and twenty-seven; however, right after the war the upper limit was set at thirty-six years old and was successively lowered each year. Every recruitment to a preliminary year or a preparatory course was preceded by a press campaign encouraging people to take up university studies. It was emphasized that extra preparation for studying was no shame. Enrollment was encouraged with additional benefits such as accommodation, scholarships, access to workshops, libraries, and teaching aids. It was not without significance that during the subsequent recruitment drive for degree courses a quota was reserved for those who had completed preparatory courses. In 1947, *Głos Robotniczy* described the situation as follows:

> This made a difference, for example, the course in Łódź, initially totaling around 700 persons finally had a clear social face, which was working-class and peasant. I hope it keeps this face and the preliminary year, because out of 500 applicants this year to the preliminary year, 75 percent are learners on the preparatory course. (*Synowie robotników*, GR 02/47)

By 1949, only two-year preparatory courses were offered, part of which was the preliminary study year. A place on this course meant the award of a seven-year scholarship (that is, for the two-year course followed by the five-year, two-stage university degree) as well as a place in a dormitory.[17] It comes as no surprise to learn that a high number of people from the working class attended these courses. It was also these students who joined the Union of Polish Youth more frequently than others. However, the number of applicants soon started to fall, and every year it was increasingly harder to fill all the places on offer.

Research on course participants was first conducted as early as 1946 by a team of sociology students (later, professors of the University of Łódź, including Jan Lutyński, Wacław Piotrowski, and Antonina Kłoskowska) under the supervision of the historian Nina Assorodobraj.[18] The study covered around 750 people from the course with the country's highest intake, in Łódź, and a smaller one in Warsaw. In 1947, when the first year of the researched group was taking entrance exams at the University of Łódź, there were already more than 8,000 regular students, made up of 22 percent workers, 18 percent farmers, 10 percent craftsmen, and 43 percent intelligentsia (according to the University of Łódź's report).[19] (See table 5.1.)

The majority of course participants, on the other hand, were skilled workers. Unskilled workers constituted 10 percent, the same number as came from the intelligentsia. Nearly all of them already had jobs and as many as 35 percent were even employed as white-collar workers despite having no formal education. Their social advancement was hence already underway, and the courses were only supposed to reinforce their position or to enable further promotion in the workplace. There were also people who had previously held official posts, but at the time they took the course, they were blue-collar workers. The course was supposed to protect them from downward mobility and to reintroduce them to office work in new circumstances.

Those participating in the study were the last intake before the implementation of a new system of studies. They had been born in the early 1920s and brought up in a prewar environment. They were young people from unprivileged homes, primarily from a working-class and peasant background, with poor educational opportunities, both before and during the war. The surveys conducted over the next few years suggested that these course participants did not view educational advancement as an opportunity to gain prestige or a better salary. Neither were they driven by an aspiration to improve

TABLE 5.1 THE SOCIAL MAKEUP OF THE PREPARATORY COURSE PARTICIPANTS AT THE UNIVERSITY OF ŁÓDŹ, 1947–1956*

	PARTICIPANTS OF PREPARATORY COURSES IN ŁÓDŹ—SOCIAL ORIGIN											
	TOTAL		WORKERS		PEASANTS		INTELLIGENTSIA		CRAFTSMEN		OTHER	
YEARS	NO.	%	NO.	%	NO.	%	NO.	%	NO.	%	NO.	%
I 1946/47	541	100	224	41.4	129	23.8	68	12.6	46	8.5	74	13.7
II 1947/48	301	100	138	45.8	64	21.3	42	14.0	28	9.3	29	9.6
III 1947/49	194	100	89	45.9	61	31.4	18	9.3	12	6.2	14	7.2
VI 1950/52	257	100	95	37.0	143	55.6	2	0.8	6	2.3	11	4.3
X 1954/56	184	100	80	43.5	84	45.7	10	5.4	6	3.3	4	2.2
TOTAL	1,477	100	626	42.4	481	32.6	140	9.5	98	6.6	132	8.9

*On the basis of *Ze studiów humanistycznych* . . . , table 12.

their lifestyle. Their goal was to obtain qualifications and a good profession, and then return to their hometowns.

The most interesting materials from this collection are the statements written by the participants in the form of short essays. After completing the course, during the entrance exam, they were asked to reflect on the following subject: "I am older, it is the year 2000—how do I see my life?" The future professor Jolanta Kulpińska, at the time a student of sociology in Łódź, made a selection of essays by those who had undertaken the course in the previous three years. How did they picture the future? The papers' authors saw themselves (naively, comments Assorodobraj)[20] as inventors and great thinkers: One wanted to split the atom; another to become a professor; and yet another to build increasingly more novel and efficient machines for their factory. They held academic studies in great esteem, often expressing gratitude to the Polish state for the opportunity to be educated. Another participant wrote that initially, he had not believed the declarations made after the war. He had not believed in words such as "People's Poland," "democracy," or "freedom," but he had changed his mind:

> They started to open schools, to call on working and peasant youth to get an education, which seemed impossible, how were we supposed to learn, we, poor folk, but it happened. [...] Only today do I see how backward our fathers, grandfathers, and so on, were, how much they had to toil, century after century.[21]

The essays can be divided into two groups. The first are utopian visions of the future when, having harnessed the energy of the atom, humanity can control the climate and travel through space. The second outlined more down-to-earth, realistic plans focused on the writer's own future. The latter essays are particularly interesting, giving at times moving accounts of the aspirations and visions of the participants' career paths. One of them wrote about his intention to study law and return home as a qualified lawyer to counsel simple, impoverished people and "investigate if some wealthy landowner was going to hire young boys, when their place should be in school." He concluded with the words: "On my deathbed, I will be at peace" (this is a recurring motif in many essays; there was a strong conviction that once privileges such as education and social benefits had been won, they would never be lost). "You can pass away peacefully knowing that future generations are no longer at risk."[22] Another author dreamed that he would return to his village as an agricultural engineer and for the following forty years would run a cooperative with his neighbors. Yet another looked back from the perspective of the imagined year 2000, confident that "we did not disappoint the state because having completed our studies, we scattered ourselves around villages and cities contributing to socialism with our work."[23] Though lofty at times, the written words convey great hopes as well as a sense of responsibility connected to the democratization of education and the creation of the socialist country's prosperity.

The essays are written in simple language, often contain mistakes, and reverberate with postwar turns of phrase from speeches and press talk. As mentioned earlier, this was a language rooted in the prewar working class. The essays, written only two years after the end of the war and before things took off on a strong political trajectory, are primarily a poignant testimony of advancement and faith in a bright future: one's own and that of future generations. Like postwar memoirs submitted in public competitions, the essays could be easily criticized as propaganda written for the political purposes. However, I would defend them along the lines of a recent revival of memoirs as a source for the people's history of PRL and treat them with "patience, attentiveness, but also openness"; there are no pure and innocent sources, and while analyzing the biographical materials of the time we should be led by a "critical empathy."[24]

The fate of the course participants is unknown. Obviously, none of the authors split the atom or programmed the climate into an everlasting summer. Probably only one in three people completed their studies.[25] It was not until a decade later that another sociological study addressing the issue of the fate of postwar students was conducted.

AT THE UNIVERSITY

Once the first regulations governing the recruitment process had been introduced in the late 1940s, the university application procedure involved the submission of documents issued by the candidate's secondary school. These included "a certificate of social origin, skills and social work of the school-leaver/first-year applicant," as well as information about the parents' occupations (based on statements from the municipality), their workplaces, and their salaries. Such certificates were produced by the School Recruitment Commission, which at that time had to include a representative of the ZMP.[26] A quota of seats was at the discretion of the ministry, which selected as many as 20 percent of the applicants to the most prestigious and popular faculties. With the introduction of the "Small Constitution" in 1952, a large number of intelligentsia children were refused a place at university in order to boost social background statistics in favor of working-class and peasant entrants.[27] However, such forced and short-term changes were only tokenistic.

When the Stalinist period came to an end, it was time to assess, sum up, and critically examine the effects of the 1948 reforms. Discussion about the intelligentsia, the role of the university, and the achievements of earlier higher education transformation resumed. The 1956 Thaw brought about many changes, which also meant revising a number of policies. For instance, the two-stage system of studies was abolished, and the rector was again elected by the university senate and not by a government official. Also, the former system of academic degrees was reinstalled. Higher education institutions regained some of their lost autonomy, and overall, this period was a time of regeneration for the University of Łódź after its previous marginalization.[28] The aforementioned revival of institutional sociology had its impact not only in relation to the university's structure but to its political life as well. Aside from symbolic events, such as the participation of Józef Chałasiński, Jan Szczepański, and Tadeusz Szczurkiewicz (only the latter was a member of the PZPR, while all three were Znaniecki's protégés) as expert sociologists in the Poznań trial,[29] the possibility of resuming research and obtaining funding were again open.

The government too needed reliable diagnoses of the social situation and scientific tools to verify the achievements and failures of the previous years. One of these endeavors was broad research into higher education, launched at the end of the 1950s.[30] Its aim was to evaluate the results of the reforms, to check how the socialist university was put into practice. Due to the impact of Łódź sociology and the size of the city itself, Łódź was often the subject of research. Consequently, today there is a substantial number of resources that have enabled research from that period to be revisited from a contemporary perspective. With regard to the topic of this present study, it is the "post-Thaw" research on higher education that carries the most value. This research was conducted in Łódź and offers a precise and reliable diagnosis of the University of Łódź as well as the lives of its students and graduates. It was also supervised by one of Chałasiński's closest associates, and, coincidentally, the third presiding rector of the University of Łódź, the sociologist Józef Szczepański.[31]

The research included a section devoted to preparatory course students, that is, those who were to become the flag "product" of democratizing education, and the advance from factory halls and farmhouses to a working intelligentsia. Szczepański's research illustrated that such advancement was not easy.[32] Those who had undertaken preparatory courses made up around 30 percent of the university student body. Most students had followed the standard path, completing secondary school and passing the final exam. For preparatory course participants, entering an academic environment was already a challenge due to the class context and the need to quickly familiarize themselves with the dominant culture. Moreover, as the research suggests, they were met with hostility from some students and faculty, who defended the idea of an elitist university. This took the form of rather cruel harassment and class discrimination that would today be described as bullying.

Documents reveal that preparatory course graduates were called names, and their knowledge and sense of self-worth were demeaned. They even found it hard to perform everyday activities. For instance, students in one of the dormitories barricaded the doors so as not to let in the first-year course students. One of the course participants described her difficulties in establishing relationships in the new environment. While she had several new acquaintances, "the rest teased her, making it hard for her to use the bathroom, iron her clothes, calling her a yokel, trash, etc."[33] This was not tacit hostility but, rather, calculated action clearly dictating who had a place in the student community and who did not. A large number of individuals researched wished they could change the environment. There were even times when such abuse was one of the reasons they dropped out of university. One of the researched groups recalled: "Everyone here gives us dirty looks; we prefer not to say where we come from. They make fun of us and say that we've enrolled at university straight from elementary school. This hostility is everywhere. [...] They keep saying that trash has been allowed to study after only seven grades." The following statements reveal the breadth of this phenomenon: "In cafeterias, not only were we given dirty looks by secondary-school graduates, but wherever you looked, you could see graffiti showing a double-zero[34] [preparatory course] student writing 2 + 2 = 5, or of one sitting on a potty, stringing together the letters a . . . b . . . c . . ."[35] Course participants were referred to by their fellow students as "trash" and depicted as childlike and ignorant. This conflict had a strong class dimension, which grew even stronger when the privileged position of "regular secondary school graduates" was threatened. However, university entrance exams results and, later, end-of-course exam results were the same for preparatory course participants as for other students.

Between 1946 and 1958, 22,000 people enrolled in courses in Łódź and Warsaw: 14,850 completed them, but only 7,000, that is, less than 32 percent, obtained higher education diplomas.[36] Although this may seem like a moderate achievement, it should be noted that at the same time, out of ninety-one researched course graduates as many as eighty-seven later held managerial functions in the state apparatus.[37] A section of them were already party activists and had continued their education only because they had been encouraged by the party.

Preparatory courses were a radical project for social change; moreover, they were devised from the bottom up in the academic environment. From the outset, they were viewed with great skepticism by conservative members of the academic community and the authorities, too. From the perspective of the majority of their fellow students, those who had done the preparatory course were seen as threatening newcomers attempting to invade the university through their political connections. The presence of these participants had no major impact on the social profile of students in general nor on shifting the social imaginary regarding the university and its students. According to Szczepański, these antagonisms evaporated in later years. The courses themselves had served their purpose. The idea of the courses had partly stemmed from the vision of the socialist university as well as from a pressing imperative to improve the education of an entire generation following the turbulence of the war. From 1953 onward, enrollment plummeted and the whole initiative lost its importance.

POSTWAR STUDENTS

Szczepański's research conducted in Łódź sought to examine the first generation of "socialist professionals" entering the workforce. The period of the study, which covered over 1,500 people, was the moment when the graduates of the reformed university entered adult life. At the very time the researched group was studying, a key change was supposed to have been taking place—the liberal university was to become the socialist university. The percentage of working-class students was increasing, which was reflected in the structure of the examined group: 27.7 percent came from working-class families, 19.6 percent from a peasant background, and 40.2 percent from the intelligentsia. The lowest number of working-class students were to be found enrolled in scientific subjects (mathematics, physics, chemistry), and the highest in the reformed law course. The following years brought improvements since those who had completed preparatory courses (where as many as 76 percent came from the working class) started applying to universities (with preferential treatment).[38] Szczepański's series of studies gives insight into exactly what was happening during the first postwar years, a time of fast and often spectacular social advancement for many. The postwar gaps were rapidly filled, new residents populated the cities, and new faculty were hired at universities.[39] Promises of advancement and being part of the modernizing project were attractive for a number of reasons.

A study of the first attempt to develop generations of students during the first decade of the PRL used the materials collected over several years by Szczepański's team at the University of Łódź. Three waves of students, who subsequently went on to study after the war, were singled out.[40] Szczepański's findings confirmed generational divisions present also in literature and comments from the examined period.

1. Young people of the occupation years, a type that filled university halls right after the war, people able to recall interwar Poland, with a set worldview shaped by the war. This first generations to enroll at university were often young people mature beyond their years, hungry for stability and a chance for a "normal" life. A number of them were decidedly against the new reality, while others had clearly left-wing views (which did not necessarily win them the sympathy of the new authorities). Some of those radical leftist young people came from the intelligentsia and were seen as "the pimply-faced," "wild," or, referring to the French Revolution, the "sans-culottes," which by itself might reveal how their engagement was seen by contemporaries.[41] The exceptions in this group were people such as the researched course participants. Although they belonged to an older generation, their profile fitted more with the next group, embarking on their studies between 1948 and 1952.

2. "Revolution enthusiasts" (also profiled by later researchers),[42] that is, young people who longed for the country to be reconstructed, supporters of the six-year plan, searching for their own generational experience. It is noteworthy that after 1949, between 65 percent and 80 percent of those comprising the Union of Polish Youth were students. One of the narrators, a future professor who had just begun her studies (and who was later active in the opposition), described her involvement during that period as follows:

> The influence of Marxism and Leninism was still immense. [. . .] I belonged to the generation which didn't get to participate in [. . .] the resistance. After the war, we really wanted to change something, to change the world. These notions of free education, free health care, equality, equal treatment—in the country, I saw how hired hands were treated—all of this really resonated with me. (LA 08)

This slightly younger group, later often described as the "ZMP generation," joined the project of building socialism in search of an identity experience, an origin story that would channel their thirst for changing the world.[43] A younger generation whose memory rarely reached back to the time of the war, the "ZMP generation" or "generation of falcons" would form the new intelligentsia in years to come.[44] It is interesting, as Agnieszka Mrozik shows, that the workers and peasant members of the Polish Youth Union have been marginalized and forgotten (especially when class origin intersected with gender), and it is rather the intelligentsia biographies that have established the black legend of the "ZMP generation."[45] Both these generations, prewar and postwar, formed the cornerstone of the socialist modernizing project. Rapid changes and the particular historical moment made the end of the 1940s and beginning of the 1950s a time of intense engagement in the socialist modernizing project for the postwar youth. However, some came too late.

3. "Revolution skeptics," who also wished for reconstruction, but by the time they entered higher education, the difficulties of the modernizing project and the implemented model for development (the failure of the six-year plan) had already become apparent. These were working-class, revolution-oriented, and politically engaged young people who had already had firsthand experience of the system's shortcomings. They could be called belated enthusiasts; one-third were not admitted to their first-choice program due to restricted admittance. At the same time, they viewed a university degree as a personal and economic investment that would provide them with a profession, a good salary, and prestige as well as an exemption from physical work. Although socialism was supposed to make physical

> work equal to and just as prestigious as intellectual work, the latter was still decidedly more attractive, even if there was little difference at the level of wages. The prewar model, "from peasant to gentleman education," still prevailed.

It is worth recalling that right after the war, the traditional university model, the liberal university, still prevailed as a concept. For students it meant a free choice of subjects; emphasis on self-study; a high expectations set (like knowledge of foreign languages); just a handful of examinations throughout the entire program, which could be taken at any time, and multiple times; several-hours-long seminars; and the master-student dynamic. The first postwar generation felt the shortages the most intensely and had to redress the war backlog. The average age of graduation in 1952 was still thirty-four. Conditions for studying had had to change due to the influx of working-class young people, who were not only less prepared but also had no notion of what a university was. Solutions such as a fixed course of study, specific timetables for individual years, work discipline (checking student attendance, mandatory consultations, and repeating material), and organizing self-help associations and student groups with leaders were primarily geared at making the academic environment more inclusive. Whereas the liberal model of the university sought to foster a creative and independent personality, the socialist university aimed to prepare its students to perform a specific profession in the planned economy and to guarantee jobs right after graduation. The former model ensured freedom of study, independent growth, and mature selection. However, it was not sustainable as a higher education model for those who did not know how to study and what university actually is.

Interestingly, Szczepański's research suggests that the "revolution enthusiasts" spoke very highly of the liberal university system and viewed the reforms introduced after 1948 negatively. This happened even though many of them probably would not have been able to study if not for the reforms, nor would they have been successful doing so because of the elitist manner of their studies' organization. A critical approach toward the socialist university was a result of two existing tensions. The first related to the discrepancy between the vision of the socialist society and the actual surrounding, everyday reality. This failed to live up to their expectations and generated dissonance between experience and its description, for instance, in press discourse. These students were beginning to experience the split that would later be described as one that characterized the entire social system of the PRL—a split between private and public life, two levels of values, truths, and principles. The second tension, described also by Szczepański, referred to the professional life of the graduates. Today, we would say that the job market the latter generation faced was not absorbing the new waves of educated specialists well, and after graduation, most young people were faced with disappointment. For the first wave of graduates, everything was "wide open," as had been promised in the press and speeches. However, the next generation experienced more difficulty finding a suitable job.

WORK AS PRIVILEGE AND OBLIGATION

One of the system's promises was a job for everyone. The founding premise of the top-down socialist state of prosperity was to tackle unemployment. In the planned economy, everyone was promised work, which was viewed as a privilege after the turmoil of the twenty-year interwar period. At the same time, employment was obligatory in the modernizing country, and after 1950, it was directly regulated and supervised by the Council of Ministers. Once the job guarantee was introduced, the act of March 7, 1950, on "the planned employment of the graduates of secondary vocational schools and universities" regulated the tasks of the job allocation committee in close cooperation with the state commission of economic planning. In the 1950s and 1960s, the Ministry of the Interior published an annual internal bulletin that listed individual fields of studies along with the number of students "produced." Departments and workplaces could communicate their demand for workers, which later determined the number of students accepted at the university and the distribution of job allocations. How did this work in practice, though?

Research by Szczepański's team revealed not so much the inefficiency of the job allocation committee but rather the effectiveness of traditional mechanisms for obtaining work. In the case of the preparatory course research, it revealed that participants more often than other students later took advantage of the job guarantee. The remaining students managed without state assistance: 41 percent of the general population did not take advantage of the job guarantee while another 24 percent came to the committee with their own ideas of where to work.[46]

Another important insight was a study of the graduates of (1) technical schools, (2) secondary school graduates who did not go on to higher-level education, and (3) several faculties at the University of Łódź in the late 1950s. Although the concept of the committee itself was positively evaluated by the students, its implementation fell short of expectations. This was reflected in the actual, real-life decisions made by the students: They rarely entrusted their future employment to the committee and found a workplace in advance by themselves. The committee only approved it.[47] This graduate impulse to protect oneself against the decisions of the committee also stemmed from fear of "exile to the provinces, where the intelligentsia goes to die."[48]

Several other elements of the system also triggered graduate discontent and frustration. They pointed to injustice, which was very noticeable. The clash of various reasonings and regulations produced unfair and sometimes ridiculous situations. Technical school graduates with near-identical qualifications and job allocations went on to hold an extremely diverse range of positions, in terms of both competencies and pay. university graduates whose professions were tagged as "unproductive," despite longer periods of study, received lower-paid positions than those in "productive" occupations. This happened in spite of the unambiguous message they had received during their studies, that they were just as necessary, that they were the country's future and the cornerstone of building socialism. For instance, only 18 percent of history graduates worked in their profession. There were also cases when the degree earned was an obstacle, rather than an advantage in finding work.[49] Although all of the studied graduates made more money than their less-educated peers, there were complaints about salaries that did not satisfy their ambitions and promises of prosperity upon completing their studies. While only 4 percent of the graduates of "productive" chemistry made less than 1,000 zloty a month, this was the salary of only one in five sociologists and philologists. Women made 300–400 zloty less despite obtaining better results during their studies. The committee barely considered any individual achievements, putting everyone under the same heading within the common category of university graduate. While individual achievement had no bearing on outcomes; class differences were stark; for example, working-class historians would more often end up working in schools, whereas an academic career was most prevalent among those from the intelligentsia and least among graduates of peasant descent.[50]

In the late 1950s, concern about the overproduction of an intelligentsia resurfaced, a problem that was seemingly impossible in times of a planned economy. However, the main issue was not overproduction but rather the mismatch between graduates' education profile and the demands of workplaces (nearly half of them did not anticipate hiring any degree holders). Another factor was student expectations. Since nearly half the graduates found work independently, over a third of graduates were not hired according to their profession (the data for the academic year 1956/1957).[51] The more strongly one had believed in the opportunity for advancement and the project of a socialist intelligentsia, the more one trusted in state-guaranteed privilege or could not rely on any other, the more bitter was the disappointment. Graduates of the reformed socialized university were qualified, but workplaces had already been saturated and postwar shortages met by the previous graduates.

The first wave of students had the most opportunities. However, for the second and the third wave options were shrinking. They expected state guidance and support, but this led to employment that was far from their dream jobs. The 1956 Thaw additionally undermined their faith in socialism. A sense of disillusionment deepened. What had previously been instilled in them began to ring hollow. One preparatory course participant remembered being convinced: "At the time, we were told that we would be pioneers of progress, education, new ideas. [...] That's what I wanted to be!"[52] However, as he recalled, there was nothing but disappointment. Those who had the most to lose following the socialist dream experienced the most disillusionment. As the research suggests, young people from the working class were even more critical of the party than the intelligentsia. Furthermore, people with higher education were more supportive of socialism as a system.[53]

The people who had advanced in the dynamic postwar period and taken high positions, often without formal higher or even secondary education, feared the wave of new intelligentsia with university diplomas. At that point, their positions were sufficiently high not only to effectively block the careers of young graduates but even to prevent them from being hired.[54] By the end of 1945, as many as three thousand workers held managerial positions (from foremen up).[55] Skilled workers with prewar experience had the highest chances of promotion. The nature of their advancement was more about filling in gaps and satisfying the "hunger for professionals" than any conscious social politics (although at the same time, it served this purpose). After 1949, along with an intensification of political activity, there was another wave of promotions, this time with a political profile. Prewar specialists, who not so long ago had been quite scarce, were suddenly faced with being replaced by political management who also had agitation functions. Aside from displaying the correct ideological attitude, they also served as an example of the great opportunities available and the possibility of advancement offered by the PZPR. The percentage of working-class directors, which was already substantial, grew from 33 percent in 1948, to 53 percent in 1949, and to 68 percent in 1954/1955.[56] In 1952, 36,000 workers held managerial positions. The scale of the change was enormous, even more so if we consider the significant number of workers who rejected positions. The reason for these rejections was a sense of having insufficient qualifications. However, it was also dictated by financial issues—a higher position typically meant a pay cut compared with the positions of manual workers. At the time, the pay system stipulated a wide range of wages that depended on the position held, although the qualifications demanded might have been the same. In the late 1950s, this caused frequent conflicts between university graduates and management as well as between other informal groups in workplaces. The young people studied often changed jobs, searching for a position that would allow them to make the most of their abilities.

All these elements not only resulted in a "waste" of well-educated young people in the theoretically well-greased machine of the planned economy. University education, or even choosing a general secondary school over a technical school, did not fulfill the promise of socialist modernization. Unsurprisingly, subjective satisfaction from work was found to be lowest among secondary school graduates who did not complete their studies, that is, the people who embarked on the educational path that was supposed to lead to higher education but who for various reasons were unable to complete it. For comparison's sake, the group that was most satisfied with work were the graduates of technical schools, who also had a secondary education but one more aligned with their aspirations. While universities were able to educate a generation of a new intelligentsia, workplaces were unable to continue this task and often even reversed the effects achieved at universities. At the same time, the proclaimed success of universities was not entirely obvious, and it is hard to say if they produced the new intelligentsia effectively. Institutions such as universities, companies, and schools learned to operate in the new state-socialist system. The prewar grade system was reproduced, which was too great a challenge for the students who had come from technical schools or crash courses, for instance. The system, resistant to change, regulated itself. Professors found various ways to get around dictates issued from above. For instance, they kept quiet about allocated vacancies in order to select candidates according to their own criteria, rather than offer places as a result of open competition or in response to pressure from the PZPR's university unit—which will be discussed further in chapters 7 and 8.

Sociological research after the Thaw revealed numerous deficiencies in the education system and the limitations of the reform. Some of these arose from the country's economic and administrative situation: the rapid pace of change and bureaucratic failures as well as macroeconomic difficulties. The majority, however, stemmed from social tensions. On the one hand, there was not enough support from academic circles and students themselves for changes that were too rapid or for the project of the socialist university. On the other, the staff from the first wave of postwar advancement feared better qualified "new staff." The supporters of the new order, that is, the generation seeking employment several years later, lost their enthusiasm for revolution because of the conservatism of both new and old elites. The "revolution enthusiasm" partly came up against the first postwar promotions and emerging pathologies of the system, such as the overgrowth of bureaucracy and the inefficiency of the economy. After the first decade of the PRL, the mechanisms of school selection based on social background underwent significant change, but they were not eliminated altogether. The socialist meritocracy of the new staff was still a long way off.

6

EDUCATIONAL DESIRES

Schools are agencies whose task is to test, select and distribute.[1]

"BEFORE THE WAR, WHAT WOULD HAVE HAPPENED TO THE WIDOW STEFANIA Binkowska—a mother of two? Would it have mattered that she is an amazing spinner?" pondered *Głos Robotniczy* in 1953. The answer was clear: "The widow Binkowska would have ended up like the other 60,000 officially unemployed workers in Łódź in 1939. Homelessness, a shortage of food and housing, illiteracy, and death were wreaking havoc." The reader, however, encounters Mrs. Binkowska several years after the war:

> Stefania Binkowska's eyes glided over the words while she struggled to understand the content of the letter. At the top—the company's green stamp; at the bottom—the fancy signature of the executive director of the Armia Ludowa ZPB [Cotton Industry Plant] and the date 16 March 1950. What does it say? The voice of Walenda, the head of staff, was reaching her as if from afar, although he was right there beside her. He was looking at her, smiling. —The secretary of the Staff Committee and myself have decided to send you on a two-semester weaving and spinning course. Are you on board? (*Rośnie socjalistyczna nowa Łódź*, GR, 05/53)

Stefania was about to start the course with "pride and earnestness." Her story, published on the second page of *Głos Robotniczy*, served to illustrate the availability of education and show that the system would support everyone who wanted to get educated. Workers were expected to improve their qualifications, develop their skills, and advance. As early as 1949, it was estimated that around 15,000 workers had advanced to managerial positions (in 1945, as mentioned in the previous chapter, it was three thousand),[2] and in 1961, only one in ten white-collar workers continued to have the same education they had received before the war.[3] The rest obtained their education in the years after the war. It was assumed that as the PRL and the idea of the socialist university developed, 80 percent of each class year would complete a higher education course.[4] With every generation entering the education system in the PRL, further reforms were introduced and numerous policies were being tested. Educational desires were roused, but who went to universities and who went to vocational schools? Who resigned from studying and why? Who wanted to study but could not? Throughout the entire PRL period, the gross enrollment ratio[5] at the level of higher education never exceeded 10 percent and in 1990, it stood at 9.8 percent. In contrast, in 2008, as a result of the political transformation and the emergence of private universities, the threshold of 40 percent was exceeded (compared with the postwar plan, this was hardly a great achievement), and it remains at this level today.[6]

This chapter follows school reforms of earlier stages of education in the PRL, further reforms of higher education, and their results across the country. Despite various attempts and quite sophisticated tools and policies democratizing access to education, the PRL's entire modernization project, including the preliminary year, preparatory courses, part-time and evening courses, as well as university consultation centers in small towns, was not catching on. Differences in educational aspiration (as well as disbelief in the attainability of the goal), economic factors (expenses at the level of the state and at home), demographics (struggles with adjusting the infrastructure and politics to the fluctuations), inequalities in accessing culture, and often failed educational policies continued to shape the selection mechanisms.[7]

DROPOUTS AND SIEVES

The reforms in higher education were just a part of the broader change in the educational system. One of the problems with the attempt to engineer social mobility via education was that early streaming took place during selection for places at middle school level, which then determined the likelihood of continuing education to university level. After 1945 only minor amendments were made to the prewar system and curriculum. Slight changes included, obviously, the history of World War II, as well as the foreign language requirement. Religion remained obligatory. It was with the educational reform of 1948 that a new state-socialist curriculum was introduced, with Russian becoming the mandatory foreign language; religious classes were removed from the school program. Elementary education was still based on the seven-grade school system (ages seven to fourteen), and the number of schools was doubled. Vocational training was favored over the general lyceum (general secondary school). The number of vocational schools also grew, especially those that offered training for skilled workers lasting only a few months or in some cases up to two years. In 1956 compulsory education was extended to sixteen-year-olds, and religion was brought back but in the form of extracurricular classes. From 1959 to 1965, thanks to the "Thousand Schools for the Millennium of the Polish State" project, in opposition to the celebration of the Christianization of

Poland, over 1,200 schools were built. Fortuitously, this occasion coincided with the postwar baby boomers' entrance into the education system.

Educational reform in July 1961 extended elementary education to eight years (ages seven to fifteen); the same legislation sought to curtail grade repetition for those who had not passed end-of-year exams and to encourage high school enrollment. Compulsory schooling was then extended to seventeen-year-olds. Only in 1965 was a system introduced of awarding points for social origin as part of enrollment in universities. The 1971 reform sought to overcome early selection. There was a plan to introduce a ten-grade school such as existed in the USSR and to further unify the educational system. After the ten-grade public school, pupils would either go on to a two-year profiled high school, which prepared them to enter colleges and universities, or to a two-year vocational school, which would be the final stage of their educational path. Plans for this reform were abandoned in 1981.

While in the early years of the reform in the 1950s university selection mechanisms favored young people from the working class, this did not last long. The difference between the percentage share of applicants from the working class and the accepted students was positive. This means that out of all the applicants, proportionally more representatives of the lower classes were accepted at university. However, while in the 1951/1952 academic year 77.8 percent of accepted candidates completed their courses, in subsequent years this rate began to drop; in 1955/1956 it fell to 73.4 percent, and in 1958/59 to 68.2 percent.[8] In the 1960s and 1970s, there was only an absolute growth in the number of working-class students, along with a general growth in the number of students. Throughout the entire period of the PRL, there was a relatively strong relationship between parents' education and occupation, and the education of their children. While the general pool of students increased, disparities remained at a similar level.[9]

The problem was that changes in the student body mostly referred to the young people admitted to universities but not graduates. While Szczepański writes that in the 1970s as many as 40 percent of each year's school leavers started higher education, Jan Kluczyński writes of only 30 percent of the year group. In comparison to the prewar 3 or 4 percent, this was an improvement, but less impressive than what the reforms had hoped to achieve. Furthermore, in both cases, the data are overly optimistic because they refer to the moment at which the socialist system of education was operating on a mass scale, educating over half a million students, of whom one in three studied in a technical field.[10] Every year, the incidence of dropping out and the mechanism of sieving affected the social structure. Between 20 to 60 percent of students dropped out of university after their first year. The proportion of young people from a peasant background remained the same throughout the entire program while the share of the intelligentsia grew, hence, it was primarily working-class people who gave up.[11] The processes occurring at the University of Łódź were no different from the changes across the rest of the country.[12]

Graduates offered the following reasons for giving up their courses: insufficient preparation, motivational and organizational difficulties (for instance, lack of information), difficulties with the mode of instruction, financial hardship such as a shortage of housing, and commutes.[13] The dean's office primarily couched this in terms of a lack of aptitude. Both the press and scientific reports at the time suggested that the scale of the problem could have been alleviated if academic faculty had "taken better care of the young people." Szczepański even argued that the financial losses connected with dropping out were so acute that it would have paid off to hire more faculty who could have provided students with more individualized care instead of offering impersonal teaching alone.[14] Young people from cultural contexts other than the intelligentsia had difficulty finding their place in the new environment. It was a key problem in the 1950s, despite Stalinist reforms, and remained unsolved. Different research from the early 1980s indicated that parents' education continued to have the most influence on the educational careers of individuals.[15]

During the whole period of state socialism access to schools was growing but only up to secondary education. Past that, obstacles were not decreasing but increasing.[16] Even among the generation who completed their secondary education between 1957 and 1960 (that is, who were educated entirely after the war), only 10 to 12.7 percent of those who had completed elementary school were later accepted at universities.[17] In the 1960s, a significant disproportion between access to education in the city and in the country, and between different regions of Poland, instead of decreasing, continued to largely determine educational paths.[18] The highest number of dropouts were among girls from rural areas who not only experienced difficulties in accessing educational infrastructure but often had to defy the social expectations of their families and communities. As late as the mid-1960s, fewer girls than boys were also pursuing secondary education. In addition to the prospect of working on the family farm, taking a job in traditionally female occupations like domestic help or childcare was still an attractive alternative to education.[19]

Initially, the majority of research on education and social mobility in the PRL focused on selection mechanisms. One of the first methods was to record the number of school years between generations according to the pattern that the more years spent at school, the higher the position in the social structure, in accordance with the meritocratic translation of education into life success. In the first few years after the war, the illiteracy level was also not without significance. The research that used these relatively simple criteria seemed to confirm the success of the educational leap. The rate of illiteracy was going down, the average time at school was increasing, and each subsequent year the citizenry was getting more education.[20] However, the optimistic picture painted by the press and by the authorities' public speeches did not fully correspond with research results. With the introduction of slightly more complex research tools, the so-called early selection thresholds became an issue.[21] In the 1970s, increasingly more research on disparity was conducted along with potential solutions based on models and large quantitative studies.[22] The notion of "thresholds" became popular, Mare's[23] selection mechanisms and his "school of educational crossings."[24] In his view, the education system is composed of a series of stages, with a selection of learners taking place at each stage. Disparity is measured not according to the total number of school years but the structure of choices: Is education continued and in what form?

In interwar Poland, the dropping out and sieving out of young working-class people took place as early as at the elementary level of education, after the four mandatory grades of elementary school.[25] In the postwar period, the point of selection took place at one level higher up. Choosing a secondary school was a key decision on the educational path. The simple fact of attending a general secondary school put one on the path to higher education. However, this was only temporary. Aside from the prewar generation, who took advantage of the aforementioned postwar openness of the social structure, the degree of disparity remained at a stable level. The selection mechanisms were the most stringent in the early stages of education. Only in the 1950s and 1970s did this point move temporarily to the level of secondary schools.[26]

It is noteworthy that these two moments were a result of the most restrictive top-down policies: this affected the generations educated after the Stalinist reform in 1948 and its amendment, when points for social origin were introduced in the mid-1960s (something that had not been practiced even in the Stalinist period). Additional points were awarded to applicants with a high grade point average (GPA) in secondary school as well as candidates who were socially engaged, working, and studying in colleges (if they were reapplying). Furthermore, in 1975, academic Olympiad and competition finalists were accepted without having to pass exams.[27] The nature of exams changed too. Written tests and essays were introduced. This allowed for anonymity, which previously had not been an option with oral exams. All these procedures tallied with the 1948 regulation, that is, they were aimed at standardization, the introduction of simple criteria limiting the reproduction of the intelligentsia, and a more effective management of an increasing number of students. A rather convoluted points system was also developed, but again its effects were minuscule and temporary. The structure of the student body became more egalitarian in technical fields, and after ministry involvement, also at the faculty of law and economics.

Other forms of study also became available for working individuals, that is, part-time and evening courses. These modes of study developed in the 1950s and continued to attract students.[28] Even though these forms were established at the University of Łódź as well, the early 1970s saw a drop in the number of students taking these courses.

It was at this time that the so-called consultation centers outside Łódź were established. These enabled part-time modes of education to be run in small provincial towns, closer and cheaper in comparison with large cities. Hence part-time, evening, and extramural courses became a channel for working people to obtain higher education. In Poland in 1977, evening and part-time degree courses were completed by as many as 274,900 people.[29]

Capped admittance was a major factor limiting the opportunity for advancement via higher education. Rooted in the Second Republic of Poland, fear of an overproduction of the intelligentsia reemerged in the 1960s. Every year, over 20,000 graduates of higher education institutions were ready to enter the workforce.[30] This number continued to grow so much that in the 1980s it was decided to limit the opportunity of access to higher education by people who were working. There was a lack of unskilled workers, not university graduates.

However, as with the 1948 reform, as soon as the policy stopped being rigorously enforced, the student social composition returned to its previous state. The assignment of points for origin at university enrollment, that is, at the third stage of education, may have been a suitable tool but it was introduced too late. The effective selection had already taken place when the type of secondary school was being chosen.[31]

SECONDARY SCHOOLS

The key to increasing the number of working-class and peasant students lay therefore at the earlier stages of education, above all the point at which the type of secondary school was selected. Young people had three choices: attend the most elitist type, the general secondary school (lyceum); attend the more common technical school; or attend the most easily accessible vocational school. The attempt to increase the number of young working-class people at general secondary schools only resulted in their being filtered out at a later, higher level. Even if the share of this group of young people was growing, it was impeded after the Thaw.[32] During the school year of 1959/1960, young working-class people totaled 43 percent in the general secondary schools in Łódź. Peasant youth did not exceed 3 percent of the students. At the same time, over half the students at the university came from the intelligentsia, despite the fact that Łódź was an industrial center with a historically underdeveloped and negligible intelligentsia. In the same academic year, out of 1,140 secondary school graduates, only 486 were accepted at universities.[33] This included nearly half of all general secondary school and technical school applicants. Graduates of vocational schools usually finished their education at the middle level. Therefore, not only were there relatively fewer working-class and peasant young people at the middle level but also almost all were rejected when attempting to continue their education.[34] As a result, general secondary schools had a more elitist character than the wider society, and if working-class and peasant young people made up half of the secondary school student body, this was already considered a great achievement.

During the period of the PRL, the class profile of students at general secondary schools, which offered the greatest opportunity for progression into higher education, was much more diverse than today (although already in the 1960s, the share of working-class students in general secondary schools had started to drop). The remaining types of secondary schools were often dead ends and did not prepare students well for passing the school-leaving exam, the *matura*.[35] This was also pointed out as one reason for the educational disparities. The necessity of choosing one's future educational path at such an early stage, that is, after eight grades of elementary school, bifurcated educational paths too early.[36] Along with the elitism of general secondary schools, as early as the 1980s there were discussions about diversifying the criteria of university admittance. Reformers wanted to offer those who had completed vocational schools a head start in the form of additional points on their application.[37]

While it is true that in 1960 over two million people (out of a population of 29,88 million) had completed a secondary education,[38] even in the 1980s, a common secondary education was yet to be achieved. Research showed that the social composition of elementary school pupils was decidedly different from that of university students and that it was at the secondary level of education that the difference first became apparent. General secondary schools attracted the most able students, in particular the vocational schools, which were the first and the safest choice for both women and men. Until the 1970s, 45 percent of the workforce for industry was educated in vocational schools.[39] However, they were usually the choice of pupils with the lowest grades or those who needed to start work as early as possible. Some people did not continue their education beyond the elementary level at all.[40] Hence, for the majority of the postwar generation, the path to advancement was not higher education but secondary education—more precisely, vocational schools.

It was these institutions that became the main path for the advancement of the working class. The second available option was technical school. Higher education institutions like universities afforded advancement only if they offered practical faculties and the opportunity to enter the workforce quickly. Technical universities came next, and the most elitist universities last. Selection was the least stringent in the recruitment process of vocational schools. They were also the most popular choice of secondary education among young people. Their number skyrocketed: in 1937, there were 1,489; in 1952, 2,552; and in 1965, 8,780.[41] From 1945 onward, nonaffluent students constantly and unwaveringly chose vocational schools.[42] It was these institutions that promised a steady occupation in a short time and class-wise, they were familiar with these jobs. The cultural hegemony these schools offered was closer to that of the working class, compared with that which prevailed at the universities. Also in Łódź in the 1960s, when over three times as many people completed elementary school than before the war, while 75 percent of pupils continued their education at the secondary level, most of them did so at vocational schools (in the school year of 1960/1961, there were over 25,500 students).[43] Given the ruralization of urban culture after the war and the peasant-background profile of the city's population,[44] it was vocational schools and not the socialist University of Łódź that constituted a channel for advancement.

The secondary education system, furthermore, created differences in educational paths between genders.[45] Despite being a side effect of educational policies planned as emancipatory from a class, not a gender, perspective, the system created a visible structural pattern: a high feminization of general secondary schools (visible in Czechoslovakia, Romania, and Hungary as well) and therefore containing a higher number of female than male students. While most boys studied in vocational schools preparing them for typically male working-class jobs, it was girls who more often obtained higher education, studying to become clerks, teachers, or health care workers.[46] Aside from running farms, these were the jobs available to them in the countryside. Industry did not really have a place for them.

The disproportion was such that even as late as 1967, the Ministry of Science and Higher Education introduced a minimum quota for female pupils along with instructions to treat female candidates more leniently than male. An informational campaign followed, aimed at encouraging girls to enter technical education—at the same time as some technical and vocational schools did not permit female enrollment. A similar campaign was planned but for male pupils in general secondary schools.[47] While vocational and technical schools were well financed and developed, their offer was not attractive to women, who more often chose general secondary schools and therefore had the opportunity to continue on to university.[48] Indeed, women enrolled and graduated more often from universities (while there were large differences in the feminization of students depending on the discipline). Vocational and technical secondary education proved more attractive for their male counterparts, as such courses were shorter, thereby offering the prospect of earning and providing for a family earlier as well as guaranteeing a higher income.[49] If girls were choosing vocational schools it was rather trade or gastronomy over mechanic or electric profiles, and indeed some facilities did not even have female toilets.[50] Initial encouragement for women to enter traditionally male occupations waned from the mid-1950s onward. As many researchers have already pointed out, there was a conservative shift toward women's reproductive role and their part as wives and mothers rather than as frontline workers.[51]

The project of transforming the social imaginary from the 1950s, even if successful, did not reach the target results. Education was commonly considered to be valuable but in later years, degree courses were no longer considered a good career choice. In Poland, where a network of secondary technical and vocational schools was developed early on, these became an important channel for advancement through education. Despite such changes as the introduction of part-time and evening degree courses, until the 1990s, more than half of secondary-level pupils attended vocational schools, and most did not continue their education upon completion.[52] At the same time, the socialist economy did not even need the number of graduates that it was able to produce. By the early 1960s, a higher education had been completed by over 300,000 graduates nationwide, including 35 percent of working-class and 20 percent of peasant origin. At the same time, the number of white-collar workers in 1959 totaled as many as 2,100,000, which in 1959 constituted 8.1 percent of the general workforce.[53] To what extent did having a white-collar job mean becoming part of the intelligentsia? For sure, it was an advancement from manual work, but it did not equal obtaining a higher education. As mentioned earlier, in the interwar period, around 1 percent of the population had a higher education while in 1970, this had already grown to 2.7 percent of 32.5 million people.

Therefore, there were shortages of unskilled workers and staff in the most basic positions. This was a global process that occurred both in capitalist and socialist countries. One aspect of this change was an increase in the number of people with a technical education: graduates of technical universities and other higher education institutions of this type.[54] Randall Collins observes with regret that in Western countries, the educational system did not correspond to the economic structure in a functionalist way but came to be used pragmatically by the elites to maintain their prestigious positions, that is, as Bourdieu would put it, to defend the hegemony and preservation of cultural dominance.[55] In the meantime, the socialist economy and educational system were based on vocational schools, and this was the main channel of advancement for the children of unqualified workers and peasants (at that time, now farmers). These channels of education were not the domain of the intelligentsia.

ENGINEERS

In terms of the employment structure, the model of the socialist economy needed low-skilled workers and technicians with secondary technical education. Since 1949, government resources had mainly been poured into technical sciences.[56] These were also developing more rapidly than other fields.[57] As early as 1946, *Głos Robotniczy* reported:

> Young working-class people in Łódź are more willing to attend the polytechnic and want to continue their forefathers' and fathers' professions but as engineers or chemists working in factories co-owned by the people of democratic Poland. Today, who

knows if material conditions also don't play a major role [in this decision]. (*Uniwersytet u progu nowego roku . . .*, GR, 09/46)

The production of numerous specialized professionals accorded with the vision of the new socialist elite,[58] where it was engineers and not pharmacists or lawyers who were supposed to be the cornerstone of the intelligentsia. The cult of the engineer as a socially useful occupation grew along with the aforementioned desire to have a "profession" after the experiences of war. In addition, these occupations were closer to the experiences of the working class. Staff were needed, however, and higher education above the bare minimum was too much of a burden and an unnecessary delay in the taking up of paid work both for the interested parties and their families as well as wider society. This type of rhetoric was also intensified by "the six-year plan." While the University of Łódź kept losing faculty and students, lost its status, and was labeled a provincial university, the Łódź University of Technology thrived.[59] It is noteworthy that the damage at the University of Łódź was less severe in scientific disciplines.

Although universities and institutions such as the Institute for Academic Faculty Training were supposed to educate people to shape Polish culture and politics, the whole educational system was primarily set up to educate professionals for industry: chemists, mechanics, and technicians. The new intelligentsia might have received an education at universities but the new professionals did this at technical schools, specialized colleges (for instance, of economics or of teaching), and, last but not least, vocational schools. The notions of a new intelligentsia and new professionals, though often used interchangeably, need to be distinguished to better understand the successes and failures of the PRL's modernizing project. Compared with the new intelligentsia, the new professionals coped better in a country undergoing modernization.

One of the most crucial shifts within higher education was this focus on new professionals and the development of technical education. Before World War II, young people looking for higher education had primarily selected universities. In 1935, technical studies (in all fields) attracted only 11.4 percent of students while elitist law—24.3 percent. In 1956, the share of future lawyers had dropped to 3.2 percent whereas technical studies attracted as many as 36.4 percent of students.[60]

Disappointment with reforms, economic stagnation, and the social unrest of the late 1960s and early 1970s also affected the educational system. In 1971, the Ministry of Science and Higher Education formed a committee of experts to produce a report on the state of education. The endeavor was supervised by none other than Jan Szczepański. The goal was the diagnosis of the condition of education in the PRL.[61] According to the drafted report, Poland was considered a "country of people who studied." This meant that a common elementary education had been established, but there was less success in the area of secondary education and the least in the popularization of higher education.[62] The report recommended that the authorities focus on the promotion of kindergartens (as the earliest selection threshold) and secondary schools (where selection was the most stringent). There were also suggestions to open collective municipal schools instead of scattered elementary schools in which teaching took place in poor conditions. At the level of higher education, the report encouraged an expansion of three-year vocational universities along with four- to six-year master's studies as well as the introduction of doctoral studies, that is, a two-year course for candidates in the sciences.[63] Although reforms instituted by the ministry largely deviated from the report's recommendations, the focus on vocational rather than university education remained a common element.

Studies revealed a peaked interest in educational aspirations. However, in most cases, these aspirations stopped at the secondary level.[64] A parent's level of education was not without significance in this process. While lower-class families were primarily driven by a desire to provide their children with a better future and help them "escape" their class of origin, intelligentsia parents placed the bar much higher. Their ambition was to provide their children with an opportunity to have a scientific or scholarly career—"to get an academic post," which was the pinnacle of achievement in their view.[65] For lower-class families, it was enough to avoid physical labor and to move up into the category of white-collar workers, and not necessarily to pursue further scientific or scholarly ambitions (if they existed at all), which could be undertaken during free time, rather than via professional development. In the 1950s and 1960s, efforts to leave the working class peaked; most of all this was about avoiding physical labor in jobs requiring low qualifications. However, in the majority of cases, the working class, similar to the intelligentsia, was reproduced. In the 1960s, thousands of working-class children still worked in the same factories where their parents had worked.[66] Working-class and peasant families mainly dreamed about secure, light work for their children. A handful had ambitions to give their children a "from-peasant-to-gentleman education" while an equally small group wanted to see their children become engineers dedicated to building socialism. Again, most wished to protect their children from work in the fields or the monotony of work on a production line.[67]

As other studies indicate, it was young women who continued to dream about a university education. Naturally, educational aspirations were the highest among young people from the intelligentsia: 65 percent planned to obtain a diploma from an institute of higher education while only 39 percent of people of peasant origin wanted the same education for themselves.[68] These figures come from the responses given in surveys conducted at state agricultural farms (PGRs). They also revealed a strong preference for the professions of doctor, teacher, and engineer, and a complete lack of interest in the future of their children as, for example, members of the creative intelligentsia like artists or filmmakers.[69] Either that remained outside of their imagination or it was seen as impractical if not dangerous. Faced with a relatively wide spectrum of job opportunities that demanded only a low level of education, the vast majority of young peasants, especially young males, had no aspiration whatsoever to continue their education. Nearly half wished to stay in the countryside and around 36 percent planned to work in agriculture.[70] Technical occupations, which were most desirable to young males living in cities (61 percent), were the second most attractive career paths for those living in the country.

At the level of the decisions made by individuals and the situations of specific families, these were mainly shaped by (a range of) underlying ideas about the value of making a long-term investment in a child's education.[71] Other studies on educational aspirations from the late 1970s show that the intelligentsia strove to educate their children by any means, regardless of their predispositions or the family's material resources. At the same time, young people from the intelligentsia were more motivated to take up their studies. Not only did they not want to lose their parents' position but they also wanted to secure economic and cultural capital. The children of the intelligentsia were in a way forced into higher education.[72] Individuals from families with a higher education were more likely to experience psychological discomfort and confidence issues. They were driven to obtain a diploma not only for reasons of prestige but to maintain a sense of self-worth.[73]

To sum up, the divide between the intelligentsia and the working class was exacerbated by the disparate aspirations of the younger generations. Working-class young people cared about early self-reliance and favored obtaining a profession, working, and supporting themselves over studying.[74] Considering the above-mentioned negligible salary differences between graduate and nongraduate work, and the growing prestige of technical professions, the choice to study at university was not an obvious one. For intelligentsia families, an educational path that did not lead to higher education equaled degradation. An educational path other than the aforementioned "getting an academic post," for instance, going to a vocational school, would mean failure. For working-class families, on the other hand, this was considered an advancement.

WHAT DOES ADVANCEMENT MEAN?

If a technical education (also that at the secondary school level) offered the main channels of advancement, why, from the very outset, was it universities that were at the center of the debate? Why did they embody a promise of change, and why were they the main point of reference with regard to educational desire? If the university operated simply as a symbol orienting people's actions but not necessarily the real target for the thousands of working-class children and their parents wanting a better tomorrow, what was social advancement, and how closely was it linked to education and the university as an institution of advancement? The popularity of vocational and technical schools cannot only be explained in terms of selection mechanisms, even if they are viewed broadly and include educational desires and aspirations. Their appeal was also linked to a shift in how advancement was understood.

In a socialist state, the very notion of advancement itself is problematic. A vertical change of social position could be an advancement criterion in capitalist countries dominated by the market and individualist values. The idea of socialist advancement meant a shift in the range of the hierarchy and the elevation of the position of the working class. The aim was to flatten the social ladder as much as possible, both at the level of salaries and prestige and also of social security.[75] Hence, socialist advancement hinged on creating a sense of social equality and an appreciation of work, and not inducing direct hierarchical mobility. Socialist modernization could not offer advancement by suggesting that people move from the working class to the intelligentsia.

At the same time, working-class people were quick to adopt the lifestyle of the intelligentsia and their distinctions, thereby distancing themselves from their own families of origin. Interestingly, this distance was generated not by embarrassment or deep resentment[76] but rather by the high expectations of the family itself. Sending a child to university to get the "peasant-to-gentleman education" was supposed to result in a specific outcome. Families expected refinement and tangible results as had traditionally been the case following long years of study. By contrast, the socialist university of the second half of the 1950s aimed to level out social differences. Aside from clothes worn at work, visible differences were fading. What might be called "a petite-bourgeois style" became widespread thanks to the mass and uniform production of furniture, apartments, the payroll system (which was diversified in other respects), and so on. "Ladies and gentlemen" were no longer particularly visible, and graduates, even if they managed to enter the working intelligentsia, rarely visited their families in the countryside by pulling up in a car, wearing a new suit or tailor-made two-piece. Only the creative intelligentsia, with artistic bohemian aspirations, still stood out from the rest of the society (although this was scarcely the distinction parents had in mind). A professional intellectual blended in with other workers. Later studies show that class differences at the level of lifestyle still remained considerable, although not as ostentatious as before the war.

Subsequent generations were not as convinced that education should be the path to social improvement. In the 1970s, it was believed that what divided society was salary levels, hence the idea of socialist meritocracy had not caught on. While in the 1960s half the respondents considered education to be a factor shaping social inequalities, ten years later this opinion was held by only a third of respondents.[77] Education was no longer viewed as a reliable means of improving the quality of one's life. Research showed that although from the late 1960s young people with aspirations still prioritized education, it was treated instrumentally, as a means to get a job and higher status.[78] The earlier research on first-year students at the University of Warsaw and the University of Łódź in the 1961/1962 academic year revealed that even this rather elitist group did not feel that it was essential to obtain a degree to become a person of culture. The majority thought that the purpose of a degree was to help a person become a qualified specialist. Students expected their course to offer them intellectual growth,[79] but above all, to give them a social position, in terms of both economic reward and prestige.[80] Numerous studies pointed to a shift in professional prestige. Along with the jobs of doctor and professor, those of miner and farmer were included in the group of most valued occupations, while those of merchant and priest lost their once high positions.[81]

First in 1965 and later in 1967, Włodzimierz Wesołowski and Kazimierz M. Słomczyński conducted research on social mobility in industrial Łódź. Despite the official line, enforced by the authorities, that society was classless, the study established that social advancement, understood as climbing the social ladder, was present in the PRL. It applied a model of equal opportunities and investigated deviations from the assumed mobility paths between classes. The social categories employed in the study were the intelligentsia, office workers, technicians, "white-blue collar" workers, craftsmen, and manual workers. The results revealed a stable, vertical structure where advancement occurred rung by rung between adjacent categories. The intelligentsia were shown to be the group with the most intergenerational stability—56.2 percent of representatives of the intelligentsia in Łódź had maintained the position of their intelligentsia parents.[82] Furthermore, this group also included the children of office workers and, to a lesser degree, skilled workers. The children of "white-blue collar" workers and craftsmen, on the other hand, had mostly moved into the technicians group. The second most stable group after the intelligentsia was that of manual workers. Most children had remained in the same group as their parents. The degree of mobility assumed in the model approximated the research results across all groups, except for white-collar workers (the intelligentsia, office workers, and technicians as a group), who maintained their position over time. Within this subgroup, the intelligentsia remained the group that was impenetrable. After a short period of postwar openness, it once again became a group that basically self-recruited.[83] Furthermore, advancement was most beneficial for the intelligentsia and also (relatively) for unskilled workers who had started from the worst positions. Meanwhile, the level of education among peasants and unskilled workers was still very low. In 1972, 93 percent of independent farmers (i.e., not working on collective farms) had only completed an elementary education or in some cases had not even completed this. It is not surprising that this situation was hereditary.[84]

Other social groups, too, started to believe that the number of years spent at school did not later translate to a better income. As a matter of fact, by the 1960s, it was more the type of work you did, and not your education, that affected income.[85] According to comparative analyses conducted between the prewar period and the situation in 1960, manual workers' wages grew by 45 percent, and white-collar workers' decreased by 25 percent.[86] In the first few years after the war, manual workers would sometimes refuse an offer of a higher position as they would earn less than if performing manual work. The gap between the salaries of blue- and white-collar workers closed in later periods, and as a result, the wages of skilled workers were only slightly lower than the salaries of the intelligentsia.[87] This situation did not change until the 1980s, when income differences increased, depending on education.

Salary, however, did not determine lifestyle, structure of expenses, or family consumption preferences. The income gap might have been closing, but the status differences were not. Aside from individuals' wages, what also needs to be compared is the average income per family member, the impact of women taking up jobs, and the number of children. Although the aforementioned prewar distinctions regarding clothes and home decor lessened, structural inequalities were preserved. Various kinds of privileges, such as the allocation of an apartment, access to a car, or domestic appliances, were supposed to bridge the gap between classes and level social differences. However, the research shows that living conditions, especially in terms of housing (the sewage and central heating system, the number of people per room), significantly favored intelligentsia families over those of the working class. The average number of rooms in an apartment was the highest for the intelligentsia—3.29. The family of a skilled worker lived on average in 2.78 rooms, and as many as half the respondents lived in small one- or two-room apartments. The intelligentsia more often resided in new apartments and had central heating, a sewage system, as well as better domestic appliances: People with higher education most often had a refrigerator, a washing machine, or a vacuum cleaner. Only technical workers were more likely to have a TV set.[88]

The example of academic faculty, undoubtedly part of the intelligentsia, seems to confirm that. For instance, in 1964, the University of Łódź, together with the Łódź University of Technology, undertook the project of building apartments for faculty at 79 Narutowicza St.[89] In the 1970s, the housing co-operatives in Łódź agreed to make an annual transfer of a pool of apartments to be at the disposal of the University of Łódź.[90] Affiliation to the intelligentsia continued to offer a certain guarantee of a rather comfortable life, higher and more stable salaries, and social prestige. At a more general level, a high position correlated with education. For example, company directors and specialists had on average completed fifteen years of education, compared with a manual worker's seven. The political elites were also dominated by people with a higher education but in most cases, these were the people who had been educated in the immediate postwar years.[91] In the late 1960s, the intelligentsia totaled 9.8 percent of the population, but it received 16 percent of the salary quota of society as a whole.[92]

Changes that were noticeable at the level of society as a whole (that is, including all age groups) would not be observed until much later. As those educated in the PRL reached increasingly higher levels of education, the result was that around the year 2000, 10 percent of the population had completed a higher education (hence, the youngest people who could have completed their studies had been born in the early 1980s).[93] In Poland, social advancement, classically understood as climbing the social ladder, applied to between 24.4 to 35.6 percent of the postwar population.[94] Most people had obtained a higher education during the period of the PRL and they primarily became engineers.

BLEACHING BLUE-COLLARS

The arduously construed new professional class was riddled with contradictions, and just as contradictory, if not dialectic, were the factors that shaped its creation. In the 1960s, the two strongest currents shaping the social structure were the shift from peasant to working class, hence the migration to cities and blue-collar workers taking the positions of white-collar workers.[95] As we have seen, at this time, the main channel of advancement for working-class people was not university but secondary schools such as the technical school for factory workers in Łódź. Its students were delegated by the Ministry of Light Industry (61.4 percent of students came from a working-class background and 21.3 percent had a peasant origin). This was the place for people who had no interest in becoming "an intellectual."[96] In fact, it could be seen as a kind of working intelligentsia for those satisfied with their secondary education—these were the new professionals. However, as research on technical school graduates indicates, their behavior and values corresponded with the traditional intelligentsia. They had traditional values and did not display much interest in politics or political activity as new socialist professionals engaged in building a better world should have done. The socially advancing groups aspired to models of behavior associated with the purportedly higher social classes. They were not the avant-garde of transformation. They were interested in family, stability, apartments, and cars as well as sending their children to university. On the other hand, among the 2,000 textile workers surveyed in 1963, 70 percent wanted their children to have a higher education, although in most cases, they were unable to specify the preferred degree subject.[97] According to the sociologist Mirosława Marody, the emergence of traditional values among the people who had advanced largely coincided with the withdrawal into the private sphere, that is, a sphere of family life and stability, which can easily be framed as a turn toward conservative values or the adoption of bourgeois values.[98] As the number of educated people grew, social advancement became less spectacular. Open educational doors mattered less than frustration at a lack of choice or restricted career opportunities at higher levels of professional development (where rules lacked transparency). The new elite owed its success to resourcefulness and toeing the party line rather than education.[99]

Matters were similar in the USSR. Sheila Fitzpatrick's research on socially advancing workers also revealed that they led lifestyles that mirrored traditional bourgeois models, reproducing or even enhancing the distinctions that had been characteristic of the prerevolution period (for instance, by sending their children to piano lessons).[100] Furthermore, high-ranking Stalinist elites also held rather conservative values.[101] An analogous process occurred in Poland. While in postwar Poland and in postrevolution Russia a rhetoric of austerity and sacrifice to rebuild the country prevailed, in the later periods it was stability and even satisfying consumer appetites that gained importance. The project of building a new culture became overshadowed by previously elitist models. These models, however, were less those of high culture or an intelligentsia ethos[102] and more bourgeois models creating the foundation of the Polish middle class.[103] Edward Gierek's success and relative political stability rested on his capacity to enable people to realize these models—getting their own two-bedroom apartment, a washing machine, and a TV set.

Despite the passage of time, the aforementioned differences in the aspirations of parents changed only slightly in the 1960s. In the early 1980s, that is, after almost forty years of the socialist modernizing project, 84 percent of secondary school graduates from intelligentsia homes wanted to go to university but only 32 percent of graduates whose fathers had professional training wanted to make the same move. Although both groups had obtained their secondary school–leaving certificate, the level of aspiration inherited from the family home proved to have a stronger influence than school.[104] The expectations of blue-collar workers' children were similar: Only 20 percent wanted to do a degree course. In the case of farmers' children, the figure was only 12 percent.[105] Perhaps their parents, as had been the case of textile workers in Łódź surveyed in the 1960s, wanted them to go to university, but this was too abstract an aspiration to shape later decisions. Or maybe it was at odds with other values instilled at home?

While education may have continued to be highly valued by Poles, this did not have to take the form of a university education. As further research suggested, education was treated instrumentally as a means to obtain an interesting job and a higher salary. Other long-running research on the values held by students during the PRL period also confirmed that what was most highly valued was stability, family, and professional standing, and not political engagement.[106] The vision of an egalitarian society in which almost everybody was a state employee and played an equally important role, whether as first secretary or worker on a production line, did not favor costly educational investments. Naturally, this vision had little impact on actual social divisions.

Another aspect of socialist advancement was the growing importance of political capital. Following the transformation of the social structure and its increasing rigidity, literature on the USSR started to use the term "nomenclature." This referred to party members as well as officials at all levels (local authorities, administration, industry) appointed by party authorities.[107] Aside from the Chinese socialist university, where cultural capital overlapped with political capital,[108] in Russia and Central Europe, education was only one element on the path of advancement to the nomenclature. Often, it was enough to take a short course or enroll in a party school to climb the career ladder. As a result, it was not intellectual talent but formal indicators that provided access to power.[109] Not only was university not a sure path to accessing the ruling class, but the ruling class also did not identify with the academic intelligentsia. Throughout the entire PRL period, the number of academics, together with the more loosely defined intelligentsia in the party, was rather insignificant. This way, along with the educational path offered by university, there were other equally attractive advancement opportunities offered by vocational and technical schools, as well as by short preparatory courses and the party career. However, that was a path for rank-and-file party members.

Actually, already in the late 1940s, the party started to create separate channels of educational advancement for its elites, which were supervised only by the "progressive" intelligentsia. And it was not happening at the socialist University of Łódź. The "professorate's active members," led by Stefan Żółkiewski and Adam Schaff, moved from Łódź to Warsaw after 1948. There, they created parallel structures directly subject to the Ministry of Education (and later, the Ministry of Science and Higher Education), such as the Central Party School at the Central Committee of the PZPR. Its short, two-year, accelerated program was supposed to train people for party work, and over time, the school even awarded PhD degrees and habilitation degrees.[110] It offered basic-level courses for election agitators, school inspectors, municipal secretaries, and even mechanics.[111] On the other hand, the Institute for Academic Faculty Training (later, the Institute of Social Sciences at the Central Committee of the PZPR) attracted the progressive intelligentsia and had a broader mission that was not solely geared to educating party functionaries.

The listed institutions formed parallel structures that operated as an alternative to traditional academia and comprised a small and elitist circle with select political views. Such an educational path was essentially elitist, whatever the PZPR branded it. The difference was that while traditionally oriented universities favored candidates from an intelligentsia background, in this case loyalty to the party was the selection criterion. These were small institutions that did not aspire to function as an egalitarian socialist university, as did the University of Łódź. They were never aimed at mass education—on the contrary, their task was to forge political elites and not thousands of specialists.

DEMOCRATIZED EDUCATION

During the first twenty years after the war (1945–1965), during the period of socialist transformation, the social structure of Poland was relatively open. In the first years of the PRL, the primary goal of higher education was to satisfy a "hunger for staff," which was so severe that factories themselves tried to train their own specialists.[112] The second goal was the production of political support for the new system. A new intelligentsia was being formed and the first successes were noted with pride. The ratios were good, especially compared to the prewar period. The first reconstruction plan, the so-called Three-Year Plan (1947–1949), would at a later period be considered the most reliable and comprehensive project for the reconstruction of the economy in the entire Eastern bloc.[113] The next one, the Six-Year Plan, however, modeled on the prewar production plans of the USSR was less successful. The period of the "gentle revolution" was conducive to the formation of a wide coalition of support for a number of top-down reforms (like preparatory courses). However, faculty, even the left-leaning faculty, continued to view the changes with skepticism.[114]

The intelligentsia underwent a profound change. While in the two interwar decades 80,000 students had been educated, during the PRL period as many as two million people were awarded higher education diplomas.[115] This was also a time of increased educational mobility, that is, successive levels of education obtained by people from various classes and social backgrounds. However, possibilities were shrinking. From the end of the war until the mid-1960s, every other first-year student came from an intelligentsia family. Each year, a working-class or peasant student, who initially had similar chances of studying, found themselves at a greater disadvantage. In the 1983/1984 academic year, every eleventh first-year student came from a working-class family and every twenty-third from a peasant background; by the 1989/1990 academic year the figures had fallen to every fifteenth and every twenty-ninth, respectively. This was—and remains—a result of a system of inherited social position, which had grown more entrenched by the time of the transformation, and the end of the PRL, when both economic processes and the rhetoric of the free market and self-reliance reinforced social disparities.[116] Comparison of the distances between professional categories from the years 1981 and 2005, 15 years after the 1989 transition, indicates that in the PRL they were distributed more evenly and that social polarization started to grow in the 1990s. Selection mechanisms also became stricter. When the moment of the strictest selection was pushed to the secondary level of education, after 1989, the chances of getting into secondary school increased, but not the chance of progressing to a higher level.[117] The distances between school types increased considerably. While previously categories of parental profession had been evenly distributed among all types of school (vocational, technical, general education, etc.), by 2005, general secondary schools had become elitist in terms of their students' social backgrounds.[118]

Alicja Zawistowska's studies on educational mobility between four generations, that is, of those born before 1929, in 1930–1944, 1945–1959, and 1960–1979, show that the children from the oldest cohort were subject to the most rigorous selection at elementary school level, and the majority of the people who passed this critical moment later obtained a higher education. Over the subsequent generations, the moment of the most rigorous selection kept moving up to higher levels of education. In the fourth generation studied, although elementary schooling had become universal, selection at the further levels became tougher than ever. Social origin was the most crucial factor for the group of those born before 1929, when the children of high-positioned employees were seven times more likely to be awarded a higher education degree than were working-class children. This generation was born too early to take advantage of the higher education reform implemented straight after the war and, in the case of young people from the working class, of the incentives introduced along with the education reform in 1918. In the case of the two middle generations (born between 1930 and 1959), social origin was of less significance and the distance between classes also diminished. The first beneficiaries of the reform were the generation who started their education after the war, that is, in the years after 1940. This generation experienced stable educational trajectories, and this was when the likelihood of reaching postelementary levels of education for working-class children was at its highest.[119]

At the end of the PRL period, the reproduction mechanisms became more visible once again. In the 1980s, it was children from intelligentsia families who had the highest chances of continuing their education past secondary level, whereas those with working-class or peasant origins most often correlated with dropping out of school and the threat of unemployment.[120] Those researching that period tend to believe (and this has been supported by broad research) that these changes did not reduce disparities. While the distribution of the levels of education and wages became more egalitarian, disparities not only did not decrease but in fact kept growing.[121]

During the post-PRL transformation, it was capitalism that roused hopes of creating an egalitarian society. Although time has shown that this could not have been more wrong, it is the period of the PRL that has been viewed as a time of educational failure, when scientific growth was stunted by political pressure, censorship, and limited access to the world's scientific community, as well as the inefficiency of the educational system at earlier levels. Meanwhile, twenty-five years after the transformation, it became clear that social disparities were growing drastically and that the solution was not access to higher education. Perhaps access to good-quality higher education could do something to halt the disparity; this has become the domain of the chosen few. Vertical disparities have transformed into horizontal ones. According to Alicja Zawistowska, the author of the previously discussed study comparing the educational achievements of four generations of Poles, it was the last generation that once more experienced strong divisions. Social origin resurfaced as a selection criterion while social differences deepened.[122]

Currently, only 1 to 2 percent of students at public higher education institutions come from impoverished families and from small towns and villages.[123] Obviously, the share of these types of families in society as a whole is much lower than it was in Poland in the immediate postwar years. Young people from the intelligentsia still choose to attend general secondary schools more often than their peers from working-class or peasant backgrounds. Hence, the offspring of intelligentsia families are overrepresented in higher education while the offspring of peasant and working-class families are underrepresented. If the latter do go on to higher education, they do so at private or fee-paying colleges, which offer a much lower level of education. As a result, nonaffluent students are doubly disadvantaged—they have to pay for something that offers them neither a chance of work nor authentic knowledge. Nevertheless, European rankings still place the Polish educational system among the most egalitarian (although still at a relatively low level). The differences between urban and rural young people are growing starker while social origin is again gaining importance.[124] Inequalities are growing in higher levels of education and are emerging very early.[125]

The children of the most poorly educated parents rarely go to kindergarten and later obtain the worst results in middle school examinations. Often, at this level, classes are already streamed and students divided into better and worse: 57 percent of young people whose parents have only a basic education do not continue in education at a higher level (50 percent in the case of parents with professional training), while nearly 90 percent of children whose parents have higher education go on to study at higher education institutions.[126] At the same time, general secondary schools are no longer a guarantee of further success and a certain channel of advancement. The moment of selection has simply moved and the role of higher education has fragmented.[127] Young people from the most affluent backgrounds study law and medicine, as in contemporary France or Great Britain, and also interwar Poland.[128]

To recapitulate, the effects of the postwar transformation of higher education appear in their best light when compared with the interwar period. While in the 1937/1938 academic year, for every 10,000 residents, there were 14.4 students, in the first year of rebuilding the country, the 1945/1946 academic year, the figure already stood at 23.1. The number of students increased in nearly all social groups. Thereafter, this proportion continued to grow: In the year 1950/1951, it had grown to 50.0 and by 1960/1961 to 55.4.[129] In 1960, 415,000 people had a higher education and in 1988, that had grown to 1.8 million.[130] At that time, 378,000 people were studying for a degree (after the transformation of the system and the rise of private higher education, only a decade later, there were about 735,000 more—1,112,500).[131] The change also had a qualitative character. The profile of higher education was different during the PRL—fewer students selected law, economics, or humanities, and more of them chose medicine and primarily technical subjects. Increasingly more women were getting an education and so were young people from working-class and peasant backgrounds (from 19 percent before the war to 44.5 percent in the 1960s[132]). Action taken to democratize higher education was rigorously implemented after the educational reform of the late 1940s right up to the mid-1960s, when "points for [social] origin" were introduced. Although the changes planned never came close to the anticipated results, there were some successes. Thanks to initiatives such as the preparatory courses and, more generally, the shift in the social imaginary, discrimination against working-class children diminished, and the number of white-collar workers' children among the student body shrank too.[133]

However, change was most pronounced at the secondary level. The real places of advancement were the vocational schools and, to a lesser degree, the polytechnics, not the universities. New professionals, technicians, and engineers lived in blocks of flats with central heating and went on company holidays, their children went to public schools, and they received state health care and insurance payments if they fell sick. Looking back, it is the lines, empty shelves, and corruption that often springs to mind as the main image of the PRL, but for the generations born in the 1920s and 1930s, especially for many working-class people, it was a modernizing project that offered them a real improvement in living conditions. However, while the new professionals were designing machines, writing out applications, filling in charts, and managing production, academics remained at their lecterns. Did the change reach them as well?

The vision of an egalitarian and democratic university did not appeal to the most ambitious. The socialist model of the university brought an inevitable massification of education. However, at the same time, academic circles atomized into elitist groups that cultivated the model of the traditional university, and higher vocational schools for new professionals. The academic field demarcated the limits for social advancement, a subject that will be elaborated in the next chapter. The processes of democratization and a certain uniformity of studies and students triggered defection and attempts to create niches where the elitist nature of studying and university could be preserved—not as a value in itself but as a recognized system of values and distinctions where the academic intelligentsia felt most comfortable. It also remained attractive to aspiring students who dreamed of the intelligentsia as an elitist group and searched for their place there, and not among the crowds of the professional intelligentsia. Despite attempts to depict elitist higher education as a land of useless aesthetes disconnected from the needs of society, it seems that the narrative of education as the peak of human thought and a temple of science had not been entirely erased after all.

7

ACADEMIC BIOGRAPHY

Fundamentally important to me was my fortunate birth as a child of an eminent scholar.[1]

IN 1952 AN ORPHANED PEASANT BOY FROM A VILLAGE IN CENTRAL POLAND walked into the building housing the University of Łódź rector's office, clutching a certificate of academic excellence. He headed for the enrollment committee on the first floor, entered shyly, and ventured politely:

"Gentlemen, I would like—"

Only to be cut off:

"There are no gentlemen here, we are all colleagues!"

This scene was recalled by a retired professor,[2] who at that point was just setting out on his academic career. Born in 1934, the prospective biology student was one of the few future professors with peasant origins. He was an example of the greatest achievement of the system that created the "new intelligentsia"—after all, what might have been an exception, a miracle,[3] in the interwar period was supposed to become the norm. The children of peasants and workers were to have equal access to a career, be that as a mechanical engineer or a classics professor. However, the new intelligentsia occupied a very uneven position depending on their type of profession, and among the academic professors born in the 1920s and 1930s, there were far fewer "colleagues" than "gentlemen."

So far, I have sought to trace three areas of change in postwar academia: first, the formation of the socialist university model vs. the liberal one—as they were labeled in the postwar debates. Second, the attempts to reconstruct the social imaginary through the discourses of the local daily press. Third, the reforms of the higher education system, their course, and their limits based on research undertaken at the time. In this section, I shall examine the course of the democratization and modernization attempts in the most elite social field, that of university faculty. The social structure of student enrollment changed radically, just as the education profile and path of graduates transformed. After completing their degrees, young working-class people became engineers, chemists, teachers, managers, or representatives of the authorities at various levels. But what actually happened within the main instrument of educational change—within the very institution that was supposed to provide knowledge and skills to thousands of workers and peasants?

The question of the democratization of the academic profession is essentially about the limits of social change and the crux of selection practices. Since the education reforms of 1948, the "shackled" and "captive" scholars of prewar lineage had the task of educating a new intelligentsia, including academic faculty. Academic teachers were a key element of the postwar reconstruction of the imaginary, in almost a dual sense—first, as part of the intelligentsia, and second, as those able to nurture new academics: They "knew how to build locomotives."[4] Before the war in Poland, 2,460 people held posts as professors, adjunct professors, and assistants, with another 3,409 contracted to teach courses.[5] In the 1945/1946 academic year, despite losses of almost 40 percent of professors and 20 percent of other faculty, some 5,464 people were employed, including 1,166 professors and 3,034 adjuncts and assistants.[6] Institutional development was likewise impressive—there were a total of 928 departments at thirty-three higher education institutions, most of them built from scratch and creating new academic environments. By 1949, this figure had risen to sixty-seven, and by 1954 to eighty-four higher education institutions. Over the next few years, the number of professors would fall considerably, but that of other faculty would rise to over 10,000 scholars.[7]

Obviously, the excessively rapid rise in the number of colleges and students meant that there was a shortage of academic staff, and in some departments, positions remained unfilled. The pace at which degrees were being acquired was not as fast as the aging of the professorial community. Figures reveal the speed of generational change, with assistant professors soon beginning to constitute the core of the faculty. The situation in higher education in the first half of the 1950s appeared to have been following the model of the socialist university.

Quantitative data does not much help to understand the cultural shift that was supposed to happen. Accordingly, I am here going to focus on biographical analysis and examine a few dozen stories of postwar students who went on to become university professors. However, only a handful of the more than fifty life stories of postwar professors available were of those of urban or rural working-class origin. It was exceptional to overcome barriers not just on the prewar but also the postwar biographical path—a university professor from the working classes was a rarity, although their academic career would develop in a remarkably similar way to the general model of academic biography. How was this able to happen in the supposedly captive university and within the context of controlled recruitment? Were the results of vast press campaigns, government reforms, and leftist reformer efforts really that inefficient? Did the socialist university produce socialist professors? The postwar generation educated in the reformed university system was to become the "new intelligentsia." The individuals who had been advanced from their peasant and worker families were to have been the most loyal to the authorities. And those very chosen ones, were they true representatives of the new university? How did they experience the socialist emancipation? Did they realize the dream of a new intelligentsia?

First, I will reconstruct a typical academic biography for a professor, following their career through the PRL. The majority of professors were of intelligentsia or noble origin, and a typical academic career was highly elitist. In the next chapter, I will then compare the above findings with several biographies of professors of modest class origin, who were supposed to build the socialist university model and to constitute and shape the new academic intelligentsia. My aim is to discover whether a nonelitist academic career would be that different from the typical academic model presented here. John Connelly notes that it was a planned party policy to build elites out of people who were potentially the most faithful to the system, who had not previously had a chance of an academic career;[8] similarly the construction of the ZMP generation assumes that those who experienced social advancement thanks to state socialism supported the system. The academic paths of urban and rural working-class professors indicate the extent to which this experiment of the socialist university was successful.

INTELLIGENTSIA HEGEMONY

What is specific about Poland, and in part for Central and Eastern Europe as a whole, is on the one hand the social revolution of World War II that changed the social structure and modified the cultural hegemony. It rebuilt the social imaginary, disturbed the cultural dominance of the upper classes, and enforced higher education reforms geared toward its democratization. On the other hand the regional specificity includes the role of the intelligentsia and its ethos,[9] in particular the strong influence of the Warsaw-based, formerly noble intelligentsia, which hegemonized Polish national culture and viewed history through the lens of the Russian partition.[10] This intelligentsia heritage shaped the intellectual elite of the interwar period and consequently the postwar formation of universities.

Most Polish scholarship on the postwar period and its universities focuses on legal changes and terror. Nevertheless, two important voices focus on biographical and cultural changes among the postwar intelligentsia. I wish to examine them more closely as great examples of intelligentsia hegemony, which defined public opinion and shaped memory policies in post-1989 Poland (chapter 1). Let us take a closer look at the paradigm interpretations of the postwar intelligentsia concerning the generations born in the 1920s and 1930s in the first postwar decades.

In her book on the new intelligentsia, sociologist Hanna Palska analyzes the diaries of peasants, who were, to use her words, the subjects of a “communist educational experiment."[11] The book's argument frames this experiment as rooted in not symbolic, but actual violence. This direct violence resulted in "submissively indoctrinated" individuals, naively believing in the communists' "beguiling promises." The socially advancing group, with their habitus shaped by the postwar system, were a cheated and manipulated generation, their history devoid of any emancipatory potential for change or chance for social advancement (other than the opportunity to "vent their resentment").[12] From her perspective, the communists are a sinister, totalitarian force, concentrating solely on retaining power. Palska interprets the recollections of her protagonists with the aid of Jan Kuchta's 1933 book *The Psychology of the Rural Child* (*Psychologia dziecka wiejskiego*),[13] which argues that children's development in the countryside is the reason for their disadvantage. They are raised with a shortage of stimuli, in a dialect incapable of describing more abstract issues, and with limited ways of spending time. Based on Kuchta's deterministic thesis from sixty years previously, the book presents the rural community as unable to offer any alternative narrative to that of the communists (completely ignoring interwar agrarian political and social movements). Elsewhere the power of the church and local traditions seems not to play a role. Similarly, the rural children's contact with nature as something providing "cognitive stimuli," evident in the materials collected for this book, is ignored. This purported restricted development of rural children is claimed to result in an authoritarian personality characteristic of individuals with a disturbed sense of security and displaying dogmatic inclinations that make it easier to accept Stalinist Marxism as the first abstract code explaining the world that they encounter. This elitist and anthropologically deterministic view almost entirely rules out the possibility of emancipatory social change, meaning that the appearance of professors of rural origin educated before the war is nothing short of a miracle.

In a similar vein, albeit considerably more convincingly in methodological terms, Hanna Świda-Ziemba's *Interrupted Flight* (*Urwany lot*) seeks to reconstruct the worldview and "key concepts for being in the world of young intellectuals" born in the late 1920s and early 1930s, based on private sources such as diaries, correspondence, and notes.[14] The author argues that the generation of "prewar" young people retained an intellectual ethos (or academic habitus), unlike their counterparts born in the 1930s and educated after the war. She portrays a well-educated cohort of young people, contrasting them with the "generation of ZMP ideologists,"[15] a new elite mainly populated by young beneficiaries of social advancement. The prewar ethos of the generation of young well-educated people supposedly comprised a strong impulse for self-improvement and strong will: "People who were profoundly attached to a worldview, be it Catholic or Marxist-socialist, pursued a particularly rigorous demand for work."[16] She notes that engagement in the postwar changes, despite doubts regarding the communists' project and the USSR's role, appealed not only to those with left-wing views but also simply to those with social sensitivity, a sense of the failure of the prewar system, a desire for public life and generational rebellion, and a need for emancipation from the values of parents and teachers. I can agree with that, yet she argues that whereas this generation retained a certain unimpaired core of prewar values, the "ZMP generation" succumbed to, or was seduced by, communist ideology and forgot the prewar ethos.

Both books' approach focuses on the influence of the political field on the formation of students' habitus, attributing a sinister and all-encompassing character to it. The so-called authoritarian personality explains everything, and not only in relation to postwar peasants but also nonelite groups whose motivations and social worlds differed from those of the intelligentsia milieu. Once again, this takes us back to dominant narratives about oppression and seduction, and also the story about the reproduction of the intelligentsia.

THE MODEL OF THE ACADEMIC BIOGRAPHY

Every individual biography is characterized by a biographical path defined by the rules of the field, dispositions, and reproduction.[17] This is understood as the social history anticipated for a specific habitus. In social reproduction, a key mechanism underpinning the endurance of structures and preventing social change is educational work and the reproductive effect that it engenders.[18] Therefore, the teaching work essentially entails replacing the habitus taken from home with a new, secondary habitus. A teacher or professor, apart from knowledge, also unconsciously transmits to his or her students the rules of the field, thereby allowing them to remain unnoticed and transparent but, nevertheless, highly ideological, and thus sustaining the traditional structures of the system. The course of an individual biography can even be used to measure social inequalities, just as one can do so by estimating the probabilities of children from various social backgrounds passing through the successive stages of education. The elimination taking place at each stage of education also shapes the biographical path.[19] It is not class origin that corresponds directly to social inequalities, but the pertinent educational career.

The autobiographies penned by professors and narrative interviews constitute an excellent reservoir of information on the academic field and the paths of academic careers. It was for this reason that I chose biographies as the main research material for this chapter. The cases selected for biographical analysis were only those by professors of the University of Łódź born in the 1920s and 1930s. In total, of 1,516 pages of 59 autobiographies in the series My Path to Science published by the Łódź Scientific Society, 32 cases met the criteria. Additionally 20 narrative interviews with retired professors of the University of Łódź were gathered by the research team in the 2010s. Some of the interviews were conducted with people who had also published their life stories. An additional context was provided by publications containing interviews with professors from Cracow and Warsaw, and also other cities: interviews with members of the Polish Academy of Arts and Science (PAU),[20] and collected reminiscences of deceased professors from the journal *Życie Nauki/Życie Szkoły Wyższej*. Finally, 52 life-stories (autobiographies and narrative interviews) of University of Łódź professors were analyzed here.[21] The older group was mostly undergraduates, and even writing their master's dissertations during the occupation, while the younger group was beginning their degrees around the time of the higher education reforms. (See figure 7.1.)

Let me stop for a moment to look briefly at the context material, the interviews with mainly the Warsaw and Cracow professorship published in four volumes by PAU. In this collection there are very few interviews with women in the PAU materials—just 17 out of a total of 138. Most of the interviewees come from noble, intellectual families, followed by military, doctors', and teaching families. There are precisely sixteen people from other backgrounds, all men (including the sons of: an educated farmer from Kashubia, a forester, a salesman, and a steelworker from Silesia, an inn owner, a large farm owner, and a craftsman). One of them calls himself "homo novus," the first in the family to go to university. In all cases, their education at secondary level took place in the postwar period and was therefore free, for many families a significant factor. It is

CULTURAL CAPITAL

ECONOMIC CAPITAL	1	2	3	5	6	7	8	9	10	TOTAL
10							1	2	3	6
9									2	2
8						1	5	4	1	11
7						6	7	1		14
6					3		2			5
5					1	2				3
4			1	1						2
3			1							1
2		3								3
1	2	1	2							5
TOTAL	2	4	3	1	4	9	15	7	6	

Figure 7.1 Distribution of economic and cultural capital in the analyzed biographies. The numbers in the individual fields signify the number of interviewees of a given level of economic capital compared to the cultural capital in the family home. This level was estimated on the basis of the interviews and autobiographies compared to each other among selected authors of memoirs and narrators (in total 52 people). Dark gray indicates those with the lowest number of both capitals; light gray indicates the largest groups.

not surprising that, in the context of documenting academic life, the PAU interviewer asked scholars about individuals associated with academia in their family, or other elite family members (landowners, politicians, artists); however, it was striking that those questions were never posed to professors of less elite families and family members. The interviewees themselves either refer to their nonintelligentsia families fairly briefly or emphasize the difficulties encountered on their educational path (such as walking many kilometers to school, the nature of the obligation to or difficulties with reconciling work and studies). Those from elite families, meanwhile, are encouraged by the interviewer to underline their lineage, sometimes even three generations back. This is a mutual recognition of intelligentsia habitus, a pedigree recognized and legitimating one's place in academia.

Nevertheless, the biographical collection analyzed here focuses on University of Łódź professors only. In the entire set of autobiographies and narrative interviews, which for simplicity's sake I group together and call biographies or life stories, only a few belonged to people from the working classes. Among the professors, there can be found individuals from impoverished teachers' homes, frequently forced by their family's economic situation or wartime events to work from a young age, as well as those raised in manor houses or in professorial homes filled with books. The feature that unites the poor houses of teachers or clerks and those of judges and professors is not that they possess economic capital, however, but rather cultural capital. My objective was to track the social space of the family of the future professor by defining its economic and cultural capital (figures 7.2 and 7.3).[22] Only a few belonged to people from the rural or urban working classes, or, as it was termed at the time, to people of worker or peasant origin. Most had a farm background, and only one a blue-collar one, but this was a well-situated family with relatively high social capital.[23] In a few cases there was no direct reference to the interviewees' origin, which could not be determined from the contextual information provided either—therefore it was too risky to locate the social space of the family.

Most of the professors whose biographies I compiled were "cultural capitalists." Bourdieu calls intellectuals "cultural capitalists" endowed not with economic, but cultural capital.[24] Despite the sizable economic diversity of professors' families, especially on account of the turbulence of war (loss or death of family members, resettlements, forced work, time spent in a camp, etc.), their cultural capital not only remained resistant to these changes but often also protected many families from economic demotion. Most importantly, though, it gave them the opportunity to choose and an awareness of an open educational path—the questions that these young people asked were where (with whom) to go for education, and possibly how to pay for it, but not whether to do so at all. Alongside professorial, noble (and landowning) families, we can therefore add to the group of professions with high cultural capital military families along

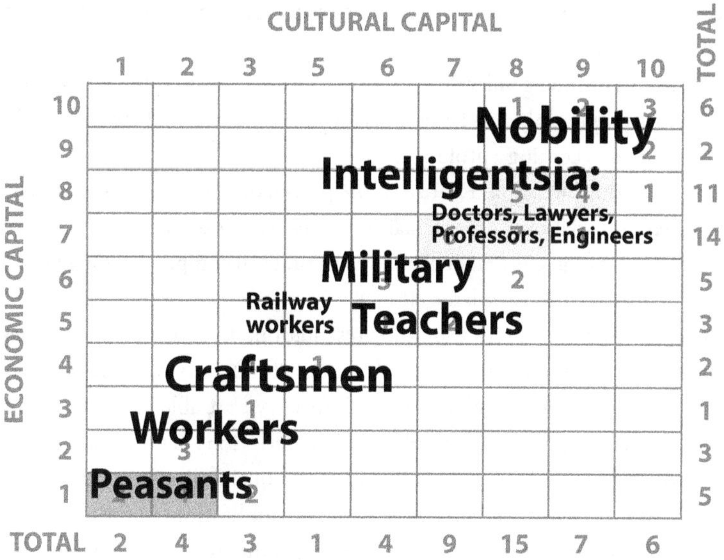

Figure 7.2 Distribution of economic and cultural capital divided into professional groups of family of origin.

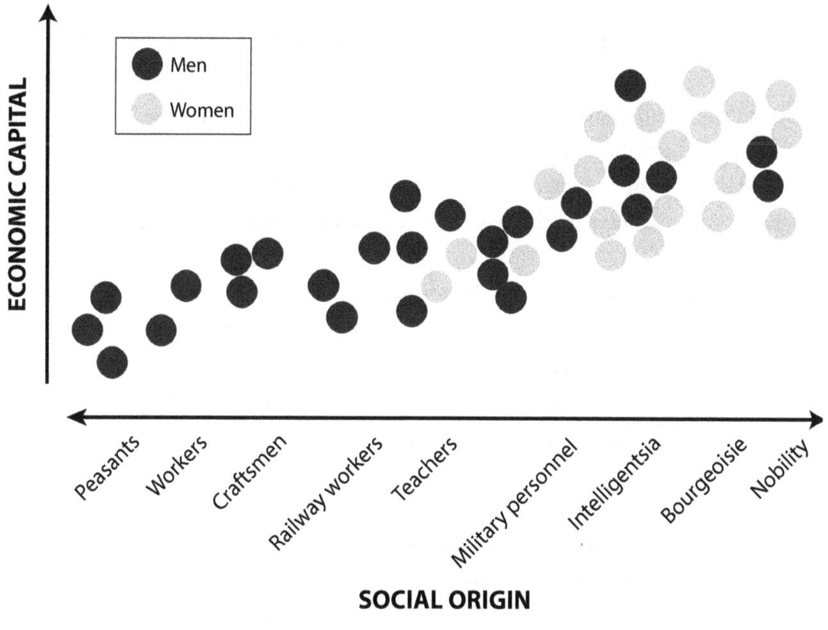

Figure 7.3 Gender distribution by social origin in analyzed biographies.

with those of teachers, doctors, lawyers, mid- and high-ranking state officials, foresters, and engineers.[25]

Interestingly, distinct gender differences can be observed in academic career opportunities. For example, only girls from so-called "good homes" had the chance of going to university and becoming a professor.

At the same time, we should note that the proportion of women is relatively large but the different social spaces that female scholars occupy at the beginning of their careers indicate that high cultural or economic capital can compensate for gender disadvantage.[26] I return to this issue later.

In their structure, topic selection, and presentation, the academic biographies illustrate the rules of the academic field and the criteria for occupying a position within it. By tracking the construction of biographical stories, we are able to see the path of the academic biography. Its various stages, such as descriptions of family life and first interests, choice of degree, course of studies, and subsequent career stages also reveal the criteria and values of the academic field. Reviews, publications of articles and books, and participation in organizations all correspond to the stratification of the academic field, and at the same time are a weapon in the struggle for one's position in the field.[27] At the same time, though, in the academic field paths are conditioned by dispositions that result from class origin.

The collected biographical materials—autobiographies, narrative interviews, but also biographies written by students as recollections of deceased professors—have a specific and fairly constant structure. This is most visible with written materials when their author is in full control of the material. At the same time, as a public, official biography, it creates and also discloses the rules of the academic field. It is worth noting that all the biographical materials under consideration were gathered after 1989, when the PRL had been defined as a purely oppressive totalitarian state. The model of academic biography reconstructed on this basis is ordered according to a schema:

1. Family home—stage of reconstruction of the first inspirations, recognition of the predispositions that would be decisive and prepare the individual for an academic career, revealing the likelihood, rather than chance or nature, of the future career. At the same time, they reveal the work of cultural capital and the importance of class factors in the educational paths of future professors.
2. University studies—the obvious continuation of education after secondary school—middle school (*gimnazjum*) and high school (*liceum*). The choice of degree is an important moment in the process of occupying a position in the field and the formation of the academic habitus. In this case, the course usually finishes with employment at the university; generally, with a "mentor"[28] who has already played an important role in the future academic's life.

3. Academia—At this stage of the life story, several elements recur: successive academic degrees and organizational functions held, publications and conferences, foreign travel, and the building of a network of cooperation.
4. Completion—usually meaning retirement. A time of summing up achievements, which reveals an academic's status through official farewells, jubilee conferences, and publications, students continuing the professor's research interests, awards, and distinctions. Further academic activity is also emphasized.

These elements are present in most biographies, and thus mostly concern people with high cultural capital. The interesting differences that occur in peasant biographies will be discussed in the next chapter.

FAMILY HOME

Almost all the biographies begin by recalling the family home, often presenting potted biographies of the parents, and in a few cases grandparents too, when they made a positive impression in the academic field or history of Poland (as a professor, member of Parliament, head teacher). The descriptions of the family home usually refer to the presence of books, the beginnings of the passion for learning, and interest in the world. The role of parents is underlined as those who introduced their child to the world and shaped the traits that would come to be of use in academic life. Apart from a love of books or reading in general, these include diligence, industry, and other qualities required in a later academic career, such as "curiosity about the world" or "love of the truth."

The homes of teachers, doctors, lawyers, and the nobility guarantee security and the possibility of education. This effect is augmented in the case of professorial homes—an upbringing "in the shadow of the department"[29] at a parent's university was said to have an inevitable impact on children's future. The narrators themselves often emphasized this: "It was probably significant that I come from an intellectual family, attended a good school and did not have to work during the war,"[30] or "The family traditions, atmosphere, and upbringing demanded that I learn,"[31] and "Growing up in this kind of academic atmosphere, it is no surprise that I wished to continue the research interests of my father [a prewar professor and dean in Vilnius]."[32] Choosing an academic career is presented as almost natural, as one of the authors stresses:

> Fundamentally important to me was my fortunate birth as a child of an eminent scholar [...] and a teacher of languages. [...] Owing to my parents' high level of education and profession as teachers, I was naturally a privileged child.[33]

The atmosphere, the existence of a library, subscriptions to magazines (even if they were the trade publications of the father, a forester), listening in on adult conversations, and visitors to the house were all hugely important, which is often cited in the biographies. If "in our home it was easy to speak fluently in English, French, German and Russian,"[34] this meant that children got a feel for language. Furthermore, much attention was devoted to their development in a planned and deliberate way: reading together, good schools, sometimes a governess, music lessons, organization of free time, that is, reproduction mechanisms lasting generations.[35] In the atmosphere of the family home, emphasis was not only placed on contact with books, but also on the beauty of nature[36] and the world of art. These are areas of high value—of course, appreciating beauty and the forces of nature, interest in art, and a love of nature are intrinsic characteristics of a person who has been well brought up, a member of the intelligentsia. These elements also lay the foundation for later intellectual achievements and the exceptional sensitivity required in the academic field, manifested in a love of beauty and order. For example,

> I used to be interested in nature, concentrating on botany, zoology, perhaps more on biology, and this stemmed from my reading, and I would say also to a great extent from my father, who, though a humanities scholar, was interested in nature, especially ornithology, birds; and during walks with him—and he liked to take my sister and me for walks—it was probably to expose me to and sensitize me to bird calls.[37]

Several biographies also contain the motif of frail health or chronic illness, which kept the future academic at home for a long period, sometimes even in bed, making reading books their main diversion. Such individuals, with nothing else to do, devoured the resources available at home and from public libraries and spent a lot of time thinking; often they had few friends, which led to their isolation from the world of their peers. One interviewee spent several years in hospital, which meant that he was lucky to survive the war without being exposed to air raids or participation in the underground. This motif, found in some biographies, seems to conflict with the image of the athletic academic nurturing both mind and body, the aficionado of mountain hikes and climbing. Reading the diaries of Jan Szczepański, a sociologist of peasant origin, we find numerous descriptions of gymnastics, rambles, and swimming, activities meant to counterbalance brain work,[38] yet in many cases, it was in fact the onset of illness or physical problems that served as an additional factor steering someone in the direction of an intellectual career.

Support for the cultural capital acquired at home comes from social capital—a family's connections and friendships are sometimes crucial to the course of the academic biography. Friends of the parents of a girl from an intellectual household about to take her school-leaving exams arrange for her to meet two well-known professors, the philosopher Władysław Tatarkiewicz and the social educationalist Helena Radlińska, to discuss her options for choosing a degree course.[39] A future student's father calls a professor he knows to find out whether the atmosphere in the young man's chosen area of studies might be politically improper (it is not—prewar professors work there, all "the right sort"[40]). In another case, when the doctoral examiner is unable to arrive on time, he is brought to Łódź by his friend, who is also the candidate's uncle—with the promise of lunch and the reimbursement of all costs by her father; as a result, they succeed in holding the defense sooner.[41] All these stories are described in the autobiographies as a natural element of the educational path. Going to university itself is presented as a natural decision, with only the choice of degree subject or discipline sometimes needing justification.

POSITION IN THE FIELD

The next constant element that provides structure to an academic biography is of course the course of study itself—first starting out, becoming acquainted, and then finding a place in the academic field, as well as the first attempts to take up a position based on the institution's status and contacts with other scholars. Here, an overview of the eminences whom the young novice earlier encountered at lectures, or even in university corridors are often mentioned. This is noted discreetly, for example by saying, "The biographies of these professors can be found in every encyclopedia!"[42] This is when the interviewees first begin to find a place in the network of academic relations, by drawing on the authority of established figures in the field. However, academia is sensitive to and highly values awareness and knowledge acquired outside the classroom, such as knowledge of works of art that is not taught at school and known only to those with an everyday familiarity with high culture. Only those familiar with the canon can question it, and this is actually expected at higher levels of education. School prepares its pupils in a narrow, schematic fashion, and this is the only educational channel available to the lower classes.[43]

Mention is often made of the intensiveness of the degree course and the eminence of the scholar's cohort to underscore other students' success—especially those who also went on to become professors. The exceptional quality of the postwar cohorts was apparently noted by the lecturers themselves, who "pointed to the zeal with which we embraced knowledge. After all, to reach the highest positions in the administration and economy, it was not essential to possess a higher education certificate."[44] Here we see the idea of academia as a unique area of human activity not confined by economic constraint, a notion also discussed later. Moreover, descriptions of a convivial meeting years later at a conference, or even by chance at the station, are supposed to emphasize the intimacy of the relations, the individuals' mutual memory of themselves as future scholars who promised much even as undergraduates, stressing the solidarity of people of knowledge.

In the stories of those who studied during the period before and during the reform, several references were made to the liberal university model (as discussed in chapter 3) and its difficult, demanding format, and in stories of those who started their degrees within the reformed system, to the high quality of their courses, despite the new rules. As one narrator who started university in 1945 recalls:

> What I perceived to be the main feature of that university system was the student's ability to control his path. The quota of hours that we were obliged to show evidence of in our record books in order to move up to the next academic year was ten hours per week. The departments of the Institute in charge of the subject offered particular courses from which the student had to choose—to be honest—somewhat as he saw fit. This concerned specifying what had to be done—and how many papers one needed to account for participation in one's chosen classes. Our student brains became rather scrambled by the difficulties posed by answering the question: how was one to set about this study lark.[45]

According to the material, this challenging atmosphere demanded that students demonstrate independence and organizational skills, as well as reinforcing a sense of longing for the prewar atmosphere of, purportedly, unconstrained discussions and meetings for which the starting time might be set, but not the finishing time. Constraint was said to come not so much from any growing political control, which had little impact on seminars with selected members, but rather from the modern pace of learning and the lack of time for sitting down together in the department common room and for never-ending meetings. The same narrator notes that conducting a seminar until the discussion exhausted itself "was the absolutely understood, undisputed norm, appropriate for academic study."[46] By pointing to the "undisputed norm" of the time, he shows that this transparency of certain rules had been lost, leaving a certain wistfulness, albeit not without a measure of criticism:

> Furthermore, I perceived our first years as the continuation of a certain way of conducting academic learning, invoking the prewar past with all its positives, but also shortcomings. Here I am thinking of the partial elitism of those studies, and also a certain kind of feudalism of internal relations. [...] Those first years taught us thrift, loyalty, and solidarity—one might say a "Conradian"[47] faith in enterprise.[48]

The postwar reforms and increased access to learning were, from the formal angle, at odds with the prewar study model recognized by the academic field—a system that as a whole was working to weaken the university democratization process.[49] Research on graduates in the late 1950s documents the prevalence of negative opinion with regard to the reforms in academia—opposition to the two-stage organization of degrees and discipline of studying and complaints about the fragmentary nature of the knowledge acquired[50] were elements of the habitus people assimilated during their studies. The format of prewar academia, when contrasted with the postwar changes, threw into starker relief many elements present before the war.

The independence that was required (students had to work through their own reading list, prepare papers, and write reviews) and the high level of individualism had a reverse side in the form of elitism. One narrator, who studied in Lviv (then Lwów) in the 1930s, notes that many students could not cope with the wide choice of subjects and put off taking exams, which then accumulated, thereby preventing them from ever completing their degree. The narrator herself, despite being very well prepared at earlier stages of her education and supported by her landowning family, struggled to prepare for classes. Her mentor's seminar, she recalls, was dominated by the children of professors: "This type of super-liberalism was the most dubious aspect of university."[51] Similarly ambivalent was the figure of the mentor and, as the previous narrator put it, "a kind of feudalism of internal relations."

On the basis of the research discussed in the previous chapters, Jan Szczepański argues that the higher education reform led to a change in the balance of relations between mentor and pupil. It was not possible to retain this aspect of a liberal university, he continues, and accordingly, the socialist university became an extension of secondary school (except that the subjects were more plentiful and harder).[52] In the stories that are constructed, including those of people starting university during the reform, this change disappears from view. A student usually mentions the mentor in question as early as during the first stage of his or her university career, devoting much space to this mentor's biography and presenting their relationship as familiar, almost that of parent and child. Many professors address their charges using the diminutive form of their first name, a mark of extreme familiarity, and even as "son" (the feminine form, in fact, does not figure in the materials), and in response, the student calls them "Professor" or "Madam Professor" (thereby symbolically excluding the existence of other professors), as well as simply "Mentor." Senior doyens of the discipline are referred to using rather affectionate terms such as "Grandma" (in the case of Prof. Helena Radlińska—pedagogy, or Dr. Krystyna Tryuk—mathematics) or "Gramps" (Prof. Józef Kostrzewski—archaeology). The familiarity of the relationship appears in many forms in the biographical recollections, for example, tangible material help (provision of accommodation, winter boots, decent clothes) or admission to the scholar's domestic sphere (inviting students home, introducing them to the family, or the extreme example of a professor sending a young graduate to the chemist to queue for medication for his mother-in-law). Chałasiński's wife—Krystyna Chałasińska, an employee of the Sociology Library—purportedly had the habit of asking assistants, before organizing the professor's name day celebrations: "Kids, what do you want this year: bigos or tripe?"[53]

The structure of one biography was dictated almost entirely by the names, written in bold, of important people, mentors at a given stage of the author's career.[54] However, the mentor-student relationship was often somewhat monogamous, presented as a profound and lasting bond. One interlocutor conveyed this sense by stressing that she "guards like a talisman" the correspondence with her mentor.[55] Sometimes there are anecdotal elements to the stories about the mentor or other important professors, as in this example:

> There's an anecdote attributed to many professors, not only our professor, about how plants identify an environment. If one knows the requirements of a plant, then if they are present, without testing the soil one can tell if it is humus soil, or sandy, calcareous, moist, wet, fresh, dry, and so on. And so . . . the professor comes along, grabs a marsh marigold, and says, "Here you see, this is a marsh marigold. If this plant grows, that means there must be water somewhere." And he himself is up to his knees in water.[56]

In *Homo Academicus*, Bourdieu cites a similar anecdote about Wittgenstein, who, lost in thought, walked onto a flower bed, and, when asked by the gardener what he was doing there, retorted, "What are we all doing here?"[57] The purpose of this example is to reveal the disposition to eccentric behaviors characteristic of the academic habitus. A certain eccentricity—an oddity, perhaps—is forgivable, and even strengthens the image of a person devoted to higher purposes, for whom a tidy flower bed or even his own trousers are secondary to the noble goals of understanding and scholarship. At many points, the academic field is defined as an area of super-reality, a unique area whose distinctness requires special treatment.

The figure of the mentor also legitimizes the position, or aspirations thereto, in the field, while the status of the institution where one studied and the broader conception of the academic community play a similar role. Like one's fellow students and the mentor, members of the wider academic community discretely transmit the desired values of the academic field. The *universitas* is meant to inspire and support, to subject the ideas of individual researchers to debate, and in a synergic endeavor build the progress of knowledge.

The memoirs often cite rather lengthy passages from diverse external sources, such as reviews of articles, recommendations, descriptions of the narrator from correspondence, speeches, or even overheard rumors. Such outside perspectives act as a measure of the position obtained in the field and serve to somehow objectivize the author's subjective narrative. So, when writing about the defense of a master's thesis, they often include extensive extracts from the examiner's report in an attempt to persuade the reader of the objective value of their work and head off any allegations that their own judgments are arbitrary.

Particularly early in individuals' academic careers, external evaluations are quoted as a verification of the effect of their work. These do not only consist of reports concerning the completion of a degree, but also comments on the first public presentation (a paper at a seminar, a conference), and even overheard comments or encouragement received in the corridors from people already recognized in the field. Such external opinions show appreciation that the person in question is modest and submits to expert assessment, rather than relying on naive self-belief. Negative opinions and reviews are also a common element in the constructed biography. Like an awful teacher at high school, they represent a hurdle on the academic path, which posed a threat but was successfully negotiated, thus confirming the correct choice of path.

Academic teachers, with their pedagogical authority, are responsible for establishing this secondary habitus, and—as Bourdieu concludes—this is done in the name of modernization and rationality. The academic habitus and its values are presented as universal and also rare, but they are arbitrary, and the status of universality is at best a usurpation. This is because of their dominant position in the field. As Bourdieu argues, the academic habitus acquired by young students and, in turn, demanded by them at the later stages of their academic career, constitutes nothing but the struggle to retain class inequalities and the status quo.[58] The success of socialization and young people's acquisition of the academic habitus means that individuals also fulfill their destiny—the realization of their biographical path.

ACADEMIA

For obvious reasons, the professors' stories devote the most space to research topics. They seldom reconstruct the details of the content and are instead satisfied to outline the areas they covered and any potential outcomes. As one narrator put it, this information is adapted to "the level of an intelligent high school pupil." The main part of the biographies comprises reconstruction of the professor's academic career. The rules of the academic field here act with full force, ordering the academic biography in each of the stories into recognizable (albeit of varying intensity) markers of position. These are the academic degrees obtained, organizational functions held, stipends and trips (especially abroad), networks and collaboration, publications, conferences, awards, alumni, and tributes paid upon retirement. After an outline of the professor's own family background, entry to the academic field through the choice of discipline, inclusion in academic networks via the lecturers of the given institution and its status, and particularly the figure of the mentor, the life story arranges itself into an academic career mapped out by the criteria mentioned above. Today, at a time when state-socialist practices have been replaced by capitalist parameterization and reporting, these areas are made apparent in every report or job application. They might therefore seem obvious, yet it is in this obviousness, or transparency, that the rules of the academic field and the habitus that is subject to them are concealed.

Elements of the academic's everyday work, such as research, field trips, and the drudgery of writing, are mainly expressed in terms of the aforementioned indicators such as publications, conferences, and reviews. A few passages, however, refer directly to research work per se: "I like working at night when the world is asleep. I have the feeling that I'm in control on Earth then."[59] Moments of breakthrough and discovery that are characteristic of the natural sciences are in particular reflected in the biography. The same narrator writes about the recognition of a new species of algae: "I don't think anybody can imagine my experiences." Another scholar relates with satisfaction the discovery of a previously unknown work as "a find that shocked the University of Łódź humanities faculty."[60] Yet these are isolated moments, and the details of the day-to-day research do not take up much room in the constructed stories in comparison with the effect and impact of the work, and hence the life stages are defined rather by academic degrees and other achievements.

The offer of an assistantship (a US assistant professorship, a tenure track position) is presented in a broad context and usually in the passive voice. The status of this event and its ennobling dimension are highlighted by circumstances in which the professor has to search for or even chase after the young academic novice. Such stories discreetly highlight the fact that the narrator was not chosen by chance or without due consideration but was valued, important and worth special effort:

> I was walking with him [his son] to the doctor, to the clinic on Moniuszko Street. There was a children's clinic there that was operating very efficiently at the time.... Wooden stairs, and I hear behind me a shuffling on the stairs, a patter on the stairs, and heavy breathing. The professor was a rather corpulent older gentleman. He'd seen me walking with my child, chased after me, caught up with me, and on those stairs of the clinic on Moniuszko Street he said, "Dear fellow, dear fellow, I've just received tenure, would you be interested in a position with me?" [laughs].[61]

Yet it is not pure talent or ability that is responsible for the success that something like earning a university degree represents, but rather the upper classes' better command of language and appropriate style. Pure talent does not exist; it is always constructed and must be recognized. This process intensifies with degree devaluation, a powerful phenomenon in France in the 1980s and 1990s that has also reached Poland in recent years. Educational capital without cultural capital is hard to turn into economic and social capital.[62] In state-socialist Poland, the system directed young people from working-class and peasant families to an array of newly opened vocational schools and numerous colleges (agricultural, teaching, or economics), which offered the prospect of the completion of higher education in just two years, and then to polytechnics, which recognized the value of the abilities to deal with material and tools that the working-class students brought from their homes. Universities held practical skills and collaboration with industry at a distance and maintained high demands regarding propriety, self-expression, views about "well-brought-up people," and remained the most closed to youth of the working classes.

In the collected materials, the rhetoric of charisma is relatively rare. It is not individual aptitude, but rather a significant other such as a father, or sometimes mother, a teacher, or the first mentor who are described as key factors in later success. The narrator's own talents, if stressed at all, surface rather discreetly in the opinions of others, in rational explanations or anecdotes. One woman showed a meticulously kept diary that she had written at the age of six and asked rhetorically how it was that such a young child could record everything, including the date and place of entry—"Whoever heard of such a thing?" she concluded. Another professor accounted for his success during his studies by saying that he had previously lost out on several years of learning, and his guilty conscience had led him to try harder than his peers.[63] External factors often cited include a higher force or the aforementioned natural order—this is frequently God or fate that has wisely guided the interviewee's life course, and sometimes chance that led to the outcome. What is emphasized, therefore, are factors independent of individual, natural capacities, with hard work being the fundamental individual factor. The professors' biographies do not mention the operation of charisma, which works through a certain blindness toward social inequalities and the attribution of school successes to individual abilities—a natural gift that guarantees good results.[64] This may be partly to do with a cultural difference associated with the social demand for modesty and humility in presenting one's own life. If we were to seek some kind of dominant sentiment masking the mechanisms of social reproduction, it would be that of gratitude. Each biography identifies some significant others to whom the professors owe their achievements. This participation varies greatly, from igniting a passion to recognizing and polishing aptitude. The paths of the academic biography are reconstructed as nonindividual, particularly in relation to the mentor.

Another important feature of the academic path is international fellowships and contacts. Young academics would get the chance to go abroad often even during their doctoral research, and sometimes after. A scholarship at Lomonosov University in Moscow was by no means the most popular—they also went to Cambridge, New York, or Paris (foreign stipends were funded by the Rockefeller Foundation, for example, which only officially commenced operations in the PRL in 1985, and also by the Ministry of Foreign Affairs, which launched a special scholarship program in the 1960s[65]). Almost all the interviewees took trips abroad for both short conference stays and research stipends lasting many months or sometimes years. The results of academic teachers' research in the 1980s showed that, while in general most trips were to socialist countries, in the case of people with the title of professor working at universities, the majority of trips were to countries in the so-called West. As Dariusz Stola's research on business travels from the PRL reveals, a gradual increase in the number of trips occurred after Stalin's death; already in 1954, 12,578 people traveled to countries of the Soviet bloc on business and 2,064 to capitalist states. A greater increase in trips was recorded after 1956, rising quite steadily throughout the 1960s, until a dynamic growth in the 1970s.[66] Apart from the benefits associated with developing one's own research and building networks, a scholarship, research fellowship, or later trips to give guest lectures were a value that ensured a better position in the field. A separate category is research field trips (biological excursions to Antarctica or archaeological digs in Egypt), yet these fulfilled analogous functions.

Simply mentioning fellowships, ideally abroad, is, therefore, a value in itself, but also an additional asset—they were used for increasing one's network of contacts. A compulsory point in the academic biography is an overview of the Polish and international institutions with which the protagonist worked and which recognized the true scholar he or she was: "These contacts with specialists at home and abroad is something that I regard as an essential condition of creative work."[67] The histories of correspondence, joint projects, and exchanges of ideas are often supplemented with stories of long-term friendship. Apart from the substance, also very prominently displayed is the building of interpersonal relations, again, for better or worse, and with their emotional dimension.

The next ordering element in the biographies, which also conveys the criteria of the position in the field, is diverse conferences, conventions, and seminars. Again, as in the case of lengthy scholarships and research fellowships, they are worth noting in their own right, but can also bring additional effects. One author summed up each of her papers given at conferences by citing the number of later requests for copies (noting the institution from which the inquiry was addressed). She explains, "I always attached a great deal of importance to conventions and congresses,"[68] and cites an anecdote according to which it was easier to find her at an academic convention than anywhere else.

The "publish or perish" principle also applied, though not in the quantified form present today. Still, publications were an indicator of one's position in the field. The authors of the biographies devote separate space to their first publication, underlining external verdicts on it (reviews, requests for copies, the debates it triggered). They usually just mention their major books, especially when accompanied by extra events, such as those related to censorship, and less often refer to journal publications. But there are also references to invitations to contribute to edited volumes or a book series, when the invitation alone ennobles them, representing recognition of the community as an expert in one's field. There are fairly frequent passages describing the technological process of producing a publication at a time not only without computers, but also often without typewriters. One female professor recalls that, after recklessly using a typewriter for the descriptions of the illustrations in her article, for many years she was in charge of a variety of writing for her department, as nobody else owned such a machine (not to mention being proficient at typing). Illustrations, reprints, copies, hand-drawn graphs, and tables were much more valuable material than they are today. One author relates how she transported the manuscript of her own book to its foreign publisher in person, fearing that the precious copy might be damaged during transit.

Above all, the academic career is timeless. Historical events or the political context are presented as interventions from outside the field, distractions from the world of academia. The education reform, the Thaw, 1968, and student strikes are seldom mentioned. In the interviews, the narrators discussed these issues when asked, but in the sample of recorded and therefore fully controlled materials, such questions are scant. Also treated episodically and briefly are censorship, the secret service, or problems with travel. They figure mostly in anecdotes, as harmless, external interventions in the academic field. And yet the criteria of advancement in the field were tightly regulated by the central authorities, debates raged on, and a succession of reforms was implemented. The 1948 reform regulated the period required for writing the various degree dissertations and the rules of faculty selection, transferred to the ministry the right to confer the titles of professor and associate professor, briefly introduced the title of candidate of sciences, and connected titles to academic degrees. From 1954, some of these moves were abandoned, and the next reform, in 1958, again changed the regulations in the field—the degrees of doctor and associate professor were awarded by the Faculty Board, professor by the State Board, appointments as tenured associate professor were made by the minister, and the position of senior lecturer was also introduced. In the narratives and biographies, this topic is barely present. Academia is presented as a timeless and apolitical entity, and the political context only intervenes sporadically in the order of the field.

A more general political influence, like historical events, seems to be of little importance. As one scholar explains: "It was becoming clear that, by making skillful use of historical and dialectic materialism and adroitly choosing quotations from the classics one can defend a number of just causes."[69] Many tried to avoid restrictions or keep to one side: "without overstepping the permissible line, trying to work well in all conditions"[70] as one narrator states, citing the motto of her mentor.

One of the memoirs invokes the figure of sociologist Stanisław Ossowski, a prewar colleague of Chałasiński's with whom the latter fled during the war from the sentences of the rightist underground, given for spreading dangerous left-wing views.[71] Owing to his publications, support for Jan Strzelecki and the conception of "socialist humanism," and his "excessively liberal" attitude, he fell into disfavor with the authorities and was dismissed during the higher education reform. Ossowski figures as an uncompromising, inimitable model, presented as a counter to the more pragmatic approach of the academic community.[72] The university field in the professors' biographies is almost free of conflict, tension, and complication. Academic careers are the result of hard work and good cooperation. The political complications of promotion are only present in the case of problems with being granted it. The influence of the political field is therefore either absent or negative in character.

The absence of politics is doubtless mainly related to the representation of the model of the academic biography as a conflict-free process without any tensions or disputes. Apart from the rules of construction of the academic biography, the minimal politicization of academia may also be a cause of this. As John Connelly notes in his numerous publications,[73] Polish academia was incorporated into the party structures to a lesser degree than was the case in East Germany and Czechoslovakia. According to Connelly, communist scholars were "ghettoized" in departments of Marxism-Leninism and had little influence on the academic community.[74] In the most frenzied period of Stalinism, in 1953 9 percent of students[75] and 10.7 percent of professors belonged to the party; in 1958 the figure for students was just 2.5 percent, but the percentage of party members among faculty had risen to 11.4 percent[76] (or according to other estimates, 19.9 percent; at the University of Łódź it was lower, 15 percent).[77] In the German Democratic Republic, Czechoslovakia, and Poland too, local parties were adept at constructing the new elites. But whereas in the first two countries they focused on young academics and successive intakes of students, in Poland the process was more complex. Hostility to both communism and Russia was rife among most of the academic community, which is usually explained by historical events[78] and the community's social structure and background. The party initially opted for a conciliatory policy, and the majority of prewar scholars who survived the war and came back to Poland returned to high positions, regardless of their views. Loyalty to the academic community was dominant, not loyalty to the party. The appointed rectors tended to be faithful to their universities, playing the role of mediators between political pressures and the independence-seeking academic community. In the Soviet Union and the German Democratic Republic, the academic community found itself in a far worse position,[79] and also in comparison with Czechoslovakia, the ideologization of scholarship was less pronounced.[80]

COMPLETING THE BIOGRAPHY

The final parts of the academic biographies often contained references to the professors' students. Sometimes these take the form of an account of the master's and doctoral theses defended under the professors' supervision, and elsewhere they simply express the hope that their students will remember them as a good teacher. There are also some mentions of protégés continuing the professor's field of interests and consequently forming their own school. In many instances, the moment of retirement appears to be of particular significance—while analogously, the moment when the professor's own mentor stepped down or withdrew from the spotlight is also remembered as discernible and important. With this comes fear and a sense of being "orphaned" (once again the language of family bonds), but at the same time, it also brings the possibility of change and of introducing one's own priorities. This is not declared outright, but appears in the guise of new research issues or organizational changes implemented as an independent researcher. The final stage of the academic biography is one of summing up and bidding farewell—the academic community should see its members off appropriately. Often, though, it is the less ostentatious gestures that are more important than the jubilee galas or doctorate renewal ceremonies. These might offer the opportunity to continue working part-time, continue participation in department or institute meetings, and also be students' memories and a continuation of their teacher's interests.

When reconstructing their academic biography, the authors of memoirs and narrators emphasize their continued academic activity (often hindered by worsening health). One author wrote of the fear brought on by the end of her professional work, using the expression "the time of non-existence in retirement"[81]—which neatly conveys the meaning of disconnection from the mainstream of academic life. The end of an academic career often tested the strength of bonds in the academic community. One narrator recalls proudly that, despite retirement, he retained the use of his office at the university; another relates how other faculty intervened when he lost his sight to allow him to remain in his position, but without a teaching load—despite the unusual situation, his gratitude led him to write about this in his official memoirs.

Departures could also bring disappointment and conflict, although such statements can only be found in the interviews and not the autobiographies. One of the interlocutors concludes: "I experienced a kind of defeat. Because in my department, my interests were already being continued to a certain extent, and tensions surfaced between my colleagues."[82] The narrator designated a controversial successor, to the chagrin of department members senior to him—she herself calls this an infringement of the "rule of seniority"; furthermore, the appointed successor eventually left her mentor's school altogether, even changing the name of the department. Reconciled to her fate, the narrator describes her situation in retirement: "When I'm walking along the corridor and see so many publications in glass cabinets, I don't even know them, nobody even remembers to give me them [laughs], you can see that various good things are going on in the institute. It's normal, that's the way it has to be, starting again." The bonds that are emphasized so many times are, after all, meant to be characterized by a certain monogamy, faithfulness, and loyalty: a relationship with the mentor for better and for worse, with the university and one's own department. This attachment is presented not as a flaw, but as the greatest asset. In this context, the proud summary of one professor comes as no surprise: "Sixty-one years at one university and in one department!"[83]

References to activity outside of the university are rather uncommon; for example, participation in the economic life of the country or region in the case of economists, work as a critic for film studies scholars, or educational activity among professors of pedagogy. There are quite a few moral evaluations of the subjects' own lives, remaining true to their own principles or the common good. The absence of reference to teaching as a key scholarly activity is striking. One should keep in mind that teaching was a focal point of the socialist university, even more important than research. This silence would be strange in any academic context, but within this particular generation of the PRL it points to the great distance there was between the imagined and desired activities of the scholar and those that were actually implemented by the government project.

When reconstructing their careers, the professors never leave their roles. Their stories tend to be grandiloquent rather than small-minded, engaged, not distanced, and serious, not jocular (apart from the numerous anecdotes that often appear). Of course, this tone is not surprising in the additional materials—recollections of the deceased—but is rather puzzling in the professors' own biographies. As the interviews were being collated, it could often be seen that interventions had been made in the recorded interviews, fragments deleted or even the whole text subjected to editing. Perhaps the biography was so shaped and ordered by the academic career path and the academic habitus so dominated the rest that a critical distance from one's own biography and the institution of the university proved impossible.

This quality reveals the academic habitus and its foundation, the belief in the inseparability of the life and the work, a life that cannot shut out the professional sphere, and a profession that permeates the entire life and experience. The whole of the academic field seems to be an area of certain superior principles and values—substantive, cultural, and even ethical. This superiority reinforces the cultural arbitrary as universal. The values of academia that are presented are imperative for everyone, they are practically a guarantee of humanity. The academics speak in favor of the university as a temple of knowledge and scholarship as a value in itself. Other research, concerning the ethics of academic teachers among other matters, confirmed scholars' strong conviction that "science is a quest for the truth."[84] Barbara Post's research on the ethos of Warsaw academics reached similar conclusions, identifying truth, honesty, and universalism as the principal values.[85] Somewhat bombastic expressions about the scholar's mission, work, or superior values can be found in many autobiographies, such as this female professor's somewhat prophetic summary:

> From this difficult, laborious, and risky path I took away two, not so much benefits as, observations. The first is that the academic path is strewn with many thorns, and requires "Benedictine" toils and sacrifices. The second is that those embarking on this path will have no peace and will not abandon their muse. For they know that they are in its control. Yet woe to those who for opportunistic purposes disregarded its instructions. They'd have been better off staying silent forever.[86]

There cannot be many better guarantees of one's own privileges and maintaining the hegemony of a given group in society. Attributing superior values to scholarship and a unique mission to academics has a very clear class function—it is a distinction that ensures the reproduction of the cultural arbitrary of the dominant classes.[87] One female narrator concludes that what is most precious in scholars is their ability to distinguish true values and remain true to them—yet they are the ones who are responsible for the criterion of this truth. After all, there are no concrete denotations behind universal expressions like "proper" and "decent," to use the language of professors.

INTERSECTION OF CLASS AND GENDER

When we enquire about women's participation in academic life and their functioning in the modern academy, we come face to face with series of depressing data that confirm our worst fears. We learn that, according to pessimistic predictions, the higher the institutional position—the fewer women. The higher the academic title—the fewer women. The more elite the institution—the fewer women. Studies show that female scholars not only feel unequally treated, but they occupy less prestigious positions, take more years to develop their careers, and finally, more of them leave academic career altogether. We regularly hear about the systemic difficulties of female academics: from the "glass ceiling" or "sticky floor," impostor syndrome, the Matilda effect, to "ghost advising."[88] One by one, as studies in different countries show, at each stage of the career ladder gender matters. Looking for a job? It turns out that letters of recommendation for female researchers are shorter and are more often about their personality, while recommendations for male researchers focus on abilities and achievements.[89] Further, marriage: Yes, it affects careers. It leads to rapid progress and success, but for men. Women's careers slow down. The higher up the hierarchy, the more single or divorced women.[90] Similarly, children: Women with offspring are treated as less serious candidates for admission and are offered lower salaries than men with children. Academic career advancement is at odds with the biological clock, which primarily affects women. It is easier for men with children to obtain and maintain a permanent position in academia after earning a doctorate than for women, and those without children have 30 percent more chance to do so—for men, children are a career stabilizer; for women, a career inhibitor.[91] In the assessment of achievements, the number of articles only translates into faster career progression for men; in women's careers, the number of publications statistically has no effect on promotion. With gender-diverse co-authorship, merit is more often attributed to the male co-writer(s). The long-term consequences of such bias to recognize merit in a given field of research are devastating for female authors. All in all, gender in academia does matter profoundly and so does a class background.

During the Polish People's Republic, illiteracy declined spectacularly among women, and they entered education and increasingly college. Female scholars experienced better work conditions too, especially in comparison with the interwar period; more positions were open and available—especially after the war losses and rapid postwar modernization. In contrast to those achievements, as research by Jolanta Kolbuszewska and Renata Siemieńska reveals,[92] the advancement of women in academia was limited and grew much more slowly than the proportion of female students. The higher up the academic hierarchy, the fewer women were present. In the 1970s the feminization of faculty reached 30.7 percent, in the 1980s, 35–36 percent, but among professors it was only 8.6 percent and 11.2 percent, respectively.[93]

Under state socialism, female scholars took more time to obtain academic degrees than men, engaged more in administration, and it was rare for them to take prestigious positions. Women were expected to bear a "triple burden," that is, to be active in the workplace, in the home, and in political life.[94] However, in the less politicized realm of academia, the triple burden took the form of female academics tending to undertake administrative work as the third factor. In a few cases analyzed by Kolbuszewska, female historians were also involved in political activism, but overall, this was a rather uncommon choice. Interestingly, she also shows that for female historians it was easier to find a stable position at the newly established universities like the University of Łódź, and specialization in labor and economic history—well-supported and popular research themes from a political perspective—could accelerate female careers.[95]

According to material analyzed in this chapter, many of the female narrators, who comprised almost half the interviewees, had no children and shared household duties with their husbands (still, not a widespread partnership model), frequently with the help of other family members, or simply domestic help. The vast majority of them were from homes in which servants were not unusual—as was pointed out before, cultural and economic capital compensated for gender disadvantage. Furthermore, the subject of family was raised most often in the women's biographies, with managing the household and raising children seen as a challenge requiring good organizational skills and resourcefulness. Among the women with children, this was often something worthy of note—they frequently stressed the difficulties that the children caused, how they hampered them from attaining their scholarly objectives: "My duties as a mother were no less absorbing [than the academic ones]. I left home feeling anxious, leaving my child in the care of a nanny, and came home anxious too."[96] Another professor, a mother of two, mentioned special "leaves" for research, negotiated with her husband—something by no means transparent but valued and fought for. Even one male scholar mentioned the difficulties he had had with developing academically, as his department was full of women burdened with domestic duties, which resulted in a greater organizational workload for him.[97] In one professorial family, it was the wife who organized holidays with their children, and she was rarely joined by her husband, who found them boring, preferring to spend the time doing fieldwork.[98]

To a great extent, the private sphere was subordinate to the academic career—one author of memoirs declared that, after defending her master's thesis, "I did my duty to my mentor. Only then did I decide to get married."[99] One of the passages cut during authorization of the interviews contained a story that I will quote, keeping the interlocutor entirely anonymous, about her dramatic breakup with her fiancé. Since the narrator had been certain that she would end up solely as a wife at her husband's side, she decided to end the happy relationship in order to devote herself to her academic career. She never had a family, but devoted her life to academia.

Those who decided otherwise could remain in the field of academia, but without finding themselves in the elite group of interviewees—retired professors esteemed in their fields. A group of biographical interviews conducted by Kartarzyna Andrejuk with a similar cohort of people outside of academia but experiencing educational advancement proves that women tended to prioritize family over careers. Women talked about the family context more often and more extensively than men.[100] Similar findings were revealed by Agnieszka Mrozik, who analyzed biographies of prominent female communists: writers, politicians, activists, and educators. Her research exposes the power of patriarchy evident from the level of personal relationships like division of chores, to work relations and public recognition. Furthermore, Mrozik's eponymous female "architects of the PRL" become mothers, wives, or sisters instead of public figures with agency. Relegated to the domestic sphere, their roles and achievements must be drawn out with special attention today; women's histories have to be specially found in the state.[101] In my research, female professors mentioned a family context more often than their male counterparts, but by contrast their professional lives were equally or more important to them than was the case for their female counterparts in Andrejuk's study. Male interlocutors, on the other hand, rarely mentioned family context or children at all. Several narratives also contained thanks to the professors' wives for taking on domestic responsibilities and child-rearing, thus allowing their husbands to develop their academic career, for example:

> Throughout my activity, she [the wife] supported me not only with advice but in the initial period also in material terms. By sparing me from family duties, she enabled me to dedicate myself totally to my academic work, especially when I was writing treatises for academic degrees and during my long stays abroad when she was responsible for our son's care.[102]

This determinant of the academic biography is also worth bearing in mind. The academic career is not a matter of simply individual endeavor, but a family investment, and its costs are borne by people from outside of academia—not just the professor himself or his mentor and community, but the family too.

As can be seen in the material discussed above, despite the tools of educational advancement designed to equalize class differences, and emancipatory rhetoric focusing on gender inequality, the overlap of class and gender disadvantages effectively blocked women's academic careers. Kolbuszewska analyzed biographies of successful female scholars with habilitation in the interwar period, all of whom came from the upper classes, which is not surprising. Furthermore, her analysis of female historians with habilitation after 1945 confirmed my findings about the intersection of class and gender. In staff questionnaires, almost all female historians declared their class origin as "working intelligentsia" (*inteligencja pracująca*), a wide term that could hide many biographical paths: from landed gentry or nobility to petty bourgeoisie, such as a local state official or teacher parent. The most elitist background was deliberately hidden.[103] A closer analysis of selected cases reveals that a working-class background was extremely rare and exceptional—miraculous.

THE LIBERAL UNIVERSITY AGAIN

The educational system conceals its nature. Likewise. the liberal university concealed its nature and the rules that governed it, and at the same time, it transmitted the cultural arbitrary. In professors' everyday gestures, from giving praise and teaching seminars to ceremonies and conferences, but also jokes or body language, self-reproduction of the system takes place, under the spell of the practice repeated by their students. Without adopting the whole of the academic habitus, it is hard to attain a position in its center. Through elements of the academic career, as it were, in the "objective" and measurable criteria of hard facts, such as academic degrees, trips abroad, publications, and so on, the less tangible values of the academic field are located. It is difficult to point out what is specific to the Polish or the Eastern European context. To be sure, elements such as para-feudal relationships within the department, a strong intelligentsia ethos, staying in a role at the cost of self-reflexivity or over-modesty appear to be more characteristic of this historical context than others. Above all, I am interested in the vision of the university and the model of scholarly pursuit that emerge from the professors' biographies.

The vision present in professors' biographies is decidedly closer to the liberal university as seen by Tadeusz Kotarbiński than the socialized university promoted by Józef Chałasiński (cf. chapter 2), or the socialist university implemented by reforms and presented in the postwar press (cf. chapter 3). Yet it was the socialist model that was supposed to be the setting for the formation of the academic habitus of the narrators who were undergraduates between 1945 and 1956. There were more critical and derisive remarks from the professors on the subject of the 1948 reform (two-stage degrees, parameterization, referrals to courses,[104] and work) and strategies for coping with pressure from the party. The picture of academia painted in the analyzed biographies had even less in common with that presented in the press, and certainly with the advocated model of study, the formation of new faculty, and the democratization of the university.

The main elements to which Chałasiński refers in his critical reconstruction of the liberal university model are the pursuit of pure science and disinterested scholarship, detached from society in the sense that it is situated beyond the needs of everyday life, economic benefits, and other circumstances. A widespread view among the professors is of the university as a temple of knowledge, an autonomous institution that should remain a self-regulating and autonomous community of scholars.

With the ideal of pure scholarship comes the need to devote oneself totally to this field—a recurrent motif in many biographies is dedication to academic work, regardless of the economic and political benefits and even personal (dis)comfort. In several narratives, the choice of the academic path is emphasized to varying degrees, despite its economic unattractiveness: "For the sake of being true to the realities of those times, I would like it to be known that to take up the position of assistant at a salary of 2,600 zloty, I left a job as an official in nationalized industry, where my pay had been four times higher."[105] Another narrator leaves his work as a chief accountant for an assistant's post, which, he says, meant demotion in terms of both salary and prestige.[106] And yet another professor speaks admirably of her colleague who "had no hesitation in leaving a well-paid position and starting academic work at a very modest assistant's wage."[107] It was even proposed that academics' salaries should be kept low to discourage people engaging in academia for profit from joining the profession, thus keeping it the preserve of the enthusiasts who were true scholars.[108]

Therefore, academic work is presented not merely as work, an area of professional activity, but also one of vocation and sacrifice. This is possible because of the unique status accorded it at the level of ethical values, its exceptional role in civilization, and the autotelic value of cognition itself. As Chałasiński derisively put it, academia is "the esoteric domain of the intellectual aristocracy." Although each of the professors would likely balk at this cutting definition of their work, at many points in their narratives an understanding of academia as a para-religious sanctuary of superior purposes and values emerges. Scholarship is pursued for cognition's sake per se, and therefore—as an adherent of the socialist university model might add—isolated from the needs of society, but only thanks to that same society's effort and work. The biographies contain several warnings against external factors interfering in scholars' research activity. The best way for scholarship to develop is for it to be unfettered by any limitations—neither economic nor political demands. The status of scholarship itself is therefore interwoven with para-sacral values, the university presented as a "temple of knowledge," and as a consequence professors bear an additional load of demands of a moral nature.

The second key foundation of the liberal university was the "craft model," as Chałasiński termed it, the mentor-student relationship. As one author of memoirs noted, this was characterized by "a certain feudalism of relations" at odds with the ideas of teamwork and the university-factory with set rungs of a career and criteria for promotion of a young academic. It was the importance of interpersonal relations, criteria not based on merit but rather mutual affections and antipathies, and the appointing of heirs, that sustained the traditional system of relations. University posts, though awarded by a work order, were in fact subject to an intrinsic internal regulation. Only one narrator remembered receiving a referral to work at the university at the beginning of their academic career. All others were chosen and appointed by their professors, who applied for a position to be made available in their departments or who were quite readily able to hand out posts.

This dyadic relationship never transformed into a more corporate model, and indeed Chałasiński himself contributed to this, in a way, in his own department by inviting assistants round for tripe. At first, he was unable to employ another assistant from the intelligentsia, because his department was made up entirely of intelligentsia-origin faculty and the party did not approve.[109] At the same time, he faced little opposition in canceling a contract with an employee at another department because of her landowning origins and "reactionary views."[110] In the 1940s, Chałasiński, himself born in 1904, inveighed against the elite composition of academia, and yet the generation of his protégés, born in the 1920s and 1930s, were scarcely different from this generation, in terms of both class origin and their ideas about the university. The mentor model continued to operate.

The work ethos is what seems to be a common component for both models of the university. Industrious professors work through the night, burdening their partners (and if they can afford it, their servants and governesses, too) with reproductive costs (in gender theory terms). They claim to be willing to endure any hardship for the sake of scholarship. One professor recalls that for several days after following his mentor to Łódź, he slept at the railway station, and when the matter came to light, he found a more comfortable residence in a departmental storeroom. Another recalls with pride a colleague who "wrote his master's thesis working day and night, sometimes sleeping in the library,"[111] while another author of an autobiography, who would arrive at work at eight in the morning, cited the ritual question of a professor who would bid her farewell at 6 p.m. by asking "You're leaving already?"[112] She had family and young children at home.

All in all, the socialist university model was supposed to change the very manner of studying and acquiring knowledge, Yet the future professors remember the period of reform as a negative reference point. As I have mentioned, reference was made to the satisfaction that came from having started one's degree before the reform, and some passages almost defend their author's own competencies, stating that despite studying in the reformed system, their academic work was of a high quality. Similar declarations are also given in the form of a less direct appreciation of independent work, their own reading, the hard-to-satisfy demands of professors (for example, managing to complete the set readings in German or French, independent preparation for a very difficult exam).

Many of the aforementioned elements might be considered common for postwar academic faculty internationally, but the reference point of the socialist university is crucial here. Historical circumstances, which purportedly oppressed scholars and kept them captive, are of minor importance in the reconstructed biographies, as is the model of the socialist university. Instead, professors' stories are rendered through a prism of an ideology of pure science and disinterested scholarship, rooted in the liberal university, and seem to be blind to knowledge production contexts, as well as class and gender intersection. Academic biography appears to be governed by unspoken rules about invisible construction, neutral meaning, narrative objectivity, and a transparent agenda. All appears natural, inevitable, and apolitical. At least for those who understand how not to break the social consensus about what it means to be a professor.

8

NEWCOMERS TO ACADEMIA

Is it fair that my path to the University will be barred just because I am not a doctor's son?[1]

THE INHERITORS BEGINS WITH A QUOTATION FROM MARGARET MEAD REgarding visions among the Omaha Indians.[2] The visions, whose authenticity was judged by the community, were theoretically an egalitarian means by which the elite families emerged. All the young men in the society would describe their dreams, which a local council assessed to gauge their authenticity. Yet the "true" visions were in fact confined to the children of the appropriate families, who already belonged to the clan elite. In the 1960s in France, the chances of a child of peasant origin completing university were 1 percent, whereas for children from a professional background the figure was 60 percent.[3] In the PRL, the democratization of education had taken place twenty years earlier, with extremely large-scale attempts to change the social structure as well as the social imaginary. Nevertheless, as I showed in the previous chapters, this was a complex process, and inequalities did not vanish. It was necessary to monitor the social profile of the student body on a top-down basis throughout, and inequalities appeared even at secondary school level, and then through screening and students dropping out. As a result, the social makeup of graduates constantly confirmed the more rigorous selection of young working-class people.

Apart from the well-known and often deployed Bourdieusian concepts of reproduction, field, and habitus, I would like to focus on the less common notion of hysteresis, which might prove useful in analyzing the changes in postwar Polish academia. This term, borrowed from the language of physics, is crucial for understanding social change. In *Distinction*,[4] Bourdieu refers to hysteresis as simply meaning "lack."[5] It refers to dissonance between the conditions of acquisition and those of using the rules of the field, for example attributing to devalued titles values to which they are no longer eligible, as in the case of noble titles.[6] The crux of every change in social practice is hysteresis, or rather overcoming it—this is the nonreducible element of the relationship between habitus and field.[7] It is the inclination to sustain structures corresponding to the conditions in which they were formed, which takes place, for example, during rapid transfers in the social structure. This is a structural delay between possibility and disposition, noticeable, for instance, in opportunities not taken, the impossibility of thinking of certain events in a way that is later obvious. Because of learned schemas, feeling at home, aversion to, and failure to understand change, humans are inclined to stick with what they are accustomed to. The field has changed, but the expectations and horizons of possibilities of the actors dealing in it mean that they are unable to make use of, or even recognize, this change. In sum, hysteresis is, therefore, a tool for thinking through change, transformation of the field, and the subjective nature of changes—an individual response or change in habitus. It occurs at many levels; for example, the case of children of the working classes entering universities, but also that of prewar professors tasked with building the socialist university.

According to Bourdieu, it is the representatives of higher classes who find it easier to make use of changes and adapt to them—their competencies and networks allow them to recognize the situation and fit in more quickly. The result of this is that people of success achieve success (the Matthew effect), while the lower classes are those afflicted most strongly with the inertia of the habitus.[8] The dispositions of these people become dysfunctional, leading to a greater lack of fit in the field. Yet another example of the hysteresis effect also shows the reverse possibility of a loss of agency by people with higher positions in the field as well as less privileged people demonstrating better adaptation to the changes in it. This was because, during the period of higher education reform in France, the middle generation of faculty accumulated symbolic capital according to the "old principles" and the logic that had been in place for decades in the academic field. They did not perceive the opportunities (and thus threats) associated with the "massification" of education, and their safe positions went on to be occupied by younger, more entrepreneurial graduates geared toward new values and criteria of the field. The younger generation was able to recognize the new possibilities and quickly adapt to the changes, without bearing the burden of the costs that came with acquiring a position according to the principles that had bound academics before higher education was opened to the masses.[9] In a similar vein, Jane L. Curry describes a corresponding mechanism among Hungarian and Polish academic scholars, the majority of whom, after the systemic transformation in the 1990s, were unable to take advantage of the new opportunities for the commercialization of research or international collaboration.[10]

Was a similar mechanism at play in the first postwar years at the University of Łódź? Those who had least fitted the academic field in the interwar years—too liberal or leftist, opposing anti-Semitic excesses and feudal customs, and consigned to marginal institutions such as the Free Polish University—were the quickest to find a place for themselves in the postwar turmoil and began to build their own institutions. Then, we observe a top-down change in the rules of the academic field. New criteria were introduced, along with new rules of advancement and new objectives, but the traditional habitus of academics remained relatively unchanged.

Limiting privilege refers precisely to the work of hysteresis, which serves as a tool for analyzing the construction of the socialist university. It leads us to ask about the change in the academic habitus under the influence of changes in the political field. This field enforced transformations in the academic field, imposing a new social structure and economic order—the privilege of working classes, protected by the state and popularized in the press. The reforms, the repressions of the time of Stalinism, or even the simple influx of students from the working classes and the massification of universities would open up new opportunities for academic careers and reconstruct the academic habitus. At least, this would seem to be the intuitive interpretation from the perspective of today's view of that period as a time of a captive and shackled academia and the idea of the formation of a new intelligentsia. In the light of the collected materials, however, this question appears to be not so much improper as an obscuration of another dimension of the work of hysteresis—the traditional privilege of elites, in particular the intelligentsia, and social reproduction. My proposal is not to examine the process whereby the habitus of academics was adapted to the changed rules of the field (which also took place), but to consider the changing habitus of people entering the academic field on the back of those changes. Accordingly, the question I pose concerns the adaptation of the "select few"—the people from lower classes who embarked on the path of a university career. These individuals, who began their studies in the late 1940s and the 1950s, entered an academic field that was subject to conflicting logics—traditional and socialist privileges.

The hysteresis effect, therefore, operated at two levels and in contrasting directions so the privileges abolished each other, creating paradoxical situations on both sides. The first level was that of the adaptation of the academic field to political changes and the simultaneous opposition of the prewar academic habitus, which took the form of an aspiration to rebuild the traditional university. The changes on this level excluded many prewar professors from institutional life; it rather enabled careers supported by political capital (understood not only as party membership, but also fitting in the modernization project), and finally it opened up huge opportunities to the working classes as the new intelligentsia. At the same time, though, within the academic field, the hysteresis effect operated with its vector pointing in the opposite direction. Whereas the delayed reaction of the habitus to the changes in the social field continued, the doxa of the academic field remained unchanged as an enclave of elements of the former order. People entering the field as a result of political changes and wishing to occupy positions within it were also affected by a reverse hysteresis effect: Following their advancement, they began to look for paths of adaptation and came under the strong influence of the prewar academic habitus. The vectors of these forces were therefore contradictory and limited each other. Owing to the top-down reforms and aforementioned reconstruction of the social imaginary, a dual hysteresis was at play. This chapter answers the question of what consequences the clash of these forces had for the project of the socialist university.

INHERITORS, ADVANCEMENT, AND CHANGE

As we have seen, people from an intelligentsia background dominate the professors' biographies in the broadest terms—at one extreme of this social group there are the children of railway workers, foresters, and rural teachers, and at the other, the landed gentry and academic intelligentsia (see figure 7.2). Between them, we find those from military families (officers, noncommissioned officers) and the children of engineers, the impoverished nobility, and the bourgeoisie. The economic capital of these families and consequently the educational conditions of the children and the need to work varied greatly. The financial situation of these families, especially during the occupation, was almost as difficult as that of peasant or worker families. The key difference, however, lay in their cultural capital.

A classic division proposes that we distinguish between the inheritors (*les héritiers*) and the miraculous (*les miraculés*).[11] The former consist of children from the upper classes, whose origin endows them with qualities that are valued by the school system. The latter group are children from the rural and urban working classes, who achieve success despite adversity and who lack the qualities that the system desires. For the inheritors, the legitimate culture taught in school is their rightful inheritance, whereas for *les miraculés*, every stage of their education involves a major transformation. They are subject to rigorous selection, hence those who succeed must be exceptionally able, as well as determined to make an effort. Educational inequalities are the result of a process of elimination in which lower-class pupils and students are more liable to be removed than their upper-class counterparts. The elements discussed in the previous section compose the academic biographical path, a biography that is the "natural" result, so to speak, of the structure of the social and academic field. But where do *les miraculés* come from? As the biography of Bourdieu himself shows, alongside the biographies of "inheritors" (*les héritiers*), for whom the dominant culture is their own, there are also separate biographies that follow a deviant path.

In a sense, peasant and worker biographies in the academic field are deviant career paths, as they don't fit the system of social reproduction. The deviation concerns the incongruence of the position in the field to previous dispositions.[12] These are paths in which something has gone wrong from the perspective of the structural conditions of the field.[13] Examples of such deviant paths include both impoverished noblemen of the interwar period in search of intellectual positions and the advance of proletarian daughters to teaching roles. Their starting position and the educational path that this determined assumed a different course of the biography. To some degree, these deviations were encouraged by the socialist emancipatory project, the visions of inclusive modernization for the working classes. It was a state-guaranteed socialist privilege. However, as has now been established, this emancipation was not taking place at universities, making the few exceptional cases of upward mobility deviant not only in terms of the interwar liberal university, but also with regard to the postwar socialist model. Among the analyzed material, cases of unexpected biography are to be found in the paths taken by four peasant sons, although in the case of one of these, his parents had become workers in a small town during his childhood, along with the biographies of two sons of railwaymen (first generation—the grandparents worked on farms). I also included the life story of a female professor born outside of the age range of the study (before World War I) and a professor of medicine who only began his studies at the University of Łódź and from 1949 continued his education at the newly founded Medical University of Łódź. The lack of biographies of people of urban working-class origin might seem surprising, especially in Łódź, and certainly, these proportions would be different in the less elitist technical universities.

What brings about the reproduction of the social structure is the "school career," the educational path taken.[14] A huge role was played by early schooling in the lives of academics and by seemingly chance decisions taken early on this path. These had a tangible influence on the position they later occupied in the field. Accordingly, one professor, himself from an intellectual home, divided his fellow students after the war into "first-class passengers" who had attended good schools with good teachers and "third-class passengers" who

> were and are those who brought and today bring nothing from home, apart from the principles of honesty, and who did not experience good teaching at school. I always treated those from the third category with the greatest respect, as they obtained positive results through their own work.[15]

In the case of elite biographies, reference to the domestic context, parents and their education, and the influence of methods of upbringing form mandatory elements of the narrative structure. Things are otherwise in the stories of people of modest social origin. These often omit their childhood years or mention them only in passing, only beginning their narrative in the postwar period and with the start of high school, the passing of the school-leaving exams, or even as late as going to university.[16] One learns little about working-class professors' school education. Of course, what these biographies have in common is a completely different family home context from that of children of the nobility and intelligentsia. In contrast to lengthy references to "our manor houses," "devoted servant,"[17] or the huge library, visits by painters and professors for dinner or trips to museums and bedtime stories about ancient mythology,[18] passages discussing the family home are limited in narratives by those from rural, working backgrounds.

What characterizes the narratives of those from the rural and urban working classes is that the most important moment is the break that takes place in the biographical path. Among the professors, this often entails their father's promotion, for example to the position of a machine operator in a factory or a railwayman, a state official with a stable wage. In other cases, what made the difference was the parents' determination to provide their children with a better life than their own through educational advancement. The elementary school period falls in the interwar or wartime years. Although this stage is a predictable element of the biography, especially after the introduction of compulsory schooling in 1919, every subsequent level of education is problematic and cannot be taken for granted. Financial difficulties associated with transport or boarding (commonly a cheap private lodging) are as difficult to overcome as the initial deficits in knowledge. Especially in the prewar period, newcomers know nothing about school, what it was, or how one should behave, nothing is obvious, there is no map for a family to follow. Postwar education research shows that during the war in some cases clandestine schooling exacerbated and intensified selection mechanisms, thereby consolidating elitism, especially in the case of higher education, but in other instances, access to education improved for young people from rural areas. The latter occurred as many teachers and lecturers spent the war in the countryside, teaching and giving private instruction to the local young people.[19] Those unexpected meetings of peasant children with the urban intelligentsia, forced by the war, also resulted in disrupting the peasant educational path.

In the postwar period, it becomes far more obvious what higher educational paths can be taken as a result of free education, numerous scholarship programs, a developed infrastructure including facilities such as boarding schools, halls of residence, the opening of thousands of schools, as well as information campaigns and the reconstruction of the social imaginary. This was still not an obvious or easy path, but at least it was possible to imagine and more accessible than before. The example of those undertaking preparatory courses, discussed in an earlier chapter, is the best proof of this.

BREAKING THROUGH

The first interviewee from a peasant family, born in 1929, opens his narrative[20] by talking about the start of his degree course, only later returning to his childhood. Immediately, however, he distances himself from assessing today's perception of interwar Poland, stressing that for him it was

> a republic in the wake of the three partitions, terribly poor, and primitive in technical terms, with many deficiencies. The position of my family in this country was not much lower than the average level, so it was neither at the social bottom nor was it at any kind of apex.[21]

His parents had completed elementary school after World War I and were thus, despite everything, relatively well educated for villagers from central Poland. He begins his education at elementary school in the late 1930s, only for this to be interrupted by the war. During the occupation, he manages to continue his education after his family is resettled, reads a great deal, and after liberation starts middle school and then attends pedagogical high school. He avoids the work order and is awarded a place to study in Łódź. He is sent to Warsaw for the second stage of his higher education and there completes his master's degree before receiving another referral, this time to work as an assistant at the University of Łódź. The importance of this moment lies in the absence of the figure of the mentor and in fact, throughout the story, the reference point is the more general scholarly community rather than specific individuals. Ministerial policy and the referral system, not an informal academic community, shape the professor's educational path and career.

The other interviewee of peasant origin is a war orphan from a small village in central Poland. This was the student told at registration that "we are all colleagues," rather than gentlemen. Born in 1934, he only began his education after the war and, as in the previous case, completed a pedagogical high school and—again—managed to avoid the work order. Owing to the poor health of the only other family member to survive the war, he refuses the referral to study in the USSR and instead begins a degree in Łódź, the closest option to his hometown village. Immediately after defending his dissertation, he receives a job offer from his mentor (the one mentioned in an earlier chapter, offering him the job on the stairs at a clinic). A textbook academic career ensues, made all the more stable by his starting a family at an early age. Like the previous narrator, he remains grateful as well as also somewhat sentimental toward the state-socialist era. Apart from the starting point being that of entry into academic life, this narrative follows the pattern of that of the classic academic biography.

The other narrator is a professor of mathematics born in 1929. His family runs a small farm, and both parents have elementary education: "They could read, but they couldn't write or count very well."[22] His father subscribed to a farmers' weekly, but otherwise, "in my family home, apart from my elder siblings' textbooks, there were no books."[23] Before the outbreak of war, he completes several years at a provincial school, where the teaching method consists of corporal punishment. During the occupation, he does physical labor in various trades, and as part of his self-education he only manages to read "a few adventure books." After the war, he continues learning at an accelerated rate, and from

1947 he quickly passes through his lyceum years, emphasizing the good fortune he had with his teachers. He begins his studies within the two-stage system (a three-year BA and a two-year MA), receiving a referral to undertake his second stage at the University of Warsaw before being referred back to work in Łódź after completing his master's degree—in exactly the same way as the first interviewee. He then embarks on a standard career, which he sums up years later in the context of being awarded a professorship: "The path to this title was neither easy nor straightforward. Hard work, persistence, and tenacity accompanied me all the way along the path."[24]

Another professor's family was active in the rural community. The author presents his father as a skilled, self-taught man and his mother, though illiterate, as sensitive to literature and music. At home, he says, "There were dreams of sending me to school," and later, "My parents also dreamed of educating me—as one said in the countryside—'as a gentleman.'"[25] After studying at underground classes set up by his father, he became involved in the "Wici" agrarian youth organization.[26] This was a formative event, as there he encountered a completely different milieu, including better-educated activists. They exchanged reading matter, he had access to a library, and, as he put it himself, "As the first high-school graduate in the family, I sat on a magic carpet that carried me off to the Faculty of Medicine." This metaphor of flight is also present in the motto of his mentor, who says to him, "My son, academic work will allow you to fly high."[27]

The final person was born in 1925 in the former borderlands of the Prussian and Russian partitions and raised in a family with peasant roots, who made ends meet with seasonal work in Saxony. The author of the autobiography saw with his own eyes how his father advanced socially, first to being a railway worker, then a driver's assistant—that is, from his own farm to a stable state position. The path of this biography is somewhat similar to the aforementioned histories of railwaymen's families, but what is especially notable is the speed of this narrator's advancement and his memory of his peasant origins. His father's advancement stands out as a formative event, his parents pay their debts, and above all, they can afford to pay tuition fees and to educate their son beyond the mandatory four years of school. In 1938 the author goes into town with his father to buy supplies for school, and the tailor addresses the peasant boy as "honorable young gentleman." The boy is inordinately surprised by this, but his father explains how much money he had given the tailor. School fees are similarly high, as "almost everybody is the son of state or local government workers with a permanent salary with which they could cover fees, railway tickets, and other small expenditures."[28] His education is interrupted by the war, during which he does physical labor, afterward continuing his education at a free pedagogical high school (with a newly opened boarding house in former monastery buildings). In the meantime, he becomes involved in the scouting movement, and in a way, this leads to a change in his degree subject. After a year of studying law, he switches to geography in 1950, receiving an offer of work from his mentor just before his defense. His career then proceeds in a standard fashion, apart from his refusing an assistant professorship after March 1968 (he is a party member),[29] which he receives only several years later.

Additionally, I would like to include one prewar narrative, that of a female professor born in 1914, which forms a certain counterpoint to the narratives of people born in the 1920s and 1930s. What is worth underlining is the uniqueness of her case, not only as a woman but also as a person of peasant origin in her region. The prewar history of this future university professor begins in a peasant family who own a small farm that is not sufficient to keep the family. Her father also had an apprenticeship with a master craftsman and makes extra money in his trade. Her mother taught herself to read and write, and expertly ran the household "frugally, but not poorly." Both parents took part in the public life of the village: the father in the cooperative and fire brigade; the mother in the Rural Housewives Society. Despite their limited resources, the cultural capital in this family can be said to have been relatively high. The mother taught all six children to read and write, and they all attended elementary school, although only after the introduction of compulsory schooling. At home, it was the custom to read aloud in the evenings, mostly novels from the village library, and the father helped with homework. The school was less than a mile away, and the teacher kept up the narrator's interest in learning. In order to continue education at a higher level, the future professor spent a long time persuading her parents, who finally consented: "As I remember it today, this involved strong resolution on my part and a huge sacrifice from my parents."[30] The narrator walked over three miles every day to her new school, in winter sometimes turning back because of snowdrifts. She wanted to carry on learning and went to middle school, but at this stage, her parents did not know what to do and how—they had no conception of how to organize their daughter's further education. They approached the mother's brother, who had moved to the city, for advice. Thus it was that the narrator set off to her uncle in Łódź to start middle school:

> In the vast hall at break time, there were girls in smart uniforms walking in pairs. All of them taller than me—young ladies, among whom I looked like a lost child. I was overawed and alarmed. My first contact with the teacher began with instructions regarding dress, school items, and textbooks. And I was thinking about how much this would cost and where my parents would get so much money from. [. . .] I myself decided that I wouldn't be going to this school.[31]

After a year's break, the family managed to find another school, somewhat less costly (they were given a partial fee waiver). This was the modern, state institution, the Women's Teaching College (Seminarium Nauczycielskie Żenskie) run by progressive educationists of the time. Although the girl lived in poor conditions, in private lodgings rather than the modern boarding house (which she could not afford), she declares that she did not feel too bad. She then went to the pedagogical high school, where she passed her school-leaving exams in 1934. Following the Jędrzejewicz reform,[32] she was unable to find work and got by on private tutoring. She learned that there was a branch of the Free Polish University in Łódź, but could not afford to study there. The tide turned with a loan from the head of her previous school, who said: "You'll repay it when you have a job—you must study."[33] At first, she understood little of the lectures, and so she sat in the first row, where she started to be recognized, and one of the university professors then helped her to obtain a tuition fee waiver. At the same time, she worked as a teacher in a small town, but once the war broke out, fearful of roundups, she left for Warsaw. There, she took part in underground education, continuing her learning thanks to her contacts with Free Polish University professors and defending her dissertation in history as part of the underground at a bridge table in a professor's flat. The same professor later offered her a position as an assistant after the war, by now at the University of Łódź.

This part of the story, along with the professor's experiences of the war and participation in the Warsaw Uprising, occupies almost two-thirds of the entire biography, the rest of which then resembles a classic academic career, albeit one begun with a delay. Although she completes high school at the age of twenty, it takes her another decade to obtain a master's degree. In contrast, several interviewees from intellectual homes began their education a year earlier, and one of them had even skipped the first year, and so they had a time advantage even over their peers with a similar background. Furthermore, in the following story, the author writes a great deal about teaching, which seems to be her main area of interest and source of greatest satisfaction, while this is marginalized in most biographies.

In the case of this biography, it is the events of the war that allow the narrator to go to university. Thanks to underground classes, she gains her master's degree, and the postwar transformation and reforms do not have an undue influence on her academic career. By 1945 the narrator is a member of the academic community with close ties to her mentor and an academic degree; she just needs a job, which in the war-ravaged country she would no doubt have found in any case. What happened in her case was a remarkable leap, at the price of the endeavor and sacrifice of the protagonist and her parents, and accompanied by fear, doubt, and often humiliation. Despite this huge effort, before the war, a teaching position in a small town would have been regarded as the greatest achievement; further career paths only opened up with the war (although her father died in Auschwitz, and she herself faced danger on many occasions). The difference between this biography and other peasant narratives is the point at which the educational path begins. Despite this, it was wartime events that enabled her to commence her studies following her advancement to the position of teacher. What in many cases might have been an obstacle became an advantage, allowing her to overcome class and gender handicaps. The other professors of peasant origin examined here began their education at middle and high school after the war, with the changing system lowering some of the interwar barriers. They were therefore not threatened by the selection mechanisms in operation at the most problematic levels (middle school, high school) of education for prewar working-class and rural children.

The greatest of the numerous obstacles in the career path of working-class children took the shape not only of material restrictions and available infrastructure, but of making bad decisions, wasting time gaining skills that were useless from the perspective of university education, and making choices forced on the young person by their material situation or need for social security. In the biographies of people from these classes, as the biographies of those from rural backgrounds make clear, advice on the matter of course and subject choices was not the domain of parents, but of teachers. Parents neither knew enough about the subject nor were sufficiently familiar with the field to know how to shape their child's educational path. Even caring for a child's elementary education made them exceptional. This was why the mother of the oldest interviewee had to consult her brother on how to go about sending her daughter to middle school. In the other cases, it is the teachers who nurture their pupils' thirst for education and encourage them to continue, even—as in one of the cited cases—funding further study themselves. Yet their role might be overestimated; a person who has managed to advance "tends to make his school-mentors over-important, since they are the cashiers in the new world of brain-currency,"[34] yet the biographical guardian, in the form of a headmaster or teacher, provides an important point on the peasant biographical path, making breakthrough easier. Neither parents nor children from the peasant class were oriented toward educational success, let alone an academic career.[35] In most of the cases, children internalize their initial failures and interpret them as their own deficiencies. The system generates mechanisms that neutralize its own aberrations, which means, at the level of practices, that people make objectivized possibilities into subjective limits of expectations. This was why the postwar reconstruction of the social imaginary and generation of a desire for education was so important in postwar Poland.

AVOIDING PRIVILEGE

Several common strands run through the deviant academic biographies. In the context of the family background, it is the appearance of additional factors that permits a change in career path. This might be the parents' above-average activity and desire for their children to be educated to a higher level than the rest of their class, or their appropriate placement in the postwar education system (all narrators but one complete pedagogical high school and obtain an exceptional permit for further study).

Interestingly, advancement in the PRL, even for people of the "right" origin, was strictly controlled and not easy. In the planned economy and with heightening parameterization, social mobility was also planned and controlled (cf. chapter 4). In certain cases, newly gained political capital based on class origin worked unexpectedly—top-down regulations meant that their origin could give some candidates access to higher education, and, even without active participation in the ZMP or the PZPR, even a job too.[36] Young people were subject to work orders, university referrals, and other mechanisms regulating social advancement. Also, factory-funded scholarships were more attractive options for the working classes than the intelligentsia; by collecting such a stipend, the student was obliged to repay it as a qualified worker at the given work establishment. Future professors often had to avoid "privileges" such as guaranteed workplaces to continue their education. As one interviewee recalls:

> One person per class, sometimes two, could be excused a work order if they were going to university, but they had to distinguish themselves in some way at school. And I was fortunate enough to be excused the work order, but my 18-year-old friends, girls and boys were referred to rural schools, and here—in central Poland and the western territories. Low wages, very tough working conditions. But what is really worth mentioning is that they were not afraid of that hardship, they did not shirk it.[37]

On top of this came even more curious situations, when the very mechanisms meant to facilitate education and guarantee work on its completion brought about the opposite effect at the level of individual practices.[38] Similarly, another professor had to avoid being awarded a scholarship in order to go to university at all.

> After completing middle school, I then completed high school, and they tried to give me a work order at a school, because as a pupil, despite all the difficulties and arrears that there were, I had caught up on a lot of things and distinguished myself appropriately. I belonged to a sort of class elite, one of the best pupils. I decided to go to university. Since it was a pedagogical high school, there was a lack of teachers after the war, so they tried to rope me in, the money would be useful, and I was awarded a scholarship by the department and they tried to force me to accept it. But a couple of months before the leaving exams. I refused to accept the scholarship, anticipating that if I took the money, there'd be a condition, I'd have to work it off. And as a result, I got into university.[39]

These unusual situations that came about were the avoidance of privilege—the theoretically better and safer conditions of a career guaranteed by the state represented an obstacle to continuing one's education, which was so highly sought-after. The reproduction process was reinforced by the tendency of representatives of the rural and urban working classes to make "bad" choices on the way to higher education. Some of these might have resulted from ignorance, but they also occurred because of the need for security. For example, from the perspective of a peasant's daughter, choosing a vocational school rather than a high school was a safer choice, as it provided her with a guaranteed trade, but it also reduced or even eliminated her chance of studying at a higher level. As mentioned, almost all the interviewees from peasant backgrounds completed pedagogical high schools, which meant that they should immediately start work and thus earn a living. A change to their educational path, and therefore also biographical path, came only through good fortune. In the case of the academic biography model, an individual completing a good middle school and then a general high school was predestined for further, higher level, study. Inequalities were thus reinforced—on top of social origin came the choice of secondary school, then courses chosen and degree subject taken. As documented in Bourdieu's works on the French educational system, the highest success rate was recorded for students with a classical education—not because this developed skills that would prove to be of use later, but because this was a course chosen by pupils with strongly internalized values of school institutions and the requirements they set.[40]

The narrators in question chose history, biology, and geography as their subjects. These disciplines are popular among students from the working classes, and especially those with rural origins. What initially triggered interest in these fields can be traced back to the topics of lectures at prewar people's universities, the memoirs of self-taught individuals, and the holdings of public libraries in villages and workers' districts.[41] An interest in biology and geography seems to be related to close contact with nature; as one of the interviewees recalls: "I spent a lot of time in my youth by the river, in the forest. So, I knew about nature, understood it, but didn't have names for it."[42] History, meanwhile, was of interest because of its relatively high accessibility through oral family histories and popular literature available in local libraries, such as Józef Kraszewski's and Nobel Prize–winner Henryk Sienkiewicz's historical novels.[43] As one of the narrators born in the 1940s remembers:

> My parents, as I've mentioned, although they were not educated people, read a lot. In fact, in our house, I read books—Mickiewicz's *Pan Tadeusz*, Sienkiewicz's books, *With Fire and Sword*, *The Deluge*, and others—as soon as I learned to read, very early. Later I read all the history books available in the so-called school library, then the district library.[44]

Many intellectuals who had advanced socially had met many obstacles on their paths; sometimes their origins determined their later interests. Prefaces and introductions to Bourdieu's works almost always mention his social background[45] as a factor explaining his later interests. Deborah Reed-Danahay underlines the similarity between his biography (Bourdieu was the son of a provincial postal worker) and the life stories of socially advanced intellectuals like the Breton writer Pierre-Jakez Hélias, the American writer Richard Rodriguez,[46] a folklorist and the son of rural immigrants (who focused on ethnic distinctiveness), and Richard Hoggart, whose interests in the working class are closely enmeshed in his own biography.[47] Antonina Kłoskowska uses a similar analogy in the introduction to the Polish edition of *Reproduction in Education, Society and Culture*, comparing Bourdieu's biography with that of Józef Chałasiński. Their different writing style notwithstanding,[48] Bourdieu's argument (like that of Hoggart) is similar to that made forty years earlier by the Polish sociologist.

In his book *Młode pokolenie chłopów* (The Young Generation of Peasants),[49] Chałasiński distinguished between the "pupil model" and the "shepherd model," the latter involving social advance, which leads to the peasant becoming disinherited from his own cultural context. This leaves him with three potential paths: (1) submitting to the system and abandoning attempts to overcome the deprivation caused by advancement; (2) despite submitting, attempting to achieve individual success within the system; (3) rejecting—to use Bourdieu's terms—the arbitrary of legitimate culture. This last option entails an attempt to position one's own value system against the dominant culture and the institutions that underpin it. Only this path leads to true emancipation. Chałasiński himself sought to follow it as an interwar agrarian and then founder of the socialized university model. Bourdieu, meanwhile, only seems to see an emancipatory potential in replacing the former culture with a new one, with new rules of the arbitrary and its own set of legitimate values (in the spirit of modernists or Proletkult activists). The policy of the previously dominated fluctuates between that of appropriating the cultural heritage passed down by the dominant classes/nations and that of rehabilitating the remnants of the dominated culture. This is starkly visible in the Soviet debates of the 1930s.[50]

CRAFT

Both interwar and postwar research on peasant students at the post-Habsburg Jagiellonian University in Cracow underlined their tenacity, assiduity, or even a "fanatic devotion to work taken from home."[51] Education was seen as an escape from hard work in a field, and many young people not only knew perfectly well how much effort was taken by their families to assure their education, but also needed to prove that they worked just as hard, but differently.

A strong work ethos is present in all the professors' narratives despite their social background, yet this is an ethos associated with the intelligentsia mission, a search of discovery, or an irresistible passion for pure knowledge . . . but not with work in the sense of craft. The latter is the understanding of the work ethos that seems to emerge in the narratives of people from the working classes. As one of the professors says, "I treated my studies as work—you get nothing without working for it, so I studied." He was a hard-working and conscientious student (otherwise he would not have been there), who also illustrates his attitude to his studies with a story about a student award:

> As was the case then, there were a lot of exams, I was surprised in the autumn because I got into university in 1949, so in the autumn of 1950 my colleagues informed me that I was on the list, I'd received a prize for passing the exam, so I couldn't really understand at all how you could be given an award for something that you were obliged to do.[52]

Another interviewee of peasant origins even uses factory terminology, explaining:

> In academia, you never feel your shift is over, as there's always something you have to do. Even when you come home from work, you get away at any time to sit at a desk or table and read, write, make notes, do something.[53]

The craftsman's work ethos involves satisfaction at getting the job done. All the interviewees were aware of their advancement:

> The awards I have are absolutely enough for me, what I've achieved in my life, for someone who went to a third-rate elementary school in [name of small town], I've accomplished a great deal, I never dreamed of all that, actually I only ever dreamed of one thing: to complete high school, to get that far, and everything else, I just treat as a bonus. There was a chance, so I took it, I went to university. There was a chance, so I did my doctorate. [. . .] Professor Szczepański was asked to tell us how he had put together such a body of work. So, he says, like a highlander: if you spend several decades getting up at five every morning and doing something, it all adds up. And it added up for him.[54]

The interviewees climbed the educational ladder with great determination, as is particularly clear in the case of the professor born in 1914. Each successive choice, like attending pedagogical high school, taking the risk of not responding to the work order, or turning down a stipend in order to go to university, were all turning points away from a socially anticipated career, their biographical path determined by the family's social space.

GENERATIONS AND CLASS

In addition to having a craftsman's work ethos, the interviewees are often activist types like their parents, whose social engagement and desire for education allowed them to change their children's educational path. This kind of relish for the city, the university, and cultural possibilities was typical for the peasant student emigrating to an educational center.[55] One interviewee relates his wonder at the opportunities that living in a city brings, and how he grabbed the cultural opportunities offered by Łódź with "both hands," as well as getting involved in the Union of Polish Youth and participating in building student dormitories. He became an activist—a real Subbotnik,[56] the first to turn up at a meeting or to dig foundations for new tram tracks. But at the time, he was never quite aware of the complexity of the situation. He cites a heroic action that must have taken place around 1953–1954:

> There was an election. I don't remember if it was to Parliament or the national councils. And at school, not far from the Jaracz Theater, there was a polling station. One of the lads ran up and said that some hooligans were making trouble there. And . . . instantly, without being provoked, students, who held a range of views and were not always enthusiastic about what was then called the new or present reality, that is, the People's Republic, but hearing that something was going on at the polling station, straightaway they all set off to help. Before the police could arrive, we'd quickly dealt with those hooligans, and order was restored.[57]

It is of course possible that those hooligans were just some drunkards, and what was happening was not an opposition demonstration. The interview took place in the 2010s after a number of political purges, a revival of a totalitarian paradigm, and an anticommunist memory policy offensive.[58]

Owing to their origins, different habitus, and the "ZMP generation" context, these narrators are more inclined to oppose elements of the liberal university model—yet these tend to take the form of minor comments on its aberrations, rather than any comprehensive critique. One of the obligations of the academic field, reinforced in the case of autobiographies, is to present the field as coherent and tension-free. This is visible in the biographies of people of working-class origin too. Conflicts sometimes arise in the context of an exchange of ideas, in arguments and free debate, but rarely as personal animosities, or even excessively heated paradigmatic battles. Of course, there were conflicts, which presumably often determined somebody's career path, accumulating with academic and political disputes. The absence of such differences in these narratives probably reveals the obligation to construct a conflict-free biography.

The narrators' biographies are torn between elements of the peasant habitus and the rules of the academic field. The often-described rupture in the biography, a rupture relating to advancement,[59] takes on another dimension in the context of socialist modernization. Social engagement and the significance attached to teaching might be associated with a sense of owing a debt to one's class of origin. The professors usually completely lose touch with the rural community from which they come. They feel grateful to the system or society as a whole for offering them the chance to study. This might be described as a sense of guilt toward the community that they left, something present in people who have advanced.

Both Bourdieu and the aforementioned Pierre-Jakez Hélias touch upon the motif of the divided world that results from leaving home. Bourdieu calls this cleavage resulting from upward mobility, *habitus clivé*[60]—meaning a kind of formative experience of being an outsider in both the class to which one aspires and one's class of origin, to which a return is no longer possible. Hoggart calls such cases—such as himself, Bourdieu, Chałasiński, and Szczepański—"scholarship boys,"[61] and Chałasiński uses the term "the shepherd model." Like Bourdieu, they each emphasize the sense of loss and exclusion that comes with their advancement, "full of unease and uprooted from the soil," people who forever feel an inner anxiety that comes with not belonging to any group. According to Hoggart, the alienation is especially acute for averagely capable people (although he writes only of "boys") who lose their bond with their community of origin and receive little in return—as he puts it, "They have, in some degree, lost their hold on one kind of life, and failed to reach the one to which they aspire. The loss is greater than the gain."[62] In the biographies of professors—after all, the most able group, or at least the group making the fullest use of the structural possibilities provided by the PRL—the gain is enormous.

SELECTION AND LANGUAGE

Although the postwar social imaginary draws different possibilities, new career paths, and the generation of educational desire, the change remained incomplete. In the retired professors' narratives, their differences from the habitus are no longer discernible, but these reveal themselves on the margins of the story and in the form it takes, including its language and narrative structure. In her book on the new intelligentsia, Palska quotes Stefan Żeromski: "A snobbish attitude will lead this new wave of intelligentsia away from the peasantry, naturally ashamed of their domestic commonness and contemptuous of the speech of their uncouth fathers, to overdo things when cultivating a lordly, urban and worldly manner of speech."[63] In addition to their restricted linguistic code,[64] children from rural backgrounds faced the problem of their dialect;

this concerned not just vocabulary, but also an intonation and accent that they had to lose. This issue is hardly mentioned by the interviewees, with one exception: "Quite soon, probably thanks to appropriate reading, teachers and the whole community, I lost all trace of my dialect."[65]

Another consequence is the hypercorrectness characteristic of those who have undergone social advancement.[66] For a person experiencing upward mobility, "a hundred habits of speech and manners can 'give him away' daily."[67] Often during the interviews, it was people from intellectual homes who would make language errors, while the few interlocutors from families with lower cultural capital were greater linguistic purists. One of them, from a railwayman's family, not only paid close attention to the correct construction of his own oral statements, later re-editing the entire interview, but also corrected the slightest mistake made by other people, including me, the interviewer.

Indeed, language plays an important role in selection mechanisms. In the debate on linguistic deficit, the issue of educational opportunities and the role of language has also been explored.[68] Language is one of the first obstacles or first transparent facilitators on the educational path. For children from homes with high cultural capital, correct pronunciation and syntax, as well as a rich vocabulary, are an obvious, although often invisible, privilege. For peasant and working-class children, dialect, accent, and grammatical errors are one of the earliest perceptible obstacles that distance them from the academic biographical path. Linguistic deficits are significant even at the earliest thresholds of school selection. From this somewhat deterministic perspective, educational failure is closely related to linguistic competencies. First, the way one experiences the world is closely conditioned by the linguistic code one uses. Second, dialect does not belong to the dominant culture and is depreciated—both urban and rural working-class children must stop using it to function effectively in the school system. In addition, academic teachers tend to wrongly assume linguistic manifestations of intelligence, resulting from "class ethnocentrism."[69] One of the methods that the institution of the university employs to generate distance is academic language, which is marked by a casual ease, colorful metaphors, and oratorical embellishment that there is no need to teach. So, while the first step to advancement involves dropping local dialect and provincial accents and expanding one's vocabulary and linguistic structures, the next, much harder one is to learn academic language.

There is a closed circle of mutual recognition of the institutions and the people enjoying educational success. It is easier for people with a high cultural capital to experience this, as educational institutions are an element of their culture—they recognize them as legitimate and are in turn recognized as legitimate, which reinforces their educational success. The associated belief in the uniform social background of pupils and students translates into a learned ignorance of the selection processes. The assumption of students' equality in the system means that possessing talent (intelligence, sensitivity, skill) or otherwise is perceived as the only cause of inequality, and class origin is ignored. The education system transforms the predispositions brought from home into supposed endeavor and sacrifice.[70] Academia itself rejects its own academic nature by punishing excessively scholastic statements from working-class students. It places eloquence and appropriate tastes and the ease and linguistic structures of the upper classes before diligent preparation. The tastes and ease of the upper classes thus become more important than preparation—learning by rote, being true to teachers' interpretations or a certain orthodoxy toward the official interpretation. At the same time, precisely the same traits that gave working-class children their place in the school system are depreciated at high school level and entirely undesirable at university.

STABILITY

The next common element of the working class and peasant professors' biographies is their poverty as students contrasted with their later stability. Undergraduate days and the first years of work as an assistant are a time of lack of money and privation. References to scarcities are balanced by later successes, or rather the scale of success is determined with reference to the wretched starting point:

> When I started work, as I said, I got married earlier, we had children earlier, and we lived, I'd say, modestly and poorly. My shoes were, not to put too fine a point on it, not Paris fashion, or even Łódź or [name of a small town] fashion. The professor once stared at those shoes and said: "Young man, but you can't wear those shoes in winter." "Aw, Professor, I'm not ill, I can wear them." He took 500 zloty out of his wallet: "Young man, off you go to the shop right away [. . .] and buy yourself some decent shoes."[71]

This story also depicts the familiar relations with one's mentor. What is significant here, though, is the contrast between the initial situation and the portrayal of the later comfortable life:

> During the week we'd eat lunch in the canteen, and the children. when they were small, would have theirs at nursery school, but on Sunday we could afford to take the whole family out for lunch at a good restaurant. Often at the Grand Hotel in the blue room, which was cozier than the raspberry room. Or at other good restaurants.[72]

The restaurant in question was not only good, but one of Łódź's most exclusive venues. Other interviewees not only particularly valued being allocated a flat or owing a car, but also other, simpler events such as having milk delivered to their door by the Społem (Together) Consumers' Cooperative.[73]

The postwar years were difficult for a whole generation and poverty was underlined in most of the stories. Hardships were a common experience among all social strata; for a brief historical moment it was not restricted to the lowest classes. By no means was it a race to the bottom caused by a new government, but rather a short period when economic capital didn't come into play. Even cultural capital could not be made to operate efficiently as symbolic capital. On the one hand postwar equality in poverty allowed those few determined pupils to get through another selection barrier, on the other it served as a reference point to further stabilization provided by the entrenching People's Poland. Thus, the approaching stabilization was bringing a modernization project with working classes in its center.

The narrators tend to express gratitude toward the PRL, albeit some more explicitly than others. At many points, a strong affection for and idealization of this period is stated even though it was being devalued by the public when the materials were gathered. In general, the professors of modest origin certainly benefited from the preceding political system, and some were party members or members of the ZMP during their student days. During this period, they benefited from scholarships, free accommodation, and subsidized canteens, and at the same time, the reconstruction of the social imaginary led to their being valued citizens and showed them new possibilities. This group was supposed to be the foundation of the rebuilding and the loyal new intelligentsia. One interviewee underscores the duty placed upon him as a professor educated with public money: "I grew up in an atmosphere in which you make use of the benevolence of society, and need to give something back to society for all that," adding elsewhere:

> On the whole, I must say that life was more interesting and perhaps more creative, and I'm not quite able to understand that Poland has been born twice. It was baptized once,[74] and then again in 1989. Because I remember my dream, you see, as a little kid, what I thought of Poland. Whatever it was, for it to be Poland.[75]

In state-socialist Poland, the lives of ordinary people were also supposedly different: "Relations between people, I must say, were full of goodwill back then,"[76] or further on: "There was a great sense of social security. People were poor, but everybody was poor. So, it didn't hurt so much as when you're poor and you see the undeserved wealth of others. Second, there was discernible progress from year to year." It is worth noting that it was the same narrator who ate Sunday lunches at the Grand Hotel who said this.

The narrator who graduated in medicine from the University of Łódź[77] makes an interesting remark. Aware of the political situation in the context of his background, he writes:

> I wish to express my deep-rooted conviction, that comes from my family background and community, and not as the result of indoctrination, that I consider myself a beneficiary of the social transformations that took place in our country after liberation and allowed me and others like me access to knowledge.[78]

Another interviewee praises not only the flat awarded to him or the aforementioned bottle of milk delivered to the door by the consumer's cooperative, but also the money allocated him for conducting research and business trips permitted "without restrictions, when needed."[79] Many of the professors from outside the selected peasant biographies stress the favorable financial situation of academia. At the same time, far more frequent mention is made of issues such as obstacles to trips, excessive bureaucracy, difficulties with getting hold of publications from the West, or long waits for reagents ordered in exemplary fashion.

Apart from substantial scholarships, the democratization of higher education—and not simply from the individuals' own perspective—is also presented as a key postwar accomplishment: "I share the joy [. . .] that after 1945, rural youth swarmed to middle schools. [. . .] Today I regret that this swarm has come to a halt."[80] Interviewees from the intelligentsia, though left-leaning party members, also comment on the scale and significance of this phenomenon:

> Sometimes when I listen to the recollections of young people, the reflections of young journalists or young politicians, on the darkness that hung over the land in communist times, I feel a little uneasy, and I'm extremely critical toward all historical materials. I must say that I'm a huge skeptic when it comes to so-called historical studies because I look at what gets written about the People's Republic at the moment and I'm able to judge what happened and compare it with the opinions that are now coming out on the subject. I certainly didn't feel any . . . perhaps I'm applying another comparative scale here. A young man [himself], who, from the level of school libraries and everything found in bookshops, immediately entered a world of, indeed, very intellectually significant people.[81]

Another interviewee notes: "Although we are talking here of the lives of individuals, after the war, the move from a squalid hut, with collectivization, electrification, it was, after all, an amazing revolution. Certainly, for those people, it was an exceptional leap."[82] In one autobiography, an author from an intellectual background takes issue with negative evaluations, not so much with the communist era as with Stalinism, arguing that what is forgotten today is the need to rebuild one's own life. In her opinion, the disavowal and negative assessment of Stalinism that took place in the 1990s are analogous to the condemnation of the Warsaw Uprising that occurred at that time.[83] In this context, the verdict on the transformation of 1989 is decidedly critical.

MINOR DIFFERENCES

According to the collected biographical materials, there are only minor differences distinguishing the academic careers of people of intelligentsia origin from those of the working classes. All had a strong work ethic and participated in extra activities, whether as scouts, party or ZMP members, or just in student life more generally. They all also broke through the limitations of their class (gaps in knowledge, language), sketching in their biographies a path from a rural cottage to the department. The distinguishing features of the biographies were:

1. The role of the family home—low cultural capital and the significant role of external factors such as the schoolteacher, an organization (scouts, "Wici"), or the influence of the state-socialist institutions.
2. The choice of a pedagogical high school as a relatively safe path, guaranteeing a career after graduation, and also not closing the path to higher education, in contrast to vocational or technical high schools.
3. The need to avoid privilege—The postwar system created paths of advancement for the new intelligentsia only up to a certain rung of the social ladder. To climb higher, right up to the most prestigious positions, it was necessary to break away from the socialist past of the new intelligentsia's biographical path created by the institutional framework by avoiding a work order or not accepting a scholarship that would need to be paid off later by working.
4. Significant nonacademic activity—The interviewees were active in university life, party members, and often engaged in social actions. An interesting context is provided by research on academic teachers carried out in the 1980s.[84] This showed that certain characteristics of individuals hardly correlate at all—type of university, community and origin—and the remaining correlations do not form any pattern. The only exception was if someone's father was educated to a level lower than the average in the community, then there was a positive correlation with membership of the PZPR and ZMP, and a negative one with belonging to independent organizations. This data is confirmed by observations from the qualitative analysis of the interviews and autobiographies.
5. A positive attitude toward the PRL, a sense of gratitude for the political changes of the postwar period, disappointment at the transformation, and a critical view

of the post-1989 period, as well as contemporary evaluations of the communist era.

One of the interviewees used the final lines of Ignacy Krasicki's poem *Prostak* (The Simpleton) to describe his own biography. The whole of this poem provides a good summary of the structural conditions of peasant academic biographies:

> Happy wise men; and we, simpletons / So can we too be happy? / Everything comes easily to them, to us from toil / Yet we live on the same Earth. / They in their merits have a team, / They think as they wish, and I as I can.
>
> Simpleton, as father and mother said, / I fulfill it in my simplicity. / I see that the others have studied more, / I hear that they speak highly of virtue. / I don't know how; when will I step up, / Wishing to be virtuous, I do what I can.
>
> I don't have the honor of being a Capuchin, / But I have the privilege of being a good chap; / And so I simply follow the crowd, / I follow fate, I follow the age, / And the beaten path chosen, / I say what I think, I do what I can.[85]

However, the differences mentioned are only points in the whole biography, which are essentially no different from the others—they too are ordered by academic degrees and other markers of the field. Despite the initial contrast of the educational paths, the widely varying conditions in the family home, and the lack of economic and social capital, the structure of peasant biographies follows almost the same track as the intelligentsia ones. The academic doxa encompasses all professors. (See table 8.1.)

HYSTERESIS

It was those who experienced the remarkable leap from the "squalid hut" to higher education who in later years would fill factory offices, hospitals, courts, and schools. However, they were far less likely to end up in university departments. Those who did manage to do so entered a milieu alien to them. In the academic field, it was still rather a liberal than a socialist university model that was in place. It continued to be the prewar academic habitus that was valued, and the structural changes in the political field were viewed as hostile outside interventions. Young novices arrived at university with a very hazy idea of what studying meant and what a university and scholarship were. They were beneficiaries of the transformations and believed in the system and the opportunities it gave them. They were ideal material for the new socialist faculty. So why is this not what they became? Why are their biographies so similar to those of the

TABLE 8.1 ACADEMIC CAREER MODEL WITH DIFFERENCES RESULTING FROM PROFESSORS' PEASANT ORIGIN

HOME AND CHILDHOOD	STUDIES	ACADEMIA	COMPLETION
	TRAJECTORY OF ACADEMIC BIOGRAPHY		
Family origins First inspirations First mentor (parent/teacher) Predispositions	Conscious and free choice of subject Occupying place in the field Followed by employment	Successive academic degrees Networking Trips and stipends External opinions Teaching	Students and schools Prizes and awards Valedictions and tributes Continued activity Distinguished place in the field Further employment
	DIFFERENCES IN PEASANT BIOGRAPHIES		
Low cultural capital External factor changing the trajectory	Safe career choices Avoiding privilege in the Polish People's Republic	Engagement and active participation in political life	Sentiment for previous era Criticism of transformation post-1989

others—both at the structural level and that of the presented rules of the field? Why did the model of traditional academia and its values, which had been compromised in public discourse, become their model?

On the one hand the academic field was meant to adapt to political changes. This led to resistance from the prewar academic habitus and attempts to reconstruct the traditional university modeled on the liberal university. As we have seen, changes at this level excluded many prewar professors from institutional life, enabled careers supported by political capital, and finally opened up huge possibilities for the urban and rural working classes as the new intelligentsia. Hysteresis slows these changes down—the inertia of the habitus delays change. On the other hand, the hysteresis effect also worked within the academic field with its vector pointing in the opposite direction. The doxa of the academic field remained unchanged. The young university novices wishing to take their place in it had to adapt to the habitus of prewar academia. Therefore, on the one hand the postwar social system provided new paths of social mobility. It offered a change in the structures of the academic field through pressure from the political field and unveiled new possibilities to the actors, especially those who had previously been excluded, who had been most affected by the selection mechanisms. On the other hand, after embarking on the academic path, the beneficiaries of the socialist transformations went on to adopt the traditional academic habitus almost entirely. The radical modernization project did not have an impact on either the internal rules of the field or the traditional university model.

The narrative of the captive university and shackled knowledge represented in some of the intellectual biographies and in the historical discourse on the PRL has concealed the highly conservative nature of the academic field. In fact, it was extremely resistant to change. To a large degree, the academic field preserved its autonomy and its well-established body of values and criteria, enabling a position to be taken within it. In this way, the hysteresis effect plays out not between the political field and academic's habitus, but between the permanence of the academic field and the habitus of the working classes. The academic habitus always demands some work from those entering the academic field, yet its scope varies depending on the individual's initial distance from the field itself—which is greatest and most difficult to cover for the working classes. The academic field remained sufficiently autonomous for the habitus of those entering it "illicitly" to undergo a stronger hysteresis effect than the traditional entrants—this was shown by Chałasiński in the interwar peasant biographies. This still occurred despite radical attempts to rebuild the entire education system.

In one of his books, Terry Eagleton cites an anecdote about Professor Arthur Quiller-Couch, who in the 1920s would begin his lectures at Cambridge with the phrase "Gentlemen," although the lecture group largely consisted of women.[86] This is how the hysteresis of the academic habitus works. In 1960s France, education was popularized, but not democratized. The respective proportions of the social profile of students had remained the same. One might well expect that the influx of a larger number of worse-prepared students would have meant that academic instruction would have adapted to its level of sophistication, especially as many teachers had benefited from social advancement too, and also would have had to assimilate to the academic habitus from the outset. Yet this did not happen. Teachers who had undergone advancement were all the more zealous to defend the traditional values and esoteric language of academia to prove their authenticity and legitimacy in the field. They acknowledged the outward signs of mastering knowledge (like linguistic correctness), being awarded titles and subtle status symbols, and perceived all attempts at change as a threat.[87]

The same thing could be seen in postwar academia in the PRL—the prewar university, haunted by the vision of itself as a liberal university, defended itself from an "invasion by the barbarians." The changes introduced with the building of the socialist university were only a facade. At the level of the field as a whole, there was little change in the education system. To put it too crudely: socialist privilege has yielded to the traditional one. The emphasis placed on educating young people (born in the 1920s and 1930s) to be the new intelligentsia did not reach the academic field. For example, one of the authors of the analyzed autobiographies mentions that during the Stalinist period, as a young assistant, she was dismissed from her job. Yet this did not harm her academic career much, since when she wrote her memoirs, she was a professor at the same institution. According to Connelly, of eleven assistants dismissed as a result of the 1948 reform, nine of them continued their academic careers. Furthermore, in 1951–1954, the titles of professor and associate professor were awarded to 302 people, only 41 of whom were party members.[88]

As the example of Chałasiński and sociology shows, the names of departments, lectures, and research were changed, but the content remained practically the same. Academia managed to stay largely unaffected by the top-down changes. Among the academic faculty studied in the 1980s, out of 2,000 academic teachers, 68 percent of teachers at universities were from an intelligentsia background (59 percent at polytechnics), while among students surveyed in 1979, the majority of those wishing to continue an academic career were from intelligentsia homes.[89] It is important to remember that, once an academic career had been embarked on, selection mechanisms continued to operate, limiting the possibilities of occupying a position in the field, right up to the acquisition of the title of professor—and the autobiographies, memoirs, and interviews summing up academic lives concerned only professors.

Contrary to public opinion, it was not simply political pressures that determined one's opinions and views about the university; of equal importance was the position one held in the academic field. It was the "pariahs" of the prewar system,[90] consigned to the margins of the academic field before the war, who wanted to build the socialist university. This is who Chałasiński and Szczepański were. Neither the influence of the political field nor social background fully explains practice or events in the biographies.

The anticipated biographical path for people from working classes had been forsaken, but the new one demanded sacrifice and the adoption of a new habitus. The new intelligentsia, the "hawk generation,"[91] were able to adopt the model of the socialist habitus—thanks to the socialist privilege they then took up positions as specialists, the technical intelligentsia, and no doubt also faculty at technical and agricultural colleges. To occupy a position at the apex of the academic field, however, among the adherents of the elite of traditional academia pursuing pure science and disinterested scholarship, they had to adapt to the rules in place there. The educational system is capable of sustaining the social structure, and also of ensuring controlled mobility through the selection of a few people from the working classes. They are only admitted into the academic world with the proviso of assimilating the habitus of the traditional university. The academic field fended off any influx of new faculty with a socialist habitus. Narratives about captive or shackled academia lose sight of the key dimension of the change—the symbolic violence of the political field was not as strong as that within the academic field. John Connelly is therefore right when he writes of the defeat of the communists in their confrontation with the Polish professorship;[92] however, his argument does not take into account internal struggles in academia and the initial potential of places like Łódź.

To simplify Bourdieu's perspective somewhat, the function of pedagogical conservatism is for a small group of the dominant classes to defend their position. They protect their positions from the invasion of barbarians, their weapon in this fight being the defense of the social order and higher culture (with the cultural arbitrary hidden as universal). Just as the intelligentsia in the Soviet Union aspired to the values of the dethroned bourgeoisie, sending their children to piano lessons and filling their dining rooms with heavy sideboards and cabinets,[93] so too the young scholars entering the world of academia also desired the attributes of power and prestige of a world that was supposed to have disappeared. To a great extent, this is not a generational conflict as much as a conflict of classes—of their values and languages.[94] This tension had already become visible in interwar Poland, and socialist modernization only exposed it more, rather than overcoming it. The conflict between the intelligentsia and the working classes appeared at many levels: aesthetic taste, life orientation, attitude to faith, and so on.[95] In the case of the narrative about "captive academia," the political dimension of change obscured all the others. This concentration on institutions and their policies typifies not only the totalitarian paradigm but conventional history in general.[96] The hysteresis effect worked on two levels, but only one was prominent.

At the same time, discourse about the PRL was primarily produced by the intelligentsia, who regarded, as well as experienced, state socialism as regressive. Their hegemonic position in cultural production was threatened by the socialist modernization project. This helps explain the dominance of the narrative of darkness, captivity or Homo Sovieticus. Perspectives that viewed Poland's postwar history as a modernization project, one of emancipation or the empowerment of thousands of people were easily marginalized as the sentimental visions of party people, the effect of unconscious indoctrination, or the seduction of the young by totalitarian propaganda. Indeed, the project failed. Bourdieu tries to show, in *The State Nobility* for instance, that the presence of *les miraculés* in higher education does not demonstrate the democratization of the system, but rather that the uniqueness of this particular group reveals that the reproduction mechanisms operate from the earliest school years.[97] In the case of postwar Poland and peasant children advancing to become university professors, this meant their inclusion in the huge modernizing machinery of postwar reconstruction and Stalinism. It was not possible to change the social system, including the rules of reproduction, without changing the whole education system[98]—which was why there was an upturn in the number of students from urban and rural working-class backgrounds, but not a permanent one. The controlled mobility of outside individuals essentially underpinned the social structure.

Factors such as the social consequences of the revolution and the successes of democratization meant perhaps greater egalitarianism for the next generations of professors, those born in the 1940s and 1950s—not so much in higher education, but at lower levels. Yet the academic field as a whole retained its conservative character, and the criteria and rules for holding a position, the declared values, an idealized vision of academia, and the desired mentor-student relations survived. It is astounding that the field was able to absorb and neutralize all manifestations of the postwar attempt to change its structure, labeling them as captivity or including them in the doxa of the discipline. For example, Chałasiński is today presented above all as a doyen of sociology, rather than a radical reformer and pioneer of the idea of the socialized university.[99] The social revolution of 1939–1956 and the socialist modernization project created opportunities for advancement on an unprecedented scale. Only to a limited extent, however, did it transform the academic field in terms of values, rules of the field, and the university model. This is how the state-guaranteed socialist privilege for the working classes has been limited by the traditional privilege of the intelligentsia and its reproduction.

CONCLUSIONS

THE RAPID POSTWAR MODERNIZATION UNDERTAKEN IN POLAND TRIED TO industrialize, urbanize, and electrify the country; encourage more frequent handwashing; get people to leave the church; and emancipate women, all within one lifetime. The final collapse of the largest "deliberate social experiment" has been framed by some as the "end of history" and the final victory of liberal democracy; by others as the twilight of an industrial era and modernity as such.[1] Other explanations focus on axiology and a failure to build common socialist values.[2] Reformists' efforts became "modernization without substance."[3] The newly established institutions never achieved cultural hegemony.[4] While this seems true with regard to universities and professors, it does not diminish the scale of upward mobility including that of future faculty.

Modernization attempts can be totalitarian and based on force. However, the case of postwar Poland seems much more complicated, even paradoxical. This modernization project was designed to reshape society and turn marginalized groups into citizens. This paradoxical citizenship did not offer freedom of speech or civil rights, but rather a socialist welfare state with public health care, pensions, paid holidays, public kindergartens, and access to universities. Educational reforms were designed to include rather than exclude, serve the people's state, and conduct engaged research. This provided traditionally marginalized groups with a central position in the social imaginary, as well as a vision of a decent life and open possibilities. State socialism was an integral and indivisible—even dialectical—part of Western capitalism, a crucial player in decolonization, and a reference point for social and political thought; this fruitful and eye-opening perspective has been growing in recent scholarship.[5]

In the book's introduction, I claimed that the narrative about the political field's domination of the academic field appears far less secure once we start to trace the reproduction of prewar traditions and structures. More precisely, my argument undermines two main narratives about postwar universities in Poland and Eastern Europe: a story about captivity and a story about seduction. In this narrative, the university's traditions and values are undermined by political forces, which demand the production of specialists, which appeal for support for industrial development and expect the implementation of positive discrimination in favor of young people of working-class origin, and so on. Likewise, the postwar generation of students is considered to have been seduced by the vision of a new society and the creation of the "new intelligentsia."

As we traced the development of the socialist university, we saw what a complicated, even paradoxical process it was. Political reforms introduced in the late 1940s indeed profoundly influenced the organization of higher education, but they did not yet result in redefining its role and values. Academia was "parameterized," which means all its activities were measurable and countable by the Ministry of Higher Education. Universities were obliged to respect assigned quotas of students and graduates—as many as the planned economy needed. Courses became compulsory, and in opposition to what was called the "aristocratic manner of studying," students were supposed to work like workers in a factory: with almost eight hours per day of classes, roll call, and supervision of their efficiency. The first three years of study were designed to prepare students for practical tasks, and an additional final two years to give them more advanced skills and the *magister* (master's) degree. Contact between a student and a future workplace was encouraged during the course in order to obtain work experience. Universities were thus to become part of a production process aimed at training skilled specialists (with the humanities training future teachers and office workers). Censorship was reinforced, international cooperation strictly controlled, and many disciplines—like sociology—were labeled "bourgeois" and simply abolished.

Awareness of the changes that were implemented in the United States and Western Europe during the postwar decades throws into relief the transnational aspects of the Stalinization of higher education. The democratization of universities was a global phenomenon as was the coupling of higher education with the economy. Solutions like internships in future workplaces or efforts to produce the professionals needed in industry might even seem more like capitalist than socialist solutions. The socialist university was different but not in the way that many picture it, as a captive, state-controlled, and highly censored institution. Yes, the central planning, state management, and political control were more direct, strict, and exposed. However, the most crucial difference was to be found in the declared goals of reforming universities under state socialism, namely their promotion of equal access to higher education and its benefits for the rest of society. It was these values and the vision of future society as well as the role of the university within it that made this model of the socialist university an alternative to a capitalist one. Discursive declarations—in the daily press and political speeches—that championed the universities' accessibility and their responsibility to wider society more strongly define the socialist university model. They were not just empty promises, but their realization was impossible to pursue. The role of the state was to shield these values from market-driven logic. To what extent political pressure like censorship was a side effect and to what extent a necessary condition of operation remains an open question.

The first stage of the spectacular postwar reconstruction brought about certain effects: the formation of numerous universities, a higher number of students and graduates, and also an increase in the number of students from the working and lower classes. However, following the postwar cohorts and individual biographical paths, one can see how limited that change was. The relatively egalitarian distribution of the student social profile, which is a key index from the perspective of educational democratization, turned out to be only temporary. The peak achievement occurred with the proportions of students in the first half of the 1950s. During that period, despite—or perhaps because of—the most stringent education policies, the best ratios of young working-class people were obtained: nearly 50 percent of all students. The same was the case with the situation for women.[6] The Stalinist period meant more possibilities of advancement for the working classes, while the Thaw meant a return to more traditional values, both at the gender as well as the class level. As Szczepański's research discussed in chapter 5 has shown, the window for upward mobility was short and narrow.

At a general level, it should be noted that universities did not evolve into the main site of the educational revolution. Everyday classism, the system's inefficiency, and traditional class divisions remained strong among professors and students. Change happened in trade schools and technical colleges rather than at universities. Despite this, the university still served as a symbol of open opportunities. Upward mobility was experienced above all by those at the two extremes of the social structure: the intelligentsia and the unskilled workers (who had started from the lowest position). While in 1957 one-third of Polish citizens were still unable to read and write and 7 percent of adults had never attended school, a new generation was graduating from universities. After thirty years of the socialist experiment, when the population of Łódź exceeded 850,000, over 95 percent of its citizens had a higher or at least secondary education. Before 1989, the number of graduates nationwide reached almost two million. Every next generation brought up during the PRL had a greater chance of attaining a higher level of education, and educational inequalities were decreasing.

Along with the intensification of educational policies, a number of measures that had been put in place in the immediate postwar period and were driven by the authentic engagement of their creators, and not by an imposed top-down structure, started to disintegrate. This applied to the preparatory courses as well as the Democratic Professorship Club. Empty slogans increasingly eclipsed real action. The image of the new intelligentsia, depicted from the outset in the press and in speeches, not only emphasized its substantive preparation, but also its ideological profile. Commitment was needed as much as knowledge. The success of modernization was only possible if there was mobilization for the cause.[7]

Simultaneously, the youngest generation of postwar Polish society showed significant support for the entire project of socialist modernization—the socialist privilege. At least during that period, students were its infrastructure. According to studies conducted at the University of Warsaw between 1957 and 1958, and repeated in 1978 and

1983, 70 percent of respondents strongly agreed with the question: "Would you be in favor of the world moving toward some socialist form?" In the later period, support for the project had been maintained whereas support for the authorities had declined.[8] It is often mentioned that the main goal of the socialist systems was the creation of "the new man."[9] Despite the relatively high participation of students in the ZMP (the Union of Polish Youth) during the first half of the 1950s, only 10 percent of students were members of the PZPR. That percentage was even lower among the professorate and did not exceed 7.5 percent.[10] While the idea that the ZMP generation and the new intelligentsia had been "seduced" may accurately describe the sentiments of that period or the specificity of certain narrow groups, it totally fails to illustrate the generational change or the wider social transformations taking place at the time. What really shaped society and its structure were established frameworks, both imaginary and institutional.

As was shown in the last chapters, the failure to produce a new academic intelligentsia was a problem not only of given generations but rather of given classes: their values and languages. For example, a profound difference in educational aspirations shaped the choices of worker and intelligentsia families. While the working classes wished for their children to simply avoid physical labor, the intelligentsia aimed at an academic career for their children—becoming a professor was the dream biographical plan. In the 1980s, 68 percent of academics teaching at universities were of intelligentsia origin, as were the students planning an academic career. The radical project of social reform did not influence the inner-ruled academia. The socialist privilege yielded to the traditional one. The narrative of a captive university produced by the totalitarian paradigm masks the highly conservative nature of the academic field and its high level of autonomy, especially with regard to values and the criteria for granting positions to newcomers. Interwar academia, seeing itself as an imagined liberal university, defended itself from the wave of "barbarians at the gates." Cultural capital—the domain of the intelligentsia—was endangered by political capital, but the academic field both defended its inner autonomy and managed to maintain hegemony over knowledge production. This is how state-provided socialist privilege tried to limit social reproduction and inevitably was limited by the traditional privilege of the intelligentsia.

The University of Łódź, planned as a center of the modernization project, an egalitarian institution open to the working classes, participated in the process of the reproduction of traditional academia. We can only surmise whether similar processes took place at universities with prewar traditions. It is possible that while in Łódź the city's working and revolutionary traditions did not work in favor of the university's development, they appear to have played a certain role. This city's traditions did not influence successive generations of professors, as did factors prevalent at the borders of the partitions. Maybe tradition had a stronger influence on other universities. Despite its initial ideological declarations, various educational measures, and political reforms, the

University of Łódź became an element of traditional academia. Compared with other Polish higher education institutions, its position and prestige were weak owing to its brief history and compromised—from the perspective of academia—workers' heritage. As an institution, it was able to successfully compete for a number of new investments, for which there was a chronic lack of money, and other quantitative indicators.[11] However, it never became the alternative type of university envisaged in the postwar modernization dream: a socialist university. It never became a place of educational advancement for the working classes to any greater degree than elsewhere in the country.

In conclusion, the mobility ladder for postwar cohorts was the trade schools, and even though a considerable number of working-class children did enter the universities, these were still definitely a minority. On the one hand the socialist university built a new intelligentsia on which the political system would depend. However, on the other hand this reproduced the liberal intelligentsia ethos that would eventually challenge that system. Classism among students and faculty, fears about academic degradation, and visions of pure and disinterested scholarship shaped the postwar university alongside political pressure, implemented reforms, and press campaigns. Symbolic power works not only by reproducing the academic habitus but, more than that, by producing historical discourses about the postwar period and the socialist university as such. Therefore, the story of social advancement and its limitations has been eclipsed by the martyrology of the intelligentsia and its heroic struggles for academic freedom.

Our peasant student, Mr. Temptation, probably did graduate from the university. He probably got a stable job in one of Łódź's factories. He probably got a small apartment in a block of flats in one of the newly built city districts like Widzew or Teofilów. His vaccinated children went to a nearby kindergarten and later a primary school built to mark the Millennium of the Polish State in 1966. Probability also indicates that they too had a good chance of getting into a general secondary school and finally obtaining a higher education degree. Mr. Temptation probably retired in the 1980s and received a state-guaranteed pension, just when state socialism was crumbling. It's easy to dismiss this image as postsocialist nostalgia. But it is tempting to think in terms of these probabilities.

APPENDIX

During the period under consideration in this study, statistics collated to better understand and document higher education did not include ethnicity, religion or, in most instances, gender. Tables were organized according to class background, as declared by the student or determined by the father's job status, or by level of education, or by rural/urban origin.

The dozens of archival statistics and tables surveyed were carefully drawn by hand. In the first postwar years, because of material shortages, these were drawn on reused paper, with some sheets even bearing swastikas from the previous regime. Later, the quality of the paper was so poor and fragile that the sheets were falling apart. In all cases, class was the main criterion of social division.

TABLE A.1 INCREASE IN NUMBERS OF ACADEMIC WORKERS IN POLAND IN SELECTED YEAR*

ACADEMIC LEVEL	NO. OF ACADEMIC WORKERS AND LECTURERS IN POLAND BY ACADEMIC YEAR				INCREASE IN % COMPARED TO 1937/1938
	1937/1938	1947/1948	1957/1958	1968/1969	
Professors and associate professors	907	2,044	2,954	4,968	325.7
Adjuncts and assistants	2,107	5,223	12,888	17,218	611.7
Lecturers and senior lecturers	157	391	1,525	2,672	971.3
Total	3,014	7,267	15,842	22,186	525.6

*On the basis of *Informator 1969*. . . , table 2, p. 1; *Rocznik statystyczny 1980*, op. cit.

TABLE A.2 THE SOCIAL MAKEUP OF THE FIRST GENERATIONS OF STUDENTS AT THE UNIVERSITY OF ŁÓDŹ/THE ŁÓDŹ UNIVERSITY OF TECHNOLOGY*

ACADEMIC YEAR	SOCIAL ORIGIN IN %			
	WORKERS	PEASANTS	INTELLIGENTSIA	OTHER
1947/1948	16/13	18/14	40/40	26/33
1948/1949	22/33	18/17	41/34	19/16
1949/1950	29/39	19/21	40/38	12/4

*On the basis of *Ze studiów humanistycznych*. . . , table 24 i 25, pp. 167–68.

TABLE A.3 THE SOCIAL MAKEUP OF STUDENTS AT THE UNIVERSITY OF ŁÓDŹ IN SELECTED YEARS BETWEEN 1945 AND 1969*

	SOCIAL ORIGIN IN %			
ACADEMIC YEAR	WORKERS	PEASANTS	INTELLIGENTSIA	OTHER
1945/1946	21	26	39	14
1948/1949	22	18	41	19
1951/1952	36	19	40	5
1954/1955	33	18	44	5
1957/1958	33	21	40	6
1960/1961	29	16	48	7
1963/1964	31	14	49	6
1966/1967	35	12	48	5
1968/1969	36	12	47	5

*On the basis of *Uniwersytet Łódzki 1945–1970*, p. 206.

TABLE A.4 NUMBER OF STUDENTS PER 10,000 CITIZENS FROM 1937 TO 1969*

ACADEMIC YEAR	POPULATION	STUDENTS	NO. OF STUDENTS PER 10,000 CITIZENS
1937/1938	34,515	49.5	14.4
1947/1948	23,929	94.8	39.6
1957/1958	28,540	162.7	57.0
1968/1969	32,426	305.6	94.2

*On the basis of *Informator 1969*, table 7, p. 10.

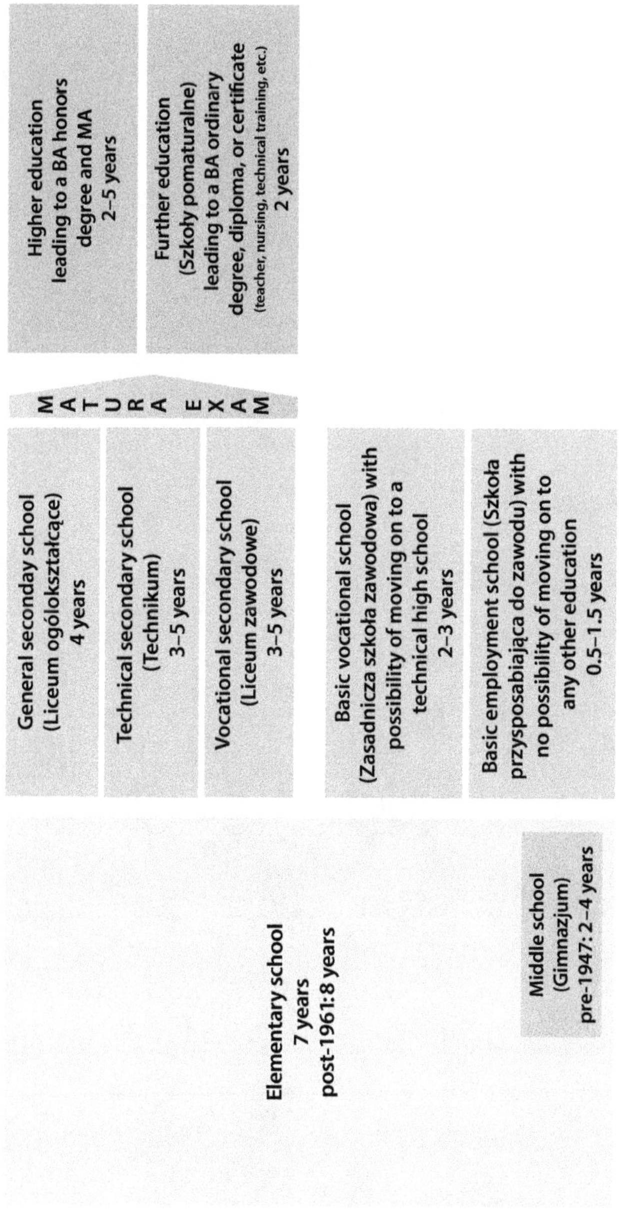

Figure A.1 Educational system in Poland 1945–1989.

NOTES

ACKNOWLEDGMENTS

1. Kaja Kaźmierska, Katarzyna Waniek, and Agata Zysiak, *Opowiedzieć uniwersytet* (Łódź: WUŁ, 2015).
2. Agata Zysiak, *Punkty za pochodzenie. Powojenna modernizacja i uniwersytet w robotniczym mieście* (Kraków: Nomos, 2016).

INTRODUCTION

1. "The Cockney University" was a satire on the newly established University of London printed by the conservative "John Bull" in 1825.
2. Preparatory course—accelerated training to prepare students for the university exam.
3. By working class I mean here both the urban proletariat and peasants, as the term was used in the period (*klasy pracujące*).
4. Intelligentsia is a status group characteristic of Eastern Europe and Russia: an educated and professionally active social strata with a self-inscribed symbolic role as cultural and moral leaders (particularly important during the partition period).
5. Here I am translating the Polish term *cham*, i.e., usage referring to Noah's second son, Ham. In Polish the word has a deep genealogy in the rationalization of class distinctions. The Polish version of the Hamitic hypothesis sought to explain differences between peasants and the nobility as racial: Kacper Pobłocki, *Chamstwo*, Wydanie I (Wołowiec: Wydawnictwo Czarne, 2021), chap. 6; Adam Leszczyński, *Ludowa Historia polski: historia wyzysku i oporu: mitologia panowania* (Warszawa: Wydawnictwo WAB, 2020), chap. 1.
6. Referring to *les miraculés*—Pierre Bourdieu and Jean Claude Passeron, *The Inheritors: French Students and Their Relation to Culture* (Chicago: University of Chicago Press, 1979).
7. Piotr Hübner, *I Kongres Nauki Polskiej jako forma realizacji założeń polityki naukowej państwa ludowego* (Wrocław: Zakład Narodowy im. Ossolińskich, 1983), 172.
8. Henryk Słabek, "Wychodźstwo robotnicze: awans społeczny jednostek i zubożenie klasy?," in *Komunizm: ideologia, system, ludzie*, ed. Tomasz Szarota (Warszawa: Neriton, 2001), 267.
9. I am using established periodization to help my narrative be navigated and understood. One needs to be aware of the artificiality and oversimplification of such divisions, but their functionality and intelligibility nevertheless remain.

10. Agata Zysiak et al., *From Cotton and Smoke: Łódź—Industrial City and Discourses of Asynchronous Modernity 1897–1994* (Łódź: WUŁ, 2018).
11. John Connelly, *Captive University: The Sovietization of East German, Czech and Polish Higher Education, 1945–1956* (Chapel Hill: University of North Carolina Press, 2000).
12. John Connelly and Michael Grüttner, *Universities under Dictatorship* (University Park, PA: Penn State University Press, 2005); Connelly, *Captive University*.
13. Edward Hallett Carr, *The Soviet Impact on the Western World* (Macmillan, 1947), http://archive.org/details/sovietimpactonth008238mbp.
14. Johanna Bockman, *Markets in the Name of Socialism: The Left-Wing Origins of Neoliberalism* (Stanford: Stanford University Press, 2011); Susan Buck-Morss, *Dreamworld and Catastrophe: The Passing of Mass Utopia in East and West* (Cambridge, MA: MIT Press, 2002).
15. Martin Müller, "In Search of the Global East: Thinking between North and South," *Geopolitics* 25, no. 3 (May 26, 2020): 734–55, https://doi.org/10.1080/14650045.2018.1477757; James Mark and Paul Betts, eds., *Socialism Goes Global: The Soviet Union and Eastern Europe in the Age of Decolonisation*, new edition (New York: Oxford University Press, 2022).
16. Daniel Bertaux, Paul Richard Thompson, and Anna Rotkirch, eds., *On Living through Soviet Russia* (London: Routledge, 2004), 2.
17. Charles Gati, *The Politics of Modernization in Eastern Europe: Testing the Soviet Model* (Westport, CT: Praeger, 1974); Mark G. Field, ed., *Social Consequences of Modernization in Communist Societies* (Baltimore: Johns Hopkins University Press, 1976); for the overview see: Sheila Fitzpatrick, "Revisionism in Soviet History," *History and Theory* 46, no. 4 (December 1, 2007): 77–91.
18. In defining modernization, as well as other grand and ambiguous terms in this book, I follow usage and meaning used by the actors and discourses in the discussed time periods.
19. Michael D. Kennedy, *Professionals, Power and Solidarity in Poland: A Critical Sociology of Soviet-Type Society* (Cambridge: Cambridge University Press, 1991), 146.
20. L. R. Graham, "Big Science in the Last Years of the Big Soviet Union," *Osiris* 7 (1992): 51.
21. J. L. Peschar, *Social Reproduction in Eastern and Western Europe: Comparative Analyses on Czechoslovakia, Hungary, the Netherlands and Poland* (Nijmegen: Institute for Applied Social Sciences, 1990); Göran Therborn, *European Modernity and Beyond: The Trajectory of European Societies, 1945–2000* (London: Sage, 1995).
22. Zoltan D. Barany and Iván Völgyes, eds., *The Legacies of Communism in Eastern Europe* (Baltimore: Johns Hopkins University Press, 1995); Jacek Kochanowicz, *Backwardness and Modernization: Poland and Eastern Europe in the 16th–20th Centuries* (Aldershot: Ashgate Variorum, 2006).

23. Johann P. Arnason, "Communism and Modernity," *Daedalus* 129 (2000): 61–90.
24. Valentin Behr, *Powojenna historiografia polska jako pole walki: studium z socjologii wiedzy i polityki* (Warszawa: Wydawnictwa Uniwersytetu Warszawskiego, 2021).
25. Stephen Kotkin, "1991 and the Russian Revolution: Sources, Conceptual Categories, Analytical Frameworks," *Journal of Modern History* 70, no. 2 (June 1998): 384, https://doi.org/10.1086/235073.
26. Achim Siegel, *The Totalitarian Paradigm After the End of Communism: Towards a Theoretical Reassessment* (Amsterdam: Rodopi, 1998).
27. Maria Nikolaeva Todorova, ed., *Remembering Communism: Genres of Representation* (New York: Social Science Research Council, 2010).
28. Andrzej Friszke, "Epilogue: Polish Communism in Contemporary Debate," in *Stalinism in Poland, 1944–1956*, ed. A. Kemp-Welch (Warszawa: Macmillan Press; New York: St. Martin's Press, 1999), 146.
29. Valentin Behr, "Historical Policy-Making in Post-1989 Poland: A Sociological Approach to the Narratives of Communism," *European Politics and Society* 18, no. 1 (2016): 81–95, https://doi.org/10.1080/23745118.2016.1269447.
30. Michael Geyer and Sheila Fitzpatrick, *Beyond Totalitarianism: Stalinism and Nazism Compared* (Cambridge: Cambridge University Press, 2009); Kristen Ghodsee, "A Tale of 'Two Totalitarianisms': The Crisis of Capitalism and the Historical Memory of Communism," *History of the Present* 4, no. 2 (October 1, 2014): 115–42, https://doi.org/10.5406/historypresent.4.2.0115.
31. Malgorzata Fidelis, *Women, Communism, and Industrialization in Postwar Poland* (Cambridge: Cambridge University Press, 2010); Padraic Kenney, *Rebuilding Poland: Workers and Communists, 1945–1950* (Ithaca, NY: Cornell University Press, 2012); Katherine Lebow, *Unfinished Utopia: Nowa Huta, Stalinism, and Polish Society, 1949–56* (Ithaca, NY: Cornell University Press, 2013); Brian Porter-Szücs, *Poland in the Modern World: Beyond Martyrdom* (Oxford: Wiley Blackwell, 2014), chap. 8; Anna Artwińska and Agnieszka Mrozik, eds., *Gender, Generations, and Communism in Central and Eastern Europe and Beyond*, Routledge Research in Gender and History (Abingdon: Routledge, 2020); Katarzyna Stańczak-Wiślicz et al., eds., *Kobiety w Polsce 1945–1989: Nowoczesność—Równouprawnienie—Komunizm* (Kraków: Towarzystwo Autorów i Wydawców Prac Naukowych Universitas, 2020); Katarzyna Chmielewska, Agnieszka Mrozik, and Grzegorz Wołowiec, eds., *Reassessing Communism: Concepts, Culture, and Society in Poland, 1944–1989* (Budapest: Central European University Press, 2021).
32. Hanna Palska, *Nowa inteligencja w Polsce Ludowej: świat przedstawień i elementy rzeczywistości* (Warszawa: PAN, 1994).
33. Piotr Hübner, *Polityka naukowa w Polsce w latach 1944–1953: geneza systemu*, Problemy

naukowe współczesności (Wrocław: Zakład Narodowy im. Ossolińskich, 1992); Piotr Hübner, *Siła przeciw rozumowi—: losy Polskiej Akademii Umiejętności w latach 1939–1989* (Kraków: Secesja, 1994); Piotr Hübner, *Nauka polska po II wojnie światowej—idee i instytucje* (Warszawa: COM SNP, 1987).

34. Janina Chodakowska, *Rozwój szkolnictwa wyższego w Polsce Ludowej w latach 1944–1951*, Monografie z dziejów oświaty, t. 26 (Wrocław: Zakład Narodowy im. Ossolińskich, 1981); Bolesław Krasiewicz, *Odbudowa szkolnictwa wyższego w Polsce Ludowej w latach 1944–1948* (Wrocław: Zakład Narodowy im. Ossolińskich, 1976).

35. Rafał Stobiecki, *Historia pod nadzorem: spory o nowy model historii w Polsce. II połowa lat czterdziestych—początek lat pięćdziesiątych* (Łódź: Wydawnictwo Uniwersytetu Łódzkiego, 1993).

36. Krzysztof Baranowski, *Oddział Wolnej Wszechnicy Polskiej w Łodzi: 1928–1939* (Warszawa: PWN, 1977); Bohdan Baranowski, ed., *Uniwersytet Łódzki. Historia. Teraźniejszość. Perspektywy* (Łódź: Uniwersytet Łódzki, 1978); Bohdan Baranowski, "Pierwsi Rektorzy Uniwersytetu Łódzkiego," *Życie Szkoły Wyższej*, no. 7/8 (1980): 87–91; Bohdan Baranowski, *Uniwersytet Łódzki 1945–1980* (Łódź: Uniwersytet Łódzki, 1980); Bohdan Baranowski and Krzysztof Baranowski, *Trudne lata Uniwersytetu Łódzkiego: 1949–1956* (Łódź: Wydawnictwo UŁ, 1990).

37. Quoted in Rafał Stobiecki, "Z dziejów pewnego projektu. 'Socjalistyczny Uniwersytet w robotniczej Łodzi'," *Rocznik Łódzki* LXI (2014).

38. Jan Szczepański, *Dzienniki z lat 1945–1968* (Ustroń: Galeria Na Gojach, 2013), 29.

39. Palska, *Nowa inteligencja w Polsce Ludowej*; Hanna Świda-Ziemba, *Człowiek wewnętrznie zniewolony: problemy psychosocjologiczne minionej formacji* (UW, 1998); Zdzisław Zblewski and Filip Musiał, eds., *Komunizm w Polsce: zdrada, zbrodnia, zakłamanie, zniewolenie* (Kraków: Kluszczyński, 2005); Patryk Pleskot and Tadeusz Paweł Rutkowski, eds., *Spętana Akademia: Polska Akademia Nauk w dokumentach władz PRL* (Warszawa: IPN, 2009); Ryszard Herczyński, *Spętana nauka: opozycja intelektualna w Polsce 1945–1970* (Warszawa: Semper, 2008).

40. György Konrád and Iván Szelényi, *The Intellectuals on the Road to Class Power* (San Diego, CA: Harcourt Brace Jovanovich, 1979); Ivan Szelenvi, "The Intelligentsia in the Class Structure of State-Socialist Societies," *American Journal of Sociology* 88 (1982): S287–326; Eric Hanley, "A Party of Workers or a Party of Intellectuals? Recruitment into Eastern European Communist Parties, 1945–1988," *Social Forces* 81, no. 4 (2003): 1073–1105.

41. Joel Andreas, *Rise of the Red Engineers: The Cultural Revolution and the Origins of China's New Class* (Stanford: Stanford University Press, 2009), 4–5.

42. Connelly, *Captive University*; Benjamin Tromly, *Making the Soviet Intelligentsia: Universities and Intellectual Life under Stalin and Khrushchev* (Cambridge: Cambridge University Press, 2014).

43. Dorota Mycielska, "Drogi życiowe profesorów przed objęciem katedr akademickich w niepodległej Polsce," in *Inteligencja polska XIX i XX wieku: studia, t. 2*, ed. Ryszarda Czepulis-Rastenis (Warszawa: PWN, 1981); Bohdan Jaczewski, "Nauka," in *Polska odrodzona 1918–1939: państwo, społeczeństwo, kultura*, ed. Jan Tomicki (Warszawa: Wiedza Powszechna, 1982), 507–53.
44. At that time a leftist or left-winger could mean a social democrat, a communist, a Christian democrat, or an agrarianist—there was a powerful pro-peasant movement in interwar Poland; but a leftist could also mean a labor movement activist like a Bund member. In this book I usually follow this wide usage of the term *leftist*, meaning in general pro-labor, egalitarian, and pro-social.
45. Jan Tomasz Gross, "War as Revolution," in *The Establishment of Communist Regimes in Eastern Europe, 1944–1949*, ed. Norman M. Naimark and Leonid Gibianskii (Boulder, CO: Westview Press, 1997), 17–34.
46. Igal Halfin, *Language and Revolution: Making Modern Political Identities* (London: Routledge, 2004).
47. Connelly, *Captive University*, 198.

CHAPTER 1

1. Józef Chałasiński, *Społeczna Genealogia Inteligencji Polskiej* (Kraków: Czytelnik, 1947), 54.
2. Janusz Żarnowski, *O inteligencji polskiej lat międzywojennych* (Warszawa: Wiedza Powszechna, 1965).
3. In the early 1930s, the rural population still accounted for 73 percent of the general population and was the base for radical social movements and educational demands. Jan Szczepański, *Polskie losy* (Warszawa: Polska Oficyna Wydawnicza "BGW," 1993), 15–16.
4. Mycielska, "Drogi życiowe profesorów przed objęciem katedr akademickich w niepodległej Polsce."
5. Krzysztof Baranowski, *Alternatywna edukacja w II Rzeczypospolitej: Wolna Wszechnica Polska* (Warszawa: Towarzystwo WWP, 2001); Zofia Skubała-Tokarska, *Społeczna rola Wolnej Wszechnicy Polskiej* (Warszawa: PAN, 1967).
6. Warsaw's nonpublic universities were the Higher School of Humanities, the School of Political Studies, and later the Wolna Wszechnica Polska (Free Polish University). See also: Baranowski, *Oddział Wolnej Wszechnicy Polskiej w Łodzi: 1928–1939*, 10.
7. Krzysztof Leja, *Zarządzanie uczelnią: Koncepcje i współczesne wyzwania* (Warszawa: Wolters Kluwer, 2013), 44–45.
8. The Józef Mianowski Fund, which financed multiple research projects, received profits from the oil reserves in the Caucasus.
9. Piotr Hübner, *Zwierciadło nauki: mała encyklopedia polskiej nauki akademickiej* (Kraków: PAU, 2013), 221.

10. Bohdan Jaczewski, ed., *Życie naukowe w Polsce w drugiej połowie XIX i w XX wieku: organizacje i instytucje* (Wrocław: Zakład Narodowy im. Ossolińskich, 1987).
11. The Józef Mianowski Fund (Kasa im. Józefa Mianowskiego—Instytut Popierania Nauki), the biggest philanthropic organization supporting scholarship and research, was established in 1881 and was still powerful in the interwar period. However, by that time it depended more on public and government support.
12. This term was introduced by Romuald Mankiewicz in 1919 on the publication of his article of the same title in *Nauka Polska*. The whole statement defended the unconditional autonomy of scholarship: Hübner, *Zwierciadło nauki*, 49.
13. Hübner, 50.
14. It is noteworthy that the demands he had put forward were eventually implemented after 1948 during the wave of the Stalinist reforms, although in a quite different setting. Shortly afterward, Prof. Borowik himself took the position of office director of the First Congress of Polish Science, which took place in 1953.
15. Best known for *The Polish Peasant in Europe and America* (1913), co-authored with W. I. Thomas.
16. The term is taken from the word meaning sanation or purification, and roughly translates as "national moral regeneration." The Sanacja regime was the government bloc of Józef Piłsudski, which after the 1926 coup d'etat developed into authoritarian rule.
17. Jaczewski, *Życie naukowe w Polsce w drugiej połowie XIX i w XX wieku: organizacje i instytucje*, 233.
18. During the second term, it was eight deputies and three senators from the National Democracy, four connected with the Christian Democracy, three each with the Sanacja regime and the Democratic Party, and one each with the People's Movement and the Polish Socialist Party (the PPS). Hübner, *Zwierciadło nauki*, 43–44.
19. Porter-Szücs, *Poland in the Modern World*, 95–101.
20. Named after Janusz Jędrzejewicz, the minister of education from 1931 to 1934.
21. Jaczewski, *Życie naukowe w Polsce w drugiej połowie XIX i w XX wieku*, 167–75; Jarosław Jastrzębski, "Reforma Jędrzejewicza w państwowym szkolnictwie akademickim II Rzeczpospolitej. Wzmocnienie prerogatyw władzy państwowej," ed. Artur Patek, *Prace Historyczne* 138 (2011): 159–76; Joanna Sadowska, *Ku szkole na miarę Drugiej Rzeczypospolitej: geneza, założenia i realizacja reformy Jędrzejewiczowskiej* (Białystok: Wydawnictwo Uniwersytetu w Białymstoku, 2001); Janusz Tymowski, *Organizacja szkolnictwa wyższego w Polsce* (Warszawa: PWN, 1980), 27–30.
22. Andrzej Gawryszewski, *Ludność Polski w XX Wieku* (Warszawa: PAN, 2005), 323.
23. Urszula Jakubowska and Jerzy Myśliński, eds., *Humanistyka polska w latach 1945–1990* (Warszawa: Fundacja Akademia Humanistyczna, 2006).
24. Bohdan Jaczewski, *Polityka naukowa Państwa Polskiego w latach 1918–1939* (Wrocław: Zakład Narodowy im. Ossolińskich, 1978), 149.

25. Żarnowski, *O inteligencji polskiej lat miedzywojennych*, 120.
26. Szymon Rudnicki, *Obóz Narodowo-Radykalny: geneza i działalność* (Warszawa: Czytelnik, 1985), 72–73.
27. Ghetto benches (*getto ławkowe*)—an institutionalized form of segregation of Jewish students who were officially required, under threat of expulsion from the university, to sit in a separate section of lecture rooms.
28. Monika Natkowska, *Numerus clausus, getto ławkowe, numerus nullus, "paragraf aryjski": antysemityzm na Uniwersytecie Warszawskim 1931–1939* (Warszawa: Żydowski Instytut Historyczny, 1999); Natalia Aleksiun, "Together but Apart: University Experience of Jewish Students in the Second Polish Republic," *Acta Poloniae Historica* 109 (January 1, 2014): 109–37, https://doi.org/10.12775/APH.2014.109.06.
29. Jolanta Kolbuszewska, *Kobiety w drodze na naukowy Olimp . . . : akademicki awans polskich historyczek (od schyłku XIX wieku po rok 1989)* (Łódź: Wydawnictwo Uniwersytetu Łódzkiego, 2020), 76, 79, 111.
30. Violetta Rodek, "Kariera naukowa kobiet w II Rzeczpospolitej jako Przykład Pokonywania Barier Na Drodze Ku Równości Obu Płci," in *Działalność kobiet polskich na polu oświaty i nauki*, ed. Dorota Żołądź-Strzelczyk and Wieslaw Jamrozek (Poznań: Wydaw. ERUDITUS, 2003), 65, quoted by: Kolbuszewska, *Kobiety w drodze na naukowy Olimp . . .*, 78.
31. Halina Wittlinowa, *Atlas szkolnictwa Wyższego* (Warszawa: Nasza Księgarnia, 1937), 4; Kolbuszewska, *Kobiety w drodze na naukowy Olimp . . .*, 77.
32. Żarnowski, *O inteligencji polskiej lat miedzywojennych*, 148.
33. *Głos Nauczycielski* 1926 no. 5, quoted in Żarnowski, 124.
34. Janusz Żarnowski, *Społeczeństwo Drugiej Rzeczypospolitej, 1918–1939* (Warszawa: PWN, 1973), 20.
35. Mycielska, "Drogi życiowe profesorów przed objęciem katedr akademickich w niepodległej Polsce," 254–57.
36. Jaczewski, *Życie naukowe w Polsce w drugiej połowie XIX i w XX wieku*, 233.
37. Out of 520, 320 professors opted to protest. Ryszard Herczyński, *Spętana nauka: opozycja intelektualna w Polsce 1945–1970* (Warszawa: Semper, 2008), 25.
38. Among others, Stefan Czarnowski, Ludwik Krzywicki, Tadeusz Kotarbiński, Maria and Stanisław Ossowscy, and Józef Chałasiński—the next chapter will elaborate on this subject.
39. Andrzej Mencwel, *Etos lewicy: esej o narodzinach kulturalizmu polskiego*, Idee, no. 19 (Warszawa: Wydawnictwo "Krytyki Politycznej," 2009).
40. First published in 1971, the book discusses the development of intelligentsia opposition on a whole political spectrum. Bohdan Cywiński, *Rodowody niepokornych* (Warszawa: PWN, 2010).
41. Baranowski, *Alternatywna edukacja w II Rzeczypospolitej*.

42. Asa Briggs, *Victorian Cities* (Berkeley: University of California Press, 1993), chap. 3; Harold L. Platt, *Shock Cities: The Environmental Transformation and Reform of Manchester and Chicago* (Chicago: University of Chicago Press, 2005).
43. Wiktor Marzec and Agata Zysiak, "Miasto, morderstwo, maszyna. Osobliwe przypadki we wczesnonowoczesnej Łodzi," in *Rekonfiguracje modernizmu: nowoczesność i kultura popularna*, ed. Tomasz Majewski (Warszawa: Wydawnictwa Akademickie i Profesjonalne, 2009); Agata Zysiak, "The Desire for Fullness. The Fantasmatic Logic of Modernization Discourses at the Turn of the 19th and 20th Century in Lodz," *Praktyka Teoretyczna*, no. 3 (13) (December 20, 2014): 41–69.
44. Wiesław Puś, *Dzieje Łodzi przemysłowej: zarys historii* (Łódź: Muzeum Historii Miasta Łodzi, Centrum Informacji Kulturalnej, 1987), 533.
45. Edward Rosset, *Łódź miasto pracy* (Łódź: Wyd. Magistrat miasta Łodzi, 1929), 12.
46. Jan Augustyniak, *Życie naukowe Łodzi* (Warszawa: Wydawnictwa Kasy im. J. Mianowskiego, 1933), 173.
47. Ludwik Mroczka, *Fenomen robotniczy Drugiej Rzeczypospolitej: studia z dziejów społecznych łódzkiej klasy robotniczej (1918–1939)* (Łódź: Wydawnictwo Naukowe WSP, 1987), 145–47.
48. Kamil Piskała and Agata Zysiak, "The Postwar: Social Justice for Proletarian City?," in *From Cotton and Smoke* (Łódź: WUŁ, 2018), 102.
49. Piskała and Zysiak, 113.
50. Ludwik Stolarzewicz, *Literatura Łodzi w ciągu jej istnienia: szkic literacki i antologja* (Łódź: S. Seipelt, 1935), 22.
51. Baranowski, *Oddział Wolnej Wszechnicy Polskiej w Łodzi: 1928–1939*.
52. Jan F. Choroszy, *Poglądy etyczne Tadeusza Kotarbińskiego: studium historyczno-analityczne* (Wrocław: Wyd. Uniwersytetu Wrocławskiego, 1997); Jaczewski, *Życie naukowe w Polsce w drugiej połowie XIX i w XX wieku*, 233.
53. There was no requirement for candidates to have a school-leaving certificate—important for those who had completed technical schools or those who weren't able to take the school-leaving exam because of their radical views (those who did not complete a general secondary school had to go through a special *matura*—school-leaving exam—commission). I draw most of the information on the Free Polish University, the WWP, in Łódź from this publication: Baranowski, *Oddział Wolnej Wszechnicy Polskiej w Łodzi: 1928–1939*, 22.
54. Baranowski, 116–18.
55. Józef Chałasiński, "Początki uniwersytetu robotniczej Łodzi," in *Tranzytem przez Łódź*, ed. Irena Bołtuc-Staszewska (Łódź: Wydawnictwo Łódzkie, 1964), 54.
56. Marek Groński, "Sprawy kultury w działalności łódzkiej Rady Miejskiej 1928–1934," in *Studia i materiały do dziejów Łodzi i okręgu łódzkiego: dwudziestolecie 1918–1939*, ed. Pawel Korzec (Łódź: Wydawnictwo Łódzkie, 1962), 183–84.

57. Baranowski, *Oddział Wolnej Wszechnicy Polskiej w Łodzi: 1928–1939*, 74.
58. Kolbuszewska, *Kobiety w drodze na naukowy Olimp . . .*, 104.

CHAPTER 2

1. "Łódź," *Dziennik Łódzki*, January 2, 1945, 1.
2. Gross, "War as Revolution," 17–34.
3. Tadeusz Łepkowski, "Myśli o historii Polski i Polaków," *Zeszyty Historyczne* 68 (1984): 120–29.
4. Michael Fleming, *Communism, Nationalism and Ethnicity in Poland, 1944–50* (London: Routledge, 2010), 9; Kenney, *Rebuilding Poland*, 4.
5. Krystyna Kersten, ed., *The Establishment of Communist Rule in Poland, 1943–1948* (Berkeley: University of California Press, 1991); Andrzej Leder, *Prześniona rewolucja. Ćwiczenie z logiki historycznej* (Warszawa: Wydawnictwo Krytyki Politycznej, 2014).
6. Hugh Seton-Watson, *The East European Revolution* (Westport: Praeger, 1961), 232–34.
7. Only in the Baltic States were proportions similar. Jan Tomasz Gross, *Upiorna dekada. Trzy eseje o stereotypach na temat Żydów, Polaków, Niemców i komunistów 1939–1948* (Kraków: Universitas, 1998), 10.
8. Edward Rosset, *Oblicze demograficzne Polski Ludowej* (Warszawa: Państwowe Wydawnictwo Ekonomiczne, 1965), 31–40.
9. Kersten, *The Establishment of Communist Rule in Poland, 1943–1948*, 8–9.
10. Stanisław Ciesielski and Włodzimierz Borodziej, eds., *Przesiedlenie ludności polskiej z kresów wschodnich do Polski, 1944–1947* (Warszawa: Neriton; Instytut Historii PAN, 1999); Jacek Kochanowicz, "Gathering Poles into Poland. Forced Migration from Poland's Former Eastern Territories," in *Redrawing Nations: Ethnic Cleansing in East-Central Europe, 1944–1948*, ed. Philipp Ther and Ana Siljak (Lanham: Rowman & Littlefield, 2001), 134–54.
11. Marcin Zaremba, *Wielka trwoga. Polska 1944–1947. Ludowa reakcja na kryzys* (Kraków: Znak, 2012).
12. Andrzej Bolewski and Henryk Pierzchała, *Losy polskich pracowników nauki w latach 1939–1945: straty osobowe* (Wrocław: Zakład Narodowy im. Ossolińskich, 1989); Rafał Habielski, *Polityczna historia mediów w Polsce w XX wieku* (Warszawa: WAiP, 2009), 171.
13. Stanisław Mauersberg, "Nauka polska i szkolnictwo wyższe w latach wojny 1939–45," in *Życie naukowe w Polsce w drugiej połowie XIX i w XX wieku: organizacje i instytucje*, ed. Bohdan Jaczewski (Wrocław: Zakład Narodowy im. Ossolińskich, 1987), 238; Stobiecki, *Historia pod nadzorem*, 38–39.
14. Kersten, *The Establishment of Communist Rule in Poland, 1943–1948*, 9.
15. Stanisław Mauersberg, "Nauka polska i szkolnictwo wyższe w latach wojny 1939–45," in *Życie naukowe w Polsce w drugiej połowie XIX i w XX wieku: organizacje i instytucje*,

ed. Bohdan Jaczewski (Wrocław: Zakład Narodowy im. Ossolińskich, 1987), 237; Marian Walczak, *Szkolnictwo wyższe i nauka polska w latach wojny i okupacji: 1939–1945* (Wrocław: Zakład Narodowy im. Ossolińskich, 1978).

16. Josef Krasuski, "Education as Resistance: The Polish Experience of Schooling During the War," in *Education and the Second World War: Studies in Schooling and Social Change*, ed. Roy Lowe (London: Falmer Press, 1992), 135; Kenneth R. Wulff, *Education in Poland: Past, Present, and Future* (Lanham, MD: University Press of America, 1992), 11–14.
17. Stobiecki, *Historia pod nadzorem*.
18. Adam Bukowczyk, biographical interview, 2010, Archiwum Wspomnień Łodzian.
19. Leszek Olejnik, "Mniejszości narodowe w Łodzi w 1945 r.," in *Rok 1945 w Łodzi: studia i szkice*, ed. Joanna Żelazko (Łódź: IPN, 2008).
20. Isaiah Trunk and Robert Moses Shapiro, *Łódź Ghetto: A History* (Bloomington: Indiana University Press, 2006); The tragic phenomenon of the ghetto is widely recognized by Western and Polish historiography, but its history has also triggered many controversies. See: Andrea Löw, *Juden im Getto Litzmannstadt: Lebensbedingungen, Selbstwahrnehmung, Verhalten* (Göttingen: Wallstein, 2006); Gordon J. Horwitz, *Ghettostadt. Łódź and the Making of a Nazi City* (Cambridge, MA: Harvard University Press, 2009); Adam Sitarek, *"Otoczone drutem państwo." Struktura i funkcjonowanie administracji żydowskiej getta łódzkiego* (Instytut Pamięci Narodowej, 2015); Michal Unger, *Reassessment of the Image of Mordechai Chaim Rumkowski* (Jerusalem: Yad Vashem, 2004).
21. Tadeusz Bojanowski, *Łódź pod okupacją niemiecką w latach II Wojny Światowej, 1939–1945* (Łódź: Wydawnictwo Uniwersytetu Łódzkiego, 1992).
22. Leszek Olejnik, *Zdrajcy Narodu? Losy volksdeutschów w Polsce po II wojnie światowej* (Warszawa: Trio, 2006); Benno Kroll, *Tak było: wspomnienia łódzkiego Volksdeutscha* (Łódź: Biblioteka "Tygla Kultury," 2010); Krystyna Radziszewska and Monika Kucner, eds., *Miasto w mojej pamięci. Powojenne wspomnienia Niemców z Łodzi* (Łódź: Wydawnictwo UŁ, 2014).
23. Edward Rosset, "Stosunki ludnościowe," in *Łódź w latach 1945–1960* (Łódź: Wydawnictwo Łódzkie, 1962), 28.
24. Janusz Wróbel, "Bilans okupacji niemieckiej w Łodzi 1939–1945," in *Rok 1945 w Łodzi: studia i szkice*, ed. Joanna Żelazko (Łódź: IPN, 2008), 26.
25. Puś, *Dzieje Łodzi przemysłowej: zarys historii*, 104.
26. Connelly, *Captive University*; on Łódź's first postwar years: Przemysław Waigertner, *Czwarta stolica: kiedy Łódź rządziła Polską (1945–1949)* (Łódź: WUŁ, 2019).
27. Tony Judt, *Postwar: A History of Europe Since 1945* (New York: Penguin, 2006); Frank Biess and Robert G. Moeller, eds., *Histories of the Aftermath: The Legacies of the Second World War in Europe*, 1st ed. (New York: Berghahn Books, 2010).

28. The term was proposed in Jerzy Borejsza, "Rewolucja łagodna," *Odrodzenie*, no. 10–12 (January 15, 1945) and is often used to describe the first postwar years; Nina Kraśko, *Instytucjonalizacja socjologii w Polsce 1920–1970* (Warszawa: PWN, 1996); Jakubowska and Myśliński, *Humanistyka polska w latach 1945–1990*; Eryk Krasucki, *Międzynarodowy komunista: Jerzy Borejsza, biografia polityczna* (Warszawa: PWN, 2009); Henryk Słabek, *O społecznej historii Polski 1945–1989* (Warszawa: Książka i Wiedza, 2009).
29. Porter-Szücs, *Poland in the Modern World*, 193; Fleming, *Communism, Nationalism and Ethnicity in Poland, 1944–50*, 20.
30. Translation as in Porter-Szücs, *Poland in the Modern World*, 193.
31. Barany and Völgyes, *The Legacies of Communism in Eastern Europe*, 6.
32. Adam Leszczyński, *Skok w nowoczesność: polityka wzrostu w krajach peryferyjnych 1943–1980* (Warszawa: Wydawnictwo Krytyki Politycznej, 2013), 27.
33. The Polish Committee of National Liberation was officially proclaimed in Lublin on July 22, 1944, by Polish communists under the auspices of Moscow, in opposition to the Polish government-in-exile.
34. Krystyna Śreniowska, "Kartki z dziejów Uniwersytetu Łódzkiego 1945–1989. Pamiętnik," *Tygiel Kultury*, no. 12 (2007).
35. Rosset, "Stosunki ludnościowe," 33.
36. Anita Wolaniuk, *Funkcje metropolitalne Łodzi i ich rola w organizacji przestrzennej* (Łódź: ŁTN, 1997), 46.
37. Władysław Welfe, *Łódź i ziemia łódzka w badaniach Uniwersytetu Łódzkiego w latach 1945–1970* (Łódź: Uniwersytet Łódzki, 1970).
38. Józef Kądzielski, "Czytelnictwo gazet, czasopism i książek wśród dorosłej ludności miasta," in *Łódź w latach 1945–1960*, ed. Edward Rosset (Łódź: Wydawnictwo Łódzkie, 1962), 419–26.
39. Krystyna Ratajska, *O niezwykłych łódzkich kawiarniach. U Roszka, Fraszka, Honoratka* (Łódź: Księży Młyn Dom Wydawniczy, 2018).
40. Puś, *Dzieje Łodzi przemysłowej: zarys historii*, 9.
41. Władysław Bieńkowski, "Przemówienie p. Wiceministra Władysława Bieńkowskiego Na Uroczystej Inauguracji Roku Akademickiego Na Uniwersytecie Łódzkim Dnia 13 Stycznia 1946r.," *AUŁ, Biuro Rektora*, no. sygn. 1856 (1946).
42. Leder, *Prześniona rewolucja. Ćwiczenie z logiki historycznej*; Jan Tomasz Gross, "Geneza Społeczna Demokracji Ludowych (o Konsekwencjach II Wojny Światowej w Europie Środkowo-Wschodniej)," *Krytyka*, no. 32–33 (1990): 155–67.
43. Jerzy Jedlicki, "Proces przeciwko miastu," in *Świat zwyrodniały: lęki i wyroki krytyków nowoczesności* (Warszawa: Wydawnictwo Sic!, 2000); Jan Sowa, *Fantomowe ciało króla: peryferyjne zmagania z nowoczesną formą* (Kraków: Universitas, 2011); Kacper Pobłocki, *The Cunning of Class: Urbanization of Inequality in Post-War Poland* (Budapest, 2010).
44. Kenney, *Rebuilding Poland*, 10–16.

45. Józef Spychalski and Edward Rosset, *Włókniarze łódzcy: monografia* (Łódź: Wydawnictwo Łódzkie, 1966).
46. Marta Fik, *Spór o PRL* (Kraków: Znak, 1996); Winicjusz Narojek, *Socjalistyczne "welfare state": studium z psychologii społecznej Polski Ludowej* (Warszawa: PWN, 1991); Agata Zysiak, "Socjalizm jako modernizacja—powojenna historia Polski w perspektywie rewizjonistycznej," *Przegląd Humanistyczny* 61(2 (457)) (2017): 135–45.
47. Porter-Szücs, *Poland in the Modern World*.
48. Joanna Marszałek-Kawa, ed., *Politics of Memory in Post-Authoritarian Transitions* (Newcastle, UK: Cambridge Scholars Publishing, 2017), 111.
49. Charles Taylor, *Modern Social Imaginaries* (Durham, NC: Duke University Press, 2004).
50. "Łódź," *Kurier Popularny*, January 18, 1946, no. 18.
51. J. Dąb-Kocioł, "The Speech of the Minister of Agriculture and Agricultural Reforms," delivered at the 1st National Convention of Farm Workers, which took place in Szczecin, December 19, 1947, in "Przegląd Rolniczy," 1948, 1, quoted by Ewelina Szpak, "Female Tractor Driver, Labour Heroine and Activist: Images of New Socialist Rural Women in the Polish Communist Press (1950–75)," in *Imagining Frontiers, Contesting Identities*, ed. Steven G. Ellis and Lud'a Klusáková (Pisa: PLUS—Pisa University Press, 2007), 414.
52. Loren R. Graham, *Science in Russia and the Soviet Union: A Short History* (Cambridge: Cambridge University Press, 1993), 90.
53. "My dopiero musimy wychować naszych profesorów"—I Zjazd PPR—przemówienia i uchwały. Ku nowej Polce, Warszawa, 1945, pp. 138–39, quoted in Joanna Król, "Polityka rekrutacyjna," in *Oświata, wychowanie i kultura fizyczna w rzeczywistości społeczno-politycznej Polski Ludowej (1945–1989): rozprawy i szkice*, ed. Romuald Grzybowski (Toruń: Wydawnictwo Adam Marszałek, 2004), 72.
54. R. Herczyński, *Spętana nauka*, 51.
55. Hanna Gosk, *W kręgu "Kuźnicy." Dyskusje krytycznoliterackie lat 1945–1948* (Warszawa: PWN, 1985), 83.
56. Gosk, 57.
57. Leszek Kołakowski comments thus on the views of this environment: "At that point, communism was the conqueror of nazism, the myth of a Better World, a longing for a life without crime and humiliation, the land of equality and freedom. . . . It was a goal which could justify any means," and "We weren't democrats. We believed that power had to be seized in spite of the majority because the brilliant future depended on it." Leszek Kołakowski and Zbigniew Mentzel, *Czas ciekawy, czas niespokojny: z Leszkiem Kołakowskim rozmawia Zbigniew Mentzel* (Kraków: Znak, 2008), 80, 95.
58. Jan Nosko, *Rewolucja i inteligencja: PPR i PZPR w łódzkim środowisku akademickim 1945–1971* (Łódź: Wydawnictwo Łódzkie, 1985), 43.

59. Membership in the PPR, across all universities in Łódź, was increasing. In 1948, it already totaled 400 members, but it never exceeded 2.5 percent of staff and students in any department of the University of Łódź. The exception was the preliminary year, when it reached 20 percent. This is one of the reasons why a significant section of the chapter has been devoted to this form of education. Wiesław Puś, *Zarys historii Uniwersytetu Łódzkiego 1945–2015* (Łódź: WUŁ, 2015), 239.
60. Nosko, *Rewolucja i inteligencja*, 44.
61. The society, founded by the Jesuits, was to combine studies with Christian devotion. Its operation was suspended in 1949 in response to the demands of the authorities, and resumed in 1980.
62. Nosko, *Rewolucja i inteligencja*, 50–54.
63. The PZPR's University Committee at the UŁ, AAN, file no. 33, case 1185.
64. John Connelly, "The Foundations of Diversity: Communist Higher Education Policies in Eastern Europe 1945–1955," in *Science Under Socialism: East Germany in Comparative Perspective*, ed. Kristie Macrakis and Dieter Hoffmann (Cambridge, MA: Harvard University Press, 1999), 125–39.
65. Adam Schaff, "Łódzkie wspomnienia," in *Tranzytem przez Łódź*, ed. Irena Bołtuc-Staszewska (Łódź: Wydawnictwo Łódzkie, 1964), 42.
66. This was a commonly employed reference to a book by Z. Krasiński, used as a synonym for the last conservative or even reactionary stronghold.
67. Tadeusz Chróścielewski, "W miejsce zleconego wstępu," in *Tranzytem przez Łódź*, ed. Irena Bołtuc-Staszewska (Łódź: Wydawnictwo Łódzkie, 1964), 15.
68. Bohdan Baranowski, *Pierwsze Lata Uniwersytetu Łódzkiego, 1945–1949* (Łódź: Uniwersytet Łódzki, 1985), 214.
69. Jan Lewandowski, *Rodowód społeczny powojennej inteligencji polskiej: 1944–1949* (Szczecin: Uniwersytet Szczeciński, 1991), 97.
70. Hübner, *Polityka naukowa w Polsce w latach 1944–1953*, 23 et seq.
71. Rafal Habielski and Dominika Rafalska, *Aparat represji wobec inteligencji w latach 1945–1956* (Warszawa: Oficyna Wydawnicza Aspra-JR, 2010), 29.
72. From a given year, one child went on to study per 750 children of agricultural workers (a farm up to 5 ha, c. 12 acres), per 565 children of the owners of medium-sized farms and 274 children of the owners of larger farms; however, every third child from the liberal professions, every fifth child of white-collar workers from public institutions and owners of farms over 50 ha (c. 123 acres), and every seventh child of those working in industry and rentiers. Marian Falski, *Środowisko społeczne młodzieży i jej wykształcenie* (Warszawa: Nasza Księgarnia, 1937), 55.
73. Seton-Watson, *The East European Revolution*, 282.
74. Daria Nałęcz, "Lata 1949–56," in *Czasopisma społeczno-kulturalne w okresie PRL*, ed. Urszula Jakubowska (Warszawa: IBL PAN, 2012).

75. The Polish higher education system was composed of universities, polytechnics, specialized academies (e.g., of mining and metallurgy) and colleges (e.g., of art, music, and education).
76. Jaczewski, *Życie naukowe w Polsce w drugiej połowie XIX i w XX wieku*, 231.
77. Krystyna Kersten, *Między wyzwoleniem a zniewoleniem: Polska 1944–1956* (London: Aneks, 1993), 11.
78. "Program," *Przegląd Akademicki*, no. 1 (1947): 21.
79. Jerzy Szacki, *Sto lat socjologii polskiej: od Supińskiego do Szczepańskiego* (Warszawa: PWN, 1995), 110–11.
80. Kraśko, *Instytucjonalizacja socjologii* (Warszawa: PWN, 1996), 88.
81. *Kuźnica* (1945–1948) was a Marxist social-literary weekly where major debates between members of the intelligentsia took place. In 1948, it merged with another cultural weekly, *Odrodzenie* (Renaissance/Revival) under the title *Nowa Kultura*.
82. *Wieś* (1944–1954) was a social-literary weekly for the rural intelligentsia. Focused on regional culture and education, it moved to Warsaw in 1949.
83. *Myśl Współczesna* (1945–1951) was a Marxist philosophical monthly academic journal edited by Chałasiński until 1948, then by Adam Schaff.
84. Tadeusz Błażejewski, "Z dziejów Łodzi literackiej," in *Wizerunek Łodzi w literaturze, kulturze i historii Niemiec i Austrii*, ed. Krzysztof Kuczyński (Łódź: UMŁ, 2005), 49–61.
85. Klub Demokratycznej Profesury (The Democratic Professorship Club) was first established by Adam Schaff as a leftist debating society modeled on the Anglo-Saxon tradition. It later became widespread in other cities as a Marxist self-education seminar.
86. Jan Kott, *Przyczynek do biografii* (London: Aneks, 1990), 213.
87. Irena Bołtuc-Staszewska, *Tranzytem przez Łódź* (Łódź: Wydawnictwo Łódzkie, 1964).
88. Andrzej Mencwel, *Przedwiośnie czy Potop: studium postaw polskich w XX wieku* (Warszawa: Czytelnik, 1997), 488.

CHAPTER 3

1. This quote is from Bolesław Bierut, interwar communist, prominent postwar leader, and future president of Poland (1947–1952), and comes from Józef Chałasiński's *Uczeni polscy wobec rozwoju kultury i przyszłości narodu* (Warszawa: Czytelnik, 1952), 22.
2. It should be noted that the term "socialized," from the Polish *uspołeczniony*, does not denote socialism, but rather a university that is active in the socialization process and is governed by society.
3. Choroszy, *Poglądy etyczne Tadeusza Kotarbińskiego*.
4. Baranowski, *Pierwsze lata Uniwersytetu Łódzkiego, 1945–1949*, 32.
5. Lewandowski, *Rodowód społeczny powojennej inteligencji polskiej*, 20; Jan Szczepański, *Szkice o szkolnictwie wyższym* (Warszawa: Wiedza Powszechna, 1976).
6. Szczepański, *Szkice o szkolnictwie wyższym*, 18–30.

7. The whole of Kotarbiński's speech is not available in the University Archive, but it was reprinted in *Dziennik Ludowy*. It is worth mentioning that the speech was given on the same occasion as W. Bieńskowski's speech and a controversial lecture by Józef Chałasiński, which will be discussed later.
8. Tadeusz Kotarbiński, "Dwie koncepcje równości" (AUŁ, October 30, 1946).
9. Kotarbiński, 149.
10. Józef Chałasiński, *Młode pokolenie chłopów* (Warszawa: Państwowy Instytut Kultury Wsi., 1938).
11. Gryko, *Józef Chałasiński—człowiek i dzieło*, 21; Franciszek Jakubczak, "Józefa Chałasińskiego ethos nieposłuszeństwa w myśleniu," in *Chałasiński dzisiaj: materiały z konferencji naukowej*, ed. Andrzej Kaleta (Toruń: Wydawnictwo UMK, 1996), 70.
12. Stanisław Siekierski, "Z dziejów recepcji Młodego pokolenia chłopów," *Przegląd Humanistyczny*, no. 1–2 (1986): 22–23.
13. Jakubczak, "Józefa Chałasińskiego ethos nieposłuszeństwa w myśleniu," 70.
14. Antonina Kłoskowska, "Bunty i służebności uczonego: Profesor Józef Chałasiński," in *Bunty i służebności uczonego: Profesor Józef Chałasiński*, ed. Leszek Wojtczak (Łódź: Wydawnictwo UŁ, 1992), 39.
15. The lecture given for the inauguration of the academic year took place, with some delay, on January 13, 1946. It was entitled "The Polish Intelligentsia from Its Social Genealogy Perspective" and was published as the second chapter of Chałasiński's book, *The Social Genealogy of the Polish Intelligentsia*, entitled "The Intelligentsia Ghetto."
16. Chałasiński, *Społeczna genealogia inteligencji polskiej*, 8.
17. Chałasiński, 68.
18. Rafał Smoczyński and Tomasz Zarycki, *Totem inteligencki: Arystokracja, szlachta i ziemiaństwo w polskiej przestrzeni społecznej* (Warszawa: Wydawnictwo Naukowe Scholar, 2017), 241–42.
19. Kłoskowska, "Bunty i służebności uczonego: Profesor Józef Chałasiński," 15.
20. Józef Chałasiński, "O społeczny sens reformy uniwersytetów," *Kuźnica*, no. 24 (June 17, 1947).
21. Chałasiński, *Społeczna genealogia inteligencji polskiej*, 3.
22. Chałasiński, "O społeczny sens reformy uniwersytetów," 4.
23. Herczyński, *Spętana nauka, 87*.
24. Józef Chałasiński, "Współczesne reformy szkolne a idea narodu," *Myśl Współczesna*, no. 7–8 (1947): 398–425.
25. Choroszy, *Poglądy etyczne Tadeusza Kotarbińskiego*, 12.
26. Tadeusz Kotarbiński, *Wybór pism* (Warszawa: PWN, 1958), 678.
27. Ija Lazari-Pawłowska, *Humanizm Tadeusza Kotarbińskiego* (Wrocław: Zakład Narodowy im. Ossolińskich, 1989), 13.
28. According to the daily *Głos Robotniczy*, which printed this speech given by the vice-

chancellor, the reactions of the audience were extremely enthusiastic; it was met with applause and cheers. Nosko, *Rewolucja i inteligencja: PPR i PZPR w łódzkim środowisku akademickim 1945–1971*, 44.

29. W. Sokorski, "*O demokratyzację wyższych uczelni*," *Kuźnica* 1947, no. 2.
30. The Act of Constitution passed on February 19, 1947, "on the system and scope of activities of the highest authorities of the Republic of Poland."
31. Piotr Hübner and Dorota Degen, "Instytucje naukowe, towarzystwa, biblioteki, wydawnictwa i czasopisma naukowe," in *Humanistyka polska w latach 1945–1990*, ed. Jerzy Myśliński and Urszula Jakubowska (Warszawa: Instytut Badań Literackich PAN, 2006), 17.
32. Józef Chałasiński, "Inauguracja VI roku akademickiego Uniwersytetu Łódzkiego 1950/51," 1950, syg 364649.
33. Krasiewicz, *Odbudowa szkolnictwa wyższego w Polsce Ludowej w latach 1944–1948*. See: Tymowski, *Organizacja szkolnictwa wyższego w Polsce*; Chodakowska, *Rozwój szkolnictwa wyższego w Polsce Ludowej w latach 1944–1951*; Antoni Gładysz, *Oświata, kultura, nauka w latach 1947–1959: węzłowe problemy polityczne* (Warszawa, Kraków: PWN, 1981); Hübner, *I Kongres Nauki Polskiej jako forma realizacji założeń polityki naukowej państwa ludowego*; Baranowski and Baranowski, *Trudne lata Uniwersytetu Łódzkiego*; Hübner, *Polityka naukowa w Polsce w latach 1944–1953*; Connelly, *Captive University*; Herczyński, *Spętana nauka*.
34. Tymowski, *Organizacja szkolnictwa wyższego w Polsce*, 488.
35. Herczyński, *Spętana nauka*, 118; Szkolnictwa Wyższego Dep. Nauki i, "Zatrudnienie Absolwentów," n.d., Ministerstwo Szkolnictwa Wyższego w Warszawie 1946/49/1950–67, syg 1065, AAN.
36. Szczepański, *Szkice o szkolnictwie wyższym, 18*.
37. Connelly and Grüttner, *Universities under Dictatorship*, 194.
38. Herczyński, *Spętana nauka*, 96.
39. Jan Lutyński, "Niektóre uwarunkowania rozwoju socjologii polskiej i ich konsekwencje," *Studia Socjologiczne* 195, no. 2 (1987): 127.
40. Herczyński, *Spętana nauka*, 116.
41. The decree from May 26, 1950; for more details see for example: Tymowski, *Organizacja szkolnictwa wyższego w Polsce*, 59.
42. Piotr Hübner, "Stalinowskie czystki w nauce polskiej," in *Skryte oblicze systemu komunistycznego: u źródeł zła*, ed. Roman Bäcker (Warszawa: DiG, 1997), 220.
43. Bartosz Cichocki and Krzysztof Jóźwiak, *Najważniejsze są kadry: Centralna Szkoła Partyjna PPR/PZPR* (Warszawa: Trio, 2006), 220.
44. Baranowski, *Uniwersytet Łódzki. Historia. Teraźniejszość. Perspektywy*, 11.
45. Baranowski and Baranowski, *Trudne lata Uniwersytetu Łódzkiego*, 133.
46. Jolanta Kulpińska, "Antonina Kłoskowska i łódzka socjologia. Znaczące wydarzenia," *Przegląd Socjologiczny* 61, no. 3 (2012): 29–36.

47. Bołtuc-Staszewska, *Tranzytem przez Łódź*.
48. Baranowski, *Pierwsze lata Uniwersytetu Łódzkiego, 1945–1949*, 44.
49. J. Chałasiński, *The Memorandum of the Rector on the Working Conditions and Growth of the University of Łódź*, August 7, 1950, file no. 563.
50. Chałasiński, "Początki uniwersytetu robotniczej Łodzi," 63.
51. J. Chałasiński, A lecture by Chałasiński "UŁ w 1950" [The Sejm Commission of Scholarship and Education], file no. 222.
52. Łukasz Kamiński, *Strajki robotnicze w Polsce w latach 1945–1948* (Wrocław: Gajt Wydawnictwo, 1999); Krzysztof Lesiakowski, *Strajki robotnicze w Łodzi 1945–1976* (Łódź: IPN, 2008).
53. Kłoskowska, "Bunty i służebności uczonego: Profesor Józef Chałasiński," 15.
54. Józef Chałasiński, "Od liberalnej do socjalistycznej idei Uniwersytetu," *Życie Nauki* V, no. 7–8 (1950): 537.
55. Chałasiński, 538.
56. Chałasiński, "Inauguracja VI roku akademickiego Uniwersytetu Łódzkiego 1950/51."
57. Bohdan Baranowski, "Pierwsi Rektorzy Uniwersytetu Łódzkiego," *Życie Szkoły Wyższej*, no. 7/8 (1980): 87–91.
58. Józef Chałasiński, "Memoriał Rektora ws. warunków pracy i rozwoju UŁ," August 7, 1950, Biuro Rektora, AUŁ.
59. Hübner, *I Kongres Nauki Polskiej jako forma realizacji założeń polityki naukowej państwa ludowego*, 139–62.
60. Jan Szczepański, *Socjologiczne zagadnienia wyższego wykształcenia* (Warszawa: PWN, 1963).
61. Connelly and Grüttner, *Universities under Dictatorship*, 126–28.
62. Józef Chałasiński, "Rzecz z powodu 'Humanistyki bez hipostaz,'" *Myśl Filozoficzna*, no. 2 (1952): 303–14.
63. Józef Chałasiński, "Humanizm socjalistyczny a podstawowe prawo ekonomiczne socjalizmu," *Nauka Polska*, no. 2 (1953): 50–80.
64. Kotarbiński, *Wybór pism*, 207.
65. Chałasiński, "Początki uniwersytetu robotniczej Łodzi," 79.
66. Zbigniew Jordan, "Bunt intelektualisty," *Kultura*, no. 9 (1955): 92–102.
67. Zbigniew Jordan, "O socjologii i socjologicznych czasopismach," *Kultura*, no. 5 (1957), 133–34.
68. Janina Tobera, "Józef Chałasiński, okres łódzki. Wybrane zagadnienia," in *Chałasiński dzisiaj: materiały z konferencji naukowej*, ed. Andrzej Kaleta (Toruń: Wydawnictwo UMK, 1996), 89.
69. See: John Biggart, "Bukharin and the Origins of the 'Proletarian Culture' Debate," *Soviet Studies* 39, no. 2 (1987): 229–46, https://doi.org/10.1080/09668138708411687; Zenovia A. Sochor, *Revolution and Culture: The Bogdanov-Lenin Controversy* (Ithaca, NY: Cornell University Press, 1988); Abbott Gleason, Peter Kenez, and Richard Stites,

Bolshevik Culture: Experiment and Order in the Russian Revolution (Bloomington: Indiana University Press, 1989); William G. Rosenberg, *Bolshevik Visions: First Phase of the Cultural Revolution in Soviet Russia* (Ann Arbor: University of Michigan Press, 1990).

70. Stobiecki, "Z dziejów pewnego projektu. 'Socjalistyczny Uniwersytet w robotniczej Łodzi',"' 162.
71. Puś, *Zarys historii Uniwersytetu Łódzkiego 1945–2015*, 35–38.
72. Jan Dylik and Zygmunt Dylik, "Nauka. Powstanie i organizacja łódzkiego ośrodka naukowego," in *Łódź w latach 1945–1960*, ed. Edward Rosset (Łódź: Wydawnictwo Łódzkie, 1962), 297.
73. Aleksander Kamiński, "Łódź kulturalna—uwagi wstępne," in *Łódź w latach 1945–1960*, ed. Edward Rosset (Łódź: Wydawnictwo Łódzkie, 1962), 267–68.
74. Jerzy Dziciuchowicz, "Ludność Łodzi od 1918 do lat 90. XX wieku," in *Łódź: monografia miasta*, edited by Stanisław Liszewski (Łódź: ŁTN, 2009), 228.
75. Adam Ginsbert, *Łódź: studium monograficzne* (Łódź: Wydawnictwo Łódzkie, 1962), 291.
76. March 1968 in Poland began with student protests. Harsh reaction and the suppression of the dissident movement followed. An anti-Semitic campaign was triggered too; subsequent mass emigration left vacant many academic positions. See: Sławomir Nowinowski, ed., *Marzec '68 w Łodzi* (Łódź: IPN, 2010); Konrad Rokicki and Sławomir Stępień, eds., *Oblicza Marca 1968* (Warszawa: IPN, 2004); Leszek Olejnik, "Żydzi łódzcy w latach 1956–1972," in *Społeczność żydowska w PRL przed kampanią antysemicką lat 1967–1968 i po niej*, ed. Grzegorz Berendt (Warszawa: IPN, 2009), 137–47.
77. For example: Kersten, *Między wyzwoleniem a zniewoleniem*, 297.

CHAPTER 4

1. Martin Conboy, *The Language of Newspapers: Socio-Historical Perspectives* (London: Bloomsbury Academic, 2010), 7.
2. The article refers to the newly formed Union of Polish Youth.
3. When quoting fragments from the compiled article database, I use the original spelling and a simplified bibliographic annotation (the title of the article, an abbreviated title of the newspaper, the approximate publication time: month/year).
4. Michał Głowiński, *Nowomowa po polsku*, Biblioteka tekstów (Warszawa: PEN, 1991); John Wesley Young, *Totalitarian Language: Orwell's Newspeak and Its Nazi and Communist Antecedents* (Charlottesville: University of Virginia Press, 1991).
5. The research conducted on the press materials covered the period between 1945 and 1956, and included select titles of three dailies published in Łódź as well as opinion weeklies and periodicals connected to academic circles. I primarily sought articles covering the University of Łódź and education in Łódź but also items discussing the life of academia in a wider context. Three dailies published in Łódź constitute the main research material: the local *Dziennik Łódzki* (Lodz Daily—DŁ), published between 1953 and

1956 as *Łódzki Express Ilustrowany* (Illustrated Lodz Express—ŁEI), the national *Głos Robotniczy* (Workers' Voice—GR)—both published throughout the whole research period; and *Kurier Popularny* (Popular Courier—KP), published until 1948. The most popular daily after 1948, *Trybuna Ludu* (People's Tribune), addressed the issue of Łódź and its university only to a marginal degree, and as such was omitted. The material, numbering 815 among over 1,000 initially selected articles, has been transcribed, encoded, and subjected to a qualitative analysis in order to study how the postwar social imaginary was formed and notions such the university, student, or professor emerged.

6. Charles Taylor suggests viewing the social imaginary as a way in which people imagine their social existence, their expectations, and their underlying normative assumptions. Taylor, *Modern Social Imaginaries*; Charles Taylor, *A Secular Age* (Cambridge, MA: Belknap Press of Harvard University Press, 2007).
7. Kądzielski, "Czytelnictwo gazet, czasopism i książek wśród dorosłej ludności miasta."
8. Habielski, *Polityczna historia mediów w Polsce w XX wieku*, 215.
9. Kądzielski, "Czytelnictwo gazet, czasopism i książek wśród dorosłej ludności miasta," 77.
10. Grzegorz Mnich, *Łódzka prasa codzienna w okresie stalinowskim (1948–1956)* (Łódź: Księży Młyn Dom Wydawniczy, 2014), 59–63.
11. Kądzielski, "Czytelnictwo gazet, czasopism i książek wśród dorosłej ludności miasta," 77–78.
12. Jerzy Drygalski and Jacek Kwaśniewski, *(Nie)realny socjalizm* (Warszawa: PWN, 1992), 290.
13. Maria Biernacka, "Oświata a społeczno-kulturowe przeobrażenie wsi w latach ostatniej wojny i w okresie powojennym," *Etnografia polska* 27, no. 2 (1983): 103–32.
14. Aleksander Kamiński, "Łódź kulturalna—uwagi wstępne," in *Łódź w latach 1945–1960*, ed. Edward Rosset (Łódź: Wydawnictwo Łódzkie, 1962), 267–68.
15. Kądzielski, 80.
16. Paweł Samuś, "Rola socjalistów w edukacji politycznej społeczeństwa Królestwa Polskiego w latach rewolucji 1905–1907," *Przegląd Nauk Historycznych*, no. 2 (2005): 127–46.
17. Halfin, *Language and Revolution*; Wiktor Marzec, "Rising Subjects. Workers and the Political during the 1905–1907 Revolution in the Kingdom of Poland" (PhD diss., Budapest, CEU, 2017).
18. Jane Leftwich Curry, *Poland's Journalists: Professionalism and Politics*, Soviet and East European Studies 66 (Cambridge: Cambridge University Press, 1990), 5.
19. Public opinion suspected Soviet soldiers of the sex-related murder; however, officially, the crime was attributed to the antigovernment underground. The issue was widely discussed and led to a student protest. Paweł Spodenkiewicz, "Sprawa Marii Tyrankiewiczówny," in *Rok 1945 w Łodzi: studia i szkice*, ed. Joanna Żelazko (Łódź: IPN, 2008), 251–74.
20. Polish Youth Union/Union of Polish Youth (Związek Młodzieży Polskiej)—formed

from several youth organizations in 1948 as the official and unified youth organization under the Polish United Workers' Party (PZPR). Its members wore green shirts and red ties. This group numbered 2 million members in 1955 (almost 40 percent of Polish youth at that time). It was dissolved in 1957 after the Polish Thaw. The Socialist Youth Union was established instead but never gained that mass membership.

21. Joanna Kochanowicz, *ZMP w terenie: stalinowska próba modernizacji opornej rzeczywistości* (Warszawa: Trio, 2000); Marek Wierzbicki, *Związek Młodzieży Polskiej i jego członkowie* (Warszawa: Trio, 2006); Agnieszka Mrozik, "Girls from the Polish Youth Union: (Dis)Remembrance of the Generation," in *Gender, Generations, and Communism in Central and Eastern Europe and Beyond*, ed. Anna Artwinska and Agnieszka Mrozik (New York: Routledge, 2020), 197–226.
22. Based on the research conducted in Łódź, Jan Szczepański produced a typology of postwar students. He distinguished between a scholar-student, an expert-graduate, and a sociopolitical activist. All three types were present in the press discourse, forming a general model of a socialist student. Szczepański, *Socjologiczne zagadnienia wyższego wykształcenia*.
23. This most likely refers to Prof. Ernest A. Sym (1893–1950), a biochemist and enzymologist who founded the Department of Medical Chemistry (later the Faculty of General and Physiological Chemistry at the Medical Department) at the University of Łódź; in 1946, he left for Gdańsk.
24. Lawrence S. Wittner, *The Struggle against the Bomb: Volume One, One World or None: A History of the World Nuclear Disarmament Movement through 1953* (Stanford: Stanford University Press, 1993), 184–85.
25. "Narodowy Plebiscyt Pokoju," *Polska Kronika Filmowa* 21 (1951). Repozytorium Cyfrowe Filmoteki Narodowej, http://www.repozytorium.fn.org.pl/?q=pl/node/7846.
26. The "workplace" as well was no longer a venture programmed to make a profit but rather geared to manufacturing.

CHAPTER 5

1. Taken from an exam essay from 1948, in which a working-class student describes what the future will be like in the year 2000. "Spuścizna Niny Assorodobraj-Kuli," *Dział Rękopisów BUW* 4225 (1949): 19.
2. Referring to *les miraculés* of Pierre Bourdieu and Jean Claude Passeron. Bourdieu and Passeron, *The Inheritors*.
3. Jan Szczepański, "Próba koncepcji rozwoju szkolnictwa wyższego," *Wieś Współczesna*, no. styczeń (1958): 70.
4. Lewandowski, *Rodowód społeczny powojennej inteligencji polskiej*, 122.
5. After 1950, some studies introduced the category of "intelligentsia by promotion." Lewandowski, 139.

6. The Gomułka Thaw, or the Polish October. The year 1956 was a crucial year of transition, but changes had been seen much earlier, and not only in the social sciences.
7. Bucholc, *Sociology in Poland*, 31.
8. Henryk Domański, ed., *Zmiany stratyfikacji społecznej w Polsce* (Warszawa: PAN, 2008), 8.
9. For instance: Anna Sosnowska, *Zrozumieć zacofanie: spory historyków o Europę Wschodnią, 1947–1994* (Warszawa: Trio, 2004).
10. Lutyński, "Niektóre uwarunkowania rozwoju socjologii polskiej i ich konsekwencje," 128–30.
11. Michael Burawoy, "Revisits: An Outline of a Theory of Reflexive Ethnography," *American Sociological Review* 68, no. 5 (October 2003): 645–79.
12. Zbigniew Sawiński, "Zmiany systemowe a nierówności w dostępie do wykształcenia," in *Zmiany stratyfikacji społecznej w Polsce*, ed. Henryk Domański (Warszawa: PAN, 2008), 21–22.
13. During enrollment for the 1946/1947 academic year, Rector Kotarbiński explained that the number of places in the Medical Department was limited on account of decisions made by the central authorities. The places at the ministry's discretion totaled 15 percent of the expected student body. Additionally, another third of the places were reserved for the graduates of the preliminary year, which meant that out of 150 first-year places, only 63 were available in open recruitment (*Młodzież akademicka o swoich potrzebach*, DŁ 11/46).
14. Lewandowski, *Rodowód społeczny powojennej inteligencji polskiej*, 65.
15. Jan Szczepański, *Ze studiów nad kursami przygotowawczymi: praca zbiorowa* (Łódź: Zakład Narodowy im. Ossolińskich, PWN, 1962), 45.
16. From the Russian word *Рабфак*, which originates from *Рабочий факультет* (*rabochiy fakultet*)—that is, the workers' university designed to prepare working-class people for enrollment in higher education institutions.
17. Lewandowski, *Rodowód społeczny powojennej inteligencji polskiej*, 79.
18. The collected materials and the preliminary manuscript of the research report in: "Spuścizna Niny Assorodobraj-Kuli."
19. Józef Chałasiński, "Referat Chałasińskiego 'UŁ w 1950' [Sejmowa Komisja Oświaty i Nauki]," n.d., Dział Nauczania, AUŁ.
20. "Spuścizna Niny Assorodobraj-Kuli," 19.
21. "Spuścizna Niny Assorodobraj-Kuli," 14–15.
22. "Spuścizna Niny Assorodobraj-Kuli," 17.
23. "Spuścizna Niny Assorodobraj-Kuli," 11.
24. Agnieszka Mrozik and Magda Szczęśniak, "Wstęp. Powojenne historie ludowe," *Kultura i Społeczeństwo* 66, no. 2 (September 2022): 5.
25. Szczepański, *Ze studiów nad kursami przygotowawczymi*, 181.

26. Król, "Polityka rekrutacyjna," 74–75.
27. Król, 78–79.
28. Puś, *Zarys historii Uniwersytetu Łódzkiego 1945–2015*, 35–39, 258.
29. The trials of workers arrested for taking part in the Poznań protest in June 1956. These were the first such large-scale strikes in the PRL and were brutally suppressed. Cegielski Factory workers demanded better working conditions; demonstrations reached 100,000 people and were met with violent and chaotic repression by the army using tanks, leaving fifty-seven people dead. Nevertheless, the trials were a prelude to the Polish Thaw. For more details see for example: Konrad Białecki, ed., *Poznański czerwiec 1956: uwarunkowania—przebieg—konsekwencje*, Publikacje Instytutu Historii 77 (Poznań: Instytut Historii UAM, 2007).
30. Research on higher education became institutionalized. At first, it was conducted at the aforementioned Research Unit for Higher Education at the University of Łódź, which moved in 1963 to Warsaw as the intercollegiate Department for Research on Higher Education at the Polish Academy of Sciences (PAN), subject directly to the Ministry of Higher Education. In 1973, the Council of Ministers founded a separate Institute of Political Science and Higher Education, which took over the department and other agencies of PAN. J. Kluczyński, *Szkolnictwo wyższe w czterdziestoleciu Polski Ludowej* (Warszawa: PWN, 1986), 73–78.
31. The most vital research was conducted under the supervision of Jan Szczepański at the University of Łódź at the Department for Sociological Research, PAN. The outcome was a series of publications such as: Jan Szczepański, ed., *Z badań klasy robotniczej i inteligencji* (Łódź: PWN, 1958); Jan Szczepański, ed., *Wykształcenie a pozycja społeczna inteligencji: praca zbiorowa, t. I* (Łódź: PWN, 1959); Jan Szczepański, *Wykształcenie a pozycja społeczna inteligencji: praca zbiorowa t. II* (Łódź: PWN, 1960); as well as Szczepański's own studies: Jan Szczepański, *Inteligencja i społeczeństwo* (Warszawa: Książka i Wiedza, 1957); Szczepański, *Socjologiczne zagadnienia wyższego wykształcenia*; Szczepański, *Szkice o szkolnictwie wyższym*. In 1962, the subsequent 12th volume was published: *Z badań klasy robotniczej i inteligencji*, this time devoted to preparatory courses and how their graduates later managed at the university and in professional life: Szczepański, *Ze studiów nad kursami przygotowawczymi*. The collection *Wykształcenie a pozycja*, published by the Department for Sociological Research, and the survey conducted by the Research Unit for Higher Education at the University of Łódź on the employment of the 1958 graduates were published by the Department for Planning and Organization. Salomea Kowalewska and Zdzisław Kowalewski, *Problemy zapotrzebowania i zatrudniania absolwentów szkół wyższych w przemyśle: raport z badań przeprowadzonych w 1959 roku w odniesieniu do absolwentów z 1958 r*, 1962.
32. Szczepański, *Ze studiów nad kursami przygotowawczymi*, 15.
33. Quoted in: Szczepański, 166.

34. A pejorative description of a preparatory course participant.
35. Both quotations from Szczepański, *Ze studiów nad kursami przygotowawczymi*, 165.
36. Lewandowski, *Rodowód społeczny powojennej inteligencji polskiej*, 79; Most of the students who failed to complete their studies were those that had to work or were supported by their families and depended entirely on their family situation. Between 1947 and 1950, the sifting remained at the level of slightly over 50 percent at the University of Łódź, 46 percent at Łódź University of Technology, and 42 percent at the Medical University. Szczepański, *Ze studiów nad kursami przygotowawczymi*, 181.
37. Lewandowski, *Rodowód społeczny powojennej inteligencji polskiej*, 79.
38. Szczepański, *Wykształcenie a pozycja społeczna inteligencji*, 1960, 477.
39. Kersten, *Między wyzwoleniem a zniewoleniem*, 11.
40. Szczepański, *Wykształcenie a pozycja społeczna inteligencji*, 1960, 478–79.
41. Alicja Lisiecka, "Pokolenie 'pryszczatych,'" *Pamiętnik Literacki*, 55/4 (1964): 367.
42. Hanna Świda-Ziemba, *Urwany lot: pokolenie inteligenckiej młodzieży powojennej w świetle listów i pamiętników z lat 1945–1948* (Kraków: Wydawnictwo Literackie, 2003); Palska, *Nowa inteligencja w Polsce Ludowej, X.*
43. Świda-Ziemba, *Urwany lot*, 289–91, 324, 342.
44. Palska, *Nowa inteligencja w Polsce Ludowej*; Świda-Ziemba, *Urwany lot*, 80.
45. Mrozik, "Girls from the Polish Youth Union: (Dis)Remembrance of the Generation."
46. Szczepański, *Wykształcenie a pozycja społeczna inteligencji*, 1960, 488; Szczepański, *Ze studiów nad kursami przygotowawczymi*, 191.
47. Szczepański, *Wykształcenie a pozycja społeczna inteligencji*, 1960, 488.
48. Jan Woskowski, "Losy absolwentów historii Uniwersytetu Łódzkiego," in *Z badań klasy robotniczej i inteligencji*, ed. Jan Szczepański (Łódź, Warszawa: PWN, 1958), 179.
49. Woskowski, 170.
50. Woskowski, 186.
51. Szczepański, *Socjologiczne zagadnienia wyższego wykształcenia*, 344–46.
52. Woskowski, "Losy absolwentów historii Uniwersytetu Łódzkiego," 178.
53. Szczepański, *Wykształcenie a pozycja społeczna inteligencji*, 1960, 508.
54. For instance, it was not until openings for positions were introduced in 1956 that more people with diplomas started to be hired. Szczepański, 491.
55. Słabek, "Wychodźstwo robotnicze: awans społeczny jednostek i zubożenie klasy?," 317.
56. Halina Najduchowska, *Kwalifikacje i drogi zawodowe dyrektorów przedsiębiorstw przemysłowych: studium socjologiczno-historyczne* (Warszawa: PWN, 1984); Słabek, "Wychodźstwo robotnicze: awans społeczny jednostek i zubożenie klasy?," 320.

CHAPTER 6

1. Pitirim Aleksandrovič Sorokin, *Ruchliwość społeczna* (Warszawa: PAN, 2009), 183.
2. Szczepański, *Polskie losy*, 107.
3. Adam Sarapata, *Przemiany społeczne w Polsce Ludowej* (Warszawa: PWN, 1965), 34.

4. Hübner, *I Kongres Nauki Polskiej jako forma realizacji założeń polityki naukowej państwa ludowego*, 172.
5. The ratio of the number of students (as of the beginning of a school year) at a given grade level (in a given age group) to the number of the population who qualify for the particular grade level.
6. *Szkolnictwo wyższe w Polsce* (Warszawa: Ministerstwo Nauki i Szkolnictwa Wyższego, 2013), 5.
7. Jan Szczepański, to follow then-conceptualization, defines school selection as "various social forces that in effect cut across social classes and sectors, at the level of state, local environments, families and schools, which hinder or facilitate one's path to higher education," quoted in Tadeusz Krajewski, *Dobór kandydatów do szkół wyższych: analiza czynników społecznych i pedagogicznych* (Warszawa: PWN, 1969), 37; Ireneusz Białecki, *Wybór szkoły a reprodukcja struktury społecznej* (Wrocław: Zakład Narodowy im. Ossolińskich, 1982), 157.
8. Woskowski, "Losy absolwentów historii Uniwersytetu Łódzkiego," 164.
9. Henryk Domański and Irina Tomescu-Dubrow, "Nierówności edukacyjne przed i po zmianie systemu," in *Zmiany stratyfikacji społecznej w Polsce*, ed. Henryk Domański (Warszawa: PAN, 2008), 46.
10. Six percent studied in agricultural faculties, 10 percent studied natural sciences, 13 percent medicine, 18 percent economy and law, and 22 percent humanities and social studies. Kluczyński, *Szkolnictwo wyższe w czterdziestoleciu Polski Ludowej*, 40.
11. Słabek, "Wychodźstwo robotnicze: awans społeczny jednostek i zubożenie klasy?," 367.
12. Alicja Zawistowska, *Horyzontalne nierówności edukacyjne we współczesnej Polsce* (Warszawa: Scholar, 2012), 78–85.
13. Woskowski, "Losy absolwentów historii Uniwersytetu Łódzkiego," 166–67.
14. Woskowski, 170.
15. Domański, *Zmiany stratyfikacji społecznej w Polsce*, 24.
16. Sawiński, "Zmiany systemowe a nierówności w dostępie do wykształcenia," 15.
17. Krajewski, *Dobór kandydatów do szkół wyższych*, 10.
18. Based on GUS's data from the study "Młodzież w Polsce Ludowej 1965–1970." Krajewski, 20.
19. Stańczak-Wiślicz, "'. . . być dziewczyną.' Wychowanie, dorastanie i edukacja dziewcząt," 217–90.
20. Mikołaj Kozakiewicz, *Bariery awansu poprzez wykształcenie* (Warszawa: Instytut Wydawniczy CRZZ, 1973), 17.
21. Domański and Tomescu-Dubrow, "Nierówności edukacyjne przed i po zmianie systemu," 46.
22. Władysław Adamski and Krzysztof Zagórski, *Szanse zdobywania wykształcenia w Polsce: polityka społeczna a determinanty strukturalne i kulturowe. Raport z badań*

(Warszawa: PAN, 1979); Krystyna Janicka, "Ruchliwość międzypokoleniowa," in *Struktura i ruchliwość społeczna*, ed. Kazimierz Maciej Słomczyński and Włodzimierz Wesołowski (Gdańsk: Zakład Narodowy im. Ossolińskich, 1973); K. M. Słomczyński and Włodzimierz Wesołowski, *Struktura i ruchliwość społeczna* (Gdańsk: Zakład Narodowy im. Ossolińskich, 1973); Włodzimierz Wesołowski, *Zróżnicowanie społeczne* (Warszawa: Zakład Narodowy im. Ossolińskich, 1974).

23. Robert D. Mare, *Trends in Schooling: Demography, Performance, and Organization* (Madison, WI: University of Wisconsin, 1981).
24. Zawistowska, *Horyzontalne nierówności edukacyjne we współczesnej Polsce*, 56.
25. Janusz Żarnowski's studies suggest that the children of blue-collar workers at state-owned companies had the best start among the working class. In the countryside, anything above the four years of compulsory elementary school was considered a "dandy's luxury." Zawistowska, 71.
26. Domański, *Zmiany stratyfikacji społecznej w Polsce*, 80.
27. Kluczyński, *Szkolnictwo wyższe w czterdziestoleciu Polski Ludowej*, 17.
28. Kluczyński, 21.
29. Mieczysław Pęcherski, *System oświatowy w Polsce Ludowej na tle porównawczym* (Wrocław: Zakład Narodowy im. Ossolińskich, 1981), 245.
30. Kluczyński, *Szkolnictwo wyższe w czterdziestoleciu Polski Ludowej*, 9.
31. On choosing secondary schools: Marzanna Stasińska, *Syndrom pochodzenia społecznego a wybór szkoły. Analiza kanoniczna* (Warszawa: UW, 1985); Zawistowska, *Horyzontalne nierówności edukacyjne we współczesnej Polsce*, 89.
32. Szczepański, *Socjologiczne zagadnienia wyższego wykształcenia*, 123.
33. Dylik and Dylik, "Nauka. Powstanie i organizacja łódzkiego ośrodka naukowego," 486.
34. Krajewski, *Dobór kandydatów do szkół wyższych*, 46–47.
35. Michał Pohoski, "Kariery szkolne i kariery społeczno-zawodowe a pochodzenie społeczne," *Kultura i Społeczeństwo*, no. 2 (1984); Zbigniew Sawiński and Marzanna Stasińska, *Przemiany w oddziaływaniu czynników pochodzenia na dwóch progach selekcji międzyszkolnej* (Warszawa: Instytut Socjologii Uniwersytetu Warszawskiego, 1986).
36. Domański, *Zmiany stratyfikacji społecznej w Polsce*, 31.
37. Franciszek Januszkiewicz, *Doskonalenie systemu rekrutacji na studia wyższe* (Warszawa: PWN, 1988), 31.
38. Jakub Karpiński, *Ustrój komunistyczny w Polsce* (Warszawa: Akademia Leona Koźmińskiego, 2005), 160.
39. Alicja Zawistowska, "Rozbieżność struktury wykształcenia kobiet i mężczyzn w PRL. Pomiędzy polityką państwa a indywidualnymi wyborami edukacyjnymi," *Roczniki Dziejów Społecznych i Gospodarczych* 75 (December 1, 2015): 175; Sawiński, "Zmiany systemowe a nierówności w dostępie do wykształcenia," 42.
40. Białecki, *Wybór szkoły a reprodukcja struktury społecznej*, 25–28.

41. Zawistowska, *Horyzontalne nierówności edukacyjne we współczesnej Polsce*, 72.
42. Piotr Długosz, "Społeczne skutki zmian systemu edukacji," in *Zawirowania systemu edukacji*, ed. Marta Zahorska (Warszawa: Wydawnictwo Uniwersytetu Warszawskiego, 2012), 39.
43. Ginsbert, *Łódź*, 287.
44. Bronisława Kopczyńska-Jaworska, *Łódź i inne miasta* (Łódź: Katedra Etnologii Uniwersytetu Łódzkiego, 1999), 53.
45. Zawistowska, "Rozbieżność struktury wykształcenia kobiet i mężczyzn w PRL. Pomiędzy polityką państwa a indywidualnymi wyborami edukacyjnymi."
46. Domański, *Zmiany stratyfikacji społecznej w Polsce*, 29.
47. Zawistowska, 178.
48. Zawistowska, 168–69.
49. Renata Siemieńska, "Kariery Akademickie i Ich Kontekst—Porównania Międzygeneracyjne," *Nauka i szkolnictwo wyższe* 1, no. 17 (2001): 47.
50. Stańczak-Wiślicz, "'. . . być dziewczyną.' Wychowanie, dorastanie i edukacja dziewcząt," 302.
51. Malgorzata Fidelis, *Women, Communism, and Industrialization in Postwar Poland* (Cambridge: Cambridge University Press, 2010); Natalia Jarska, *Kobiety z marmuru: robotnice w Polsce w latach 1945–1960* (Warszawa: IPN, 2015), 102; Katarzyna Stańczak-Wiślicz et al., *Kobiety w Polsce 1945–1989: nowoczesność—równouprawnienie—komunizm* (Kraków: Universitas, 2020); Agnieszka Mrozik, *Architektki PRL-u Komunistki, literatura i emancypacja kobiet w powojennej Polsce* (Warszawa: Instytut Badań Literackich PAN, 2022).
52. Sawiński, "Zmiany systemowe a nierówności w dostępie do wykształcenia," 32.
53. Michał Charkiewicz, *Kadry wykwalifikowane w Polsce* (Warszawa: PWN, 1961) quoted by Sarapata, *Przemiany społeczne w Polsce Ludowej*, 33.
54. For instance: Randall Collins, *The Credential Society: An Historical Sociology of Education and Stratification* (New York: Academic Press, 1979).
55. Pierre Bourdieu and Jean Claude Passeron, *Reproduction in Education, Society and Culture*, trans. R. Nice (London: Sage, 1990).
56. Connelly, "The Foundations of Diversity: Communist Higher Education Policies in Eastern Europe 1945–1955," 127.
57. Krasiewicz, *Odbudowa szkolnictwa wyższego w Polsce Ludowej w latach 1944–1948*, 338–39.
58. Nicholas Lampert, *The Technical Intelligentsia and the Soviet State* (New York: Holmes & Meier, 1979); Andreas, *Rise of the Red Engineers*.
59. Nosko, *Rewolucja i inteligencja*, 107.
60. Sarapata, *Przemiany społeczne w Polsce Ludowej*, 32–34.

61. Lidia Pawelec, "Raport o stanie oświaty w PRL (przedruk z 1973)," in *Oświata, wychowanie i kultura fizyczna w rzeczywistości społeczno-politycznej Polski Ludowej (1945–1989): rozprawy i szkice*, ed. Romuald Grzybowski (Toruń: Wydawnictwo Adam Marszałek, 2004).
62. Pawelec, 84.
63. Pawelec, 88.
64. Stanisław Kowalski, "Aspiracje szkolne młodzieży jako czynni demokratyzacji kształcenia," in *Naród, kultura, osobowość: księga poświęcona profesorowi Józefowi Chałasińskiemu*, ed. Antonina Kłoskowska (Wrocław: Zakład Narodowy im. Ossolińskich, 1983), 313.
65. Szczepański, *Wykształcenie a pozycja społeczna inteligencji*, 1959.
66. For instance: Halina Najduchowska, *Pozycja społeczna starych robotników przemysłu metalowego: (fragmenty opracowanych badań)* (Wrocław: Zakład Narodowy im. Ossolińskich, 1965).
67. Tadeusz Aleksander, *Awans oświatowy młodzieży wiejskiej, 1945–1970 (na przykładzie Sądecczyzny)* (Warszawa: Ludowa Spółdzielnia Wydawnicza, 1972), 124.
68. Kozakiewicz, *Bariery awansu poprzez wykształcenie*, 48.
69. Kozakiewicz, 41.
70. Kozakiewicz, 45.
71. Zawistowska, *Horyzontalne nierówności edukacyjne we współczesnej Polsce*, 87.
72. Elżbieta Wnuk-Lipińska, "Wykształcenie: cel czy środek," in *Studenci w Polsce i w Niemieckiej Republice Demokratycznej w świetle badań socjologicznych*, ed. Halina Najduchowska (Warszawa: PWN, 1987), 23.
73. Jadwiga Koralewicz, *Autorytaryzm, lęk, konformizm* (Warszawa: Scholar, 2008).
74. Kowalski, "Aspiracje szkolne młodzieży jako czynni demokratyzacji kształcenia," 314.
75. Adam Sarapata, *Studia nad uwarstwieniem i ruchliwością społeczną w Polsce* (Warszawa: Książka i Wiedza, 1965), 44–45.
76. This was true in the case of upwardly mobile peasants during the interwar period. Józef Chałasiński, *Młode pokolenie chłopów: procesy i zagadnienia kształtowania się warstwy chłopskiej w Polsce* (Warszawa: Spółdzielnia Wydawnicza "Pomoc Oświatowa," 1946).
77. Kazimierz Maciej Słomczyński, Krystyna Janicka, and Władysław Wesołowski, *Badania struktury społecznej Łodzi: doświadczenia i perspektywy* (Warszawa: PAN, 1994), 78–79.
78. Kozakiewicz, *Bariery awansu poprzez wykształcenie*, 49.
79. More specifically, it was the category "understanding yourself and the world around you" that was put first by over a third of the survey respondents as the main motivation to take up studies.
80. Szczepański, *Socjologiczne zagadnienia wyższego wykształcenia*, 145–46.
81. Szczepański, 123–35.
82. Janicka, "Ruchliwość międzypokoleniowa," 69.

83. Janicka, 89.
84. Karpiński, *Ustrój komunistyczny w Polsce*, 160–61.
85. Wesołowski, *Zróżnicowanie społeczne*, 105–6.
86. Michał Kalecki, "Porównanie dochodów robotników i pracowników umysłowych poza rolnictwem w 1960 r. i 1937 r.," *Kultura i Społeczeństwo*, no. 1 (1964): 39.
87. Lidia Beskid, *Zmiany spożycia w Polsce* (Warszawa: PWN, 1972); Grzegorz Lissowski and Michał Pohoski, "Oceny dochodów, słuszna płaca i prestiż," *Kultura i Społeczeństwo*, no. 4 (1987): 177–97.
88. Wesołowski, *Zróżnicowanie społeczne*, 107–17; Słomczyński et al., *Badania struktury społecznej Łodzi*, 58.
89. Kaja Kaźmierska, Katarzyna Waniek, and Agata Zysiak, *Opowiedzieć uniwersytet* (Łódź: WUŁ, 2015), 88; on the university's infrastructure see: Maciej Kronenberg and Karolina Kołodziej, *70 lat uniwersytetu łódzkiego w przestrzeni miejskiej łodzi (1945–2015)* (Łódź: WUŁ, 2015).
90. Puś, *Zarys historii Uniwersytetu Łódzkiego 1945–2015*, 50.
91. Edmund Wnuk-Lipiński, *Demokratyczna rekonstrukcja: z socjologii radykalnej zmiany społecznej* (Warszawa: PWN, 1996), 150.
92. These types of indexes are problematic in that the categories of "white-collar worker" and "intelligentsia" existed in parallel but were not synonymous. Furthermore, various studies defined them differently. Słomczyński and Wesołowski, *Struktura i ruchliwość społeczna*, 40.
93. Gawryszewski, *Ludność Polski w XX wieku*, 334.
94. K. M. Słomczyński, "Rola wykształcenia w procesie ruchliwości wewnątrz pokoleniowej," in *Struktura i ruchliwość społeczna*, ed. Włodzimierz Wesołowski and Kazimierz Maciej Słomczyński (Gdańsk: Zakład Narodowy im. Ossolińskich, 1973), 122.
95. Sarapata, *Studia nad uwarstwieniem i ruchliwością społeczną w Polsce*, 67–69.
96. Zdzisław Kowalewski, "Problemy kształcenia w rodzinie włókniarskiej," in *Włókniarze łódzcy: monografia*, ed. Józef Spychalski and Edward Rosset (Łódź: Wydawnictwo Łódzkie, 1966), 549.
97. Kowalewski, 555.
98. Mirosława Marody, "Przemiany postaw ideologicznych i przystosowanie w systemie komunistycznym," in *Komunizm: ideologia, system, ludzie*, ed. Tomasz Szarota (Warszawa: Neriton, 2001), 134–35.
99. Winicjusz Narojek, *Socjalistyczne "welfare state": studium z psychologii społecznej Polski Ludowej* (Warszawa: PWN, 1991), 28–29.
100. Sheila Fitzpatrick, *Education and Social Mobility in the Soviet Union 1921–1934* (Cambridge: Cambridge University Press, 2002).
101. Robert English, *Russia and the Idea of the West: Gorbachev, Intellectuals, and the End of the Cold War* (New York: Columbia University Press, 2000), 10–11.
102. Adela Hîncu and Agata Zysiak, "Socialist Culture, Participation and Expert Knowl-

edge in Poland and Romania in the Long 1960s," *European Review of History: Revue Européenne d'histoire* 30, no. 2 (March 4, 2023): 234–56.

103. Jacek Kurczewski proposes the term "communist middle class," which included professionals and specialized workers. Jacek Kurczewski, *The Resurrection of Rights in Poland* (Oxford, New York: Clarendon Press; Oxford University Press, 1993).
104. Halina Najduchowska, "Aspiracje maturzystów do wyższego wykształcenia," in *Studenci w Polsce i w Niemieckiej Republice Demokratycznej w świetle badań socjologicznych*, ed. Halina Najduchowska (Warszawa: PWN, 1987), 39.
105. Wiesław Wiśniewski, "Aspiracje edukacyjne społeczeństwa polskiego," in *Oświata w społecznej świadomości*, ed. Wiesław Wiśniewski (Warszawa: Młodzieżowa Agencja Wydawnicza, 1980), 81.
106. Halina Najduchowska, ed., *Studenci w Polsce i w Niemieckiej Republice Demokratycznej w świetle badań socjologicznych* (Warszawa: PWN, 1987), 70–74.
107. For instance: M. S. Voslenskiĭ, *Nomenklatura: The Soviet Ruling Class* (New York: Doubleday, 1984).
108. Andreas, *Rise of the Red Engineers*.
109. Ferenc Fehér, Ágnes Heller, and György G. Márkus, *Dictatorship Over Needs: An Analysis of Soviet Societies* (Oxford: Basil Blackwell, 1983), 120.
110. P. Hübner and D. Degen, *Instytucje naukowe, towarzystwa, biblioteki, wydawnictwa i czasopisma naukowe*, in *Humanistyka polska w latach 1945–1990*, ed. Jerzy Myśliński and Urszula Jakubowska (Warszawa: Instytut Badań Literackich PAN, 2006), 15.
111. Cichocki and Jóźwiak, *Najważniejsze są kadry*, 47.
112. Słabek, "Wychodźstwo robotnicze," 314.
113. T. Kowalik, *Spory o ustrój społeczno-gospodarczy w Polsce: lata 1944–1948* (Warszawa: Wydawnictwo Key Text, 2006), 90.
114. J. Connelly, *Captive University: The Sovietization of East German, Czech and Polish Higher Education, 1945–1956* (Chapel Hill: University of North Carolina Press, 2000).
115. Szczepański, *Polskie losy*, 46.
116. See for example: Maciej Gdula and Przemysław Sadura, eds., *Style życia i porządek klasowy w Polsce* (Warszawa: Wydawnictwo Naukowe Scholar, 2012); Wojciech Woźniak, *Nierówności społeczne w polskim dyskursie politycznym*, Wydanie pierwsze (Warszawa: Wydawnictwo Naukowe Scholar, 2012).
117. Domański and Tomescu-Dubrow, "Nierówności edukacyjne przed i po zmianie systemu," 54–55.
118. Sawiński, "Zmiany systemowe a nierówności w dostępie do wykształcenia," 40–41.
119. Zawistowska, *Horyzontalne nierówności edukacyjne we współczesnej Polsce*; also Sawiński, 89.
120. Domański and Tomescu-Dubrow, "Nierówności edukacyjne przed i po zmianie systemu," 71.
121. Domański, *Zmiany stratyfikacji społecznej w Polsce*, 8.

122. Zawistowska, *Horyzontalne nierówności edukacyjne we współczesnej Polsce*, 213.
123. Piotr Kozarzewski, *Wykluczenie edukacyjne*, in *Wykluczeni: wymiar społeczny, materialny i etniczny*, ed. Maria Jarosz (Warszawa: PAN, 2008), 145.
124. Przemysław Sadura, *Szkoła i nierówności społeczne* (Warszawa: Fundacja Amicus Europae, 2012).
125. Roman Dolata, *Szkoła, segregacje, nierówności* (Warszawa: Wydawnictwa Uniwersytetu Warszawskiego, 2008), 68; on inequalities in early-stage education see: Tomasz Szlendak, *Zaniedbana piaskownica: style wychowania małych dzieci a problem nierówności szans edukacyjnych* (Warszawa: Instytut Spraw Publicznych, 2003).
126. Sadura, *Szkoła i nierówności społeczne*, 21.
127. Sawiński, "Zmiany systemowe a nierówności w dostępie do wykształcenia," 32.
128. Zawistowska, *Horyzontalne nierówności edukacyjne we współczesnej Polsce*, 152.
129. GUS, *Polska w Liczbach 1944–1964* (Warszawa: GUS, 1964), 91.
130. Karpiński, *Ustrój komunistyczny w Polsce*, 160.
131. Gawryszewski, *Ludność Polski w XX Wieku*, 331.
132. GUS, *Polska w Liczbach 1944–1964*, 92.
133. Zawistowska, *Horyzontalne nierówności edukacyjne we współczesnej Polsce*, 72.

CHAPTER 7

1. JK, Narrative interview, 2011, 19, Academic Lodz Collection.
2. RO, Narrative interview, 2011, Academic Lodz Collection.
3. Referring to *les miraculés*: Bourdieu and Passeron, *The Inheritors*.
4. Referring to the Pletnev-Lenin debate in the 1920s: Graham, *Science in Russia and the Soviet Union*, 90.
5. Szczepański, *Socjologiczne zagadnienia wyższego wykształcenia*, 249.
6. Professors with habilitation (the so-called second PhD), adjuncts with PhDs, and assistants working on their dissertations composed faculty structure in interwar Poland.
7. GUS, *Rocznik statystyczny* (Warszawa: GUS, 1955).
8. Connelly, "The Foundations of Diversity: Communist Higher Education Policies in Eastern Europe 1945–1955," 126.
9. Tomasz Zarycki, *Kapitał kulturowy: inteligencja w Polsce i w Rosji* (Warszawa: Wydawnictwo Uniwersytetu Warszawskiego, 2008).
10. Bohdan Jałowiecki, *Oblicza polskich regionów*, Studia regionalne i lokalne, nr 50 (Warszawa: Uniwersytet Warszawski, 1996), 36.
11. Palska, *Nowa inteligencja w Polsce Ludowej, 114*.
12. Palska, *Nowa inteligencja w Polsce Ludowej, 119–25*.
13. Jan Kuchta, *Psychologja dziecka wiejskiego a praca szkolna (ze szczególnem uwzględnieniem "zajęć cichych")* (Warszawa: Gebethner i Wolff, 1933).
14. Świda-Ziemba, *Urwany lot*.
15. A similar division is made by Krzysztof Kosiński in *O nową mentalność: życie codzienne*

w szkołach 1945–1956 (Warszawa: Trio, 2000), 148; Hanna Świda-Ziemba, *Młodzież PRL: portrety pokoleń w kontekście historii* (Kraków: Wydawnictwo Literackie, 2010), 98.

16. Świda-Ziemba, *Urwany lot*, 204.
17. I avoid using the word "trajectory," which is widely used in the biographical research method and may be misleading, particularly when analyzing biographical materials. Henceforth I use the concepts of "biographical path," "educational path," and "academic career."
18. Bourdieu and Passeron, *Reproduction in Education, Society and Culture*, 32.
19. Bourdieu and Passeron, 119.
20. Andrzej M. Kobos, *Po drogach uczonych: z członkami Polskiej Akademii Umiejętności, t. 1* (Kraków: Polska Akademia Umiejętności, 2007), 375.
21. In this collection there are very few interviews with women in the PAU materials.
22. Michael Grenfell, *Pierre Bourdieu: Key Concepts* (Durham: Acumen, 2012), 88.
23. The author of the memoirs only writes that his family lived on the Księży Młyn workers' estate in Łódź, where skilled workers received flats and their children went to school. In this case, his interests in scholarship were supported by his parents. From the context, we can assume that this was a working elite with relatively high economic and cultural capital; the father probably held a managerial position in a factory.
24. David Swartz, *Culture and Power: The Sociology of Pierre Bourdieu* (Chicago: University of Chicago Press, 2012), 232.
25. Janusz Żarnowski estimates that the largest group among the prewar intelligentsia were teachers—around 100,000 people, followed by state officials—approximately 50,000, engineers—13,000–14,000, doctors—5,000, lawyers—8,000, journalists—3,500, and also a large group of military officers—18,000–19,000. Żarnowski, *O inteligencji polskiej lat miedzywojennych*, 69–89.
26. For gender role in the PRL and women's rights see: Susan Gal and Gail Kligman, *The Politics of Gender after Socialism: A Comparative-Historical Essay* (Princeton, NJ: Princeton University Press, 2000); Susan Gal and Gail Kligman, eds., *Reproducing Gender: Politics, Publics, and Everyday Life after Socialism* (Princeton: Princeton University Press, 2000); Magdalena Grabowska, *Zerwana genealogia: działalność społeczna i polityczna kobiet po 1945 roku a współczesny polski ruch kobiecy* (Warszawa: Wydawnictwo Naukowe Scholar, 2018); Fidelis, *Women, Communism, and Industrialization in Postwar Poland*; Natalia Jarska, *Kobiety z marmuru: robotnice w Polsce w latach 1945–1960* (Warszawa: IPN, 2015); Mrozik, *Architektki PRL-u Komunistki, literatura i emancypacja kobiet w powojennej Polsce*; Artwińska and Mrozik, *Gender, Generations, and Communism in Central and Eastern Europe and Beyond*; Stańczak-Wiślicz et al., *Kobiety w Polsce 1945–1989*; Izabela Desperak and Martyna Krogulec, *Miasto pracujacych kobiet* (Łódź: Wydawnictwo Uniwersytetu Łódzkiego, 2020); Kolbuszewska, *Kobiety w drodze na naukowy Olimp*.
27. Swartz, *Culture and Power*, 130.

28. The mentor or advisor played a role similar to a German *Doktorvater*, whose role went beyond that of solely scholar support to include protection and at the extreme, both paternalism and favoritism. However, the model was also present in the imperial scholarship in Russia. Andy Byford, "Initiation to Scholarship: The University Seminar in Late Imperial Russia," *Russian Review* 64, no. 2 (April 2005): 299–323; additionally, the role of the mentor also could be reinforced by the conspiracy education during World War II.
29. "Raised in the shadow of the university department [. . .], in an atmosphere full of culture and knowledge of the humanities, I appreciated that a so-called civilised person has to have a high degree of knowledge," OM, *Moja droga do nauki, t.3* (Łódź: ŁTN, 2000), 121.
30. JB, *Moja droga do nauki, t.3*, 37.
31. MSH, *Moja droga do nauki, t.3*, 97.
32. ZS, *Moja droga do nauki, t.6* (Łódź: ŁTN, 2011), 252.
33. JK, *Moja droga do nauki, t.6*, 19.
34. JK, *Moja droga do nauki, t.6*, 22.
35. A supplementary source also of great interest for this class dimension of the academic biographies are the photographs of professors in the five-volume collection of memoirs of members of the Polish Academy of Arts and Science. Many of these are the standard depiction against a background of books, next to a microscope or other tools of the trade, but there are also occasional shots with a background of a collection of family photographs, swords, and even a full-size oil portrait of the professor in question. Kobos, *Po drogach uczonych*, and following volumes.
36. Particular mention in many biographies is made of the beauty of and love for the mountains, with mountain hikes highlighted as a favorite pastime (alongside canoeing, sailing, and, less frequently, cycling trips).
37. KJ, Narrative interview, 2011, Academic Lodz Collection.
38. Szczepański, *Dzienniki z lat 1945–1968*.
39. JB, *Moja droga do nauki, t.3*, 42.
40. Opinions in the field meant a great deal and constituted an internal ranking list, regardless of the official data or lists of achievements. One of the PAU collection interviews mentions history at the University of Łódź. According to the Cracow professor, "Grabowska" was in charge there, numerous inspections took place, and there was a bad atmosphere; in contrast to this, he gives an example: "Wrocław had people from Lviv, a few from Vilnius. People are the most important!" Andrzej M. Kobos, *Po drogach uczonych: z członkami Polskiej Akademii Umiejętności, t. 2* (Kraków: Polska Akademia Umiejętności, 2007), 572.
41. NW, *Moja droga do nauki, t.5* (Łódź: ŁTN, 2006), 176.
42. ML, *Moja droga do nauki, t.6*, 92.

43. Bourdieu and Passeron, *The Inheritors*, 18–20.
44. ST, *Moja droga do nauki, t.6*, 204.
45. PM, *Moja droga do nauki, t.1* (Łódź: ŁTN, 1996), 259–61.
46. PM, *Moja droga do nauki, t.1*, 263.
47. In a reference to Joseph Conrad, literary references are themselves an element of the construction of intelligentsia biography: the exchange of meanings between educated people with high cultural competence.
48. PM, *Moja droga do nauki, t.1*, 272.
49. Jen Webb, Tony Schirato, and Geoff Danaher, *Understanding Bourdieu* (London: Sage, 2002), 128.
50. Woskowski, "Losy absolwentów historii Uniwersytetu Łódzkiego," 189.
51. LZ, *Moja droga do nauki, t.1*, 112.
52. Szczepański, *Wykształcenie a pozycja społeczna inteligencji*, 1960, 68.
53. WP, *Moja droga do nauki, t.1*, 271.
54. KA, *Moja droga do nauki, t.1*.
55. KJ, *Moja droga do nauki, t.5*, 60.
56. RO, Narrative interview.
57. Webb, Schirato, and Danaher, *Understanding Bourdieu*, 135.
58. Pierre Bourdieu, *The State Nobility: Elite Schools in the Field of Power* (Stanford: Stanford University Press, 1998), 367.
59. KJ, *Moja droga do nauki, t.5*, 84.
60. KA, *Moja droga do nauki, t.2* (Łódź: ŁTN, 1997), 35.
61. RO, Narrative interview.
62. Richard K. Harker, Cheleen Mahar, and Chris Wilkes, eds., *An Introduction to the Work of Pierre Bourdieu: The Practice of Theory* (Houndmills: Macmillan, 1990), 96.
63. Both cases were observed when collecting the professors' biographies, though not during the recorded interviews.
64. Bourdieu and Passeron, *The Inheritors*, 71.
65. "Whereas in 1970 of the 106,000 foreign business trips one third (36,000) were to capitalist countries, by 1973 the number of business trips had grown to almost 137,000, almost half of which (67,000) were to capitalist countries." Dariusz Stola, "Międzynarodowa mobilność zarobkowa w PRL," in *Ludzie na huśtawce: migracje między peryferiami Polski i Zachodu*, ed. Ewa Jaźwińska-Motylska and Marek Okólski (Scholar, 2001), 62–100.
66. Halina Najduchowska and Elżbieta Wnuk-Lipińska, *Nauczyciele akademiccy 1984* (Warszawa: PWN, 1990), 80–81.
67. KJ, *Moja droga do nauki, t.5*, 94.
68. KJ, *Moja droga do nauki, t.5*, 88.
69. KJ, *Moja droga do nauki, t.5*, 23–24.

70. JB, *Moja droga do nauki, t.3*, 52.
71. Franciszek Jakubczak, "Józefa Chałasińskiego ethos nieposłuszeństwa w myśleniu," in *Chałasiński dzisiaj: materiały z konferencji naukowej*, ed. Andrzej Kaleta (Toruń: Wydawnictwo UMK, 1996), 71.
72. PW, *Moja droga do nauki, t.1*, 267.
73. Connelly, *Captive University*; Connelly, "The Foundations of Diversity: Communist Higher Education Policies in Eastern Europe 1945–1955"; John Connelly, "Polish Universities and State Socialism 1944–1968," in *Universities under Dictatorship*, ed. John Connelly and Michael Grüttner (University Park: Penn State Press, 2005); John Connelly, "Communist Higher Education Policies in Czechoslovakia, Poland, and East Germany," in *The Establishment of Communist Regimes in Eastern Europe, 1944–1949*, ed. Norman M. Naimark and Leonid Gibianskii (Boulder, CO: Westview Press, 1997); Connelly and Grüttner, *Universities under Dictatorship*.
74. Connelly, "Polish Universities and State Socialism 1944–1968," 198.
75. Although from 1949 between 65 percent and 80 percent were members of the Union of Polish Youth. J. Szczepański, *Wykształcenie a pozycja społeczna inteligencji*, 477.
76. Barbara Fijałkowska, *Polityka i twórcy 1948–1959* (Warszawa: PWN, 1985), 464; Hübner, *Nauka polska po II wojnie światowej—idee i instytucje*, 174.
77. Kolbuszewska, *Kobiety w drodze na naukowy Olimp . . .*, 217 za; Fijałkowska, *Polityka i twórcy*, 468.
78. Kennedy, *Professionals, Power and Solidarity in Poland*, 16.
79. Connelly, "The Foundations of Diversity: Communist Higher Education Policies in Eastern Europe 1945–1955."
80. Zdenek Jirásek and Andrzej Malkiewicz, *Polska i Czechosłowacja w dobie stalinizmu (1948–1956). Studium porównawcze* (Warszawa: PAN, 2005).
81. MSH, *Moja droga do nauki, t.3*, 113.
82. JK, Narrative interview.
83. ST, *Moja droga do nauki, t.6*, 226.
84. Najduchowska and Wnuk-Lipińska, *Nauczyciele akademiccy 1984*, 133–36.
85. Barbara Post, "Etos warszawskich pracowników nauki—1983," in *Nauka w kulturze ogólnej*, ed. Stanisław Grzywna and Józefa Stępień, Problemy naukowe współczesności (Wrocław: Zakład Narodowy im. Ossolińskich, 1985), 215–17.
86. LZ, *Moja droga do nauki, t.1*, 204.
87. Webb, Schirato, and Danaher, *Understanding Bourdieu*, 135.
88. The Matilda effect, named after suffragist Matilda J. Gage, refers to a structural denial of recognition of female researchers whose achievements are more often ignored in favor of male scholars. Ghost advising describes the invisible and unpaid work of female scholars who supervise students of prominent male professors, providing feedback and support without public or official recognition.

89. Frances Trix and Carolyn Psenka, "Exploring the Color of Glass: Letters of Recommendation for Female and Male Medical Faculty," *Discourse & Society* 14, no. 2 (March 1, 2003): 191–220.
90. For example: Robert B. Townsend, "Gender and Success in Academia: More from the Historians' Career Paths Survey," *Prospectives on History*, no. 01 (2013), https://www.historians.org/publications-and-directories/perspectives-on-history/january-2013/gender-and-success-in-academia.
91. Martha Foschi, "Double Standards in the Evaluation of Men and Women," *Social Psychology Quarterly* 59, no. 3 (1996): 237–54, https://doi.org/10.2307/2787021; Laura W. Perna, "Sex Differences in Faculty Salaries: A Cohort Analysis," *Review of Higher Education* 24, no. 3 (March 1, 2001): 283–307, https://doi.org/10.1353/rhe.2001.0006; Mary Ann Mason, Nicholas H. Wolfinger, and Marc Goulden, *Do Babies Matter? Gender and Family in the Ivory Tower* (New Brunswick, NJ: Rutgers University Press, 2013).
92. Kolbuszewska, *Kobiety w drodze na naukowy Olimp . . .* ; Siemieńska, "Kariery akademickie i ich kontekst—porównania międzygeneracyjne," *Nauka i Szkolnictwo Wyższe* 1(17) (2001): 42–61.
93. Siemieńska, "Kariery akademickie i ich kontekst—," 47.
94. On the double and triple burden of socialist women see for example: Chiara Bonfiglioli, "Discussing Women's Double and Triple Burden in Socialist Yugoslavia: Women Working in the Garment Industry," in *Labor in State Socialist Europe, 1945–1989: Contributions to a Global History of Work*, ed. Marsha Siefert (Central European University Press, 2020), 195–215.
95. Kolbuszewska, *Kobiety w drodze na naukowy Olimp . . .*, 311–12, 325.
96. LB, *Moja droga do nauki, t.1*, 202.
97. OW, *Moja droga do nauki, t.1*, 234.
98. DA, *Moja droga do nauki, t.1*, 23.
99. LB, *Moja droga do nauki, t.1*, 199.
100. Katarzyna Andrejuk, "Awans społeczny kobiet w czasach PRL. Dynamika struktury i sprawczości," *Przegląd Socjologiczny* 65, no. 3 (2016): 157–79.
101. Mrozik, *Architektki PRL-u. Komunistki, literatura i emancypacja kobiet w powojennej Polsce*. An "effort to find women in the state" was inspired by Zheng Wang, *Finding Women in the State: A Socialist Feminist Revolution in the People's Republic of China, 1949–1964* (Oakland: University of California Press, 2017).
102. WW, *Moja droga do nauki, t.7* (Łódź: ŁTN, 2013), 136.
103. Kolbuszewska, *Kobiety w drodze na naukowy Olimp . . .*, 305–6.
104. In order to continue the course after the first two years following the introduction of two-stage programs, a student had to receive a referral to study rather than to work. This also specified the university at which the degree was to be continued.

105. PW, *Moja droga do nauki, t.1*, 268.
106. RZ, *Moja droga do nauki, t.2*.
107. KA, *Moja droga do nauki, t.2*, 27.
108. MS, Narrative interview, 2013, Academic Lodz Collection.
109. KL, Narrative interview, 2011, Academic Lodz Collection.
110. LI, *Moja droga do nauki, t.2*, 60.
111. AA, *Moja droga do nauki, t.3*, 16.
112. WZ, *Moja droga do nauki, t.4* (Łódź: ŁTN, 2002), 97.

CHAPTER 8

1. A working-class student's question to the rector, Chałasiński, around the year 1949. Józef Chałasiński, *Rewolucja młodości: studia o awansie młodego pokolenia wsi i integracji narodu polskiego* (Warszawa: Ludowa Spółdzielnia Wydawnicza, 1969), 328.
2. Bourdieu and Passeron, *The Inheritors*, 1; the cited quotation comes from Margaret Mead, *Continuities in Cultural Evolution* (New Brunswick: Transaction Publishers, 1964), 130.
3. Bourdieu and Passeron, *The Inheritors*, 2–3.
4. Pierre Bourdieu, *Distinction: A Social Critique of the Judgement of Taste* (Cambridge, MA: Harvard University Press, 1984).
5. It appears also in Pierre Bourdieu, *Outline of a Theory of Practice* (Cambridge: Cambridge University Press, 2010); Pierre Bourdieu, *The Weight of the World: Social Suffering in Contemporary Society* (Stanford: Stanford University Press, 1999).
6. Bourdieu, *Distinction*, 161.
7. Simon Susen and Bryan S. Turner, *The Legacy of Pierre Bourdieu: Critical Essays* (London: Anthem Press, 2013), 78–80; the cited quotation comes from Pierre Bourdieu, *Pascalian Meditations* (Stanford: Stanford University Press, 2000), 161.
8. Bourdieu, *Pascalian Meditations*, 161; Bourdieu and Passeron, *The Inheritors*, 82; Cheryl Hardy, "Hysteresis," in *Pierre Bourdieu: Key Concepts*, ed. Michael Grenfell (Durham: Acumen, 2012), 135.
9. Hardy, "Hysteresis," 138.
10. Jane Leftwich Curry, "The Sociological Legacies of Communism," in *The Legacies of Communism in Eastern Europe*, ed. Zoltan D. Barany and Iván Völgyes (Baltimore: Johns Hopkins University Press, 1995), 77.
11. In the original: Pierre Bourdieu and Jean Claude Passeron, *Les Héritiers, les étudiants et la culture* (Paris: Les Éditions de Minuit, 1969); Bourdieu and Passeron, *The Inheritors*.
12. Bourdieu, *The State Nobility*, 183–87.
13. Webb, Schirato, and Danaher, *Understanding Bourdieu*, 42.
14. Pierre Bourdieu, *Homo Academicus* (Stanford: Stanford University Press, 1988); Bourdieu, *Distinction*.

15. SJ, *Moja droga do nauki, t.1*, 298.
16. Based also on biographies and interviews with professors from the Polish Academy of Arts and Science.
17. Original quotations from the autobiographies.
18. Jan Parandowski's "Mythology," published in 1924, was a very popular bedtime story in intelligentsia homes.
19. Notes and essays: "Spuścizna Niny Assorodobraj-Kuli."
20. Note that this is an interview, not an autobiography written down and subjected to particular rigor or checks (including from editors and publishers).
21. SB, Narrative interview, 2011, Academic Lodz Collection.
22. ML, *Moja droga do nauki, t.7*, 89.
23. ML, *Moja droga do nauki, t.7*, 89.
24. ML, *Moja droga do nauki, t.7*, 96.
25. RJ, *Moja droga do nauki, t.3*, 139.
26. Rural Youth Association Union, "Wici," active from 1928 until its unification with the ZMP in 1948.
27. RJ, *Moja droga do nauki, t.3*, 147.
28. KT, *Moja droga do nauki, t.3*, 65.
29. After the March 1968 anti-Semitic campaign, many scholars were forced to leave Poland, which led to political promotions for associate professors without the required PhD. A "March docent" (*docent marcowy*) had negative connotations of an unfair, fast, and politically driven professional career.
30. PE, *Moja droga do nauki, t.1*, 277.
31. PE, *Moja droga do nauki, t.1*, 279.
32. The 1932 education reform named after the then minister, Janusz Jędrzejewicz; for more on this subject, see chapter 1.
33. PE, *Moja droga do nauki, t.1*, 280.
34. Richard Hoggart, *The Uses of Literacy: Aspects of Working-Class Life* (London: Penguin, 2009), 246.
35. This process also took place in Poland, as demonstrated by the research presented in the previous chapter.
36. When assistants were being employed in the 1950s, there was pressure to include people from the working classes, as well as a belief that this background led to greater support for the PZPR and greater inclination to engage in the building of the socialist university.
37. RO, Narrative interview.
38. Raymond Boudon, *The Unintended Consequences of Social Action* (London: Macmillan, 1982).
39. SB, Narrative interview.

40. Loic Wacquant, "For a Socio-Analysis of Intellectuals: On 'Homo Academicus,'" *Berkeley Journal of Sociology*, no. 34 (1989): 52.
41. Jadwiga Krajewska, *Czytelnictwo wśród robotników w Królestwie Polskim, 1870–1914* (Warszawa: PWN, 1979); Wiktor Marzec, "Proletariacka biografia i dzielenie postrzegalnego. rozmywanie granic klasowych w okresie rewolucji 1905 roku," *Folia Sociologica*, no. 41 (2012).
42. RO, Narrative interview.
43. Historical novels were the most popular reading matter in public libraries at the beginning of the twentieth century. Anna Żarnowska, *Wokół tradycji kultury robotniczej w Polsce* (Warszawa: PIW, 1986), 164.
44. WP, Narrative interview, 2012, Academic Lodz Collection.
45. Bourdieu's father, like the father of one of the interviewees, advanced from peasant stock to a state employee (postal worker) position during his son's youth.
46. Deborah Reed-Danahay, *Locating Bourdieu* (Bloomington: Indiana University Press, 2005), 32.
47. Hoggart, *The Uses of Literacy.*
48. The language Bourdieu uses in his works is rather complex (and critics have often used his own arguments against him, arguing that he reproduces the elite academic habitus), whereas Chałasiński was more accessible, without philosophical sophistication.
49. Chałasiński, *Młode pokolenie chłopów*, 1946.
50. Biggart, "Bukharin and the Origins of the 'Proletarian Culture' Debate"; Lynn Mally, *Culture of the Future: The Proletkult Movement in Revolutionary Russia* (Berkeley: University of California Press, 1990).
51. Jan Jerschina, *Osobowość społeczna studentów UJ chłopskiego pochodzenia. Na podstawie badań socjologicznych z lat 1966–1967*, vol. 25, Zeszyty PAN (Wrocław: Ossolineum, 1972), 47.
52. SB, Narrative interview.
53. RO, Narrative interview.
54. SB, Narrative interview.
55. Jerschina, *Osobowość społeczna studentów UJ chłopskiego pochodzenia. Na podstawie badań socjologicznych z lat 1966–1967*, 25:16.
56. A volunteer in state socialist countries. In the first years this was based on authentic enthusiasm, while later it often degenerated to an efficient source of unpaid labor or even a punishment.
57. RO, Narrative interview.
58. Behr, "Historical Policy-Making in Post-1989 Poland."
59. Bourdieu and Passeron, *The Inheritors*; Chałasiński, *Młode pokolenie chłopów*, 1946; Hoggart, *The Uses of Literacy.*
60. Reed-Danahay, *Locating Bourdieu*, 32.

61. Hoggart, *The Uses of Literacy*, 241.
62. Hoggart, 258.
63. See: Palska, *Nowa inteligencja w Polsce Ludowej*, 154.
64. Basil Bernstein, *Class, Codes, and Control* (London: Routledge, 2003).
65. RJ, *Moja droga do nauki, t.3*, 144.
66. Grenfell, *Pierre Bourdieu*, 29.
67. Hoggart, *The Uses of Literacy*, 249.
68. For example see: Peter E. Jones, "Bernstein's 'Codes' and the Linguistics of 'Deficit,'" *Language and Education* 27, no. 2 (March 1, 2013): 161–79; William Labov, *The Social Stratification of English in New York City*, II (Cambridge: Cambridge University Press, 2006); Carl Bereiter and Siegfried Engelmann, *Teaching Disadvantaged Children in the Preschool* (Englewood Cliffs, NJ: Prentice-Hall, 1966); Martin Deutsch and Martin Whiteman, "Social Disadvantage as Related to Intellective and Language Development," in *Social Class, Race, and Psychological Development*, ed. Martin Deutsch, Arthur Robert Jensen, and Irwin Katz (New York: Holt, Rinehart, and Winston, 1968); Zbigniew Bokszański, Andrzej Piotrowski, and Marek Ziółkowski, *Socjologia języka* (Warszawa: Wiedza Powszechna, 1977).
69. Pierre Bourdieu, Jean-Claude Passeron, and Monique de Saint Martin, *Academic Discourse: Linguistic Misunderstanding and Professorial Power* (Stanford: Stanford University Press, 1996), 8.
70. Bourdieu and Passeron, *The Inheritors*, 68.
71. RO, Narrative interview.
72. RO.
73. KT, *Moja droga do nauki, t.3*, 75.
74. The narrator is referring to the "Baptism of Poland" of 966, the coming of Christianity to the country, a highly significant date in Polish culture.
75. SB, Narrative interview.
76. RO, Narrative interview.
77. The medical faculties were separated from the University of Łódź in 1950, creating the Medical Academy, where the author of the autobiography studied for his degree and continued his academic career. The framework of the development of his career and institutional circumstances therefore differ from those at the university.
78. RJ, *Moja droga do nauki, t.3*, 146.
79. KT, *Moja droga do nauki, t.3*, 66.
80. KT, *Moja droga do nauki, t.3*, 66.
81. ZB, Narrative interview, 2011, Academic Lodz Collection.
82. BKJ, Narrative interview, 2011, Academic Lodz Collection.
83. KH *Moja droga do nauki, t.1*, 112.
84. Najduchowska and Wnuk-Lipińska, *Nauczyciele akademiccy 1984, 17*.

85. Ignacy Krasicki, *Wiersze wybrane*, trans. Ben Koschalka (Warszawa: PWN, 1964), 43.
86. Terry Eagleton, *Literary Theory: An Introduction* (Austin: John Wiley & Sons, 2011), given as an example and quoted in Webb, Schirato, and Danaher, *Understanding Bourdieu*, 130.
87. Bourdieu and Passeron, *Reproduction in Education, Society and Culture*, 95.
88. Connelly, "The Foundations of Diversity: Communist Higher Education Policies in Eastern Europe 1945–1955," 198; Connelly, *Captive University*.
89. Najduchowska and Wnuk-Lipińska, *Nauczyciele akademiccy 1984*.
90. This term is borrowed from Chałasiński; see for example: Józef Chałasiński, *Przeszłość i przyszłość inteligencji polskiej* (Warszawa: Ludowa Spółdzielnia Wydawnicza, 1958).
91. Palska, *Nowa inteligencja w Polsce Ludowej*.
92. For example: Connelly, "Polish Universities and State Socialism 1944–1968," 188.
93. Fitzpatrick, *Education and Social Mobility in the Soviet Union 1921–1934*.
94. Wacquant, "For a Socio-Analysis of Intellectuals: On 'Homo Academicus.'"
95. Swartz, *Culture and Power*, 239–44.
96. Ewa Domańska, *Historie niekonwencjonalne: refleksja o przeszłości w nowej humanistyce* (Poznań: Wydawnictwo Poznańskie, 2006).
97. Bourdieu, *The State Nobility*, 106.
98. Bourdieu and Passeron, *The Inheritors*, 66.
99. My thanks to Piotr Filipkowski for this point on Józef Chałasiński.

CONCLUSIONS

1. Michael Burawoy and Katherine Verdery, *Uncertain Transition: Ethnographies of Change in the Postsocialist World* (Lanham, MD: Rowman & Littlefield, 1999).
2. Ferenc Fehér and Ágnes Heller, *Eastern Left, Western Left: A Contribution to the Morphology of a Problematic Relationship* (Cologne: Index, 1986).
3. Augustin Stoica, "Communism as a Project for Modernization: The Romanian Case," *Polish Sociological Review*, no. 120 (1997): 313–31.
4. Fehér, Heller, and Márkus, *Dictatorship over Needs*, 283.
5. For example Mark and Betts, *Socialism Goes Global* and many other recent projects aiming at decolonizing Eastern Europe.
6. Fidelis, *Women, Communism, and Industrialization in Postwar Poland*; Stefania Dziecielska-Machnikowska and Jolanta Kulpińska, *Awans kobiety* (Łódź: Wydawnictwo Łódzkie, 1966); Kolbuszewska, *Kobiety w drodze na naukowy Olimp. . . .*
7. Maria Hirszowicz, *Pułapki zaangażowania: intelektualiści w służbie komunizmu* (Warszawa: Scholar, 2001), 85–86; Marcin Zaremba, *Komunizm, legitymizacja, nacjonalizm: nacjonalistyczna legitymizacja władzy komunistycznej w Polsce* (Warszawa: Trio, 2001).

8. Marody, "Przemiany postaw ideologicznych i przystosowanie w systemie komunistycznym," 130–31; Stefan Nowak, *Studenci Warszawy: studium długofalowych przemian postaw i wartości: praca zbiorowa pod redakcją Stefana Nowaka* (Warszawa: Wydawnictwo Uniwersytetu Warszawskiego, 1991), 127.
9. Cf. a classic study from the 1960s: Herschel Alt and Edith Alt, *The New Soviet Man: His Upbringing and Character Development* (New York: Bookman Associates, 1964); Yinghong Cheng, *Creating the "New Man": From Enlightenment Ideals to Socialist Realities* (Honolulu: University of Hawai'i Press, 2009); Victoria Hoffman, *Soviet Education and the Building of the New Soviet Man* (St. Petersburg, FL: Eckerd College, 1980).
10. John Connelly, "The Foundations of Diversity: Communist Higher Education Policies in Eastern Europe 1945–1955," in *Science under Socialism: East Germany in Comparative Perspective*, ed. Kristie Macrakis and Dieter Hoffmann (Cambridge, MA: Harvard University Press, 1999), 134.
11. For detailed information: Puś, *Zarys historii Uniwersytetu Łódzkiego 1945–2015*.

BIBLIOGRAPHY

ARCHIVES

Archiwum Akt Nowych (AAN)
Archiwum Uniwersytetu Łódzkiego (AUŁ)
Archiwum Państwowe w Łodzi (APŁ)
Archiwum PAN
Gabinet Rękopisów BUW

PERIODICALS

Dziennik Akademicki (1945–1956)
Dziennik Łódzki (1945–1956)
Express Ilustrowany/Łódzki Express Ilustrowany (1945–1956)
Głos Robotniczy (1945–1956)
Głos Uniwersytetu (1953–1956)
Kronika (1955–1957)
Kurier Popularny (1945–1948)
Kuźnica (1945–1950)
Kwartalnik Historyczny (1945–1956)
Łódź Literacka (1954–1955)
Myśl Współczesna (1946–1951)
Odrodzenie (1944–1950)
Płomienie (1945–1950)
Pobudka (1945–1947)
Po prostu (1947–1957)
Przegląd Socjologiczny (1946–1947)
Robotnik (1945–1948)
Trybuna Ludu (1948–1956)
Tygodnik Powszechny (1945–1953)
Życie Nauki (1946–1953)
Życie Szkoły Wyższej (1953–1989)

BIOGRAPHIES

BKJ. Narrative interview, 2011. Academic Lodz Collection.
JK. Narrative interview, 2011. Academic Lodz Collection.
KJ. Narrative interview, 2011. Academic Lodz Collection.
KL. Narrative interview, 2011. Academic Lodz Collection.
MS. Narrative interview, 2013. Academic Lodz Collection.
RO. Narrative interview, 2011. Academic Lodz Collection.
SB. Narrative interview, 2011. Academic Lodz Collection.
WP. Narrative interview, 2012. Academic Lodz Collection.
ZB. Narrative interview, 2011. Academic Lodz Collection.
Moja droga do nauki, t.1. Łódź: ŁTN, 1996.
Moja droga do nauki, t.2. Łódź: ŁTN, 1997.
Moja droga do nauki, t.3. Łódź: ŁTN, 2000.
Moja droga do nauki, t.4. Łódź: ŁTN, 2002.
Moja droga do nauki, t.5. Łódź: ŁTN, 2006.
Moja droga do nauki, t.6. Łódź: ŁTN, 2011.
Moja droga do nauki, t.7. Łódź: ŁTN, 2013.

REFERENCES

Adamski, Władysław, and Krzysztof Zagórski. *Szanse zdobywania wykształcenia w Polsce: polityka społeczna a determinanty strukturalne i kulturowe. Raport z badań*. Warszawa: PAN, 1979.
Aleksander, Tadeusz. *Awans oświatowy młodzieży wiejskiej, 1945–1970 (na przykładzie Sądecczyzny)*. Warszawa: Ludowa Spółdzielnia Wydawnicza, 1972.
Aleksiun, Natalia. "Together but Apart: University Experience of Jewish Students in the Second Polish Republic." *Acta Poloniae Historica* 109 (January 1, 2014): 109–37.
Alt, Herschel, and Edith Alt. *The New Soviet Man: His Upbringing and Character Development*. New York: Bookman Associates, 1964.
Andreas, Joel. *Rise of the Red Engineers: The Cultural Revolution and the Origins of China's New Class*. Stanford: Stanford University Press, 2009.
Andrejuk, Katarzyna. "Awans społeczny kobiet w czasach PRL. Dynamika struktury i sprawczości." *Przegląd Socjologiczny* 65, no. 3 (2016): 157–79.
Arnason, Johann P. "Communism and Modernity." *Daedalus* 129 (2000): 61–90.
Artwińska, Anna, and Agnieszka Mrozik, eds. *Gender, Generations, and Communism in Central and Eastern Europe and Beyond*. Routledge Research in Gender and History. Abingdon: Routledge, 2020.

Augustyniak, Jan. *Życie naukowe Łodzi*. Warszawa: Wydawnictwa Kasy im. J. Mianowskiego, 1933.

Baranowski, Bohdan. "Pierwsi Rektorzy Uniwersytetu Łódzkiego." *Życie Szkoły Wyższej*, no. 7/8 (1980): 87–91.

Baranowski, Bohdan. *Pierwsze lata Uniwersytetu Łódzkiego, 1945–1949*. Łódź: Uniwersytet Łódzki, 1985.

Baranowski, Bohdan. *Uniwersytet Łódzki 1945–1980*. Łódź: Uniwersytet Łódzki, 1980.

Baranowski, Bohdan, ed. *Uniwersytet Łódzki. Historia. Teraźniejszość. Perspektywy*. Łódź: Uniwersytet Łódzki, 1978.

Baranowski, Bohdan, and Krzysztof Baranowski. *Trudne lata Uniwersytetu Łódzkiego: 1949–1956*. Łódź: Wydawnictwo UŁ, 1990.

Baranowski, Krzysztof. *Alternatywna edukacja w II Rzeczypospolitej: Wolna Wszechnica Polska*. Warszawa: Towarzystwo WWP, 2001.

Baranowski, Krzysztof. *Oddział Wolnej Wszechnicy Polskiej w Łodzi: 1928–1939*. Warszawa: PWN, 1977.

Barany, Zoltan D., and Iván Völgyes, eds. *The Legacies of Communism in Eastern Europe*. Baltimore: Johns Hopkins University Press, 1995.

Behr, Valentin. "Historical Policy-Making in Post-1989 Poland: A Sociological Approach to the Narratives of Communism." *European Politics and Society* 18, no. 1 (2016): 81–95.

Behr, Valentin. *Powojenna historiografia polska jako pole walki: studium z socjologii wiedzy i polityki*. Warszawa: Wydawnictwa Uniwersytetu Warszawskiego, 2021.

Bereiter, Carl, and Siegfried Engelmann. *Teaching Disadvantaged Children in the Preschool*. Englewood Cliffs, NJ: Prentice-Hall, 1966.

Bernstein, Basil. *Class, Codes, and Control*. London: Routledge, 2003.

Bertaux, Daniel, Paul Richard Thompson, and Anna Rotkirch, eds. *On Living through Soviet Russia*. London: Routledge, 2004.

Bertram, Łukasz. "'Zna dobrze i nie zapomina duszy robotnika.' Akta osobowe działaczy politycznych i historia ludowa." *Kultura i Społeczeństwo* 66, no. 2 (September 8, 2022): 213–33.

Beskid, Lidia. *Zmiany spożycia w Polsce*. Warszawa: PWN, 1972.

Białecki, Ireneusz. *Wybór szkoły a reprodukcja struktury społecznej*. Wrocław: Zakład Narodowy im. Ossolińskich, 1982.

Białecki, Konrad, ed. *Poznański czerwiec 1956: uwarunkowania—przebieg—konsekwencje*. Poznań: Instytut Historii UAM, 2007.

Bieńkowski, Władysław. "Przemówienie p. Wiceministra Władysława Bieńkowskiego na uroczystej Inauguracji Roku Akademickiego na Uniwersytecie Łódzkim Dnia 13 stycznia 1946r." *AUŁ, Biuro Rektora*, no. sygn. 1856 (1946).

Biernacka, Maria. "Oświata a społeczno-kulturowe przeobrażenie wsi w latach ostatniej wojny i w okresie powojennym." *Etnografia polska* 27, no. 2 (1983): 103–32.

Biess, Frank, and Robert G. Moeller, eds. *Histories of the Aftermath: The Legacies of the Second World War in Europe*, 1st ed. New York: Berghahn Books, 2010.

Biggart, John. "Bukharin and the Origins of the 'Proletarian Culture' Debate." *Soviet Studies* 39, no. 2 (1987): 229–46.

Błażejewski, Tadeusz. "Z dziejów Łodzi literackiej." In *Wizerunek Łodzi w literaturze, kulturze i historii Niemiec i Austrii*, edited by Krzysztof Kuczyński, 49–61. Łódź: UMŁ, 2005.

Bockman, Johanna. *Markets in the Name of Socialism: The Left-Wing Origins of Neoliberalism*. Stanford: Stanford University Press, 2011.

Bojanowski, Tadeusz. *Łódź pod okupacją niemiecką w latach II Wojny Światowej, 1939–1945*. Łódź: Wydawnictwo Uniwersytetu Łódzkiego, 1992.

Bokszański, Zbigniew, Andrzej Piotrowski, and Marek Ziółkowski. *Socjologia języka*. Warszawa: Wiedza Powszechna, 1977.

Bolewski, Andrzej, and Henryk Pierzchała. *Losy polskich pracowników nauki w latach 1939–1945: straty osobowe*. Wrocław: Zakład Narodowy im. Ossolińskich, 1989.

Bołtuc-Staszewska, Irena. *Tranzytem przez Łódź*. Łódź: Wydawnictwo Łódzkie, 1964.

Bonfiglioli, Chiara. "Discussing Women's Double and Triple Burden in Socialist Yugoslavia: Women Working in the Garment Industry." In *Labor in State Socialist Europe, 1945–1989: Contributions to a Global History of Work*, edited by Marsha Siefert, 195–215. Central European University Press, 2020.

Borejsza, Jerzy. "Rewolucja łagodna." *Odrodzenie*, no. 10–12 (January 15, 1945), 1.

Boudon, Raymond. *The Unintended Consequences of Social Action*. London: Macmillan, 1982.

Bourdieu, Pierre. *Distinction: A Social Critique of the Judgement of Taste*. Cambridge, MA: Harvard University Press, 1984.

Bourdieu, Pierre. *Homo Academicus*. Stanford: Stanford University Press, 1988.

Bourdieu, Pierre. *Outline of a Theory of Practice*. Cambridge: Cambridge University Press, 2010.

Bourdieu, Pierre. *Pascalian Meditations*. Stanford: Stanford University Press, 2000.

Bourdieu, Pierre. *The State Nobility: Elite Schools in the Field of Power*. Stanford: Stanford University Press, 1998.

Bourdieu, Pierre. *The Weight of the World: Social Suffering in Contemporary Society*. Stanford: Stanford University Press, 1999.

Bourdieu, Pierre, and Jean Claude Passeron. *Les Héritiers, les étudiants et la culture*. Paryż: Les Éditions de Minuit, 1969.

Bourdieu, Pierre, and Jean Claude Passeron. *The Inheritors: French Students and Their Relation to Culture*. Chicago: University of Chicago Press, 1979.

Bourdieu, Pierre, and Jean Claude Passeron. *Reproduction in Education, Society and Culture*. Translated by R. Nice. London: Sage, 1990.

Bourdieu, Pierre, Jean-Claude Passeron, and Monique de Saint Martin. *Academic Discourse: Linguistic Misunderstanding and Professorial Power*. Stanford: Stanford University Press, 1996.

Briggs, Asa. *Victorian Cities*. Berkeley: University of California Press, 1993.

Bucholc, Marta. *Sociology in Poland: To Be Continued?* London: Palgrave, 2016.

Buck-Morss, Susan. *Dreamworld and Catastrophe: The Passing of Mass Utopia in East and West.* Cambridge, MA: MIT Press, 2002.

Bukowczyk, Adam. Biographical interview, 2010. Archiwum Wspomnień Łodzian.

Burawoy, Michael. "Revisits: An Outline of a Theory of Reflexive Ethnography." *American Sociological Review* 68, no. 5 (October 2003): 645–79.

Burawoy, Michael, and Katherine Verdery. *Uncertain Transition: Ethnographies of Change in the Postsocialist World.* Lanham, MD: Rowman & Littlefield, 1999.

Byford, Andy. "Initiation to Scholarship: The University Seminar in Late Imperial Russia." *Russian Review* 64, no. 2 (April 2005): 299–323.

Carr, Edward Hallett. *The Soviet Impact on the Western World.* Macmillan, 1947.

Chałasiński, Józef. "Humanizm socjalistyczny a podstawowe prawo ekonomiczne socjalizmu." *Nauka Polska*, no. 2 (1953): 50–80.

Chałasiński, Józef. "Inauguracja VI roku akademickiego Uniwersytetu Łódzkiego 1950/51," 1950. Syg 364649.

Chałasiński, Józef. "Memoriał Rektora ws. warunków pracy i rozwoju UŁ," August 7, 1950. Biuro Rektora. AUŁ.

Chałasiński, Józef. *Młode pokolenie chłopów*. Warszawa: Państwowy Instytut Kultury Wsi., 1938.

Chałasiński, Józef. *Młode pokolenie chłopów: procesy i zagadnienia kształtowania się warstwy chłopskiej w Polsce*. Warszawa: Spółdzielnia Wydawnicza "Pomoc Oświatowa," 1946.

Chałasiński, Józef. "O społeczny sens reformy uniwersytetów." *Kuźnica*, no. 24 (June 17, 1947), 3–6.

Chałasiński, Józef. "Od liberalnej do socjalistycznej idei Uniwersytetu." *Życie Nauki* V, no. 7–8 (1950).

Chałasiński, Józef. "Początki uniwersytetu robotniczej Łodzi." In *Tranzytem przez Łódź*, edited by Irena Bołtuc-Staszewska, 43–92. Łódź: Wydawnictwo Łódzkie, 1964.

Chałasiński, Józef. *Przeszłość i przyszłość inteligencji polskiej*. Warszawa: Ludowa Spółdzielnia Wydawnicza, 1958.

Chałasiński, Józef. "Referat Chałasińskiego 'UŁ w 1950' [Sejmowa Komisja Oświaty i Nauki]," n.d. Dział Nauczania. AUŁ.

Chałasiński, Józef. *Rewolucja młodości: studia o awansie młodego pokolenia wsi i integracji narodu polskiego*. Warszawa: Ludowa Spółdzielnia Wydawnicza, 1969.

Chałasiński, Józef. "Rzecz z powodu 'Humanistyki bez hipostaz.'" *Myśl Filozoficzna*, no. 2 (1952): 303–14.

Chałasiński, Józef. *Społeczna genealogia inteligencji polskiej*. Kraków: Czytelnik, 1947.

Chałasiński, Józef. *Uczeni polscy wobec rozwoju kultury i przyszłości narodu*. Warszawa: Czytelnik, 1952.

Chałasiński, Józef. "Współczesne reformy szkolne a idea narodu." *Myśl Współczesna*, no. 7–8 (1947): 398–425.

Charkiewicz, Michał. *Kadry wykwalifikowane w Polsce.* Warszawa: PWN, 1961.

Cheng, Yinghong. *Creating the "New Man": From Enlightenment Ideals to Socialist Realities.* Honolulu: University of Hawai'i Press, 2009.

Chmielewska, Katarzyna, Agnieszka Mrozik, and Grzegorz Wołowiec, eds. *Reassessing Communism: Concepts, Culture, and Society in Poland, 1944–1989.* Budapest: Central European University Press, 2021.

Chodakowska, Janina. *Rozwój szkolnictwa wyższego w Polsce Ludowej w latach 1944–1951.* Monografie z dziejów oświaty, t. 26. Wrocław: Zakład Narodowy im. Ossolińskich, 1981.

Choroszy, Jan F. *Poglądy etyczne Tadeusza Kotarbińskiego: studium historyczno-analityczne.* Wrocław: Wyd. Uniwersytetu Wrocławskiego, 1997.

Chrościelewski, Tadeusz. "W miejsce zleconego wstępu." In *Tranzytem przez Łódź*, edited by Irena Bołtuc-Staszewska, 5–34. Łódź: Wydawnictwo Łódzkie, 1964.

Cichocki, Bartosz, and Krzysztof Jóźwiak. *Najważniejsze są kadry: Centralna Szkoła Partyjna PPR/PZPR.* Warszawa: Trio, 2006.

Ciesielski, Stanisław, and Włodzimierz Borodziej, eds. *Przesiedlenie ludności polskiej z kresów wschodnich do Polski, 1944–1947.* Warszawa: Neriton; Instytut Historii PAN, 1999.

Collins, Randall. *The Credential Society: An Historical Sociology of Education and Stratification.* New York: Academic Press, 1979.

Conboy, Martin. *The Language of Newspapers: Socio-Historical Perspectives.* London: Bloomsbury Academic, 2010.

Connelly, John. *Captive University: The Sovietization of East German, Czech and Polish Higher Education, 1945–1956.* Chapel Hill: University of North Carolina Press, 2000.

Connelly, John. "Communist Higher Education Policies in Czechoslovakia, Poland, and East Germany." In *The Establishment of Communist Regimes in Eastern Europe, 1944–1949*, edited by Norman M. Naimark and Leonid Gibianskii, 191–216. Boulder, CO: Westview Press, 1997.

Connelly, John. "The Foundations of Diversity: Communist Higher Education Policies in Eastern Europe 1945–1955." In *Science Under Socialism: East Germany in Comparative Perspective*, edited by Kristie Macrakis and Dieter Hoffmann, 125–39. Cambridge, MA: Harvard University Press, 1999.

Connelly, John. "Polish Universities and State Socialism 1944–1968." In *Universities Under Dictatorship*, edited by John Connelly and Michael Grüttner. University Park, PA: Penn State University Press, 2005.

Connelly, John, and Michael Grüttner. *Universities Under Dictatorship.* University Park, PA: Penn State University Press, 2005.

Curry, Jane Leftwich. *Poland's Journalists: Professionalism and Politics.* Soviet and East European Studies 66. Cambridge: Cambridge University Press, 1990.

Curry, Jane Leftwich. "The Sociological Legacies of Communism." In *The Legacies of Communism in Eastern Europe*, edited by Zoltan D. Barany and Iván Völgyes, 55–83. Baltimore: Johns Hopkins University Press, 1995.

Cywiński, Bohdan. *Rodowody niepokornych*. Warszawa: PWN, 2010.

Departament Nauki i, Szkolnictwa Wyższego. "Zatrudnienie Absolwentów," n.d. Ministerstwo Szkolnictwa Wyższego w Warszawie 1946/49/1950-67, syg 1065. AAN.

Desperak, Izabela, and Martyna Krogulec. *Miasto pracujacych kobiet*. Łódź: Wydawnictwo Uniwersytetu Łódzkiego, 2020.

Deutsch, Martin, and Martin Whiteman. "Social Disadvantage as Related to Intellective and Language Development." In *Social Class, Race, and Psychological Development*, edited by Martin Deutsch, Arthur Robert Jensen, and Irwin Katz, 86–115. New York: Holt, Rinehart, and Winston, 1968.

Długosz, Piotr. "Społeczne skutki zmian systemu edukacji." In *Zawirowania systemu edukacji*, edited by Marta Zahorska, 25–46. Warszawa: Wydawnictwo Uniwersytetu Warszawskiego, 2012.

Dolata, Roman. *Szkoła, segregacje, nierówności*. Warszawa: Wydawnictwa Uniwersytetu Warszawskiego, 2008.

Domańska, Ewa. *Historie niekonwencjonalne: refleksja o przeszłości w nowej humanistyce*. Poznań: Wydawnictwo Poznańskie, 2006.

Domański, Henryk, ed. *Zmiany stratyfikacji społecznej w Polsce*. Warszawa: PAN, 2008.

Domański, Henryk, and Irina Tomescu-Dubrow. "Nierówności edukacyjne przed i po zmianie systemu." In *Zmiany stratyfikacji społecznej w Polsce*, edited by Henryk Domański, 45–74. Warszawa: PAN, 2008.

Drygalski, Jerzy, and Jacek Kwaśniewski. *(Nie)realny socjalizm*. Warszawa: PWN, 1992.

Dylik, Jan, and Zygmunt Dylik. "Nauka. Powstanie i organizacja łódzkiego ośrodka naukowego." In *Łódź w latach 1945–1960*, edited by Edward Rosset, 275–97. Łódź: Wydawnictwo Łódzkie, 1962.

Dziciuchowicz, Jerzy. "Ludność Łodzi od 1918 do lat 90. XX wieku." In *Łódź: monografia miasta*, edited by Stanisław Liszewski, 265–94. Łódź: ŁTN, 2009.

Dziecielska-Machnikowska, Stefania, and Jolanta Kulpińska. *Awans kobiety*. Łódź: Wydawnictwo Łódzkie, 1966.

Eagleton, Terry. *Literary Theory: An Introduction*. Austin: John Wiley & Sons, 2011.

English, Robert. *Russia and the Idea of the West: Gorbachev, Intellectuals, and the End of the Cold War*. New York: Columbia University Press, 2000.

Falski, Marian. *Środowisko Społeczne Młodzieży i Jej Wykształcenie*. Warszawa: Nasza Księgarnia, 1937.

Fehér, Ferenc, and Ágnes Heller. *Eastern Left, Western Left: A Contribution to the Morphology of a Problematic Relationship*. Cologne: Index, 1986.

Fehér, Ferenc, Ágnes Heller, and György G. Márkus. *Dictatorship Over Needs: An Analysis of Soviet Societies*. Oxford: Basil Blackwell, 1983.

Fidelis, Malgorzata. *Women, Communism, and Industrialization in Postwar Poland*. Cambridge: Cambridge University Press, 2010.

Field, Mark G., ed. *Social Consequences of Modernization in Communist Societies*. Baltimore: Johns Hopkins University Press, 1976.

Fijałkowska, Barbara. *Polityka i twórcy 1948–1959*. Warszawa: PWN, 1985.

Fik, Marta. *Spór o PRL*. Kraków: Znak, 1996.

Fitzpatrick, Sheila. *Education and Social Mobility in the Soviet Union 1921–1934*. Cambridge: Cambridge University Press, 2002.

Fitzpatrick, Sheila. "Revisionism in Soviet History." *History and Theory* 46, no. 4 (December 1, 2007): 77–91.

Fleming, Michael. *Communism, Nationalism and Ethnicity in Poland, 1944–50*. London: Routledge, 2010.

Foschi, Martha. "Double Standards in the Evaluation of Men and Women." *Social Psychology Quarterly* 59, no. 3 (1996): 237–54.

Friszke, Andrzej. "Epilogue: Polish Communism in Contemporary Debate." In *Stalinism in Poland, 1944–1956*, edited by A. Kemp-Welch. Warszawa: Macmillan Press; St. Martin's Press, 1999.

Gal, Susan, and Gail Kligman, eds. *The Politics of Gender after Socialism: A Comparative-Historical Essay*. Princeton, NJ: Princeton University Press, 2000.

Gal, Susan, and Gail Kligman, eds. *Reproducing Gender: Politics, Publics, and Everyday Life after Socialism*. Princeton: Princeton University Press, 2000.

Gati, Charles. *The Politics of Modernization in Eastern Europe: Testing the Soviet Model*. Westport, CT: Praeger, 1974.

Gawryszewski, Andrzej. *Ludność Polski w XX wieku*. Warszawa: PAN, 2005.

Gdula, Maciej, and Przemysław Sadura, eds. *Style życia i porządek klasowy w Polsce*. Warszawa: Wydawnictwo Naukowe Scholar, 2012.

Geyer, Michael, and Sheila Fitzpatrick. *Beyond Totalitarianism: Stalinism and Nazism Compared*. Cambridge: Cambridge University Press, 2009.

Ghodsee, Kristen. "A Tale of 'Two Totalitarianisms': The Crisis of Capitalism and the Historical Memory of Communism." *History of the Present* 4, no. 2 (October 1, 2014): 115–42. https://doi.org/10.5406/historypresent.4.2.0115.

Ginsbert, Adam. *Łódź: studium monograficzne*. Łódź: Wydawnictwo Łódzkie, 1962.

Gładysz, Antoni. *Oświata, kultura, nauka w latach 1947–1959: węzłowe problemy polityczne*. Warszawa, Kraków: PWN, 1981.

Gleason, Abbott, Peter Kenez, and Richard Stites. *Bolshevik Culture: Experiment and Order in the Russian Revolution*. Bloomington: Indiana University Press, 1989.

Głowiński, Michał. *Nowomowa po polsku*. Biblioteka tekstów. Warszawa: PEN, 1991.

Gosk, Hanna. *W kręgu "Kuźnicy." Dyskusje krytycznoliterackie lat 1945–1948*. Warszawa: PWN, 1985.

Grabowska, Magdalena. *Zerwana genealogia: działalność społeczna i polityczna kobiet po 1945 roku a współczesny polski ruch kobiecy*. Warszawa: Wydawnictwo Naukowe Scholar, 2018.

Graham, L. R. "Big Science in the Last Years of the Big Soviet Union." *Osiris* 7 (1992): 49–71.

Graham, Loren R. *Science in Russia and the Soviet Union: A Short History*. Cambridge: Cambridge University Press, 1993.

Grenfell, Michael. *Pierre Bourdieu: Key Concepts*. Durham: Acumen, 2012.

Groński, Marek. "Sprawy kultury w działalności łódzkiej Rady Miejskiej 1928–1934." In *Studia i materiały do dziejów Łodzi i okręgu łódzkiego: dwudziestolecie 1918–1939*, edited by Paweł Korzec, 159–74. Łódź: Wydawnictwo Łódzkie, 1962.

Gross, Jan Tomasz. "Geneza Społeczna Demokracji Ludowych (o Konsekwencjach II Wojny Światowej w Europie Środkowo-Wschodniej)." *Krytyka*, no. 32–33 (1990): 155–67.

Gross, Jan Tomasz. *Upiorna dekada. Trzy eseje o stereotypach na temat Żydów, Polaków, Niemców i komunistów 1939–1948*. Kraków: Austeria, 2007.

Gross, Jan Tomasz. "War as Revolution." In *The Establishment of Communist Regimes in Eastern Europe, 1944–1949*, edited by Norman M. Naimark and Leonid Gibianskii, 17–34. Boulder, CO: Westview Press, 1997.

Gryko, Czesław. *Józef Chałasiński—człowiek i dzieło: od teorii wychowania do kulturowej wizji narodu*. Poznań: WWSPiA, 2007.

GUS. *Polska w Liczbach 1944–1964*. Warszawa: GUS, 1964.

GUS. *Rocznik statystyczny*. Warszawa: GUS, 1955.

Habielski, Rafał. *Polityczna historia mediów w Polsce w XX wieku*. Warszawa: WAiP, 2009.

Habielski, Rafal, and Dominika Rafalska. *Aparat represji wobec inteligencji w latach 1945–1956*. Warszawa: Oficyna Wydawnicza Aspra-JR, 2010.

Halfin, Igal. *Language and Revolution: Making Modern Political Identities*. London: Routledge, 2004.

Hanley, Eric. "A Party of Workers or a Party of Intellectuals? Recruitment into Eastern European Communist Parties, 1945–1988." *Social Forces* 81, no. 4 (2003): 1073–105.

Hardy, Cheryl. "Hysteresis." In *Pierre Bourdieu: Key Concepts*, edited by Michael Grenfell, 126–46. Durham: Acumen, 2012.

Harker, Richard K., Cheleen Mahar, and Chris Wilkes, eds. *An Introduction to the Work of Pierre Bourdieu: The Practice of Theory*. Houndmills, Basingstoke, Hampshire: Macmillan, 1990.

Herczyński, Ryszard. *Spętana nauka: opozycja intelektualna w Polsce 1945–1970*. Warszawa: Semper, 2008.

Hîncu, Adela, and Agata Zysiak. "Socialist Culture, Participation and Expert Knowledge in Poland and Romania in the Long 1960s." *European Review of History: Revue Européenne d'histoire* 30, no. 2 (March 4, 2023): 234–56.

Hirszowicz, Maria. *Pułapki zaangażowania: intelektualiści w służbie komunizmu*. Warszawa: Scholar, 2001.

Hoffman, Victoria. *Soviet Education and the Building of the New Soviet Man*. St. Petersburg, FL: Eckerd College, 1980.

Hoggart, Richard. *The Uses of Literacy: Aspects of Working-Class Life*. London: Penguin, 2009.

Horwitz, Gordon J. *Ghettostadt. Łódź and the Making of a Nazi City*. Cambridge, MA: Harvard University Press, 2009.

Hübner, Piotr. *I Kongres Nauki Polskiej jako forma realizacji założeń polityki naukowej państwa ludowego*. Wrocław: Zakład Narodowy im. Ossolińskich, 1983.

Hübner, Piotr. *Nauka polska po II wojnie światowej—idee i instytucje*. Warszawa: COM SNP, 1987.

Hübner, Piotr. *Polityka naukowa w Polsce w latach 1944–1953: geneza systemu*. Problemy naukowe współczesności. Wrocław: Zakład Narodowy im. Ossolińskich, 1992.

Hübner, Piotr. *Siła przeciw rozumowi—: losy Polskiej Akademii Umiejętności w latach 1939–1989*. Kraków: Secesja, 1994.

Hübner, Piotr. "Stalinowskie czystki w nauce polskiej." In *Skryte oblicze systemu komunistycznego: u źródeł zła*, edited by Roman Bäcker. Warszawa: DiG, 1997.

Hübner, Piotr. *Zwierciadło nauki: mała encyklopedia polskiej nauki akademickiej*. Kraków: PAU, 2013.

Hübner, Piotr, and Dorota Degen. "Instytucje naukowe, towarzystwa, biblioteki, wydawnictwa i czasopisma naukowe." In *Humanistyka polska w latach 1945–1990*, edited by Jerzy Myśliński and Urszula Jakubowska, 39–63. Warszawa: Instytut Badań Literackich PAN, 2006.

Jaczewski, Bohdan. "Nauka." In *Polska odrodzona 1918–1939: państwo, społeczeństwo, kultura*, edited by Jan Tomicki, 507–53. Warszawa: Wiedza Powszechna, 1982.

Jaczewski, Bohdan. *Polityka naukowa Państwa Polskiego w latach 1918–1939*. Wrocław: Zakład Narodowy im. Ossolińskich, 1978.

Jaczewski, Bohdan, ed. *Życie naukowe w Polsce w drugiej połowie XIX i w XX wieku: organizacje i instytucje*. Wrocław: Zakład Narodowy im. Ossolińskich, 1987.

Jakubczak, Franciszek. "Józefa Chałasińskiego ethos nieposłuszeństwa w myśleniu." In *Chałasiński dzisiaj: materiały z konferencji naukowej*, edited by Andrzej Kaleta, 65–74. Toruń: Wydawnictwo UMK, 1996.

Jakubowska, Urszula, and Jerzy Myśliński, eds. *Humanistyka polska w latach 1945–1990*. Warszawa: Fundacja Akademia Humanistyczna, 2006.

Jałowiecki, Bohdan. *Oblicza polskich regionów*. Studia regionalne i lokalne, nr 50. Warszawa: Uniwersytet Warszawski, 1996. http://www.euroreg.uw.edu.pl/pl/publikacje,oblicza-polskich-regionow.

Janicka, Krystyna. "Ruchliwość międzypokoleniowa." In *Struktura i ruchliwość społeczna*, edited by Kazimierz Maciej Słomczyński and Włodzimierz Wesołowski, 61–102. Gdańsk: Zakład Narodowy im. Ossolińskich, 1973.

Januszkiewicz, Franciszek. *Doskonalenie systemu rekrutacji na studia wyższe*. Warszawa: PWN, 1988.

Jarosz, Maria, ed. *Wykluczeni: wymiar społeczny, materialny i etniczny*. Warszawa: PAN, 2008.

Jarska, Natalia. *Kobiety z marmuru: robotnice w Polsce w latach 1945–1960*. Warszawa: IPN, 2015.

Jastrzębski, Jarosław. "Reforma Jędrzejewicza w państwowym szkolnictwie akademickim II Rzeczpospolitej. Wzmocnienie prerogatyw władzy państwowej." Edited by Artur Patek. *Prace Historyczne* 138 (2011): 159–76.

Jedlicki, Jerzy. "Proces przeciwko miastu." In *Świat zwyrodniały: lęki i wyroki krytyków nowoczesności*. Warszawa: Wydawnictwo Sic!, 2000.

Jerschina, Jan. *Osobowość społeczna studentów UJ chłopskiego pochodzenia. Na podstawie badań socjologicznych z lat 1966–1967*. Vol. 25. Zeszyty PAN. Wrocław: Ossolineum, 1972.

Jirásek, Zdenek, and Andrzej Malkiewicz. *Polska i Czechosłowacja w dobie stalinizmu (1948–1956). Studium porównawcze*. Warszawa: PAN, 2005.

Jones, Peter E. "Bernstein's 'Codes' and the Linguistics of 'Deficit.'" *Language and Education* 27, no. 2 (March 1, 2013): 161–79.

Jordan, Zbigniew. "Bunt intelektualisty." *Kultura*, no. 9 (1955): 92–102.

Jordan, Zbigniew. "O socjologii i socjologicznych czasopismach." *Kultura*, no. 5 (1957): 133–34.

Judt, Tony. *Postwar: A History of Europe Since 1945*. New York: Penguin, 2006.

Kądzielski, Józef. "Czytelnictwo gazet, czasopism i książek wśród dorosłej ludności miasta." In *Łódź w latach 1945–1960*, edited by Edward Rosset, 419–26. Łódź: Wydawnictwo Łódzkie, 1962.

Kalecki, Michał. "Porównanie dochodów robotników i pracowników umysłowych poza rolnictwem w 1960 r. i 1937 r." *Kultura i Społeczeństwo*, no. 1 (1964): 35–40.

Kamiński, Aleksander. "Łódź kulturalna—uwagi wstępne." In *Łódź w latach 1945–1960*, edited by Edward Rosset, 265–74. Łódź: Wydawnictwo Łódzkie, 1962.

Kamiński, Łukasz. *Strajki robotnicze w Polsce w latach 1945–1948*. Wrocław: Gajt Wydawnictwo, 1999.

Karpiński, Jakub. *Ustrój komunistyczny w Polsce*. Warszawa: Akademia Leona Koźmińskiego, 2005.

Kaźmierska, Kaja, Katarzyna Waniek, and Agata Zysiak. *Opowiedzieć uniwersytet*. Łódź: WUŁ, 2015.

Kennedy, Michael D. *Professionals, Power and Solidarity in Poland: A Critical Sociology of Soviet-Type Society*. Cambridge: Cambridge University Press, 1991.

Kenney, Padraic. *Rebuilding Poland: Workers and Communists, 1945–1950*. Ithaca, NY: Cornell University Press, 2012.

Kersten, Krystyna, ed. *The Establishment of Communist Rule in Poland, 1943–1948*. Berkeley: University of California Press, 1991.

Kersten, Krystyna. *Między wyzwoleniem a zniewoleniem: Polska 1944–1956*. Londyn: Aneks, 1993.

Kłoskowska, Antonina. "Bunty i służebności uczonego: Profesor Józef Chałasiński." In *Bunty i służebności uczonego: Profesor Józef Chałasiński*, edited by Leszek Wojtczak, 7–21. Łódź: Wydawnictwo UŁ, 1992.

Kluczyński, Jan. *Szkolnictwo wyższe w czterdziestoleciu Polski Ludowej*. Warszawa: PWN, 1986.

Kobos, Andrzej M. *Po drogach uczonych: z członkami Polskiej Akademii Umiejętności, t. 1*. Kraków: Polska Akademia Umiejętności, 2007.

Kobos, Andrzej M. *Po drogach uczonych: z członkami Polskiej Akademii Umiejętności, t. 2*. Kraków: Polska Akademia Umiejętności, 2007.

Kochanowicz, Jacek. *Backwardness and Modernization: Poland and Eastern Europe in the 16th–20th Centuries*. Aldershot: Ashgate Variorum, 2006.

Kochanowicz, Jacek. "Gathering Poles into Poland. Forced Migration from Poland's Former Eastern Territories." In *Redrawing Nations: Ethnic Cleansing in East-Central Europe, 1944–1948*, edited by Philipp Ther and Ana Siljak, 135–54. Lanham: Rowman & Littlefield, 2001.

Kochanowicz, Joanna. *ZMP w terenie: stalinowska próba modernizacji opornej rzeczywistości*. Warszawa: Trio, 2000.

Kołakowski, Leszek, and Zbigniew Mentzel. *Czas ciekawy, czas niespokojny: z Leszkiem Kołakowskim rozmawia Zbigniew Mentzel*. Kraków: Znak, 2008.

Kolbuszewska, Jolanta. *Kobiety w drodze na naukowy Olimp . . . : akademicki awans polskich historyczek (od schyłku XIX wieku po rok 1989)*. Łódź: Wydawnictwo Uniwersytetu Łódzkiego, 2020.

Konrád, György, and Iván Szelényi. *The Intellectuals on the Road to Class Power*. San Diego, CA: Harcourt Brace Jovanovich, 1979.

Kopczyńska-Jaworska, Bronisława. *Łódź i inne miasta*. Łódź: Katedra Etnologii Uniwersytetu Łódzkiego, 1999.

Koralewicz, Jadwiga. *Autorytaryzm, lęk, konformizm*. Warszawa: Scholar, 2008.

Kosiński, Krzysztof. *O nową mentalność: życie codzienne w szkołach 1945–1956*. Warszawa: Trio, 2000.

Kotarbiński, Tadeusz. "Dwie koncepcje równości." AUŁ, October 30, 1946.

Kotarbiński, Tadeusz. *Wybór pism*. Warszawa: PWN, 1958.

Kotkin, Stephen. "1991 and the Russian Revolution: Sources, Conceptual Categories, Analytical Frameworks." *Journal of Modern History* 70, no. 2 (June 1998): 384.

Kott, Jan. *Przyczynek do biografii*. London: Aneks, 1990.

Kowalewska, Salomea, and Zdzisław Kowalewski. *Problemy zapotrzebowania i zatrudniania absolwentów szkół wyższych w przemyśle: raport z badań przeprowadzonych w 1959 roku w odniesieniu do absolwentów z 1958 r*, 1962.

Kowalewski, Zdzisław. "Problemy kształcenia w rodzinie włókniarskiej." In *Włókniarze łódzcy: monografia*, edited by Józef Spychalski and Edward Rosset, 548–60. Łódź: Wydawnictwo Łódzkie, 1966.

Kowalik, Tadeusz. *Spory o ustrój społeczno-gospodarczy w Polsce: lata 1944–1948*. Warszawa: Wydawnictwo Key Text, 2006.

Kowalski, Stanisław. "Aspiracje szkolne młodzieży jako czynni demokratyzacji kształcenia." In *Naród, kultura, osobowość: księga poświęcona profesorowi Józefowi Chałasińskiemu*, edited by Antonina Kłoskowska, 295–314. Wrocław: Zakład Narodowy im. Ossolińskich, 1983.

Kozakiewicz, Mikołaj. *Bariery awansu poprzez wykształcenie*. Warszawa: Instytut Wydawniczy CRZZ, 1973.

Kozarzewski, Piotr. "Wykluczenie edukacyjne." In *Wykluczeni: wymiar społeczny, materialny i etniczny*, edited by Maria Jarosz, 137–75. Warszawa: PAN, 2008.

Krajewska, Jadwiga. *Czytelnictwo wśród robotników w Królestwie Polskim, 1870–1914*. Warszawa: PWN, 1979.

Krajewski, Tadeusz. *Dobór kandydatów do szkół wyższych: analiza czynników społecznych i pedagogicznych*. Warszawa: PWN, 1969.

Krasicki, Ignacy. *Wiersze wybrane*. Warszawa: PWN, 1964.

Krasiewicz, Bolesław. *Odbudowa szkolnictwa wyższego w Polsce Ludowej w latach 1944–1948*. Wrocław: Zakład Narodowy im. Ossolińskich, 1976.

Kraśko, Nina. *Instytucjonalizacja socjologii w Polsce 1920–1970*. Warszawa: PWN, 1996.

Krasucki, Eryk. *Międzynarodowy komunista: Jerzy Borejsza, biografia polityczna*. Warszawa: PWN, 2009.

Krasuski, Josef. "Education as Resistance: The Polish Experience of Schooling During the War." In *Education and the Second World War: Studies in Schooling and Social Change*, edited by Roy Lowe, 128–38. London: Falmer Press, 1992.

Król, Joanna. "Polityka rekrutacyjna." In *Oświata, wychowanie i kultura fizyczna w rzeczywistości społeczno-politycznej Polski Ludowej (1945–1989): rozprawy i szkice*, edited by Romuald Grzybowski, 71–82. Toruń: Wydawnictwo Adam Marszałek, 2004.

Kroll, Benno. *Tak było: wspomnienia łódzkiego Volksdeutscha*. Łódź: Biblioteka "Tygla Kultury," 2010.

Kronenberg, Maciej, and Karolina Kołodziej. *70 lat uniwersytetu łódzkiego w przestrzeni miejskiej łodzi (1945–2015)*. Łódź: WUŁ, 2015.

Kuchta, Jan. *Psychologja dziecka wiejskiego a praca szkolna (ze szczególnem uwzględnieniem "zajęć cichych")*. Warszawa: Gebethner i Wolff, 1933.

Kulpińska, Jolanta. "Antonina Kłoskowska i łódzka socjologia. Znaczące wydarzenia." *Przegląd Socjologiczny* 61, no. 3 (2012): 29–36.

Kurczewski, Jacek. *The Resurrection of Rights in Poland*. Oxford: Clarendon Press; Oxford University Press, 1993.

Labov, William. *The Social Stratification of English in New York City*. II. Cambridge: Cambridge University Press, 2006.

Lampert, Nicholas. *The Technical Intelligentsia and the Soviet State*. New York: Holmes & Meier, 1979.

Lazari-Pawłowska, Ija. *Humanizm Tadeusza Kotarbińskiego*. Wrocław: Zakład Narodowy im. Ossolińskich, 1989.

Lebow, Katherine. *Unfinished Utopia: Nowa Huta, Stalinism, and Polish Society, 1949–56*. Ithaca, NY: Cornell University Press, 2013.

Leder, Andrzej. *Prześniona rewolucja. Ćwiczenie z logiki historycznej*. Warszawa: Wydawnictwo Krytyki Politycznej, 2014.

Leja, Krzysztof. *Zarządzanie uczelnią: Koncepcje i współczesne wyzwania*. Warszawa: Wolters Kluwer, 2013.

Łepkowski, Tadeusz. "Myśli o historii Polski i Polaków." *Zeszyty Historyczne* 68 (1984): 120–29.

Lesiakowski, Krzysztof. *Strajki robotnicze w Łodzi 1945–1976*. Łódź: IPN, 2008.

Leszczyński, Adam. *Ludowa historia polski: historia wyzysku i oporu: mitologia panowania*. Warszawa: Wydawnictwo WAB, 2020.

Leszczyński, Adam. *Skok w nowoczesność: polityka wzrostu w krajach peryferyjnych 1943–1980*. Warszawa: Wydawnictwo Krytyki Politycznej, 2013.

Lewandowski, Jan. *Rodowód społeczny powojennej inteligencji polskiej: 1944–1949*. Szczecin: Uniwersytet Szczeciński, 1991.

Lisiecka, Alicja. "Pokolenie 'pryszczatych.'" *Pamiętnik Literacki*, 55/4 (1964): 367–91.

Lissowski, Grzegorz, and Michał Pohoski. "Oceny dochodów, słuszna płaca i prestiż." *Kultura i Społeczeństwo*, no. 4 (1987): 177–97.

Löw, Andrea. *Juden im Getto Litzmannstadt: Lebensbedingungen, Selbstwahrnehmung, Verhalten*. Göttingen: Wallstein, 2006.

Lutyński, Jan. "Niektóre uwarunkowania rozwoju socjologii polskiej i ich konsekwencje." *Studia Socjologiczne* 195, no. 2 (1987): 127–41.

Macrakis, Kirstie, and Dieter Hoffman, eds. *Science Under Socialism: East Germany in Comparative Perspective*. Cambridge, MA: Harvard University Press, 1999.

Mally, Lynn. *Culture of the Future: The Proletkult Movement in Revolutionary Russia*. Berkeley: University of California Press, 1990.

Mare, Robert D. *Trends in Schooling: Demography, Performance, and Organization*. Madison: University of Wisconsin Press, 1981.

Mark, James, and Paul Betts, eds. *Socialism Goes Global: The Soviet Union and Eastern Europe in the Age of Decolonisation*. New edition. New York: Oxford University Press, 2022.

Marody, Mirosława. "Przemiany postaw ideologicznych i przystosowanie w systemie komunistycznym." In *Komunizm: ideologia, system, ludzie*, edited by Tomasz Szarota, 127–38. Warszawa: Neriton, 2001.

Marszałek-Kawa, Joanna, ed. *Politics of Memory in Post-Authoritarian Transitions*. Newcastle, UK: Cambridge Scholars Publishing, 2017.

Marzec, Wiktor. "Proletariacka biografia i dzielenie postrzegalnego. rozmywanie granic klasowych w okresie rewolucji 1905 roku." *Folia Sociologica*, no. 41 (2012): 177–93.

Marzec, Wiktor. "Rising Subjects. Workers and the Political During the 1905–1907 Revolution in the Kingdom of Poland." PhD, CEU, 2017.

Marzec, Wiktor, and Agata Zysiak. "Miasto, morderstwo, maszyna. Osobliwe przypadki we wczesnonowoczesnej Łodzi." In *Rekonfiguracje modernizmu: nowoczesność i kultura popu-*

larna, edited by Tomasz Majewski 187–206. Warszawa: Wydawnictwa Akademickie i Profesjonalne, 2009.

Mason, Mary Ann, Nicholas H. Wolfinger, and Marc Goulden. *Do Babies Matter? Gender and Family in the Ivory Tower*. New Brunswick, NJ: Rutgers University Press, 2013.

Mauersberg, Stanisław. "Nauka polska i szkolnictwo wyższe w latach wojny 1939–45." In *Życie naukowe w Polsce w drugiej połowie XIX i w XX wieku: organizacje i instytucje*, edited by Bohdan Jaczewski, 235–67. Wrocław: Zakład Narodowy im. Ossolińskich, 1987.

Mead, Margaret. *Continuities in Cultural Evolution*. New Brunswick: Transaction Publishers, 1964.

Mencwel, Andrzej. *Etos lewicy: esej o narodzinach kulturalizmu polskiego*. Idee, nr 19. Warszawa: Wydawnictwo "Krytyki Politycznej," 2009.

Mencwel, Andrzej. *Przedwiośnie czy Potop: studium postaw polskich w XX wieku*. Warszawa: Czytelnik, 1997.

Mnich, Grzegorz. *Łódzka prasa codzienna w okresie stalinowskim (1948–1956)*. Łódź: Księży Młyn Dom Wydawniczy, 2014.

Mroczka, Ludwik. *Fenomen robotniczy Drugiej Rzeczypospolitej: studia z dziejów społecznych łódzkiej klasy robotniczej (1918–1939)*. Łódź: Wydawnictwo Naukowe WSP, 1987.

Mrozik, Agnieszka. *Architektki PRL-u. Komunistki, literatura i emancypacja kobiet w powojennej Polsce*. Warszawa: Instytut Badań Literackich PAN, 2022.

Mrozik, Agnieszka. "Girls from the Polish Youth Union: (Dis)Remembrance of the Generation." In *Gender, Generations, and Communism in Central and Eastern Europe and Beyond*, edited by Anna Artwinska and Agnieszka Mrozik, 197–226, 2020.

Mrozik, Agnieszka. "Historia jakby nas pominęła." *Kultura i Społeczeństwo* 66, no. 2 (September 8, 2022): 39–69.

Mrozik, Agnieszka, and Magda Szczęśniak. "Wstęp. Powojenne historie ludowe." *Kultura i Społeczeństwo* 66, no. 2 (September 8, 2022): 3–7.

Müller, Martin. "In Search of the Global East: Thinking between North and South." *Geopolitics* 25, no. 3 (May 26, 2020): 734–55.

Mycielska, Dorota. "Drogi życiowe profesorów przed objęciem katedr akademickich w niepodległej Polsce." In *Inteligencja polska XIX i XX wieku: studia, t. 2*, edited by Ryszarda Czepulis-Rastenis, 243–90. Warszawa: PWN, 1981.

Najduchowska, Halina. "Aspiracje maturzystów do wyższego wykształcenia." In *Studenci w Polsce i w Niemieckiej Republice Demokratycznej w świetle badań socjologicznych*, edited by Halina Najduchowska, 39–43. Warszawa: PWN, 1987.

Najduchowska, Halina. *Kwalifikacje i drogi zawodowe dyrektorów przedsiębiorstw przemysłowych : studium socjologiczno-historyczne*. Warszawa: PWN, 1984.

Najduchowska, Halina. *Pozycja społeczna starych robotników przemysłu metalowego: (fragmenty opracowanych badań)*. Wrocław: Zakład Narodowy im. Ossolińskich, 1965.

Najduchowska, Halina, ed. *Studenci w Polsce i w Niemieckiej Republice Demokratycznej w świetle badań socjologicznych*. Warszawa: PWN, 1987.

Najduchowska, Halina, and Elżbieta Wnuk-Lipińska. *Nauczyciele akademiccy 1984*. Warszawa: PWN, 1990.

Nałęcz, Daria. "Lata 1949–56." In *Czasopisma społeczno-kulturalne w okresie PRL*, edited by Urszula Jakubowska, 63–136. Warszawa: IBL PAN, 2012.

Narodowy Plebiscyt Pokoju "Polska Kronika Filmowa," 21/1951. In Repozytorium Cyfrowe Filmoteki Narodowej. http://www.repozytorium.fn.org.pl/?q=pl/node/7846.

Narojek, Winicjusz. *Socjalistyczne "welfare state": studium z psychologii społecznej Polski Ludowej*. Warszawa: PWN, 1991.

Natkowska, Monika. *Numerus clausus, getto ławkowe, numerus nullus, "paragraf aryjski": antysemityzm na Uniwersytecie Warszawskim 1931–1939*. Warszawa: Żydowski Instytut Historyczny, 1999.

Nosko, Jan. *Rewolucja i inteligencja: PPR i PZPR w łódzkim środowisku akademickim 1945–1971*. Łódź: Wydawnictwo Łódzkie, 1985.

Nowak, Stefan. *Studenci Warszawy: studium długofalowych przemian postaw i wartości: praca zbiorowa pod redakcją Stefana Nowaka*. Warszawa: Wydawnictwo Uniwersytetu Warszawskiego, 1991.

Nowinowski, Sławomir, ed. *Marzec '68 w Łodzi*. Łódź: IPN, 2010.

Olejnik, Leszek. "Mniejszości narodowe w Łodzi w 1945 r." In *Rok 1945 w Łodzi: studia i szkice*, edited by Joanna Żelazko, 131–48. Łódź: IPN, 2008.

Olejnik, Leszek. *Zdrajcy Narodu? Losy volksdeutschów w Polsce po II wojnie światowej*. Warszawa: Trio, 2006.

Olejnik, Leszek. "Żydzi łódzcy w latach 1956–1972." In *Społeczność żydowska w PRL przed kampanią antysemicką lat 1967–1968 i po niej*, edited by Grzegorz Berendt, 137–47. Warszawa: IPN, 2009.

Palska, Hanna. *Nowa inteligencja w Polsce Ludowej: świat przedstawień i elementy rzeczywistości*. Warszawa: PAN, 1994.

Pawelec, Lidia. "Raport o stanie oświaty w PRL (przedruk z 1973)." In *Oświata, wychowanie i kultura fizyczna w rzeczywistości społeczno-politycznej Polski Ludowej (1945–1989): rozprawy i szkice*, edited by Romuald Grzybowski, 82–91. Toruń: Wydawnictwo Adam Marszałek, 2004.

Pęcherski, Mieczysław. *System oświatowy w Polsce Ludowej na tle porównawczym*. Wrocław: Zakład Narodowy im. Ossolińskich, 1981.

Perna, Laura W. "Sex Differences in Faculty Salaries: A Cohort Analysis." *Review of Higher Education* 24, no. 3 (March 1, 2001): 283–307.

Peschar, J. L. *Social Reproduction in Eastern and Western Europe: Comparative Analyses on Czechoslovakia, Hungary, the Netherlands and Poland*. Nijmegen: Institute for Applied Social Sciences, 1990.

Piskała, Kamil, and Agata Zysiak. "The Postwar: Social Justice for Proletarian City?" In *From Cotton and Smoke*. Łódź: WUŁ, 2018.

Platt, Harold L. *Shock Cities: The Environmental Transformation and Reform of Manchester and Chicago*. Chicago: University of Chicago Press, 2005.

Pleskot, Patryk, and Tadeusz Paweł Rutkowski, eds. *Spętana Akademia: Polska Akademia Nauk w dokumentach władz PRL*. Warszawa: IPN, 2009.

Pobłocki, Kacper. *Chamstwo*. Wydanie I. Wołowiec: Wydawnictwo Czarne, 2021.

Pobłocki, Kacper. *The Cunning of Class: Urbanization of Inequality in Post-War Poland*. Budapest, 2010. http://etnologia.amu.edu.pl/go.live.php/PL-H648/dr-kacper-poblocki.html.

Pohoski, Michał. "Kariery szkolne i kariery społeczno-zawodowe a pochodzenie społeczne." *Kultura i Społeczeństwo*, no. 2 (1984): 155–71.

Porter-Szücs, Brian. *Poland in the Modern World: Beyond Martyrdom*. Oxford: Wiley Blackwell, 2014.

Post, Barbara. "Etos warszawskich pracowników nauki—1983." In *Nauka w kulturze ogólnej*, edited by Stanisław Grzywna and Józefa Stępień. Problemy naukowe współczesności, 213–23. Wrocław: Zakład Narodowy im. Ossolińskich, 1985.

"Program." *Przegląd Akademicki*, no. 1 (1947): 21.

Puś, Wiesław. *Dzieje Łodzi przemysłowej: zarys historii*. Łódź: Muzeum Historii Miasta Łodzi, Centrum Informacji Kulturalnej, 1987.

Puś, Wiesław. *Zarys historii Uniwersytetu Łódzkiego 1945–2015*. Łódź: WUŁ, 2015.

Radziszewska, Krystyna, and Monika Kucner, eds. *Miasto w mojej pamięci. Powojenne wspomnienia Niemców z Łodzi*. Łódź: Wydawnictwo UŁ, 2014.

Ratajska, Krystyna. *O niezwykłych łódzkich kawiarniach. U Roszka, Fraszka, Honoratka*. Łódź: Księży Młyn Dom Wydawniczy, 2018.

Reed-Danahay, Deborah. *Locating Bourdieu*. Bloomington: Indiana University Press, 2005.

Rodek, Violetta. "Kariera naukowa kobiet w II Rzeczpospolitej jako przykład pokonywania barier aa drodze ku równości obu płci." In *Działalność kobiet Polskich na polu oświaty i nauki*, edited by Dorota Żołądź-Strzelczyk and Wieslaw Jamrożek, 61–72. Poznań: Wydaw. ERUDITUS, 2003.

Rokicki, Konrad, and Sławomir Stępień, eds. *Oblicza Marca 1968*. Warszawa: IPN, 2004.

Rosenberg, William G. *Bolshevik Visions: First Phase of the Cultural Revolution in Soviet Russia*. Ann Arbor: University of Michigan Press, 1990.

Rosset, Edward. *Łódź miasto pracy*. Łódź: Wyd. Magistrat miasta Łodzi, 1929.

Rosset, Edward. *Oblicze demograficzne Polski Ludowej*. Warszawa: Państwowe Wydawnictwo Ekonomiczne, 1965.

Rosset, Edward. "Stosunki ludnościowe." In *Łódź w latach 1945–1960*, edited by Edward Rosset, 28–55. Łódź: Wydawnictwo Łódzkie, 1962.

Rudnicki, Szymon. *Obóz Narodowo-Radykalny: geneza i działalność*. Warszawa: Czytelnik, 1985.

Sadowska, Joanna. *Ku szkole na miarę Drugiej Rzeczypospolitej: geneza, założenia i realizacja reformy Jędrzejewiczowskiej*. Białystok: Wydawnictwo Uniwersytetu w Białymstoku, 2001.

Sadura, Przemysław. *Szkoła i nierówności społeczne*. Warszawa: Fundacja Amicus Europae, 2012.

Samuś, Paweł. "Rola socjalistów w edukacji politycznej społeczeństwa Królestwa Polskiego w latach rewolucji 1905–1907." *Przegląd Nauk Historycznych*, no. 2 (2005): 127–46.

Sarapata, Adam. *Przemiany społeczne w Polsce Ludowej*. Warszawa: PWN, 1965.

Sarapata, Adam. *Studia nad uwarstwieniem i ruchliwością społeczną w Polsce*. Warszawa: Książka i Wiedza, 1965.

Sawiński, Zbigniew. "Zmiany systemowe a nierówności w dostępie do wykształcenia." In *Zmiany stratyfikacji społecznej w Polsce*, edited by Henryk Domański, 13–43. Warszawa: PAN, 2008.

Sawiński, Zbigniew, and Marzanna Stasińska. *Przemiany w oddziaływaniu czynników pochodzenia na dwóch progach selekcji międzyszkolnej*. Warszawa: Instytut Socjologii Uniwersytetu Warszawskiego, 1986.

Schaff, Adam. "Łódzkie wspomnienia." In *Tranzytem przez Łódź*, edited by Irena Bołtuc-Staszewska, 35–42. Łódź: Wydawnictwo Łódzkie, 1964.

Seton-Watson, Hugh. *The East European Revolution*. Westport, CT: Praeger, 1961.

Siegel, Achim. *The Totalitarian Paradigm After the End of Communism: Towards a Theoretical Reassessment*. Amsterdam: Rodopi, 1998.

Siekierski, Stanisław. "Z dziejów recepcji Młodego pokolenia chłopów." *Przegląd Humanistyczny*, no. 1–2 (1986): 21–33.

Siemieńska, Renata. "Kariery Akademickie i Ich Kontekst—Porównania Międzygeneracyjne | Nauka i Szkolnictwo Wyższe." *Nauka i Szkolnictwo Wyższe* 1, no. 17 (2001): 42–61.

Sitarek, Adam. *"Otoczone drutem państwo." Struktura i funkcjonowanie administracji żydowskiej getta łódzkiego*. Łódź: IPN, 2015.

Skubała-Tokarska, Zofia. *Społeczna rola Wolnej Wszechnicy Polskiej*. Warszawa: PAN, 1967.

Słabek, Henryk. *O społecznej historii Polski 1945–1989*. Warszawa: Książka i Wiedza, 2009.

Słabek, Henryk. "Wychodźstwo robotnicze: awans społeczny jednostek i zubożenie klasy?" In *Komunizm: ideologia, system, ludzie*, edited by Tomasz Szarota, 313–24. Warszawa: Neriton, 2001.

Słomczyński, K. M. "Rola wykształcenia w procesie ruchliwości wewnątrz pokoleniowej." In *Struktura i ruchliwość społeczna*, edited by Włodzimierz Wesołowski and Kazimierz Maciej Słomczyński, 103–24. Gdańsk: Zakład Narodowy im. Ossolińskich, 1973.

Słomczyński, K. M., and Włodzimierz Wesołowski. *Struktura i ruchliwość społeczna*. Gdańsk: Zakład Narodowy im. Ossolińskich, 1973.

Słomczyński, Kazimierz Maciej, Krystyna Janicka, and Władysław Wesołowski. *Badania struktury społecznej Łodzi: doświadczenia i perspektywy*. Warszawa: PAN, 1994.

Smoczyński, Rafał, and Tomasz Zarycki. Totem inteligencki: Arystokracja, szlachta i ziemiaństwo w polskiej przestrzeni społecznej. Warszawa: Wydawnictwo Naukowe Scholar, 2017.

Sochor, Zenovia A. *Revolution and Culture: The Bogdanov-Lenin Controversy*. Ithaca, NY: Cornell University Press, 1988.

Sorokin, Pitirim Aleksandrovič. *Ruchliwość społeczna*. Warszawa: PAN, 2009.

Sosnowska, Anna. *Zrozumieć zacofanie: spory historyków o Europę Wschodnią, 1947–1994*. Warszawa: Trio, 2004.

Sowa, Jan. *Fantomowe cialo króla: peryferyjne zmagania z nowoczesna forma*. Kraków: Universitas, 2011.

Spodenkiewicz, Paweł. "Sprawa Marii Tyrankiewiczówny." In *Rok 1945 w Łodzi: studia i szkice*, edited by Joanna Żelazko. Łódź: IPN, 2008.

"Spuścizna Niny Assorodobraj-Kuli." *Dział Rękopisów BUW* 4225 (1949).

Spychalski, Józef, and Edward Rosset. *Włókniarze łódzcy: monografia*. Łódź: Wydawnictwo Łódzkie, 1966.

Śreniowska, Krystyna. "Kartki z dziejów Uniwersytetu Łódzkiego 1945–1989. Pamiętnik." *Tygiel Kultury*, no. 12 (2007): 178–84.

Stańczak-Wiślicz, Katarzyna, Piotr Perkowski, Malgorzata Fidelis, and Barbara Klich-Kluczewska, eds. *Kobiety w Polsce 1945–1989: Nowoczesność—Równouprawnienie—Komunizm*. Kraków: Towarzystwo Autorów i Wydawców Prac Naukowych Universitas, 2020.

Stasińska, Marzanna. *Syndrom pochodzenia społecznego a wybór szkoły. Analiza kanoniczna*. Warszawa: UW, 1985.

Stobiecki, Rafał. *Historia pod nadzorem: spory o nowy model historii w Polsce. II połowa lat czterdziestych—początek lat pięćdziesiątych*. Łódź: Wydawnictwo Uniwersytetu Łódzkiego, 1993.

Stobiecki, Rafał. "Z dziejów pewnego projektu. 'Socjalistyczny Uniwersytet w robotniczej Łodzi.'" *Rocznik Łódzki* LXI (2014): 153–64.

Stoica, Augustin. "Communism as a Project for Modernization: The Romanian Case." *Polish Sociological Review*, no. 120 (1997): 313–31.

Stola, Dariusz. "Międzynarodowa mobilność zarobkowa w PRL." In *Ludzie na huśtawce: migracje między peryferiami Polski i Zachodu*, edited by Ewa Jaźwińska-Motylska and Marek Okólski, 62–100. Scholar, 2001.

Stolarzewicz, Ludwik. *Literatura Łodzi w ciągu jej istnienia: szkic literacki i antologja*. Łódź: S. Seipelt, 1935.

Susen, Simon, and Bryan S. Turner. *The Legacy of Pierre Bourdieu: Critical Essays*. London: Anthem Press, 2013.

Swartz, David. *Culture and Power: The Sociology of Pierre Bourdieu*. Chicago: University of Chicago Press, 2012.

Świda-Ziemba, Hanna. *Człowiek wewnętrznie zniewolony: problemy psychosocjologiczne minionej formacji*. UW, 1998.

Świda-Ziemba, Hanna. *Młodzież PRL: portrety pokoleń w kontekście historii*. Kraków: Wydawnictwo Literackie, 2010.

Świda-Ziemba, Hanna. *Urwany lot: pokolenie inteligenckiej młodzieży powojennej w świetle listów i pamiętników z lat 1945–1948*. Kraków: Wydawnictwo Literackie, 2003.

Szacki, Jerzy. *Sto lat socjologii polskiej: od Supińskiego do Szczepańskiego*. Warszawa: PWN, 1995.

Szczepański, Jan. *Dzienniki z lat 1945–1968*. Ustroń: Galeria Na Gojach, 2013.

Szczepański, Jan. *Inteligencja i społeczeństwo*. Warszawa: Książka i Wiedza, 1957.

Szczepański, Jan. *Polskie losy*. Warszawa: Polska Oficyna Wydawnicza "BGW," 1993.

Szczepański, Jan. "Próba koncepcji rozwoju szkolnictwa wyższego." *Wieś Współczesna*, no. styczeń (1958), 70–89.

Szczepański, Jan. *Socjologiczne zagadnienia wyższego wykształcenia*. Warszawa: PWN, 1963.

Szczepański, Jan. *Szkice o szkolnictwie wyższym*. Warszawa: Wiedza Powszechna, 1976.

Szczepański, Jan, ed. *Wykształcenie a pozycja społeczna inteligencji: praca zbiorowa, t. I*. Łódź: PWN, 1959.

Szczepański, Jan. *Wykształcenie a pozycja społeczna inteligencji: praca zbiorowa t. II*. Łódź: PWN, 1960.

Szczepański, Jan, ed. *Z badań klasy robotniczej i inteligencji*. Łódź: PWN, 1958.

Szczepański, Jan. *Ze studiów nad kursami przygotowawczymi: praca zbiorowa*. Łódź: Zakład Narodowy im. Ossolińskich, PWN, 1962.

Szelenvi, Ivan. "The Intelligentsia in the Class Structure of State-Socialist Societies." *American Journal of Sociology* 88 (1982): 287–326.

Szkolnictwo Wyższe w Polsce. Warszawa: Ministerstwo Nauki i Szkolnictwa Wyższego, 2013.

Szlendak, Tomasz. *Zaniedbana piaskownica: style wychowania małych dzieci a problem nierówności szans edukacyjnych*. Warszawa: Instytut Spraw Publicznych, 2003.

Szpak, Ewelina. "Female Tractor Driver, Labour Heroine and Activist: Images of New Socialist Rural Women in the Polish Communist Press (1950–75)." In *Imagining Frontiers, Contesting Identities*, edited by Steven G. Ellis and Lud'a Klusáková, 413–29. Pisa: PLUSPisa University Press, 2007.

Taylor, Charles. *Modern Social Imaginaries*. Durham, NC: Duke University Press, 2004.

Taylor, Charles. *A Secular Age*. Cambridge, MA: Belknap Press of Harvard University Press, 2007.

Therborn, Göran. *European Modernity and Beyond: The Trajectory of European Societies, 1945–2000*. London: Sage, 1995.

Tobera, Janina. "Józef Chałasiński, okres łódzki. Wybrane zagadnienia." In *Chałasiński dzisiaj: materiały z konferencji naukowej*, edited by Andrzej Kaleta, 88–91. Toruń: Wydawnictwo UMK, 1996.

Todorova, Maria Nikolaeva, ed. *Remembering Communism: Genres of Representation*. New York: Social Science Research Council, 2010.

Townsend, Robert B. "Gender and Success in Academia: More from the Historians' Career Paths Survey." *Prospectives on History*, no. 01 (2013). https://www.historians.org/publications-and-directories/perspectives-on-history/january-2013/gender-and-success-in-academia.

Trix, Frances, and Carolyn Psenka. "Exploring the Color of Glass: Letters of Recommendation for Female and Male Medical Faculty." *Discourse & Society* 14, no. 2 (March 1, 2003): 191–220.

Tromly, Benjamin. *Making the Soviet Intelligentsia: Universities and Intellectual Life under Stalin and Khrushchev*. Cambridge: Cambridge University Press, 2014.

Trunk, Isaiah, and Robert Moses Shapiro. *Łódź Ghetto: A History*. Bloomington: Indiana University Press, 2006.

Tymowski, Janusz. *Organizacja szkolnictwa wyższego w Polsce*. Warszawa: PWN, 1980.

Unger, Michal. *Reassessment of the Image of Mordechai Chaim Rumkowski*. Jerusalem: Yad Vashem, 2004.

Voslenskiĭ, M. S. *Nomenklatura: The Soviet Ruling Class*. New York: Doubleday, 1984.

Wacquant, Loic. "For a Socio-Analysis of Intellectuals: On 'Homo Academicus.'" *Berkeley Journal of Sociology*, no. 34 (1989): 1–29.

Waigertner, Przemysław. *Czwarta stolica: kiedy Łódź rządziła Polską (1945–1949)*. Łódź: WUŁ, 2019.

Walczak, Marian. *Szkolnictwo wyższe i nauka polska w latach wojny i okupacji: 1939–1945*. Wrocław: Zakład Narodowy im. Ossolińskich, 1978.

Wang, Zheng. *Finding Women in the State: A Socialist Feminist Revolution in the People's Republic of China, 1949–1964*. Oakland: University of California Press, 2017.

Webb, Jen, Tony Schirato, and Geoff Danaher. *Understanding Bourdieu*. London: Sage, 2002.

Welfe, Władysław. *Łódź i ziemia łódzka w badaniach Uniwersytetu Łódzkiego w latach 1945–1970*. Łódź: Uniwersytet Łódzki, 1970.

Wierzbicki, Marek. *Związek Młodzieży Polskiej i jego członkowie*. Warszawa: Trio, 2006.

Wesołowski, Włodzimierz. *Zróżnicowanie społeczne*. Warszawa: Zakład Narodowy im. Ossolińskich, 1974.

Wiśniewski, Wiesław. "Aspiracje edukacyjne społeczeństwa polskiego." In *Oświata w społecznej świadomości*, edited by Wiesław Wiśniewski, 66–88. Warszawa: Młodzieżowa Agencja Wydawnicza, 1980.

Wittlinowa, Halina. *Atlas szkolnictwa Wyższego*. Warszawa: Nasza Księgarnia, 1937.

Wittner, Lawrence S. *The Struggle Against the Bomb: Volume One, One World or None: A History of the World Nuclear Disarmament Movement Through 1953*. Stanford: Stanford University Press, 1993.

Wnuk-Lipiński, Edmund. *Demokratyczna rekonstrukcja: z socjologii radykalnej zmiany społecznej*. Warszawa: PWN, 1996.

Wnuk-Lipińska, Elżbieta. "Wykształcenie: cel czy środek." In *Studenci w Polsce i w Niemieckiej Republice Demokratycznej w świetle badań socjologicznych*, edited by Halina Najduchowska, 22–27. Warszawa: PWN, 1987.

Wolaniuk, Anita. *Funkcje metropolitalne Łodzi i ich rola w organizacji przestrzennej*. Łódź: ŁTN, 1997.

Woskowski, Jan. "Losy absolwentów historii Uniwersytetu Łódzkiego." In *Z badań klasy robotniczej i inteligencji*, edited by Jan Szczepański, 127–89. Łódź: PWN, 1958.

Woźniak, Wojciech. *Nierówności społeczne w polskim dyskursie politycznym*. Wydanie pierwsze. Warszawa: Wydawnictwo Naukowe Scholar, 2012.

Wróbel, Janusz. "Bilans okupacji niemieckiej w Łodzi 1939–1945." *In Rok 1945 w Łodzi: studia i szkice*, edited by Joanna Żelazko, 13–30. Łódź: IPN, 2008.

Wulff, Kenneth R. *Education in Poland: Past, Present, and Future*. Lanham, MD: University Press of America, 1992.

Young, John Wesley. *Totalitarian Language: Orwell's Newspeak and Its Nazi and Communist Antecedents*. Charlottesville: University of Virginia Press, 1991.

Zaremba, Marcin. *Komunizm, legitymizacja, nacjonalizm: nacjonalistyczna legitymizacja władzy komunistycznej w Polsce*. Warszawa: Trio, 2001.

Zaremba, Marcin. *Wielka trwoga. Polska 1944–1947. Ludowa reakcja na kryzys*. Kraków: Znak, 2012.

Żarnowska, Anna. *Wokół tradycji kultury robotniczej w Polsce*. Warszawa: PIW, 1986.

Żarnowski, Janusz. *O inteligencji polskiej lat międzywojennych*. Warszawa: Wiedza Powszechna, 1965.

Żarnowski, Janusz. *Społeczeństwo Drugiej Rzeczypospolitej, 1918–1939*. Warszawa: PWN, 1973.

Zarycki, Tomasz. *Kapitał kulturowy: inteligencja w Polsce i w Rosji*. Warszawa: Wydawnictwo Uniwersytetu Warszawskiego, 2008.

Zawistowska, Alicja. *Horyzontalne nierówności edukacyjne we współczesnej Polsce*. Warszawa: Scholar, 2012.

Zawistowska, Alicja. "Rozbieżność struktury wykształcenia kobiet i mężczyzn w PRL. Pomiędzy polityką państwa a indywidualnymi wyborami edukacyjnymi." *Roczniki Dziejów Społecznych i Gospodarczych* 75 (December 1, 2015): 167–90. https://doi.org/10.12775/RDSG.2015.03.

Zblewski, Zdzisław, and Filip Musiał, eds. *Komunizm w Polsce: zdrada, zbrodnia, zakłamanie, zniewolenie*. Kraków: Kluszczyński, 2005.

Żelazko, Joanna, ed. *Rok 1945 w Łodzi: studia i szkice*. Łódź: IPN, 2008.

Zysiak, Agata. "The Desire for Fullness. The Fantasmatic Logic of Modernization Discourses at the Turn of the 19th and 20th Century in Lodz." *Praktyka Teoretyczna*, no. 3(13) (December 20, 2014): 41–69.

Zysiak, Agata. *Punkty za pochodzenie. Powojenna modernizacja i uniwersytet w robotniczym mieście*. Kraków: Nomos, 2016.

Zysiak, Agata. "Science for Modernization: Between a Captive and Egalitarian University—The University of Lodz, 1945–1952." *Science in Context* 28, no. 2 (2015): 215–36.

Zysiak, Agata. "Socjalizm jako modernizacja—powojenna historia Polski w perspektywie rewizjonistycznej." *Przegląd Humanistyczny* 61(2 (457)) (2017): 135–45.

Zysiak, Agata, Kamil Śmiechowski, Kamil Piskała, Kaja Kaźmierska, Jacek Burski, and Wiktor Marzec. *From Cotton and Smoke: Łódź—Industrial City and Discourses of Asynchronous Modernity 1897–1994*. Łódź: WUŁ, 2018.

INDEX

Page numbers in italics indicate tables and figures

L

M

P

ABOUT THE AUTHOR

AGATA ZYSIAK, PHD, IS A HISTORICAL SOCIOLOGIST WORKING AT VIENNA University (Austria) and the University of Łódź (Poland). She is the author of the award-winning book (in Polish) *Punkty za pochodzenie* (Points for Social Origin, 2016), which served as the starting point for this book. She is also co-author of the main publication about Łódź available in English, *From Cotton and Smoke—Industrial City and Discourses of Asynchronous Modernity 1897–1994* (2018), and another award-winning project about the collapse of industry in Poland after 1989, *Wielki przemysł, wielka cisza* (Great Industry—Great Silence, 2020); a member of the Institute for Advanced Study, Princeton (2017/2018); and a cofounder of the Topografie Association, the NGO popularizing history and gathering oral histories in Łódź, which runs the digital Łódź archive Miastograf.pl.

Printed in the USA
CPSIA information can be obtained
at www.ICGtesting.com
LVHW020254151123
763991LV00003B/74

9 781612 498829